The Reconciling Community:
The Rite of Penance

*Studies in the Reformed Rites
of the Catholic Church,
Volume III*

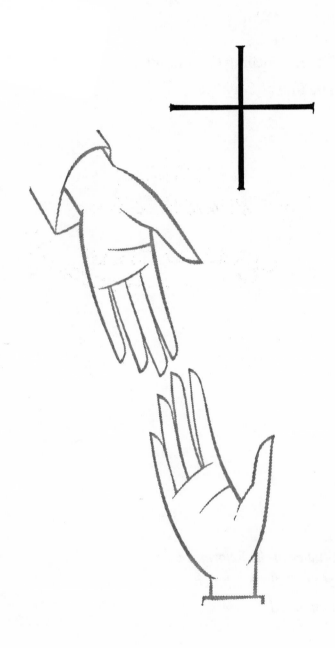

James Dallen

The Reconciling Community:
The Rite of Penance

A PUEBLO BOOK

The Liturgical Press   Collegeville, Minnesota

Design: Frank Kacmarcik

Excerpts of this book appeared as articles in *Worship* entitled, "The Laying on of Hands in Penance" and "Church Authority and the Sacrament of Penance."

Scriptural pericopes quoted from the Revised Standard Version.

Excerpts from the English translation of the *Rite of Penance* © 1974, International Committee on English in the Liturgy, Inc. All rights reserved.

Excerpts from *Documents on the Liturgy, 1963–1979: Conciliar, Papal, and Curial Texts* © 1982, International Committee on English in the Liturgy, Inc. All rights reserved.

Excerpts from *Documents of Vatican Council II* by Austin Flannery, O.P., Costello Publishing Company.

Printed in the United States of America.

ISBN 0-8146-6076-2

For my parents —
whose love first showed me
a reconciling community

Contents

Introduction

A few preliminary comments may help readers tread their way through the often bewildering history of penance and the similarly complex network of theological, liturgical, and sociological factors that are the contemporary situation of a sacrament of conversion and reconciliation.

In Part One, "Shaping the Tradition," we will examine the history of penance. The first three chapters are devoted to ancient penance. Chapter 1 will analyze its origins in the experience and practice of the apostolic and subapostolic Church. Chapter 2 will indicate how the shape of the emerging penitential institution was affected by sociological factors and internal controversy. Chapter 3 will describe the discipline and liturgy of the fully developed canonical institution. The next two chapters deal with medieval penance: Chapter 4, with the development of a private form of penance, and Chapter 5, with the gradual dominance of private confession. Chapter 6 will survey the developing character of private confession in the post-Reformation era and the beginnings of reform prior to Vatican Council II. ("Tradition and Celebration," in Chapter 10, provides an overview of the history in the form of a theory of development. It may be helpful as an exposition of my overall perspective.)

In Part Two, "The Revised Rites," we will examine the postconciliar Rite of Penance. Chapter 7 will describe the reform process from the council's call for reform to the promulgation of the new rites. Chapter 8 will analyze the doctrinal and theological foundations of the Rite of Penance and Chapter 9 will look in some detail at the rites themselves. Finally, in Chapter 10, the Rite of Penance will be assessed in relation both to the tradition and contemporary needs.

I want to express my gratitude to Aidan Kavanagh, O.S.B., for the invitation to prepare this volume; to Carl J. Peter, for the scholarship and friendship that inspired my initial study of penance; to Alfred J. Wasinger, for being a model of pastoral wisdom; and to all my colleagues and students who challenge me to live what I teach. Most of all, I thank my friends and my parents for showing me what God's unconditional love feels like.

Part One: Shaping the Tradition

Shaping the Tradition

Christian traditions are at times no more than the dead faith of those who nevertheless claim to be alive. In another and better sense, however, tradition is what survives from those who have gone before us marked with the sign of faith. It is part of us because they and we belong to the same Body. To know it is to know our place and to know ourselves. Thus, history as a way of thinking has become increasingly important for the theologian, especially in liturgy and sacramental theology. Those who share and shape worship and theology must be aware of the process of development by which they have been shaped and thus of their place as the foremost thrust of tradition.

Though penance's history is complex and sometimes bewildering, understanding it is essential for genuine reform and renewal.[1] The Church has always had to work with sinful members, assisting them to live out the implications of their baptismal conversion and recognizing them as members of its assemblies; it has always wielded power over sin, even though its dexterity and effectiveness have varied almost as extensively as the forms its sovereignty has taken. That power, the power of Christ, is equally strong today. The theologian's task is to acknowledge, understand, and explain the variety of forms that the sacrament has taken so as to disclose the underlying mystery of the Church in relation to Christ and sinners. Only then can past and present forms be evaluated in context. Only then can the Church deal adequately with how best to exercise the ministry of reconciliation now and in the future.

1

Yet tracing the origins and development of ecclesial repentance during the Church's first centuries is difficult. Ritual books are nonexistent and documents of any type are rare and difficult to interpret. We must depend on anecdotal comments, homiletic exhortations, and the passing references of polemicists to reconstruct how the Church supported the continuing conversion of its members and dealt with individuals whose baptismal repentance had faded to the point of betrayal.

Interpretation of the scanty evidence is often disputed. Most historians of penance, for example, have claimed that the apostolic and subapostolic Church dealt severely with sinners and that practice only gradually became more lenient. Careful analysis of the available data does not support this Jansenist interpretation. There was more controversy than consensus, though the communities from whom we have received the canonical scriptures seem to have been lenient. Early writers gave repentance a prominent place but did not specify Church structures to supervise or support it; they seemed ready to welcome the repentant sinner without special conditions. Only as practice developed were there criteria for gauging repentance and conditions for receiving the repentant. Thus, the interpretation proposed here is that local churches only gradually came to a consensus on disciplinary norms and liturgical practice for a formal institution of penance, without excluding other, more informal means. The struggle to respond to changing social conditions and pastoral needs and to resolve internal dissension about penance is, in fact, what gave the structures of ancient penance their distinctive character.

Polemical interests deriving from sixteenth- and seventeenth-century controversies have also heavily influenced historians of penance and particularly the interpretation of ancient evidence. The names that historians give the institution as they describe its development often suggest their assumptions. To speak, for example, of "public" penance in the first centuries may imply the absence or coexistence of "private" penance, with the two forms distinguished as radically different and discontinuous institutions. The controversy over whether private penance (identified with the familiar late medieval and modern institution of individual auricular confession of sins to a priest and his absolution of the penitent) existed in ancient times then arises. Polemicists have tried to prove or disprove its existence to show that the modern institution is the only possible sacramental form or that it is a late and illegitimate development. Yet evidence does not support such sharp distinctions and dichotomies: prior to late medieval and modern times (when only private auricular confession was regarded as sacramental) there was no single official or sacramental form of ecclesial penance. In an effort to avoid misleading impressions, period divisions will be used here. Ancient penance will refer to forms of penance in the first six centuries; medieval, in the seventh through fifteenth centuries; and modern, in the sixteenth century and after. These are, of course, rough divisions that overlap and the points of transition are particularly important.

During the first six centuries, ancient penance was slowly shaped amid crisis and controversy and then declined into obsolescence as people ignored it. During the first and second centuries, Christians lived in small, close-knit communities; any repentance beyond that of baptism was regarded as exceptional. However, during the latter part of the second century there was a growing awareness that something more was needed. The third century was the crucial period. Amid threats from without and turbulence within, postbaptismal repentance came to an institutionalized and theoretically justified form. This institution was canonically established and regulated during the fourth century and the first half of the fifth, as the Church struggled to accommodate itself to the large numbers of people who became Christian.

Since the origins and initial shape of an institution are crucial in determining its nature and the direction in which it moves, we will examine the development of ancient penance in some detail: its origins in the apostolic Church's practice of mutual correction and loving acceptance, its shaping as an institution amid controversy and dissension, and its eventual canonical regulation and liturgical celebration.

As people became increasingly alienated from canonical penance, efforts were made to meet their needs, leading eventually—though not easily—to a new form, private penance, one of several forms of medieval penance. Several factors then contributed to the growing importance and eventual dominance of private penance. Sixteenth-century controversies solidified its character and place in Catholic religious life until the twentieth century. More abundant evidence is available from these later centuries, but problems of interpretation still abound, particularly concerning the origins of private penance and modern confession.

NOTES

1. See Bernhard Poschmann, *Penance and the Anointing of the Sick* (New York: Herder and Herder, 1964) and Oscar D. Watkins, *A History of Penance* (two volumes; New York: Longmans, Green, 1920; reprinted, 1960). The best recent history is that of Herbert Vorgrimler, *Busse und Krankensalbung* (Freiburg: Herder, 1978), which has replaced Poschmann in Herder's *Handbuch der Dogmengeschichte* series. Paul F. Palmer provides texts and documents in *Sacraments and Forgiveness* (Westminster, Maryland: Newman Press, 1959), but his commentaries and interpretations must be read cautiously.

Most histories of penance are histories of its theology. Josef Jungmann's *Die lateinischen Bussriten in ihrer geschichtlichen Entwicklung* (Innsbruck: Rauch, 1932) and Mario Righetti's *Manuale di storia liturgica* (Milan: Editrice Ancora, 1950–1953) 4:170–322 are liturgical histories, but many of Jungmann's interpretations require reassessment and Righetti's focus is more on the history of theology than his title suggests.

Chapter One

Origins of Ancient Penance

The disciples who accompanied Jesus during his ministry had heard good news. Sitting with him at table, they experienced firsthand how God was making possible a new and simple intimacy of human beings with a God who was closer to them than their own parents. From his parables they learned of the counterforce of God's kingdom taking shape in unlikely places amid the chaos and turbulence of a sinful world. As they traveled with him, talked with him, and saw his gentleness with outcasts and his compassion for the suffering, they began to find a new way of looking at their past and at both present and future possibilities. The direction in which God had been leading their people became clearer. That they could deal with one another and with themselves as God was relating to them came as a revelation and a dawning of new hope.

The Easter-light of the Spirit gave new meaning and depth to the disciples' memories of Jesus. They had learned that God's love was unconditional, that the prophets before him who had spoken of God's covenant loyalty were right. Now they saw the end of what they recognized as the long reign of sin and realized that they shared his authority. The news was too good to keep to themselves. From Jesus they had learned that no one could be abandoned and left behind. All must be drawn into the new life with Christ in God. As God's ambassadors (2 Cor 5:18–6:1), they set out to make the world aware of its new situation.

This conviction of authority over sin because of what God had done in Christ was basic to the gathering (*ekklesia* or church) that began to take shape in Jerusalem, Judea, and Galilee, in diaspora Judaism, and even among the gentiles. People who had known Jesus and those who had not, Jews who saw Jesus as their messiah and gentiles who found him as their savior—all alike recognized that he gave them power over sin. "Repent and be baptized in the name of Jesus Christ for the forgiveness of your sins, and you will receive the Holy Spirit," Peter told the citizens of Jerusalem (Acts 2:38). Paul reminded the Corinthians that the reconciliation accomplished in Christ was now entrusted to them (2 Cor 5:18–20). Both the Matthaean and Johannine communities knew that they had the power to set people free from sin (Mt 9:8, 16:19; Jn 20:21–23). They had it because the Spirit had come upon them (Acts 1:8), and so, like Jesus before them, they forgave sins by welcoming sinners into their gatherings (cf. Mk 16:15–16; Lk 24:47–48) as he had brought them into his company. Theirs were reconciling communities, communities of salvation where old lines of demarcation had been erased (Gal 3:27–28).

Sinners entered the community of salvation by a baptism that showed that they had been brought to share the community's faith. It was in baptizing that the apostolic communities most clearly exercised their authority over sin and their power to overcome it. Sin no longer dominated those who entered. Sin after baptism was unthinkable, Paul reminded the Romans (6:2). Yet it existed. The story told of Ananias and Sapphira in Acts 5 shows the early Jerusalem community's disgust that such individuals could have been part of the community of saints. Paul's horror that an incestuous man remained within the Corinthian community (1 Cor 5) likewise shows the deep contradiction that he felt this to be.

Some Christians, like the Corinthians, ignored such facts. Others, like the opponents of 1 John's author, denied them, claiming an intimacy with God that made them sinless

(1:6, 8, 10; cf. Jas 3:2). But weeds were growing amid the wheat (cf. Mt 13:24–30) and churches had to deal with sinful saints.

RESPONSIBILITY FOR SINNERS

The Church was sinless and holy because of Christ's dying and rising (Eph 5:25–26), the self-offering by which he had made it holy (Heb 10:14) and a temple in the Spirit (1 Cor 3:16–17; 2 Cor 6:16). It had to be kept a community of saints. Thus, Paul did not simply encourage individuals to live lives worthy of their individual callings, for God's call was to a unity in Christ as a gathering of saints (cf. Eph 4:1–6; 1 Thes 4:7; Rom 1:6–7; 1 Cor 1:2, 9). Holiness distinguished Christians from the society out of which they had come and to which they were contrasted (cf. 1 Pt 2:9–12), making their gathering a sign of the salvation to which all humanity was called.

All were responsible to keep it holy by correcting one another as necessary, since an individual's sin diluted the Church's holiness. One person's life influenced the lives of others (Rom 14:7–8), changed the community as surely as leaven changes dough (1 Cor 5:6–8), and brought pain and loss to all (2 Cor 2:5). Thus, sins that directly affected the community, whether internally or externally, were the primary concern of the New Testament churches and called for correction.[1] The responsibility of Christians to encourage and strengthen one another (1 Thes 5:11) extended in a special way to weaker members (1 Thes 5:14; 1 Cor 8:7–13) and particularly to those who had sinned.

Though sin against the community was sin against Christ (1 Cor 8:12), the offender was by no means to be rejected and forgotten. In the New Testament, sin and community are always viewed from the perspective of mutual love and responsiveness to others' needs. Both in adding new members and in maintaining holiness, churches saw themselves serving the kingdom, humanity, and individual sinners.

In some cases they prayed that the offender would receive forgiveness and new life from God (1 Jn 5:14–16; Jas 5:16) and exercised their authority over sin through the efficacy of their prayer (cf. Mt 18:19–20). Other cases, however, called for stronger measures, for prayer was not enough for the sin that was death (1 Jn 5:16–17). Paul, for example, advised a boastful community to discipline itself and purge itself of the corrupting influence of an incestuous man. In line with the Deuteronomic norm, the brother whose membership was a lie and whose rebellion against grace contradicted the Spirit was to be expelled (1 Cor 5:7)—but he was not simply to be rejected and forgotten. Expulsion from their gatherings was intended to bring him to his senses so that he would correct the situation and then return. In the meantime, Christians were not to associate with such people and certainly not to share meals (the eucharist?) with them (2 Thes 3:6, 14; 1 Cor 5:11).

Only extreme cases called for such action. Individual Christians were neither to judge nor to exclude (Rom 14:4, 10; Jas 4:12). Such decisions were reserved to the assembled community (1 Cor 5:4; cf. Mt 18:17)[2] and to be taken only when all else failed: when the offender ignored a private warning, refused the correction of a small group, and turned a deaf ear to the plea of the whole community (Mt 18:15–17). Such a sinner was not to be treated as a pagan (1 Cor 5:10–11; cf. Mt 18:17) but rather shunned completely.

In what appears to be a ritual formula, the incestuous man was to be handed over to Satan (1 Cor 5:5; cf. 1 Tim 1:20), excluded from the community of salvation, and returned to the dominion of evil where his life-style would not be a lie.[3] Paul speaks of no other punishment; exclusion from the community of salvation was penalty enough. Perhaps he still hoped that the offender would somehow be restored to the community (as in 2 Thes 3:15) or at least finally find salvation. Paul could not forget how Jesus had dealt with outcasts—and with him. But neither could he forget the Christian community's responsibility to present a sharp sign of holiness to the pagan world.

REPENTANCE AND RECONCILIATION

While Paul's statement echoes the expulsion, exile, and death that are decreed in Deuteronomy (17:7; 19:19; 22:24), his intention is more medicinal than punitive. However, he does not indicate how the incestuous man might return to the community or hope to atone for his sin.

Contemporary Judaism's understanding and practice provides a helpful background, since the earliest Christians kept many Jewish ritual patterns. In Temple and synagogue liturgy and in private daily devotions, Jews admitted wrongdoing and prayed for forgiveness, grace, and salvation.[4] The New Testament only hints at similar practices of communal confession and prayer (e.g., Jas 5:16 and the Lord's Prayer), but we find them called for in early eucharistic celebrations and prayer gatherings (e.g., Didache 14:1, 4:14; cf. 1 Cor 11:28–31) and in such early Christian liturgies as that of Addai and Mari. Later, as in Judaism, mourning customs such as sackcloth and ashes were linked with repentance, reintegration into the community, and ritual cleansing. The laying on of hands as a gesture of solidarity was likewise borrowed from Jewish ritual.

Three means of atonement were then prominent in Judaism: sacrifice, fasting, and suffering and death. Sacrifice had only limited value, for sin-offerings generally applied only to unintentional wrongdoing, mostly in ritual or ceremonial matters. Fasting was a corporate, not individual, means of atonement and was primarily concerned with the protection and purification of the community of Israel as, for example, on the Day of Atonement. The individual's suffering and death were a last hope of atonement and reconciliation with God. In rabbinic thought, however, all these forms of atonement presumed repentance, which included determination to break with sinful ways, the admission of guilt, and the effort to make atonement to

God and undo the harm done to others. While no transgressions were in principle excluded from the possibility of repentance, rabbinic teaching recognized that some sinful situations made real repentance unlikely.

Several penitential elements from the synagogue liturgy thus seem to have entered Christian worship. However, we find no penitential liturgy as such in the New Testament and little trace of influence from the Jewish penitential liturgies or from the Jewish notion of atonement; early Christians were reluctant to borrow from rabbinic Judaism while competing with it.

Hebrews explicitly asserts that sacrifice and Yom Kippur's penitential liturgy (presumably including its corporate fast) are unnecessary because of what Jesus accomplished once and for all by his dying and rising. (Yet in the Eastern churches of the fourth and fifth centuries, the eucharist was regarded as the fulfillment of the Day of Atonement sacrifice; prayers reflected themes and contained phrases from the synagogue liturgy of that day.) Both Christians and Jews looked unfavorably on fasting and other forms of self-imposed suffering. The synoptic gospels portray Jesus as having a rather casual attitude toward fasting (Mt 9:14–15, 11:18–19; Mk 2:18–20; Lk 5:33–35), though they show him fasting in the desert before beginning his ministry as Moses had fasted on Sinai while receiving the Law (Ex 34:28). Jesus gives no prominence to fasting in forming his disciples and advises them to conceal it if they do. Paul likewise downplayed the importance of fasting and criticized the Judaizers who advocated it (Rom 14:2–6; Col 2:16–23). The early community does not seem to have fasted as a cultic or penitential practice but only as prayerful preparation for such important decisions as the appointment of apostles and elders or the reorientation of mission and ministry (Acts 13:2–3, 14:23). Yet by the second century, there are weekly fasts on Wednesday and Friday, days deliberately chosen to differ from the Jewish fast days of the time (Didache 8:1), since after the destruction of the Temple rabbis came to equate fasting with the sacrifices that could no longer be offered. The Jewish view that suffering and death provide a means of atonement and thus an avenue of forgiveness for the repentant sinner may be the background for Paul's claim that death with Christ in baptism means forgiveness and also is the key to understanding (1 Cor 5:5) where subjection to Satan and the death that is the consequence offers hope of eventual salvation.

Beyond this, the means whereby Jews atoned for their sins and were restored to the community appear to have had little or no influence on Christianity. Repentance (conversion) is therefore even more prominent than in Judaism. While Paul did not specify concrete means of forgiveness and reconciliation, he did speak often of repentance or conversion. For him, it is the indispensable condition of forgiveness and the prerequisite for restoration to the community when expulsion had been necessary. Thus, Paul advises the community to receive back, with tangible signs of affection, a repentant individual who had been ostracized (2 Cor 2:5–11). Reaffirming the repentance or conversion that had first led the person to baptism was the path to reconciliation with the community and restoration to the salvation that it signaled.

We have no evidence of other disciplinary requirements. No liturgy of reconciliation is described or even implied at this stage of development, though we can speculate. The later prominence of the Lord's Prayer as a sign of repentance and reconciliation suggest that it could have been used as a ritual prayer paralleling Jewish prayers for forgiveness and grace. A *berakah* form of prayer, eschatological in tone, the Lord's Prayer regards mutual forgiveness as the counterpart of divine forgiveness.[5] The Matthaean commentary appended to it (Mt 6:14–15) parallels the warning to accept and forgive when correcting one another (Mt 18:35). As regards a ritual gesture, Paul calls for a "proof of love"—a warm welcome and renewed friendship, presumably including the "holy kiss" with which all Christians coming to the community gatherings were greeted—as sign that the repentant sinner was received back into the community and admitted to its assemblies and meals. This could have been the beginning of a ritual of reconciliation that would later be a separate sacramental sign and is as close as we come to New Testament evidence for such a ritual.[6]

AUTHORITY IN AND OF THE CHURCH

When the Church distanced itself from the sinner, withdrawing its protection and returning the sinner to Satan's dominion, it did so not simply as discipline but as service to the promised kingdom, humanity, and the sinner. For Paul (as for the New Testament in general), the Church was the eschatological community of salvation. To be admitted to that community was to share the blessing of salvation with which God had gifted it. To belong to it was to take responsibility for making it a community of saints and a clear sign to the pagan world of God's saving work. To fail in this responsibility was to be in need of healing so that the Church might once more become whole.

This is the foundation for Paul's command to expel certain sinners, Matthew's remarks on binding and loosing, and John's statement on forgiving and retaining sins. Paul does not see expulsion as a final solution, nor do Matthew and John regard binding/retaining and loosing/forgiving as simple alternatives. Paul hopes that expulsion will lead to eventual salvation. Binding and loosing are phases of the same action, with the Church's total authority and power expressed by specifying the two extremes. The Church distances itself from sinners to maintain itself as a Spirit-filled sign of salvation and and to intensify Satan's hold on those who have given their allegiance to evil while supposedly loyal to Christ.[7] Their sin stands out against the Church's holiness. It is evident that they have ceased to walk with Jesus' disciples. The hope is that they will recognize the sin and what has been lost, that they will repent, return, and be reconciled.

None of these texts refers to the sacrament of penance as we know it, *pace* the Council of Trent. The New Testament takes seriously both conversion and reconciliation, the fundamental attitudes of sinners and Church. It does not, however, record a direct and immediate institution of the present sacrament by Christ, nor does it mandate a perennially valid way for the Church to assist and accept repentant sinners.[8] But neither are Matthew and John simply speaking of baptism, *pace* the Protestant reformers. Though Matthew 16:19 and 18:18 and John 20:23, which Catholics customarily understand as referring to the sacrament of penance, were generally referred by the fathers of the Church to baptism, this power and authority transcend both baptism and penance. What we have in all three authors is the clear affirmation that the Christian *ekklesia* is God's gathering of a community of salvation, that individuals' response to the community affects their situation before God, and that the community and its officials have authority over sin and can set down conditions for membership.[9]

The Gospels of Matthew and John reflect different systems of Church organization and different styles of Church life. These texts, variants of the same tradition, express these differing perspectives. Simply put, the Matthaean community's officials have the authority, stated in wider terms, that the Spirit has in the Johannine community.

The Jewish Christians whose faith the Gospel of Matthew reflects had organized themselves like the synagogue, with perhaps some influence from the Qumran community.[10] In some instances, the community acted as a body. Matthew 18:18, for example, speaks of the community's authority in a fashion similar to John 20:23, though the technical rabbinic phrase of binding and loosing is used. Matthew 16:19, on the other hand, uses the same terminology to describe a community official exercising authority. Certain officials, much like the rulers of the synagogue and the supervisors of the Qumran community, exercised the functions of the Twelve and Peter in supervising and regulating the life of the Matthaean community.[11] In rabbinic usage, the terminology of binding and loosing indicated the authority to determine what was permissible and what was not, of imposing obligations and of removing them, and, in extreme cases, of banishing from the community and of recalling those who had been banished. Matthew 16:19 seems primarily concerned to indicate the ability of officials to make authoritative decisions—including, for example, the admission of gentiles to the Church, a probable context for the narrative in the life of the Matthaean community—while Matthew 18:18 seems to refer primarily to condemnation and acquittal (in the sense of expulsion and reconciliation) as an action of the whole community.

John 20:23 is the same tradition, restated to apply specifically to sin rather than to authoritative decisions in general. The Johannine community appears to have placed less emphasis on the role of community officials. The Spirit, "another advocate," takes Jesus' place and continues his work. The Spirit present in believers directs their lives and the Spirit present in the Church makes it the community of salvation. The individual's response to the Spirit, either faith or unbelief, constitutes the judgment that is either forgiveness of sin or hardening in sin. In this passage, the receiving of the Spirit is the disciples' baptism. But while baptism into the community is clear evidence of faith and the sign of forgiveness, there is no compelling reason to restrict the application of the text to prebaptismal sin, particularly since the plural (liturgical usage?) appears. The text states full power over sin without distinguishing pre- and post-baptismal sin.

1 John seems to clarify an apparent ambiguity in the Johannine community's understanding of this power by insisting that communion in the Spirit of Jesus, whose sacrifice took away all sin, is the continuing source of forgiveness (see especially 1 Jn 2:1–2). This is not unlike the Qumran community's view that the Spirit of holiness cleansed from sin all who entered that community (1QS

14

3:7–8), though sins committed by members still had to be dealt with.

What is basic throughout is the conviction that the Church is the action of God, as is its activity, whether in preaching, praying, or the disciplining of its members' lives. While Paul is not as explicit on discipline as are later writers, he is clearly convinced that the community and he himself can set down conditions for membership. He quite probably has in mind the synagogal and rabbinic authority to exclude serious wrongdoers. Matthew and John make the claim that their communities exercise an authority over sin and evil that is God's. (John's passive constructions, "are forgiven" and "are retained," and Matthew's "in heaven" are equivalent Semitic circumlocutions for God's action.) Matthew states that community officials can exercise this authority. All three are alike, however, in regarding the Church as the eschatological community of salvation, with people's response to the Church and the Church's activity decisive for salvation.

CONTROVERSY OVER RECONCILIATION

Later New Testament writers, probably reflecting controversies of their times, are less optimistic than Paul about the likelihood of repentance and reconciliation. 1 John insists against his opponents that Christians do still sin and claims that prayer for the sinner brings about forgiveness, but he is hesitant to admit that all sins can be forgiven or advise prayer for the extreme offender (1 Jn 5:14–17). Hebrews forthrightly rejects the possibility of repentance in some cases (6:4–8; 10:26–31; 12:16–17), though more on psychological than dogmatic grounds, and thus witnesses to a strict policy limiting the possibility of forgiveness. Jesus' mysterious saying in the synoptics that blasphemy against the Spirit would never be forgiven (Mk 3:29; Mt 12:32; Lk 12:10) may be an indication that such rigorism existed in a number of New Testament churches with regard to at least one sin, though we cannot determine what it was.[12]

We can only speculate on the reasons for such hesitancy and strictness. Perhaps, as was the case a little later, the writers were unwilling to appear to give an excuse for sin. Perhaps, as again was the case a few years later, eschatological enthusiasm led to the fear that there would be no time for repentance. Their feeling, in any case, seems to have been that the community should not be too quick to receive back those whose way of life contradicted the community's call to holiness and damaged its character. In some cases, the betrayal was apparently considered so extreme as to rule out reconciliation, though we cannot determine why.

Most of the canonical scriptures present a different view, and Matthew's position is perhaps the most striking. Since his community was highly structured, rigidity might be expected. There was policy: Matthew gives procedures for dealing with serious sinners (18:15–18).[13] He introduces them, however, by drawing a picture of a shepherd searching for a lost sheep (18:12–14) and follows them with a statement of the unlimited power of the Church's prayer (18:19–20; cf. 6:12, 14–15) and with a portrait of Peter, the archetypal community official, asking about limits to forgiveness and being told that there are none (18:21–22). Matthew then appends the parable of the unforgiving debtor (18:23–25) as a warning to his church and its officials.

James likewise seems to set no limits to possible forgiveness (1:21; 5:19–20) and 2 Peter 3:9 reflects a similar understanding of the Lord's mercy. Luke frequently portrays Jesus forgiving sin, an emphasis not found in Mark and Matthew, and the parables of Luke 15 show that he sees the Church expressing its power not by judgment but by the proclamation of God's mercy. Revelation reflects a similar policy when it states no limits in calling churches as well as individuals in them to repentance (2:5, 14–16, 20–22; 3:1–5, 15–19).

We do not know why some writers or communities moved toward rigorism, but in general the New Testament churches wanted to rescue and save sinful members and were ready to welcome them back. The only condition was repentance and the only limit was the Lord's mercy that they had experienced. Such gospel leniency was the consequence of the good news they had heard from Jesus, experienced in his ministry, and prayed for when they prayed as he had taught.

They clearly recognized sin as a power dominating the world and struggled to set people free from it by faith and baptism and entrance into the community of salvation. Sin, as they saw it, was a much more potent and far-reaching force than simply wrong behavior and bad example, and it could once more take hold of a person who had been liberated from it. Behavior was not ignored, of course, either before baptism or after it. The New Testament churches recognized sin in their members and dealt with it, informally in most cases but sometimes, when forced to, formally. Policy statements on elements of conduct requiring correction or exclusion and lists of sins considered particularly vicious are evidence.

Controversy over reconciling sinners seems to have begun no earlier than the years in the mid-seventies and may reflect the internal tension that developed as Christianity competed with other groups in a contest to determine which would dominate post-Temple Judaism. It was, however, a controversy among Christians. All parties seem to have agreed that because the Church was the community of salvation it had authority over sin and that its prayer and decisions had eschatological implications for the sinner, just as the sinner's deeds affected the community. The question was if and when to reconcile such sinners.

Reconciliation involved receiving back the repentant sinner. There is no indication whether forgiveness was seen as granted directly in God's name or whether the Church's forgiveness was regarded as mediating divine mercy. The latter seems more compatible with the implicit ecclesiology of the canonical scriptures and with the variant expressions of "whatever you loose" and "they are forgiven." The context, in any case, was the love that Christian brothers and sisters have for one another, a love that leads them to strive to strengthen one another to build up the community in holiness.

The Church of the first two centuries existed only in small communities. Christians were a minority in a pagan milieu, sometimes in danger of being denounced, sometimes fearful of pograms initiated by hostile Jews or contemptuous Gentiles, always vulnerable to the consequences of internal weakness or division. From the viewpoint of the sociologist of religion, Christianity was a sect, with the ethical rigor, fervent enthusiasm, and high eschatological expectations that characterize such a group. Christian groups were small and close-knit, with strong bonds of affection and a loyalty to one another based on their experience of the Lord's mercy, and serious sin was considered something exceptional. In joining the Christian gathering, individuals left their former lives behind and bound themselves by the baptismal *sacramentum* (vow or oath) to live by the Spirit of Jesus. Infidelity to this commitment and thereby a return to the Jewish or pagan way of life was sin in the fullest sense; it meant losing the Spirit that was the life of the community and the bond of its peace and communion. Even as late as the mid-second century, this experience and sense of identity as a tight community was so strong that the most serious sin seems to have been the formation of factions, particularly in opposition to the bishop or presbyters who symbolized the community's oneness.

Disloyalty did happen, of course, and the churches found it necessary to deal with the fact of sin in their members, both for the sake of the sinners and to preserve the communities as witness to the kingdom and as a sign of holiness in a pagan society. The conduct of Christians was supposed to show them as God's royal courtiers and priestly servants, showing the world God's grace and holiness (cf. 1 Pt 2). At times, the Church had to confront individuals who fell short or even to exclude them from fellowship. The motivating thrust, however, was the responsibility to extend the power of Christ's victory over sin and evil: to win back the errant Christian, reintegrate the sinner into the community, and make the assembly whole and holy once again as sign and seed of what God sought for all human beings in the kingdom.

Since such grave sin was considered exceptional, each case seems to have been dealt with individually and hence somewhat informally. There is little indication of set procedures or established rituals for excluding such sinners or for welcoming them back into the assembly and no sign of limitations imposed. Repentance, a turning back from the course that had been taken, was called for. The sinner was expected to acknowledge guilt and show submission to God by a change in conduct. In such cases, as for the everyday sins that were part of each Christian's life, prayer, fasting, and almsgiving became the means for showing the repentance that marked the members of the community and obtained pardon from God. The communities, for their part, were ready to receive the sinner as God had received them. There was no debt owed other than conversion and mutual love; communion with the Church was the assurance of forgiveness and salvation.

Our earliest Christian writings speak of repentance and forgiveness much as does the New Testament. Writing to the faction-torn church of Corinth about the year 96, the Roman community, through its bishop, Clement, appeals for repentance and reconciliation, assuring the Corinthians that God's forgiveness is available (e.g., Clement to the Corinthians 48:1, 51:1) and that their community's prayer can bring about repentance and healing (56:1). A prayer like those of the synagogue (59:3–61:3) asks forgiveness for sin and seems sure of divine pardon (60:1–4):

"Thou, O Lord, has created the world, Thou who art faithful in all generations, right in Thy judgments, wonderful in strength and transcendent greatness, wise in creating, and judicious in establishing what has come into being, beneficent throughout the visible world and kind toward those that trust in Thee. O merciful and compassionate one, forgive us our iniquities and misdemeanors and transgressions and shortcomings! Do not consider every sin of Thy servants and servant maids; but cleanse us as only Thy truth can cleanse, and direct our steps to walk in holiness of heart and to do the things which are good and pleasing in Thy sight and in the sight of our rulers. Yes, Master, let Thy face beam upon us, that we may do good in peace and be sheltered under Thy mighty hand and delivered from every sin by Thy uplifted arm, and deliver us from such as hate us without cause. Grant concord and peace to us as well as to all the inhabitants of the earth, just as Thou didst grant it to our fathers when they piously called upon Thee in faith and truth; grant us to be obedient to Thy almighty and glorious name."[14]

This confession or *exomologesis* of Clement's is primarily the praise of God (26:2, 48:2, 52:1–2, 61:3), though it at least once includes the admission of wrongdoing and the apparent seeking of pardon from those offended (51:3): the presbyters against whom the one faction had revolted (57:1). If there is a set form or procedure for bringing about conversion, it is admonition, compassionate correction, and intercession in prayer (56:1–2).

The whole community is concerned (cf. 1 Clement 2:4, 6), for division and sin affect the salvation or health of the whole body. We see in Clement's letter, as in other early writings, a strong sense of internal cohesion, a vivid realization of the social character of sin and forgiveness, and the responsibility of mutual correction and acceptance. Though heresy, apostasy, and internal dissension were consequently regarded as the worst sins, even these were to be forgiven on repentance. Ignatius of Antioch also advised avoiding certain sinners (to the Smyrnaeans 4:1, 7:2; to the Ephesians 7:1), but his warning went no further than Paul or 1 John. The Letter of Polycarp explicitly insists that sinners are to be reclaimed "so that you may preserve the whole of your community intact" (11:4).

A Syrian document from the late first or early second century, the Didache, speaks of *exomologesis* or confession in the Church's assembly for worship (cf. 1 Corinthians 11:28–31):

"In church confess your sins, and do not come to your prayer with a guilty conscience." (Didache 4:14)

"On the Lord's own day, assemble in common to break bread and offer thanks; but first confess your sins, so that your sacrifice may be pure. However, no one quarreling with his brother may join your meeting until they are reconciled; your sacrifice must not be defiled." (Didache 14:1–2)

This plea for reconciliation, together with the metaphors of vine/fruit and crop/harvest in Didache 9–10, suggests that the Church's gathering parallels God's gathering into the kingdom. The eucharist as the ingathering of God's people was thus an active metaphor of salvation and the expression of hope for the final harvest. The Didache's strong Jewish spirit suggests that this public communal confession (*exomologesis-berakah*) was perhaps a prayer like those of the synagogue and that of 1 Clement 60:1–4, admitting sinfulness and asking God's forgiveness and grace.[15] Prayer alone is not enough, however, for those involved in disputes have to be reconciled (cf. Mark 11:25, which appears to be a Christian form of Jesus' saying in Matthew 5:23–24). Perhaps the kiss of peace served to ritualize such reconciliation; Justin's First Apology (65:2) shows its important position at the beginning of the eucharistic liturgy a few years later, in the mid-second century. Certainly the Sunday eucharistic meeting was the place for reconciliation.

While these early documents describe no formal discipline or ritual for dealing with sinners, there is evidence of disputes over lenient treatment. The Good Shepherd image in the catacomb art of this period, for example, may have been a protest against incipient rigorism.[16] The Shepherd of Hermas, an apocalyptic Roman work, strongly Jewish in spirit, is even clearer. Part of it, probably written near the end of the first century or the beginning of the second, is from the perspective we have seen: all sinners are called to repentance and only those who harden their hearts are excluded from pardon. Another part, however, probably written near the middle of the second century, indicates that "some teachers" are insisting that there is no repentance other than that of baptism. The angel of repentance, through whom Hermas's views are presented, cautiously opposes such rigorists.

By this time, the Roman community had grown considerably. Many of its members had been baptized as infants or young children and lacked the fervor of adult converts. The ardent yearning for an early parousia had begun to weaken. A new problem was posed, for postbaptismal repentance was no longer so easily regarded as a reversal of commitment and hence exceptional. Both a theory and a practice for disciplining lax Christians and apostates were called for, and some teachers were insisting on severity.

Like Christians before him, Hermas saw the Church under construction as the community of salvation, the place where God's pardon is present and active. Until the building is finished, he claimed, there is a last chance for repentance. This *metanoia*, as in the New Testament, is an attitude, not an institution—conversion or change of heart—and must be prompt. Time is short, and it will be difficult, if not impossible, for the insincere Christian who sins and repents repeatedly to have ultimate success (Mandate 4, 3, 1–7).[17] Hermas stresses this last chance for pastoral and psychological reasons as well as because of a sense of eschatological urgency. Roman legalism and later authors dependent on him made this "once only" as a matter of principle—as late as the fourth century some Christians regarded Hermas as canonical scripture—but Hermas himself saw forgiveness as possible for all sins through genuine conversion (Similitude 8). Even the adulterer and the apostate are able to repent and be forgiven. Hermas was more concerned with which sinners are capable of repentance than with which sins are forgivable. A preacher, not a canon lawyer, he was interested in repentant sinners rather than legal procedures for their readmission. He was convinced that God gives the power of repentance to all who are sincere (Similitude 8, 6, 2). Such apparent laxity, however, later led Tertullian to call him the "shepherd of adulterers."

Though Hermas set forth no formal penitential discipline, he does reflect the gradual evolution of institutions as the Christian "sect" became a "church" (in the sociological sense). He said nothing about procedures for reconciling sinners or about the relationship between ecclesiastical and divine forgiveness, but he did see Church elders as having the role of offering prayer for the repentant sinner (Similitude 5). Atonement for sin through self-chastisement and fasting also seem to have become more popular by this time, for Hermas criticizes reliance on fasting, insisting that what is denied oneself must be given to the poor (Similitude 5, 2, 7). No ritual for reconciliation is described, but Hermas demands that the repentant sinner be welcomed back into the Church's assembly (Mandate 4, 1, 8–9).

In the context of the community gathering, the ritual of welcome and the kiss of peace would have signified forgiveness and reconciliation. Converts were initiated and welcomed, repentant and reformed sinners were welcomed back. In both cases the assembly itself was the primary actor and celebrant. Community officials, especially the one presiding at the eucharistic gathering, undoubtedly had particular competence and responsibility—their role became increasingly prominent by the mid-third century—but in light of the New Testament documents and other early writings it would seem improper to see isolated references such as 1 Clement 57:1 affirming a power reserved to such officials. Clement advised submission to the presbyters because there had been animosity toward them, not because they were empowered to hear confessions.

For the Christians of the postapostolic age, as for those of New Testament times, the Church was the community of salvation. To be welcomed into its gathering was to receive the blessing of salvation and that in turn evoked the praise and blessing of God (*berakah* and *exomologesis*). From the mid-second century on, however, communities began to develop more formal ways of initiating new Christians and receiving back repentant sinners. In the latter part of the second century, Irenaus of Lyons spoke of the underlying meaning of this reception and was among the first to emphasize that conversion to the Church is a factor in receiving forgiveness. Few Christians would have denied this. Many, however, found it difficult to agree on whom to receive back into their community and under what conditions. Some sinners so offensively contradicted the Christian way of life that, even on repentance, they seemed to need special attention and ministry. Some factions went so far as to insist that some such sinners must be permanently excluded from the Christian assembly.

Such controversy set the stage for development. In the following centuries, the primitive practice of mutual correction gave way to strict policies requiring rehabilitation and closely supervised probation of those guilty of serious sins that were damaging to themselves and the community. From the early communal prayers for forgiveness borrowed from the synagogue and from the greeting extended to members of the eucharistic assembly grew elaborate liturgies. Simple gospel themes, played out amid controversy, became elaborate orchestrations in response to the needs of Church and sinners.

24

1. See Jerome Murphy-O'Connor's "Sin and Community in the New Testament," in *The Mystery of Sin and Forgiveness* (ed. Michael J. Taylor; Staten Island, N.Y.: Alba House, 1971), pp. 55–89. Léopold Sabourin also surveys the scriptural data in a "La rémission des péchés: Écriture Sainte et pratique ecclésiale," *Science et Esprit* 32 (1980) 299–315; for an English summary see "Forgiveness of Sin and Church Praxis," *Theology Digest* 29 (1981) 123–126. See also H. Thyen, *Studien zur Sündenvergebung im Neuen Testament und seinen alttestamentlichen und jüdischen Voraussetzungen* (Göttingen: Vandenhoeck und Ruprecht, 1970), Stanislaus Lyonnet and Léopold Sabourin, *Sin, Redemption and Sacrifice* (Rome: Pontifical Biblical Institute, 1970), and E. Cothenet, "Sainteté de l'Église et péchés des chretiens: Comment le Nouveau Testament envisage-t-il leur pardon?" in *Liturgie et Rémission des Péchés* (Rome: Edizioni Liturgiche, 1975), pp. 69–96.

2. Even Paul wanted his condemnation of the incestuous man to be ratified when the community gathered. The community's responsibility for its own discipline would thus be aligned with apostolic authority. A few years later, officials of the community would make such judgments on their own (Titus 3:10; 1 Tim 1:19–20; cf. Mt 16:19).

3. Ivan Havener examines the passage in depth in "A Curse for Salvation—1 Corinthians 5:1–5" in *Sin, Salvation and the Spirit* (ed. by Daniel Durken; Collegeville, Minn.: Liturgical Press, 1979), pp. 334–344. He concludes that temporary exclusion and eventual repentance are not what Paul has in mind but rather physical death and eventual salvation.

4. They are found, for example, in the *tefillah* which likely dates back in some form to A.D. first century. For similarities in prayer patterns, see *The Lord's Prayer and Jewish Liturgy*, Jakob J. Petuchowski and Michael Brocke, eds. (New York: Seabury, 1978). For scriptural indications of penitential liturgies, see E. Lipinski, *La liturgie pénitentielle dans la Bible* (Paris: Éditions du Cerf, 1969) and J. A. Marcen Tihista, "Liturgias penitenciales en el antiguo testamento," in *El sacramento de la penitencia* (Madrid: Consejo Superior de Investigaciones Cientificas, 1972), pp. 85–104. For post-Temple Judaism, see M. Arranz, "La liturgie pénitentielle juive apres la destruction du Temple," in *Liturgie et Rémission des Péchés* (Rome: Edizioni Liturgiche, 1975), pp. 39–56, and for the

liturgy of the Day of Atonement as precedent for contemporary communal celebrations, see John Hennig, "Die kollektive Bussfeier im Lichte der jüdischen Tradition," *Heiliger Dienst* 4 (1970) 164–169.

5. See especially Gordon J. Bahr, "The Use of the Lord's Prayer in the Primitive Church," *The Lord's Prayer and Jewish Liturgy*, pp. 149–155. He concludes that the early Church used the Lord's Prayer as Judaism used the *tefillah*. For history of liturgical use, see Ingemar Furberg, *Das Pater Noster in der Messe* (Lund: Gleerups, 1968) and T. W. Manson, "The Lord's Prayer," *Bulletin of the John Rylands Library* 38 (1956) 99–113, 436–448. See also Murphy-O'Connor, "Sin and Community in the New Testament," especially pp. 72–75.

More important than literary structure is the spirit and orientation stated at the beginning of the *berakah*. It is primarily acknowledgement or blessing of God's greatness and goodness, an expression of praise and thanksgiving, joy and admiration. After the initial blessing of God, the motive for blessing is stated (usually linked with the covenanted character of the community) and then petitions that God's goodness continue. The historical tendency, at least in Christianity, is to restrict the statement of praise and to lengthen the petitions. This is evident in penance as well as in the Eucharistic Prayer, which is derived from the *berakah*.

6. Some scholars think that 1 Timothy 5:22 (post-Pauline) witnesses to a rite of reconciliation through the laying on of hands. This interpretation is found as early as the third century. Cf. Paul Galtier, "La réconciliation des pécheurs dans la premiere épître a Timothée," *Recherches de Science Religieuse* 39 (1951) 317–322. In recent years, this has commonly been understood as referring to ordination. Joseph Coppens, *L'imposition des mains* (Paris: Gabalda, 1925), pp. 125–131, discusses the exegesis of the passage and concludes that it refers to ordination. *The Jerome Biblical Commentary* states that what is referred to is not a rite of reconciliation. Present scholarship, however, admits the possibility that the imposition of hands as a sign of solidarity with the community is a gesture of reconciliation; see Murphy-O'Connor, "Sin and Community in the New Testament," pp. 69–71. The question is whether 1 Timothy 5:17–22 deals with only one topic.

7. Herbert Vorgrimler has revived the patristic demonological understanding of binding/loosing, an interpretation that fits well with Pauline practice and also distinguishes more clearly between the power of the keys given to Peter (Mt 16:19) and the power of binding and loosing given to the disciples as a group (Mt 18:18). See "Mt. 16:18s et le sacrement de pénitence," in *L'homme devant Dieu* (Melanges offert au Pere Henri de Lubac; Paris: Aubier, 1963), pp. 51–61.

8. These positions represent the conclusions of contemporary biblical and sacramental scholarship. See, for example, Raymond E. Brown, *The Gospel According to John (XIII–XXI)* (The Anchor Bible, 29A; Garden City, N.Y.: Doubleday, 1970), pp. 1039–1045.

9. See Beda Rigaux, " 'Lier et délier.' Les ministères de réconciliation dans l'église des temps apostoliques," *Maison-Dieu* 117 (1974) 86–135.

10. See Göran Forkman, *The Limits of the Religious Community: Expulsion from the Religious Community within the Qumran Sect, Rabbinic Judaism and Primitive Christianity* (Lund: Gleerups, 1972) and J. Schmitt, "Contribution à l'étude de la discipline pénitentielle dans l'Église primitive à la lumière des textes de Qumrân" in *Les Manuscripts de la Mer Morte* (Paris: Aubier, 1957), pp. 93–109.

11. This petrine ministry is spoken of much as was that of the Qumran supervisor (*mebaqqer*, etymologically equivalent to *episcopos*), of whom the Damascus Covenant says, "he shall loosen all the fetters that bind them so that no one should be oppressed or broken in his congregation" (13:9–10).

12. Raymond Brown concludes that the sin spoken of in 1 John 5 is that of the secessionists who refuse to believe that Jesus is the Christ come in the flesh; 1 John encourages prayer for brothers and sisters who are sinners but not for *former* brothers and sisters who have reversed their steps and passed from life to death. See his *The Epistles of John* (Anchor Bible, 30; Garden City, N.Y.: Doubleday, 1982), pp. 636–637, and cf. pp. 608–619. His *The Community of the Beloved Disciple* (New York: Paulist Press, 1979) has also been helpful for understanding the Johannine community.

13. See Leviticus 19:17–18 and Deuteronomy 19:15. For a similar usage at Qumran, see 1QS 5:25–6:1; CD 9:2.

14. *The Epistles of St. Clement of Rome and St. Ignatius of Antioch* (James A. Kleist, trans.; *Ancient Christian Writers*, v. 1; New York: Newman Press, 1946), pp. 46–47.

15. In Didache 8, the Lord's Prayer is to be said three times a day, like the *tefillah*, and is deliberately contrasted with the Jewish manner of prayer; then the community's eucharist is spoken of. Texts parallel to Didache 4:14 lack its mention of the "church" (more properly, "assembly" or "gathering"); e.g., Epistle of Barnabas 19, 12; Apostolic Constitutions 7, 14, 17; the Latin Teaching of the Twelve Apostles 4, 4. For an analysis of the Didache's teaching on forgiveness and reconciliation, see Willy Rordorf, "La rémission des péchés selon la Didache" in *Liturgie et Rémission des Péchés*, pp. 225–238.

16. J. Schrijnen, "Die Entwicklung der Bussdisziplin im Lichte der altchristlichen Kunst," in his *Verspreide Opstellen* (Nijmegen: Dekker & Van de Vegt, 1939), pp. 277–294.

17. Early second-century Rome apparently had repeatable penance. See Irenaus, *Contra haereses* III, 4, 3 (PG 7: 857).

Chapter Two

Controversy and Institution

That rigorism grew in the second century was largely due to Christianity's growth and its changing social and cultural situation, which led Christian communities to reassess the informality and leniency with which they had received converts and dealt with sin and sinners. Some Christians were unsure whether numbers were a healthy sign: bonds of affection were more difficult to forge and enthusiasm was diluted. Divisions within the community, whether based on doctrinal disagreements, occupational or individual ways of life, or simple personality differences seemed more dangerous, for they weakened the community, diminished its witness, and threatened its effectiveness. Differences in interpreting and living the gospel put crucial choices before the Church, and decisions had to be made on directions to be taken if the community was to be maintained as a strong, clear, and unified sign of God's holy kingdom and if its table-fellowship was to keep its significance. Living as they did in a suspicious and often hostile society, Christians had to exercise greater care in receiving new members and in deciding whether to welcome back those who had once proved untrustworthy, for to the Roman empire the rapidly growing Christian movement was more a threat than before and it struck back with both propaganda and persecutions.

As Christians entered the mainstream of Greco-Roman culture in the mid-second century, they adopted a more conciliatory attitude toward society and were less likely to define themselves in contrast to it. Yet policy decisions had to be made on how to react to threats within and without and on how the community (and, increasingly, its officials) were to meet responsibilities in serving God's kingdom, protecting the community, and healing sinners. Procedures for forming initiates (the catechumenate) and reforming penitents developed in close parallel. Communities began to formulate policy, organize discipline, and establish liturgical rituals.

RIGORISM AND RECONCILIATION

But institutionalizing penance raised new questions. Which sinners required special attention? How was their repentance to be gauged? When were the repentant to be reconciled? Were all who sought it to be reconciled?

At times and in some places, the scandal of notoriously sinful church members was replaced by the equally scandalous situation of a community lacking in compassion and tolerance and seemingly more concerned with standards and procedures than people. Some churches questioned the practicality or even the possibility of reconciliation for certain sinners. Early second-century documents and the controversies consuming so much energy during the second and third centuries show that proponents of a stricter policy based on an elitist view of the Church were gaining ground in the West, particularly in northern Africa. By the beginning of the third century, these "puritans" were strong and numerous enough to precipitate bitter dispute and sectarianism: the heresy of Montanism (with Tertullian's writings serving as our most important source of information for the early third century), reconciliation controversies at Carthage (with Cyprian the key figure), and schisms at Rome (led first by Hippolytus and then by Novatian). All these affected the nature and direction of the developing penitential institution in the Western Church.

Controversy at Carthage

Montanism originated in the mid-second century. Its growing influence in the third century provides a convenient focus for seeing how ancient penance was shaped by controversy. Historians often refer to Montanism as "a protest against the laxity which had crept in,"[1] but this is to take too seriously the claims of what purported to be a revival movement. Earlier rigorists had laid a congenial groundwork, but the rigid asceticism, sober outlook, and strenuous discipline of Montanism stood in sharp contrast to the spirit of earlier generations of Christians. Like all enthusiasts, the Montanists (and especially their best-known convert, Tertullian) were at their best when arguing against something; they took their extreme positions because to them consistency was more important than realism.

Nowhere is this more apparent than in Tertullian's writings on repentance and forgiveness, our most important source for knowledge of early third-century practice at Carthage in northern Africa.[2] Born there about 155 or 160, Tertullian became a Christian in his mid-thirties. He was soon helping form catechumens and began his literary career as a catechist and teacher. While he did not break with the Church and become a Montanist until about 207, an earlier sternness and impatience, particularly in his writings on discipline and asceticism, show his gradual movement toward Montanist rigorism. His two most important treatises are *De paenitentia* (On Penitence), written about 203 or 204 while he was still Catholic, and his Montanist polemic against Catholic practice, *De pudicitia* (On Purity).[3] The sharpest contradiction between the two is his Catholic affirmation that forgiveness and reconciliation are possible for all repentant sinners—though only once for those subject to the penitential institution—and his Montanist denial of the Church's ability to forgive the gravest sins.

A penitential institution was apparently established at Carthage at about the same time as the formal catechumenate and developed along similar lines. Those preparing for entry into the Church and those preparing for reentry were kept in distinct groups, separate from the rest of the faithful and served by a special ministry. Neither preparation could be repeated, but the most important thing about the penitential institution is that it drew a sharp line between those who were officially sinful and those who were officially faithful, with the severity of the orthodox almost matching that of the Montanists.

The *De paenitentia* discusses penitence in general (chapters 1 to 4), prebaptismal penitence (chapters 5 to 6), and postbaptismal penitence (chapters 7 to 12). While Tertullian parallels the latter two (*De paen.* 6, 14), he is reluctant to speak of a second repentance (*paenitentia secunda*) after that of baptism for fear of seeming to tolerate or even encourage sin. This is understandable if he is speaking to catechumens preparing for baptism, for the thought of another repentance would have been scandalous to those still enthusiastically engaged in the first, though the third section seems addressed to a different audience. Like Hermas, though on psychological rather than eschatological grounds, Tertullian states that one such second chance is possible. Postbaptismal repentance is as exceptional as the anomalous sin that makes it necessary. Because this second and last penitence is so serious—how genuine is the conversion of those who have already shown themselves to be liars?—the Church must test sincerity through external manifestations, just as it does before baptism (*De paen.* 9).

Tertullian uses the Greek *exomologesis* to name the public ritual manifestation of repentance. While this word is often translated as confession, it does not mean what we usually understand by the term.[4] It is confession first of faith, then of praise, and only then of sins. *Exomologesis* acknowledges God's greatness, a greatness shown through mercy leading sinners to repentance, and breathes the same spiritual atmosphere as the Jewish *berakoth*. It is not primarily the acknowledgment of sins—this took place through presenting oneself publicly as a penitent—but rather a confession of faith, the praise of God, and an appeal for the community's prayerful support. This outlook characterizes the liturgies of penance and reconciliation throughout the ancient period.

Exomologesis went beyond inner feeling and verbal statement. Internal conversion was presupposed, at least to the extent of wanting to be converted, but a holistic view of conversion required that it be shown more through deeds than words in order to gauge its sincerity and depth. Wearing penitential garb, sinners begged for pardon and peace through the community's intercession. Seeking the Church's prayer, they knelt in sackcloth and ashes at the entrance to the place of assembly. Each Sunday at the time of worship they approached those who were gathering and pleaded for recognition as penitents and eventual reconciliation to the Church. Tertullian describes the function of this *exomologesis* in a tortuous passage in *De paenitentia* 9: "Herein we confess our sin to the Lord, not as though [God] were ignorant of it, but because satisfaction receives its proper determination through *exomologesis*, *exomologesis* gives birth to penitence and by penitence God is appeased." It is unclear to what extent sins had to be specified whether publicly (to the assembled Church) or privately (to the bishop).

For Tertullian, postbaptismal repentance is formally expressed through both Church ritual and a changed way of life. The ritual includes seeking the prayers of the Christian community and especially of the presbyters: "*Exomologesis* requires that . . . you prostrate yourself at the feet of the priests and kneel before the beloved of God, making all the brethren commissioned ambassadors of your prayer for pardon" (*De paen.* 9). The sinner's prayer becomes the prayer of the Church and thus the prayer of Christ. The changed way of life involves not only amendment but also mortification such as fasting and the wearing of sackcloth and ashes. While Tertullian's legal background is frequently evident (e.g., in his use of the term satisfaction), mortification generally functioned here as it did preceding baptism: the use of mourning customs symbolized sorrow for the past and reoriented the individual's life by establishing a revised set of priorities.

Tertullian uses several different phrases to describe reconciliation—restoration, reincorporation into the Church, peace, return to the Church's camp, reception into communion—but he gives no description of its ritual form. How he understands its manner of operation, however, is clear: the Church's prayer, because it is the prayer of Christ, unfailingly obtains divine forgiveness. Reconciliation with the Church does more than lift an ecclesiastical excommunication, for it brings about divine forgiveness.[5]

The two treatises differ considerably in stating the outcome of penitence. For the Catholic Tertullian, the Church suffers with penitents and supports them in restructuring their lives. Most important, it prays for them and, since the Church is Christ, the prayer is heard. Penitents are restored to the Church and thus reconciled with God. But for the Montanist Tertullian, there is no parallel between baptism and penance. After baptism some sins are irremissible so far as the Church is concerned; sinners must do lifelong penance, hopeful of God's forgiveness at death but condemned for life to exclusion from the Church and its sacraments.

Tertullian distinguishes remissible and irremissible sins in chapter 2 of *De pudicitia*. In chapter 4, he insists that the lifelong penance of the sinner denied reconciliation honors God and prepares the penitent to receive God's forgiveness at death. As examples of irremissible sins he gives the famous "triad" of apostasy, murder, and adultery (cf. Acts 15:29) in chapter 2 and mentions others in chapter 19: fraud, blasphemy, and other "violations of the temple of God." Tertullian thus distinguishes sins that call for *castigatio* (correction) with eventual *venia* (forgiveness) from those that call for *damnatio* (condemnation) ending in the *poena* (punishment) of death. While the Church imposes penance on both categories, some sins are so radical a break of the baptismal oath that their forgiveness must be left to God. Only the sinner's death can atone for them and cancel their penalty. Tertullian calls these sins "mortal" (3, 3; 19, 28; 21, 2) or "capital" (9, 20; 21, 14) or "greater" sins (18, 18); the others he calls "lesser" sins.

The polemics of *De pudicitia* were occasioned by a bishop's decree—perhaps in opposition to the Montanists or to similar puritans within the Church—that he would reconcile repentant sinners guilty of adultery and fornication. Tertullian does not accuse the bishop (probably Agrippinus of Carthage) of innovating but simply insists that adultery *must not* be forgiven and that murder and idolatry *are not* forgiven by the Church—a restriction on *exomologesis* not mentioned in *De paenitentia*. The edict—of which we have no other evidence—is styled "peremptory," a Roman legal term indicating that the bishop meant to end discussion, suggesting that the controversy was the latest incident in a long-standing debate.

Tertullian's polemics witness to the bishop's special role in reconciliation, just as *De paenitentia's* mention of the presbyters indicates the special value of their prayers. The harsh complaints directed at the bishop in *De pudicitia* (especially 1, 10, 21) show that the bishop supervised the whole process of penitence and made the final decision regarding reconciliation. He would also have presided over the prayer of the assembled Church that, as the prayer of Christ, embraced the sinner and won forgiveness from God.

With Montanism, the earlier controversy widened to include not only whether bishops *should* reconcile certain sinners but also whether they *could*. At one point Tertullian seems to say that the power to do so has now been withdrawn by a new revelation (*De pud.* 21), but the major thrust of his argument is that the power of the keys (Mt 16:18–19) was personal to Peter and after him belongs not to the officeholders of the visible Church but rather to the Church of the Spirit and to those filled with the Spirit.

He calls his opponents, particularly the bishop who reconciled adulterers, *psychikoi*, "unspiritual" or "sensual" (cf. 1 Cor 2:14). All parties agreed that the bishop's pardon never substituted for repentance. Tertullian, however, took a further step. He admitted the Church's role in directing penitence but insisted that some penitents were to be refused the fruit of repentance, reconciliation with the Church. They could hope for divine forgiveness only at death (*De pud.*, 4).

By the early third century, *metanoia* was being institutionalized in both prebaptismal and postbaptismal forms. Allowing more than one repentance or conversion—still regarded as exceptional—posed something of a conscience problem for the Church. It therefore began to develop a disciplinary system and a rudimentary ritual so as not to give an excuse for postbaptismal sin and not to appear lax.

The institutionalized forms of second repentance began with a public *exomologesis* or *confessio*, acknowledging God's mercy in bringing the person to an awareness of sin and a desire to return from pagan ways to the Christian community's way of life. Since sin was social and ecclesial, repentance too was social and public and had to be externally manifested long enough for the Church to offer guidance and formation and for the penitent to show reformation and disengagement from sinful ways. *Paenitentia secunda*, like the prebaptismal repentance, took place in the midst of the community, which had to be sure it could rely on its members. The whole community worked with the penitents, helping them overcome their attachment to sin by adhering more closely to the spirit-filled community of saints.

Significantly, neither Tertullian nor other early writers say much about a ritual of reconciliation or the manner whereby rehabilitated penitents were readmitted. Hippolytus (d. 235) refers to a "second baptism" in the Valentinian sect—presumably derived from the Church—which consisted of a laying on of hands.[6] However, not until the controversy over who is to be reconciled was resolved do we find authors describing the ritual of reconciliation in any detail. Then it became important that the status of reconciled penitents be publicly and officially acknowledged and celebrated.

The arguments put forward by those opposed to a more lenient practice made the discipline of irremissibility, where it existed, ambiguous. The discipline was intended to maintain the Church's holiness by indicating the Christian hatred of sin. But as puritans argued their position by denying the Church's total authority over the power of evil, rigid discipline seemed to indicate either a lack of compassion or power.

Cyprian's Solution

Cyprian, bishop of Carthage from 249 to 258, effectively ended the north African controversy and solidified episcopal control over the developing penitential institution when he initiated a dramatic and ironic policy change.

The Decian persecution in 250 was the first organized attack on Christians in 40 years and caught the Carthaginian church unprepared. Apostasy was widespread. What was to be done? Even while the persecution still raged, those who advocated a lenient treatment of apostates attempted to present Bishop Cyprian with a fait accompli. Imprisoned Christians provided apostates with letters of recommendation requesting or even granting reconciliation. On the strength of such vicarious penance, some presbyters were admitting these apostates to eucharistic communion.[7]

Though Cyprian was a devoted student of Tertullian's writings, he apparently ignored the distinction between remissible and irremissible sins and insisted that requiring penance and then refusing reconciliation would be unjust.[8] (He also disregarded Tertullian's Montanist position in *De fuga in persecutione* that escape from persecution by flight or hiding was equivalent to apostasy—Cyprian went underground during the persecution.) Nevertheless, he objected to too ready a welcome of apostates, strongly criticizing those who permitted apostates to join the eucharist without the penitential process and the laying on of hands by bishop and clergy to restore them to communion with the Church (Ep. 15, 1; 16, 2). He hoped to keep rigorists and laxists together in a unified Church and to uphold his own position as the community's chief official—overlooking the fact that his absence created the problem since he was responsible for overseeing the penitential discipline.

Cyprian's matter-of-fact references to the laying on of hands indicates that this gesture was already the most prominent ritual sign in the return to peace with the Church (the grant of the *ius communications*) as well as in the whole process of repentance. This public sign of solidarity with the Church, made by the bishop and assembled clergy (cf. Ep. 61, 3), was to precede eucharistic communion even when the penitent or sinner who had not yet begun *exomologesis* had a martyr's recommendation. Cyprian advised waiting until each case could be examined individually since circumstances varied considerably. Only in an emergency could a presbyter (or deacon, if no presbyter was available) receive a sinner as a penitent, blessing the sinner's *exomologesis* through the laying on of hands, or reconcile individuals with a martyr's letter of indulgence (Ep. 17, 2; Ep. 18, 1; Ep. 19, 2; 20, 3, 2).

After the persecution, other *lapsi,* as they were called, wished to return to the Church as quickly and easily as they had left it, and the controversy over reconciling sinners was rekindled. In a moving sermon at a celebration of the persecution's end, Cyprian took a moderate position requiring both the martyr's or confessor's letter of recommendation and a long period of rehabilitation and probation. At a synod of north African bishops held in May 251, his *De lapsis* was read and his policies confirmed;

the *libellatici* (those who had by bribery obtained false certificates testifying to apostasy) could now be reconciled if they had been doing penance; the *sacrificati* (those who had actually offered pagan sacrifice) were to do lifelong penance but were promised reconciliation on their deathbeds. Readmission to the Church's communion without the process of recovery and rehabilitation was considered meaningless, both deceptive and dangerous (*De lapsis*, 15).

This compromise solution was not completely satisfactory to either party in the controversy, but it was not to last long. Rumors spread that a new persecution was imminent. Cyprian was afraid that the penitent *lapsi* would apostasize again if they were not strengthened by the Church's Spirit and eucharist. Considering their situation comparable to a deathbed emergency, he called a council in May 252 and announced that even the *sacrificati* were to be reconciled—immediately!

The persecution never came. Ironically, Cyprian, who had first tried to steer a middle course between lenient and rigorist extremes, ended by adopting a lenient stance because of a nonexistent persecution. The result was a schism on the part of the puritans, but, so far as the Church of Carthage was concerned, the controversy had ended. Both the doctrine and the discipline of irremissibility had been decisively rejected. No penitent sinners, no matter how flawed their past, were to be left outside the Church's communion. Moreover, the principle of episcopal control over the developing penitential discipline—as opposed to the martyr's privilege—had been firmly established. Officeholders, not charismatic individuals, were to have the final say on admission to the Church's assemblies.

In speaking of the process of return to the Church, Cyprian uses *exomologesis* more broadly than Tertullian had and makes reconciliation more prominent. For Cyprian, *exomologesis* is the whole formal procedure required of those guilty of particularly grave sins before they can be reconciled to the Church. This process is a worshipful acknowledgment of God's mercy in forgiving the sinner, a lengthy manifestation of repentance through mortification, and a reform of life. Then the individual is ready to be readmitted to a full share in the community's life in the Spirit.

The ritual imposition of hands seems to have marked both the beginning of *exomologesis* and its completion in reconciliation, which explains why Cyprian sometimes regards it as exorcism and sometimes as the grant of peace with the Church. On the basis of the parallel between prebaptismal formation and penitential reformation, the laying on of hands to make a catechumen and to make a penitent both functioned as rites of exorcism—expelling the spirit of evil that had dominated the sinner. At reconciliation, the Spirit-filled community shared the Holy Spirit with the penitents through its prayer and the imposition of hands by the Spirit-filled bishop and clergy; this corresponded to bringing the newly baptized into the assembly of the faithful and the bishop's confirming and completing their baptism before they shared the eucharist. The primary significance of the rite for Cyprian, however, was not so much the direct giving of the Spirit as the giving of peace with the Church through the communion of the Holy Spirit. *Pax cum Ecclesia* was uppermost in his mind, though this is obviously closely related to his pneumatic view of the Church.

Only when Cyprian spoke of a rite for reconciling those baptized outside the Church—one that we would perhaps be more inclined to call confirmation, though it was not yet a separate sacrament—did he speak explicitly of the conferral of the Spirit through the laying on of hands. Cyprian, like Tertullian, rejected the efficacy of initiation rites performed by heretics because of the impossibility, as he saw it, of giving or receiving the Spirit outside the Church. The problem, then, is whether the imposition of hands in receiving those baptized outside the Church was that of penance and reconciliation or confirmation, though the ecclesial and pneumatic significance is the same in either case.[9] At any rate, by 256 the rite was sufficiently traditional that Pope Stephen could say, "nihil innovetur nisi quod traditum est"—no innovation, stick with tradition.[10]

This double meaning of the laying on of hands—both exorcism and grant of the Spirit—helps clarify the significance of penitential works and of reconciliation with the Church in the forgiveness of sins. Genuine repentance had to take hold and grow, and this took time. The sincerity of repentance could be doubted in those who had been disloyal, and so testing was necessary. For Cyprian and the ancient Church, true contrition was expressed in penitential deeds, just as sin was expressed in deeds. In the milieu of the time, the mortification process expressed the effort to drive out the spirit of evil by readjusting one's relationship to creation, which had been idolized by sin, and to put God first, in preference to any creature. The deeds by which repentance was made evident showed that God's pardon was received and that the penitents could be restored to the Church (Ep. 15 and Ep. 16).

This suggests that penitential works obtain divine forgiveness, but another line of thought in Cyprian's writings implies that the sinner's reconciliation with the Church is essential if penitential works are to obtain the remission of sins (De lapsis 16). The apparent paradox is due to Cyprian's ecclesial awareness that prevented him from making the later distinction between personal and ecclesiastical factors. The penitent does not obtain forgiveness simply through penitential acts nor does the bishop forgive sins directly. The whole process manifests reconciliation with God achieved in solidarity with the Church. Penitential deeds express the penitent's reattachment to the Church as the spirit of evil is overcome, and reconciliation is the grant of communion with the Church as the Holy Spirit is given.[11]

In its full sense, then, *exomologesis* is a public confession of guilt before God and the community, a way of rectifying one's distorted relationship with God and creation, a means of achieving pardon, and an appeal to the community for its prayer and support. This formal procedure was required only in extraordinary cases. Ordinary sinners followed the path of repentance through the prayer, mortification, and good works that characterized the everyday life of the Christian (cf. *De oratione*, 12). They did not need the close supervision, individualized intercessory prayer (exorcism and invocation of the Spirit), and explicit grant of peace and communion with the Church that were part of the formal process. In either situation, however, forgiveness of sins came through solidarity with the Church and through its prayer.

Schisms at Rome
The church of Carthage was not the only one racked by dissension over reconciling notorious sinners. Controversy raged in the church of Rome as well, and there too competing factions eventually split the Church. In the second century, Hermas wrote of disputes. Early in the third century, about 218, Hippolytus (d. 235) whose *Apostolic Tradition* witnesses to the bishop's role "to loosen all bonds" in its prayer for episcopal ordination, split with Bishop Callistus over the latter's alleged laxity in pardoning sinners. The schism of the rigorists lasted until 235 and was renewed under Novatian's leadership less than twenty years later.

When Cyprian wrote the Roman Church during the Decian persecution to gain support for his policy regarding the *lapsi*, Novatian was commissioned to draft the reply of the Roman presbyters and deacons, since Rome had no bishop at the time. The Roman policy, as Novatian stated it, was similar to Cyprian's at the time: reconciliation through the laying on of hands by a presbyter (or deacon, if necessary) for penitents in danger of death (Ep. 30).

A few months later, in March 251, Novatian's hope of becoming bishop of Rome failed when Cornelius was elected to that position. After Cornelius began to reconcile *lapsi* not in danger of death, Novatian reversed his earlier stance and claimed to uphold orthodox discipline by insisting that those who had apostasized be excluded for life from the community of saints.

Like Hippolytus before him, Novatian had the support of a sizable part of the Roman Church, including many presbyters and deacons, and was elected bishop in opposition to Cornelius. This schism did not end peaceably as had the earlier one, though Novatian, like Hippolytus, died a martyr for the Christian faith. While thwarted political ambitions played a part in its origin, a more prominent factor was a general dissatisfaction with developments in the Church's relationship to society, viewed by Novatian's followers as compromise and a watering down of doctrine. Concerned with maintaining rigid standards of morality, they ended by insisting that the Church could not forgive certain sins and that by admitting such sinners the Church was destroying itself. Novatian communities spread, particularly in areas where Montanism had been strong, and many of these communities of *cathari* ("puritans") lasted until near the end of the seventh century.

The long dispute with Novatianism helped the Church clarify and systematize its penitential doctrine, particularly through the efforts of bishops like Ambrose of Milan (d. 397) and Pacian of Barcelona (d. before 392), both of whom upheld the Church's complete authority over sin, an authority shown in both baptism and penance.[12] Doctrine thus came to outstrip the discipline that, in the West, permitted penance, like baptism, only once in a lifetime. The inconsistency of affirming a doctrine of complete authority over sin while limiting that authority in practice lasted until the end of the ancient period and repeatedly recurred in later centuries.

Third-century Christians in the Eastern empire seem to
have been less troubled by such controversies than those
in the West. Their understanding of penance was consequently less complicated in its development and less severe in its practice. Eastern developments in the area of
pastoral counseling and spiritual direction also paved the
way for less embarrassingly public forms of penitential
discipline.

Clement of Alexandria (d. 215) regarded all sins as remissible (*Quis dives salvetur* 38, 4–39, 2) but stressed that penance, unlike baptism, is a laborious process (*Stromata* II,
13, 56f). The process is one of dialogue between God and
the sinner assisted by a spiritual director, a holy friend
of God. While Church officials did serve as directors and
thus exercised a ministry of healing (*Stromata* II, 15),
Clement put the saintly lay director on a par with presbyter and bishop in saving sinners and forgiving sins (*Stromata* VI, 13). Though Clement did not describe the
reconciliation of penitents, the importance he gave the
Church as the community of salvation suggests that he regarded reconciliation as a prerequisite for divine pardon
of those separated from the Church by their sins.

Origen (d. 254) is the other leading witness to third-century Eastern practice and the first theologian to deal systematically with penance, listing it seventh among the
various means of remission (*In Levit.*, hom. 2, 4). Despite
his reputation for severity, he too seems to have regarded
all sins as remissible, though some sins required the public process (*In Ps.*, hom. 37, 2, 5; *De oratione* 28; *Contra
Celsum* 3, 50) and in some cases this was permitted only
once (*In Levit.*, hom. 15, 1). Sin has an ecclesial character
because it contradicts the Church's holiness; serious sin
excludes from the Church, with no need for formal excommunication by the bishop (*In Levit.*, hom. 14, 2). The
repentant sinner is to be restored to the Church, however, and in this restoration leaders of the Church and
holy members have a medicinal role in counseling peni-

tents (*Comm. in Matt.* 12, 11–14), particularly on whether or not to enter the formal ecclesiastical process. Origen applies the "praying over" of James 5:14 to the penitential system's laying on of hands—the earliest clear reference to this rite—implying that sin is a disease and this ritual gesture is the Church's prayer for healing (*In Levit.*, hom. 2, 2; *In Ps.*, 37, hom. 1, 1). Formal reconciliation through the laying on of hands was reserved to the bishop, although Origen did not specify how reconciliation is related to healing and forgiveness.

The Eastern tradition, following Clement's and Origen's lead, emphasized the Church's ministers as healers and the importance of spiritual direction. In the East, "private confession"—more a manifestation of conscience than a confession of sins—came to have a bearing on the public discipline beyond the counseling offered to penitents subject to the public discipline. People frequently did not become penitents until forced to do so by public accusation and a legal process, but Origen recommended this manifestation of conscience to other serious sinners. He advised them to go privately to a presbyter and seek his counsel on whether they needed the support of the institutionalized process of repentance (*In Ps.* 37, hom. 2). "Private confession" thus became another way of beginning penance but was not a substitute for it. Grave sins still came under the official discipline, whether the sinner took the initiative in seeking private counsel or waited for legal action.

Spiritual direction or "private confession" was also recommended to those whose sins did not call for the formal ministry of the penitential institution. They were advised to seek the counsel of Church officials or of holy individuals who could help them be healed of sin by following a path of repentance in their everyday lives. They could disclose their inner lives to such advisors, receive assistance from them in discerning the work of the Spirit, be advised on appropriate remedies for sin, and thus come to experience more fully God's liberating grace. While the intercessory prayer of both officials and gifted individuals was of value to these ordinary sinners, forgiveness came through repentance. This was, by no means, our private sacramental penance. Healing and forgiveness came by living a penitent life; the director advised on how to live such a life. There was no formal reconciliation, though prayers for forgiveness and grace were part of the regular liturgy.

A north Syrian document from the first part of the third century, the Didaskalia, describes a well-developed penitential system but one with few signs of the rigorism characteristic of many Western churches at the time. The author, probably of Jewish descent and a physician, writes for a community of converts from paganism and makes heavy use of the Didache. The descriptions of the phases of penance and the bishop's responsibilities emphasize the public nature of the ritual and the gathered community's intercessory role.

The laying on of hands appears to be a central element in the ritual, although the Didaskalia did not distinguish between this gesture as the reception of the penitent and as the reconciliation of a penitent. The laying on of hands is clearly paralleled with baptism as conferring the Holy Spirit (II, 41, 2). On the basis of this parallelism, it is likely that the laying on of hands for penance ("making a penitent") functioned as a rite of exorcism—making room for the Spirit—as did the gesture during the catechumenate. The prayer of the Spirit-filled community and the imposition of hands by the Spirit-filled bishop and clergy at the beginning and end of penance were interpreted as conferring the Holy Spirit.

The Didaskalia attaches great importance to the bishop's role. He is to expel the serious sinner from the Church—a sign of the Church's continuing hatred of sin—but he is also to grant penance and forgiveness to the repentant as a sign of the Church's love for the sinner (e.g., II, 12, 1–3). The bishop's role, then, is largely that of a judge, who, because he is responsible for the community's holiness, must examine in detail any delinquent member (e.g., II, 11, 1–2). But he is a judge whose role is also to reconcile repentants and restore them to the community. In this task, he is assisted by presbyters and deacons who pray with and over the penitents but who may not reconcile except when the penitent is in danger of death.

Interestingly, the Didaskalia does not expect sinners to come forward on their own. It assumes that the bishop or presbyters will issue the indictment or that the sinner will be denounced by someone else and then summoned before the bishop's tribunal after the charge has been verified. There is a rather extensive list of sins requiring sinners' expulsion if a warning does not lead to reform. Excommunication made clear that sinners had no right to share in the Church's assemblies since sin had extinguished the life of the Spirit in them (II, 50, 4). Those who repented and showed signs of reform were to be examined again. If the bishop was convinced of their sincerity, they were "liturgically excommunicated." They confessed sinfulness and promised reform, indicating what progress they had already made. Then, after episcopal exhortations and community intercession, they were ceremonially expelled to begin a period of penance (II, 16, 1–4). This was brief in comparison with the extensive penances of the West—only two, three, five, or seven weeks of fasting, depending on the sin. Other than the prayers over the penitents by the faithful (and especially by the widows) there is no indication of a liturgical aspect to this period of penance. However, penitents were gradually reintroduced into the heart of the liturgical assembly: first to hear the Word proclaimed (II, 39, 6–II, 40, 1) and later to share in the assembly's prayer (II, 41, 1).

In many areas of both East and West, the Church ministered to the penitents each Sunday as it did to the catechumens: through special prayers, blessings, and the laying on of hands. In the fourth century, especially in the East, the principle of progressive reformation and reintegration was further developed. Assigned times and places for the various stages paralleled the phases of the developing catechumenate and dramatized the sinner's gradual return to the Church assembled in worship.[13] The only Roman recognition of such *stationes* was at the Roman synod of 487/488 under Felix III. Basing itself on canon 11 of Nicaea, it provided for a progressive restoration to the Church of those who had apostasized during the Vandal persecutions.

According to the Didaskalia, with the completion of the period of penance the penitents were solemnly and fully readmitted to the assembly. They were exhorted not to sin again, forgiveness was declared, and then, after the assembly's prayer, peace was restored by the imposition of the bishop's hand (II, 18, 7; II, 41, 2). Apparently the penance was a condition for forgiveness, with repentance having the principal role, and the bishop forgave directly. Readmission to the Church seems to be more a consequence of the forgiveness and healing received through the bishop than a means of forgiveness and receiving the Spirit (cf. II, 18, 1–2; II, 20, 9–10), though the community's prayer in a eucharistic context is a prominent feature.

In the Didaskalia, penance and eventual reconciliation are open to all sinners who repent, including those guilty of heresy, adultery, and apostasy, and institutionalized postbaptismal repentance may apparently be repeated. Repetition was apparently prohibited only in churches influenced by Hermas and especially in those that regarded the Shepherd as canonical scripture. Generally, churches that forbade repeating penance required it only for the gravest sins. However, the Didaskalia requires it for many serious sins. The Syrian church, staying close to its Jewish roots and unaffected by rigorist controversies, maintained the temporary and repeatable character of the synagogue bann.

The churches of the East not only seem more lenient than those of the West but also more able to have a public discipline and ritual without embarrassing and discouraging penitents. The Eastern emphasis on spiritual direction, the healing function of the Church's ministers, and private counsel as a way of entering formal penance as well as a way of dealing with sins not subject to that discipline all contributed to the ease with which the Eastern Church passed from public ecclesial penance to private sacramental penance without losing an ecclesial sense. Penitential rituals, often between the homily and the presentation of the gifts (e.g., the genuflection-prayer in Serapion), continued to express communal repentance and prepare a reconciled community for eucharist. The fact that at least some Eastern churches never adopted the principle of unrepeatable reconciliation is also significant.

CONTROVERSY AND POLICY

While we have no rituals from the first four centuries and only sketchy descriptions of the evolving penitential institution, such an institution clearly existed in many churches, if not all. Ordinary sinners heard and responded to the call to repentance in their everyday lives. Informal correction, a general confession, and community intercession enabled them to experience God's mercy in the community of salvation gathered for worship. Others, however, whose sin seemed to involve a total alienation from the Christian way of life (practice varied in determining which sins did this), had to show their repentance externally and publicly long enough to prove depth and sincerity, just as the conversion of those being initiated had to be tested. Then they were formally reconciled as the others were formally initiated.

Though there were exceptions and adaptations (e.g., for the dying), ancient churches that had formal ecclesial penance presumed that some sinners lacked full membership in the Church, had to be reformed as Christians, and had to be reinstated through reconciliation. Before reconciliation could take place, however, repentance had to be manifested visibly in the Church, where members ministered to one another. All Christians had the responsibility to confront erring Christians and recall them to their baptismal pledge. All members of the community shared responsibility for penitents as well as for catechumens, though community officials had special responsibilities. The whole community shared the task of correction and intercession, observed and supported the penitents in their efforts to live a renewed Christian life, and welcomed back as brothers and sisters those who had truly reformed.

Available evidence suggests that disciplinary procedures and liturgical rituals generally took shape in the heat of controversy. During the first half of the third century, a puritanical element insisted on a stern and rigid discipline that went so far as to refuse reconciliation to certain sinners, even if they repented. Church practice gave in to these demands for a time. Discipline was tightened and public rituals developed to clarify individuals' status.

The rigorist position was rejected in the middle of the century when its proponents, both in Carthage and in Rome, insisted that their disciplinary proposals were actually a matter of doctrine. It is one of the curiosities of history that the controversy was closed not out of compassion for the penitent sinner but because the advocates of rigorism denied the Church's ability to offer forgiveness and reconciliation in such cases! But closed it was. While there would still be questions regarding the signs of repentance and the conditions of reconciliation, the policy had been established that no repentant sinner would be forever barred from the Church's assemblies.[14] For disciplinary reasons, some penitent sinners had been refused reconciliation; now, for doctrinal reasons, they would receive it. One inconsistency remained in many areas: formal penance and reconciliation were restricted to once in a lifetime.

Two ecclesiologies clashed in this third-century controversy. On one side were the Montanists, intellectuals like

Hippolytus, Tertullian, and Novatian, a minority of bishops (at least in Africa), and, in some churches, the presbyters. All these maintained an older, elitist model of a little Church, pure in the midst of a corrupt society, a small community of saints marching unswervingly toward the kingdom. No accommodations could be made, no pause to wait for the wayward. While the Church might hope for God's mercy for the sinner, it dared not relax its discipline and reconcile them. On the other side were the majority of the people and bishops. They saw the Church as a community of salvation mediating between human weakness and divine grace. That the people favored lenient treatment of repentant sinners is evident in the letters written in their behalf by Carthaginian martyrs and confessors, popular opposition to Novatian in Rome, and abundant apocryphal writings telling of the conversion of great sinners. The bishops of the period were statesmen and pastoral realists concerned with maintaining their position as leaders in the community and moderators of its discipline, but they were also ready to respond to new needs and resolve the problems that came with expansion. They made the adaptations necessary for a growing Church comprehensive enough to include both saint and sinner.

A penitential institution would probably have taken shape anyway, but the form that it took in the West was largely due to the controversies that swirled about during its formative period. Montanist and Novatianist severity were almost matched by the ecclesiastical institution. A climate of suspicion made penitents acknowledge their guilt openly and prove the sincerity of their intentions during a time of probation. A mood of condescension gave aid to the fallen but then often regarded the one-time penitent as a second-class citizen in the Church. In responding to the accusations of heretics outside the Church and the demands of rigorists within, those who supervised the community's life had to take care not to appear too lenient. In establishing their role as moderators of penitential discipline, the bishops found themselves put in the position of legislators and judges.

These effects of the penitential controversy became more evident in the fourth and fifth centuries as the institutionalization of second conversion was canonically regulated. But it is important to remember that the reluctance to grant reconciliation for fear of compromising the Church's holiness had given way to the realization that such holiness was even more clearly shown in a compassionate ministry to all sinners.

Still, rigid and severe discipline was not always due to a lack of compassion. At its base were strong convictions of Christian dignity and the need to maintain table-fellowship as experience of the kingdom. Restrictions on penance and reconciliation showed the Church's repudiation of life-styles and behavior that destroyed its dignity and showed the Church's desire to help its members live according to their call. When the discipline changed, it was to show the Christian community's complete authority over sin, its ability to assist its members in overcoming whatever power sin might have over them, and to manifest its holiness by sharing the Lord's compassion. Eschatological tension—between the "already" of a community called to live in Christ's Holy Spirit and the "not yet" of a community struggling to surrender to the Spirit—was still in evidence.

NOTES

1. Poschmann, *Penance*, p. 36. Cf. F. E. Vokes, "Penitential Discipline in Montanism," *Studia Patristica* 14 (1976) 62–76.

2. Fragmentary evidence forbids statements on the practice of "the Church" and suggests that practices varied from one church to another, even in northern Africa (cf. Cyprian, Ep. 55, 21, 2). We know that of Carthage best because of Tertullian.

3. For English translations of "De paenitentia" and "De pudici-tia" by William P. Le Saint, see *Ancient Christian Writers* 28 (New York: Newman Press, 1959).

4. For a general survey of the patristic use of *exomologesis*, see G. W. H. Lampe, ed., *A Patristic Greek Lexicon* (London: Oxford University Press, 1961) 1: 499–500.

5. For a closer examination of the relationship between excom-munication and penance in the early Church, see Jean Bernhard, "Excommunication et pénitence—sacrement aux deux premiers siècles de l'église. Contribution canonique." *Revue de Droit Cano-nique* 15 (1965) 265–281, 318–330; 16 (1966) 41–70. Excommunica-tion originated in excluding unrepentant sinners; lifting the ban after repentance enabled the person to share in the communal prayer for forgiveness that was part of eucharistic celebration. See also Rahner's essay on "Sin as Loss of Grace in Early Church Literature" [*Theological Investigations*, v. 15 (New York: Cross-road, 1982), pp. 23–53], though this 1936 essay, still heavily in-fluenced by individualistic scholastic categories, needs to be balanced by a consideration of the early Church's ecclesiological understanding of grace; cf. pp. 57–64 of the same volume.

6. *Philosophoumena* or *Contra haereses* 6, 36 (PG 16:3260); "The Refutation of All Heresies" in *The Ante-Nicene Fathers* (Alexander Roberts and James Donaldson, eds; New York: Scribner, 1926) 5: 92–93.

7. As a Catholic, in his *Ad martyres*, Tertullian had encouraged confessors of the faith in prison to maintain peace among them-selves so that they could grant it to those who had forfeited it through apostasy—presumably through their example, prayer, and recommendation, not through direct forgiveness. In *De pud-icitia*, 22 he ridicules such letters. Apologists for indulgences often appeal to these letters as early evidence for indulgences but fail to note that the practice was controversial (because it was detrimental to the growing status of officeholders in the Church), came to be strictly limited, and eventually functioned as little more than a request for leniency. The practice is only remotely related to indulgences, which grew out of the commutations and redemptions of medieval tariff penance.

8. Ep. 55. For the Latin text of the letters, see *Corpus scriptorum ecclesiasticorum latinorum* 3/2, and for the English translations,

Saint Cyprian, Letters (1–81) in *The Fathers of the Church,* v. 51 (Washington, D.C.: Catholic University of America Press, 1964).

9. *De rebaptismate* 1, written after 256 and probably before Cyprian's death in 258, also links penance and confirmation without clearly distinguishing between them—the rite is called both "penance" and "spiritual baptism" (*De rebapt.* 1, 4, 10). Those forbidding rebaptism used the rite of imposing hands both for reconciling a baptized Christian who had joined the heretics and now wishes to return as well as for reconciling someone baptized outside the Church: *"satis sit in paenitentia manum imponere"*; Ep. 71, 2. See also the *Sententia episcoporum* of the Council of Carthage, 8, 30, 63, 77, and Ep. 73, 6. For a general discussion, see C. E. Pocknee, "Confirmation and the Reconciliation of Heretics and Apostates," *Church Quarterly Review* 166 (1965) 357–361.

10. *In Cyprian,* Ep. 74, 1 (CSEL 3/2: 799).

11. Tertullian at times tended to isolate the individual's penitential activity from the Church's prayer. Cyprian unites the two more closely, seeing the value of the individual's activity as correlative with sharing the Church's Spirit. Not until Thomas Aquinas—and then only for a short time—would the personal and ecclesial dimensions again be so clearly united. For a detailed study of Cyprian's theology of penance, see Karl Rahner, "The Penitential Teaching of Cyprian of Carthage," *Theological Investigations* 15: 152–222.

12. The Church's ministry of forgiveness of sins and reconciliation in penance is frequently compared with its ministry in baptism. In his *De paenitentia* (CSEL 73: 117–206), Ambrose argues that Novatians destroy the parallel by not granting reconciliation to all who repent. Ambrose's doctrinal and procedural parallel extends to permitting both baptism and formal penance only once, though he demands formal penance only for the gravest sins. See Peter Riga, "Penance in Saint Ambrose," *Eglise et Théologie* 4 (1973): 213–226. Pacian requires formal penance only for the triad mentioned in Acts 15:29 (see his sermon on penance in PL 13: 1082–1090), though others may enter it voluntarily. He too insists, against the Novatianist Sympronian, that the Church's authority is as extensive in penance as in baptism (for the three letters, artificially grouped together, see PL 13: 1051–1082).

13. Council of Ancyra (314), c. 4, 17; Council of Nicaea (325), c. 11; Council of Laodicea (343–381), c. 2. Basil of Caesarea (d. 379) and Gregory of Nyssa (d. 398) describe how this worked in their churches.

14. Generally, at least after the Council of Nicaea, communion was given the dying who were repentant, even if discipline forbade receiving them as penitents or reconciling them. The practice has continued to this day (e.g., for a dying person whose marriage is invalid), though now absolution would be given before the eucharist.

Only particularly destructive actions or life-styles seriously at variance with that of the Christian community prohibited eucharistic participation in the early centuries. Sins that a later age regarded as excluding from eucharist were then considered indications of the Christian's need for ongoing conversion. Even when sinners had to be dealt with canonically, there was the realization that conversion takes time and that the eucharist both challenges sinners and strengthens the repentant. Thus, individuals who had not yet satisfied all the canonical requirements were often permitted to return to the eucharist. The notion of being worthy to receive communion is relatively late and probably the consequence of focusing attention more on sins than sinners. The earlier practice may offer a precedent for those who today advocate permitting people in canonically irregular marriage to receive communion. Cf. W. Stolzman, "Communion for Repenting Sinners?" *Clergy Review* 65 (1980) 322–327.

Chapter Three

Canonical Penance and Its Liturgy

By the mid-third century, a person's position as penitent was defined officially—and therefore liturgically—in all its phases; it was increasingly important that status within the community be clear, carefully regulated, and publicly known. Second- and third-century writers dealt mostly with *exomologesis*, the penitential process before reconciliation, but after the penitential controversy had been resolved in principle, descriptions of the reconciliation liturgy began to appear.

The sense of Church as a holy community gathered apart from society changed after Christianity was legally recognized in the early fourth century. Apostasy and what to do with apostates was less an issue. Other sins were downgraded to some extent as penance was allowed for the most serious sins.

Nevertheless, penance laws became more extensive and penance liturgy more elaborate. Following the controversies, discipline became more uniform on a regional basis as synods of bishops issued canonical legislation. Canons are by no means consistent with one another, but consensus on the main features of the penitential institution emerged in the fourth and fifth centuries. While we know little of the ministry to penitents apart from liturgy, the increasingly dramatic liturgy can be reconstructed on the basis of scattered evidence and what is preserved in later liturgies.

Overall, legislation and liturgy developed in tandem to make the penitents a distinct class in the Church. The names given the most prominent official form of penance in this period show its character. The extensive legislation of canonical penance distinguished it from what had preceded. Early informal procedures and interim policies of the second and third centuries gave way to an established and easily recognized ecclesiastical institution. The community's involvement was public and shown through elaborate community liturgies.

THE CANONICAL DISCIPLINE

The canonical institution, though more formal, was often less severe. During the uneasy peace that followed persecution under Emperor Valentinian (d. 260), the Church permitted occupations and entertainment it had forbidden and Christians began to enter the army, civil service, and social life. The precedent set in the treatment of apostates—reconciliation permitted for the most serious of sins—meant that life-styles once anathema to Christians were no longer sins calling for penance.

With toleration and legal status, the Church had a new freedom of operation and eventually a privileged position. Yet this new partnership of Church and empire dismantled the Christian community that had gathered apart from society to be a bright sign of holiness amid pagan darkness. With the removal of barriers to the Christian's full participation in society, the Christian's identity could no longer be determined simply by contrast with pagan society. Sin began to lose something of its public character as it was less clearly a public offense against a segregated community of saints. Similarly, as the boundaries of Church and society began to coincide and organizational dimensions of the Church increased in importance, the experience of Church community grew weaker. Sin, insofar as it was subject to formal ecclesiastical discipline, became an abstract reality determined by canonical regulations rather than a concrete experience of failing one's community.

Christians who held to an elitist ecclesiology considered the Church's new position an accommodation and compromise inconsistent with its faith. There were crowds of converts, but conversion was often superficial. The catechumenate could not work effectively with large numbers of people and this meant that pagan ways of life were being introduced into the Church. The Church was now respectable and its officials were given civil status, but some Christians questioned whether Caesar's *cursus honorum* and style of government were appropriate models for Church organization.

Canonical penance and the monastic movement can be interpreted as responses to compromise and as attempts to maintain a sharp distinction between sinners and saints. Both penance and monasticism were inclined to see the workaday world as a place of sin. Both tried to preserve a model of the Church as a separate community and maintain high ethical standards despite relaxation of discipline in the Church at large. The two interacted in this period and later to shape structures, spirituality, and ideals.

Legislation and Practice
Extensive canonical legislation in the fourth and fifth centuries tried to compensate for changes in the Church's relationship to society and Christians' relationship to Church and society. While the understanding of personal repentance underwent little change, the context within which it was expressed and experienced changed as the ecclesiastical administration of the formal process began to consist of applying impersonal laws to abstract categories of sins and as its supervisors were perceived as legislators and judges. As the ecclesial process of repentance was increasingly regulated by law, more stress was laid on ecclesiastical penalty than on strengthening community and rehabilitating sinners. In some ways, repentance became stricter as rigid law substituted for the experience of

a close-knit community. Times of penance, for example, were longer than in the third century.

Though the severity of the Synod of Elvira (dated between 295 and 314) has sometimes led to its being charged with Novatianism, its extensive regulations give an early picture of the direction taken by the canonical institution. Personal repentance, including penitential works, or temporary exclusion from the eucharist was considered sufficient for such sins as missing Sunday eucharist three times (canon 21). Other sins required entry into the formal institution of penance, probation, and supervision for a period of time—for example, one year for gambling with dice (canon 79), five years for parents who married their daughter to a Jew (canon 16). Still others required such probation for a lifetime, with communion granted only on the person's deathbed—for example, a consecrated virgin who broke her vows only once (canon 13). In some cases—at least 18!—communion was to be denied even when death was imminent; for example, a woman who had left her husband without cause (canon 8), pederasts (canon 71), a woman who had an abortion (canon 63), a person who fornicated after once repenting (canon 7), someone who falsely accused a clergyman of crime (canon 75).

Though pastoral practice mitigated this severity,[1] several inconsistencies are puzzling.[2] Canons varied considerably on which sins required formal penance. There seems to be no logical relationship between sins and the periods of time set for doing penance and no consistent pattern when various sets of synodal regulations are compared. Many grave sins were not reserved to the formal discipline and some lesser sins were. Though popular histories often single out Tertullian's triad as the sins requiring formal penance, these were sins that he regarded as irremissible—penance was to be done but reconciliation could never be granted. While his influence was such that in some churches in the fourth and fifth centuries these were the only sins reserved to the canonical institution, Elvira clearly shows that the effort to regulate the lives of Christians by canonical legislation and public penance went far beyond such limits.

The Church of this period made no sharp distinction between judicial forum and sacramental institution. Though there were sometimes differences between real and liturgical excommunication, as in the Didaskalia, an excommunicated sinner who repented was required to prove sincerity through public penance before readmission to the assembly. The public character of the *crimina* subject to the formal discipline was generally emphasized, but grave sin separated the sinner from God and the life of the Church, whether there was a sentence of excommunication or not.

Besides synodal legislation, penitential letters and sets of decrees from individual bishops also attempted to regulate ecclesiastical penance. Documents of Innocent I (d. 417), Leo I (d. 461), and Basil of Caesarea (d. 379) are particularly important for their later influence. Collections of such canons and opinions began to be made in the fifth century and provided the foundation for medieval penance handbooks and later canon law. The Gallican *Statuta ecclesiae antiqua* (from about 475) is one of the most significant.[3]

One reason for synodal legislation, of course, was the need to eliminate abuses of power and prevent arbitrary decisions. Thus, canon 53 of the Synod of Elvira and canon 16 of the Synod of Arles required the same bishop who excommunicated penitents to reconcile them, with Elvira warning an interfering bishop that he would not only cause dissent among the brethren but also threaten his own position. This probably helped to prevent "bishop shopping," but it also concentrated a great deal of power into one person's hands. In an effort to minimize this problem, canon 5 of the Council of Nicaea required the bishops of each province to meet twice a year to review excommunications. Legislation led to more legislation!

Such a situation of ever-expanding legislation moved Augustine to plead for freedom for each bishop to act with pastoral prudence according to the facts of the individual case. The Church of north Africa seems to have been more lenient and liberal than most, since institutionalization was slower there, and so the character of its penitential institution may not be typical of the time. Still, Augustine's extensive writings enable us to construct a picture of what understanding and practice was like in one Church.[4]

Augustine spoke of three types of penance or conversion: prebaptismal penance, everyday penance, and *paenitentia magna*. Adult candidates for baptism underwent *prebaptismal conversion* as they struggled to make the passage from their old life of sin and pagan ways to a totally new life as part of the faithful. The baptized faithful followed a path of *everyday penance* for the whole of their lives, seeking conversion from their daily sins. The Lord's Prayer, especially in the eucharist (which was held daily in north Africa by Augustine's time), was the primary means of pardon for their frequent, though not grave, sins. In addition to prayer, Augustine also mentioned fasting (especially in his Lenten homilies) and almsgiving. He regarded pardoning others' sins as a particularly strong indication of the charity that finds forgiveness.

Those who were properly called penitents were guilty not only of *peccata*, part of every Christian's life, but also of *crimina* calling for great penance, *paenitentia magna*, but Augustine found it difficult to specify the precise difference. In general, these sins were not everyday sins of weakness—which Augustine described as sins against the Son, against the power and wisdom of God—but rather sins of malice, against the Spirit who is the goodness of God. Whether categorizing these sins according to the classical triad or according to the Decalogue, Augustine regarded them as sins calling for the total oblation of the contrite heart in penance. Though he emphasized the penitents' separation from the faithful and their being deprived of the Body of Christ—for Augustine, Church and Christ are always correlated—he was discreet in speaking of penitential practices and rarely used the term "satisfaction."

Initiation and Penance
Augustine's correlation of prebaptismal and postbaptismal conversion (the latter consisting of everyday penance and great penance) is not the only indication that parallels between initiation and penance were maintained during the period of canonical regulation. At least at the beginning of the period, the traditional correlation of catechumenal formation and penitential reformation set the tone for legislation and guided episcopal practice. As the catechumenate disappeared and infant baptism at any time became the rule, the disintegration of the Easter sacrament obscured the relationship between initiation and reconciliation. Penance then began to upstage baptism.

The Church's concern for sincerity of conversion, particularly in candidates seeking admission to the community and in repentant sinners seeking restoration, was uppermost. In both cases, a probationary or postulancy period emphasizing transformation of life tested sincerity, and individuals were admitted to catechumenate or penance only when this was established. Both catechumens and penitents were segregated from the faithful in clearly defined groups, received special attention and prayer, and had set places within the assembly. Initiation and reconciliation both took place publicly at the end of a period of probation. The parallels, even to the point of the ritual gesture of the laying on of hands at the beginning of the period and throughout, indicate that the structures and rituals for the reformation of Christians continued to be modeled on those used for their initial formation. In the West, the principle that penance, like baptism, could not be repeated seems likewise to have been established early and was maintained until after infant baptism became the norm. This principle is maintained with such conviction and strict application, especially after the resolution of the rebaptism controversies, as to seem a point of doctrinal consensus.[5]

In the period of canonical regulation, the two institutions for assisting those engaged in conversion came to be regarded as likewise having parallel consequences: once initiated, always a Christian; once a penitent, always so marked by that experience as to be required to follow a distinctive way of life. Though penance could be received only once, its consequences were far from temporary. From one perspective, the canonical regulations made the person who had been a penitent a second-class citizen in the Church: forbidden to bear arms, engage in business, take a case to civil court, marry or engage in marital relations if already married, or be ordained. The former penitent could not hold public office and in many areas was required to continue wearing a distinctive garb.[6] But another perspective is possible. Many things required of Christians living in a pagan society maintained a distinctive identity by segregating Christians from civil society. After the Constantinian establishment, these restrictions were imposed only on Christians who underwent penance or entered monastic life. Both monks and penitents (the *conversi*) became witnesses to a way of life that had once been followed by all Christians and was still held up as an ideal.

The close relationship between initiation and penance is seen in the continuing controversy over receiving into the Church those who had been baptized by heretics and schismatics. It is often difficult to determine whether an author (Cyprian, for example) regards the imposition of hands on such a person as penance and reconciliation or as the partial repetition of the rites of initiation.[7] The laying on of hands for giving the Spirit was called for by the First Synod of Arles (314),[8] Pope Siricius (384–398),[9] and the Luciferian in Jerome's *Contra luciferianos*.[10] Clarification came only gradually.

Augustine, who is like Cyprian in emphasizing the "peace of the Church,"[11] distinguished more clearly between what we would call the sacraments of confirmation and reconciliation,[12] but he too stressed the need for union with the Church if the sacraments are to be effective and the Spirit is to be given.[13] In 404, Pope Innocent I repeated that those baptized by heretics are not to be rebaptized but only to receive the imposition of the hand,[14] and in 415 he apparently related this more directly to penance.[15] A few years later, Pope Leo the Great (440–461), however, again spoke of both *paenitentia* and *confirmatio*.[16] Not until Pope Vigilius (537–555) do we have a careful distinction: "Their reconciliation does not take place through that imposition of hands which is done through the invocation of the Holy Spirit but rather through that by which the fruit of penance is acquired and the restoration of holy communion is completed."[17]

When in 601, Pope Gregory the Great summarized the various ways in East and West of reconciling those baptized outside the Church, he referred to the Eastern practice of reconciling by anointing with the oil of the sick or, less often, with chrism.[18] The practice was also found in the West.[19] Since anointing is functionally equivalent to laying on hands, the uncertainty about which oil to use probably resulted from the twofold significance of the laying on of hands in the penitential process: healing or exorcism and the giving of the Spirit as the bond of communion. Uncertainty would have been compounded in penance for the dying, when the penitential process was necessarily abbreviated and closely related to the sacrament of the anointing of the sick.

This takes us a bit far afield, for both the reconciliation of heretics and penance for the dying (which we will see later) were exceptional adaptations of the penitential institution. They are, nevertheless, valuable points of study, since the extension of an institution into an extraordinary situation frequently expresses more clearly how it is understood. We could say from our perspective, for example, that the confirmation of those baptized outside the Church and the reconciliation of penitents (as well as of apostates and heretics) are partial repetitions of initiation. The frequent failure to distinguish between them is thus understandable. Likewise, giving eucharist as viaticum without first reconciling the dying person further emphasized penance as a reinitiation.

As baptism ceased to be the sacrament of adult conversion and faith, penance began to replace it, until, in the judgment of at least one historian, it became the basic "means of grace" in Catholicism.[20] This is increasingly evident in the medieval period, as penance is not only repeatable in theory but more frequent in fact. One clear sign that already appeared while ancient canonical penance was still strong is the period of Lent. Originally the time for the catechumenal preparation for baptism, by the fifth century it was already becoming a season of penance. By the tenth and eleventh centuries, Lent was one of the few remaining vestiges of penance's relationship to baptism, but was almost unknown as such.

THE LITURGY OF CANONICAL PENANCE

Liturgical structures were well defined even before ancient penance reached its institutional height in the fifth century. The repentant sinner was received into the order of penitents and committed to doing penance through a public liturgy, there were special intercessions by the assembly and blessings by the bishop during the time spent in penance, and then, at the completion of penance, there was the reconciliation liturgy by which the penitent was restored to full communion with the Church. While we have no formularies from this early period, prayer forms had probably grown out of the berakoth inherited from Judaism.[21] Developments in baptismal and eucharistic liturgies and the evidence of our earliest penance liturgies suggest that petitionary elements received the most attention. Set themes would have determined the content of the prayers and certain phrases would have become customary. (It is hard to imagine Cyprian praying over a penitent without mentioning the Holy Spirit and peace with the Church!) These probably began to be collected as formal written texts in the fifth century. By then, the canonical structures and discipline were well defined, the major controversies had been resolved, and the elaboration that was taking place in eucharist would have affected penance as well.[22]

Unfortunately, penance liturgy has not been studied as thoroughly as baptismal and eucharistic liturgies. From scattered references, scholars have been able to reconstruct much of the development that took place in the eucharist. Little of that kind of work has been done for the liturgy of penance and almost none of it is available in English. The difficulty is that most liturgical sources available to us date no earlier than the sixth and seventh centuries, when canonical penance was practically obsolete. We do, however, have some earlier descriptions, numerous references, and even sermons for the reconciliation service. With these we are able to construct a general picture of penance liturgy in the fifth century, and it fits closely with our oldest penance rituals, the formularies found in the Gelasian Sacramentary.[23]

An element that was not at all liturgical, so far as we can determine, is what has most interested historians of doctrine. Their question, largely framed by post-Reformation polemics, has been to what extent there was a private confession in the ancient period. They have concentrated on the would-be penitent's meeting with the bishop or priest-penitentiary delegated for that purpose. The modern scholarly debate, even in Catholic circles—between Galtier and Poschmann in this century, for example—has been complex, but it has become increasingly clear that private confession in any form even approaching our modern understanding did not exist in the ancient Church. That is, for the most serious sins there was no sacramental process leading to formal reconciliation with the Church that could be taken as an alternative to the canonical procedures with their public rituals. In one sense, confession was private, insofar as counseling is concerned (though when it became customary is conjecture), but the significant confession was public: the *exomologesis* by which the penitent heard and responded to the call to conversion and confessed the One whose merciful love had brought salvation to a sinner. Confession for the ancient Church was praising God for compassion to the sinner. The returning sinner's meeting with the bishop was no more and no less than the pastoral counseling that such a person would seek and receive today. It received no more attention in the writings of the time than the rectory door trade would be given today.

Such pastoral counseling was important, since through it the bishop (or priests assigned that responsibility in larger churches) was able to explore with the person the movement of God's Spirit in his or her life. Through this conversation, the call to conversion became clearer and the individual's desire for repentance and commitment to conversion came to be more solidly based. Then it was possible to determine whether the Church's formal assistance and ministry was needed to further the conversion that was underway. If the person's way of life had been such that extensive help was needed—if, in other words, the individual had been guilty of any of the sinful ways whose correction was reserved to the canonical discipline—then membership in the order of penitents was formally requested and arrangements were made for reception as a penitent. Otherwise, the counselor simply advised the person on how to continue spiritual growth.

While such counseling was private—Leo I in 459 was angry at hearing of penitents being required to read off a list of their sins in public and forbids it (Letter 168, 2)—membership in the order of penitents and the ecclesial conversion leading to reconciliation were not. At its beginning, repentant sinners were "received into penance" or "given penance." This is frequently termed the "blessing of penance"[24] and took place in the liturgical assembly. The Roman practice was to receive penitents at the beginning of Lent, clothe them in sackcloth, pray over them, and then exclude them from the eucharistic assembly until their time for conversion was completed. They were assigned a place among the penitents and began to live a life of penance and receive the regular blessing of penitents.[25] The ceremony was the Church's official call to conversion, the individual's commitment to respond to it, and the community's pledge to offer support through prayer, example, and love.

Sozomen, writing about 450, gives a contemporary description of entrance into the order of penitents at Rome:

". . . where there is a place appropriated to the reception of penitents, in which spot they stand and mourn until the completion of the services, for it is not lawful for them to take part in the mysteries; then they cast themselves, with groans and lamentations, prostrate on the ground. The bishop conducts the ceremony, sheds tears, and prostrates himself in like manner; and all the people burst into tears, and groan aloud. Afterwards, the bishop rises first from the ground, and raises up the others; he offers up prayer on behalf of the penitents and dismisses them. Each of the penitents subjects himself in private to voluntary suffering, either by fastings, by abstaining from the bath or from divers kinds of meats, or by other prescribed means, until a certain period appointed by the bishop. When the time arrives, he is made free from the consequences of his sin, and assembles at the church with the people."[26]

Though Sozomen does not mention it, the individual laying on of hands was an important part of this ritual.[27]

The first four prayers over the penitents given in the old Gelasian Sacramentary are probably much the same as those used as penitent blessings in Rome in the fifth century.[28]

68

"Hear, O Lord, our prayers and spare the sins of those who confess to you, so that the kindness of your pardon may release those accused by their guilty consciences.

"May your mercy come to this servant of yours, we pray, O Lord, and may all iniquities be blotted out by your heavenly pardon.

"Hear our petitions, Lord, and let not the mercy of your compassion be far from this servant of yours; heal the wounds and forgive the sins so that no longer kept away from you by iniquity your servant may always be strong enough to cling to you as lord.

"Lord our God, you do not conquer our offense but rather are appeased by satisfaction: look, we ask, on this servant of yours who freely confesses sinning against you. It is in your power to wash away crimes and to grant forgiveness to sinners, for you have said that you prefer sinners' repentance to their death. Grant this, therefore, O Lord: so to celebrate the vigils of penance before you as to correct behavior and be granted a share in celebrating the joys of eternity in your presence."

This regular blessing continued throughout the time of penance and symbolized the penitent's humility before God in seeking conversion.[29] Canon 19 of the Council of Laodicea (350) put it after the prayer of the catechumens and their dismissal; "after these [penitents] have come up under the hand" and are dismissed, the prayer of the faithful is made and the eucharist is celebrated. Augustine also speaks of the individual blessing of penitents at the community assembly, complaining of how long the line had been![30] While it is difficult to distinguish the initial blessing that "makes" the penitent from the later ones, clearly both are public liturgical ceremonies[31] and the latter are regarded as exorcisms and means of purification[32] that are to take place regularly while the person is doing penance.[33] So significant was this blessing that it became a technical term for the state of penance.[34]

During the time of penance the penitents remained in what Sozomen called "a conspicuous place." Jungmann says that their place was with the catechumens near the entrance of the church where they were able to follow the liturgy.[35] Augustine indicates that in Africa their place was on the left side of the altar, the place of sinners in the parable of the last judgment,[36] and Eligius of Noyon describes the same custom in Gaul (Sermo 8). Penitents were segregated from the community of the faithful, as were the catechumens, and given special attention by the whole assembly, for all, as Augustine says, shared in both the binding and the loosing.[37] In fifth-century Rome, the whole Church relived its baptismal conversion during Lent, and it was in this penitential milieu, focused on baptism, that the penitents returned to God, responding to God's call, with God acting in and through the assembled Body of Christ to call them back and support them in the return. Unfortunately, we know little of how the Church helped the penitents, other than by requiring prayer, fasting, and charitable service and providing special prayers and blessings in the liturgical assemblies.

Public reconciliation was insisted on, particularly in northern Africa where controversies had raged earlier. Penitents were reconciled at a public assembly, in front of the apse—generally at the bishop's chair or at the ambo—with all the people as witnesses.[38] Innocent I, in a letter written in 416, stated that Holy Thursday was the traditional day in Rome for the reconciliation of penitents,[39] and Ambrose said the same for Milan.[40] Though the mozarabic rite reconciled on Good Friday[41] and Cologne on Palm Sunday, the significance was the same: the community of the faithful was restored to wholeness in preparation for the paschal celebration and the initiation of new members.[42]

Sometimes, individuals who had not formally entered the order of penitents joined the penitents for the reconciliation ceremony. Jerome describes how Fabiola, though apparently not a penitent, took her place with the penitents on Holy Thursday—unwashed and weeping, dressed in sackcloth, waiting outside the church to be called to receive reconciliation (*communio*).[43] The language here, as in references to penance for the dying,[44] suggests a developing distinction in practice between *undergoing* conversion with ecclesial supervision and support and *receiving* the benefit of its outcome—reconciliation—something that had existed earlier only for those baptized outside the Church.

The liturgy of reconciliation took place at the close of the Liturgy of the Word after the dismissal of the catechumens, the time for the regular blessing of penitents. An analysis of the archdeacon's request to the bishop that the penitents be reconciled gives us not only a sense of the structure and setting of this liturgy but also an understanding of the roles of assembly and bishop and of the interaction of personal repentance, ecclesial prayer, and episcopal intervention.[45] This, coupled with evidence from the Gelasian and other sources, gives us a fairly complete picture of the fifth-century Roman reconciliation liturgy that marked the completed conversion and final blessing (*absolutio*) of penitents.

The setting is itself impressive. The bishop is seated on his chair, which is on a raised platform in the apse. The penitents are prostrate in tears. The people gather around, standing in witness to the penitents' return, bowing in prayer to support the petitions of the penitents, weeping in compassion and thus compensating for the baptism to which the penitents had been unfaithful. As members of the same Body, the assembled people identify with the penitents by sharing their sorrow; they have the same weaknesses, though not the same sins. By helping to carry the penitents' burden and praying for them during Lent, they had manifested God's mercy. Now they share as well in reconciling the penitents, receiving them back into the communion of the Body of Christ.

The archdeacon's address to the bishop asking him to act on the penitents' behalf emphasizes the involvement of the assembly both in the process of reconciliation as a whole and in the bishop's intervention which is the sign that the penitents are restored to the Church and forgiven by God. Though the bishop has the power of the keys and exercises an official role and decisive ministry, he does so as the one who presides over the assembly. His elevated position is the sign of his power, the power given to Peter, but it is a ministerial power exercised in and for the assembled Church. Jerome too emphasized that the bishop's ministry is oriented to the health and wholeness of the Church:

"The priest offers oblation for the layperson; he imposes hands on the one subject to it; he prays for the return of the Holy Spirit, and thus by the other public prayer he reconciles to the people the one who had been handed over to Satan for the destruction of the flesh so that the Spirit might save. And no sooner is the one member restored to health than all the members come together as a whole. The father finds it easy to pardon his son when the mother begs on behalf of her flesh and blood."[46]

The people's compassionate tears, prayer, and posture, by which they lovingly identify with the penitents, move the bishop to a similar sympathy and prayer by which he exercises his ministry to mediate between the assembly and God. Though he is distinguished from the faithful by his special relationship with God—the metaphor of the indwelling Spirit accents the stability of this relationship—the difference is one of degree and of ministerial activity; he too is part of the faithful and acts for them and on their behalf. When he prays, it is to voice the penitents' prayer which has become the prayer of the whole Church. His intercession, then, expresses the penitents' movement toward God within the context of the community's penitential progress. When he intervenes, bringing them into the Church by the imposition of hands and his sacerdotal prayer, it is as the instrument of God's compassionate movement toward the penitents, freeing them from their sins and restoring them to the eucharist.[47]

The Holy Thursday rite of the old Gelasian, though of Gallican origin, reflects the simpler and less elaborate reconciliation ceremony of fifth-century Rome.[48] Its literary quality is far inferior to the sermons just mentioned, but it uses similar themes and language. The fifth-century rite presumably consisted of the archdeacon's request to the bishop, an address by the bishop or another priest warning the penitents not to sin again, and then the bishop's prayer and laying on of hands as sign of reconciliation.

The assembled Church in its diversity of orders, functions, and responsibilities received the penitents and then celebrated the eucharist as the ultimate sign that the penitents were reconciled to God in the Body and Blood of Christ.[49] The laying on of hands seems not so much to give the Spirit directly as to restore access to the eucharist through which the penitents are once more filled with the Spirit. It is the *ius communicationis,* the right to share, which is primary: solidarity with the Spirit-filled community, expressed particularly in its eucharist.

Reconciliation thus retained something of its initiatory context and setting. Everyday penance continued to point to eucharist and participation in eucharist signified forgiveness of sins not subject to canonical penance.[50] Celebrating the reconciliation of notorious sinners immediately before eucharist[51] made eucharist the ultimate sign of their reconciliation, as it was the clearest sign of initiation into the faithful. Only with the disintegration of initiation, the detachment of eucharist from that sacramentalization of conversion, and the consequent inability of reconciliation to continue to parallel initiation did eucharist cease to be the sacramental apex of conversion and reconciliation. At that point only the juridical right to receive communion remained of the former richness.

THE PRACTICE OF PENANCE

Penance's communal foundation was weakened as both sin and repentance were progressively individualized and privatized. The growing consensus that all repentant sinners were welcome had led to a new insight into how the Church could more clearly express its holiness by healing sinners than by excluding them. A new area of pastoral ministry for Church officials thus opened up, that of spiritual counseling. As they were to be less concerned with the external aspects of penitents' lives (sin and the doing of penance) and more with their internal dispositions and motivations, the minister's pastoral and intercessory activity—counseling and supporting the individual—was distinguished from his public role as community official in reconciling penitents to the community. The penitent's relationship to the Church official became more private as the minister's role became that of a spiritual counselor inquiring into conscience as well as that of a leader regulating the life of the community. This also meant that the penitent's relationship to the community was becoming less a matter of felt experience and more a matter of abstract doctrine. As the doctrinal affirmation of the Church's total authority over sin had earlier made the discipline of irremissibility ambiguous, so now the increasing importance of a private element introduced a contradiction within the public system.

Alongside the inquiry into conscience that now had increased importance as part of the Church's canonical discipline, a private confession of shared prayer, counseling, and spiritual direction continued to develop, particularly in the East and especially among the monks, as a way of ministering to ordinary sinners. In earlier years, the call to continual repentance and the prayers for forgiveness that were a part of the liturgy, together with such private penitential practices as prayer, fasting, and works of charity, had been considered sufficient. Increasingly, however, during the third, fourth, and fifth centuries, sinners not subject to the canonical discipline or not submitting to it were urged to consult a presbyter or other holy person for advice on following the path of repentance. John Chrysostom (d. 407), among others, emphasized this practice of spiritual counseling and direction even more than had

Clement of Alexandria and Origen. In his *Peri Hierosynes* (On the Priesthood), he speaks of a divine power given priests to bind and loose, cleanse and heal by their prayer (3, 5–6). In a homily on penance (3, 4), he speaks of the church building as a physician's office, not a courtroom— a place of forgiveness where God hears the penitent's acknowledgment of guilt and plea for pardon.

This *exomologesis* was a confession to God, not the communal liturgy of the canonical discipline. Though Chrysostom knew the canonical discipline and respected its requirements, he did not always follow its prescriptions. Critics complained of his laxity in allowing repeated penance. He is quoted as offering healing even to those doing penance for the thousandth time.[52] Even more radical in his advice to those unwilling to undergo the canonical discipline, he suggested doing penance privately for at least a few days before approaching the eucharist, thereby revealing their sins repentantly to God. As a bishop who saw himself more as healer than judge, Chrysostom was in something of a bind. The severe requirements of the canonical discipline meant that it was hardly an option for most people, so much had the situation changed from the time when the institution was shaped. He did not want to keep his people from the eucharist, nor did he want them to share it unworthily. Instead of threats, then, he preached repentance and penitential works with the advice of a spiritual director.[53]

Similar advice was given in the West. Ambrose, Augustine, and other fourth- and fifth-century preachers complained about the lack of vocations to penance and about defections from that consecrated life. "Despite having been penitents," Pope Siricius (d. 399) writes, "like dogs they return to their vomit. Like pigs they wallow in the mud. They want to hold public office, to enjoy sports and recreation, to marry and enjoy its pleasures without inhibition. To publicize their lack of self-control they father children despite their vows."[54]

Young people were not permitted to become penitents, nor were those in certain occupations or professions, including the clergy. Those who were married had to have their spouses' permission. Most people, understandably, postponed penance until they were on their deathbeds. The penitential institution came to have little place in everyday life and became simply a way of preparing for death. In many areas, penitents were held up as models whereas once they had been warnings to persevere. Due to the severe discipline, maintained after the sociocultural conditions that had made it necessary had passed, few other than the most pious submitted to it willingly, but those who should have been among the most pious—the clergy—were exempt from it. Since as a rule it dealt with only the more grave sins, its public character made entering it tantamount to a public confession and in some areas such a confession was at times required. Since it could take place only once in a lifetime and since it often had consequences for the remainder of penitents' lives, people's distaste was understandable.

To add to the confusion, bishops were often unwilling or unable to enforce the canons. To call to task serious sinners not publicly known as such could subject them to punishment by the civil authorities, revenge, or social ostracism. To proceed to excommunication when sinners did not voluntarily enter the order of penitents could disrupt the community. The rapid growth of the communities meant that bishops could no longer maintain the personal contact they had once had nor personally supervise catechumens and penitents. As infant baptism became the statistical norm and as mass conversions took place, people entered the community of the faithful with little or no formation. Canonical penance was increasingly out of touch with people's needs and something new was necessary. In their pastoral hearts, many bishops knew this, but in practice most did little more than repeat the ancient rules.

Poschmann states that by the sixth century penance had come to a "dead end in its development."[55] His judgment overlooks penitential forms that stray from the straight line of development that many historians and theologians of penance attempt to draw from New Testament times to our own. So far as the canonical system and its order of penitents is concerned, however, the judgment is true enough; it had become rigid and inflexible and incapable of adapting to changing pastoral needs.

There were evident contradictions and conflicts. The doctrine of the Church's unlimited authority over sin and its ability to forgive had far outstripped the disciplinary limitation of the exercise of that power to once only for an individual. With sin regarded more as a matter of individual behavior than as a public affront to community holiness, why the order of penitents? Pastoral practice was more and more taking the dispositions of the penitent into account in assigning penance, so why should there be a structured conversion process if the individual was already inwardly detached from sin? Private confession—counseling with spiritual experts, not our sacramental form—had increased in importance. Why, then, should the penance to which it was preliminary be public?

Few people probably questioned the order of penitents so explicitly, but their dissatisfaction and fear were evident in their refusal to come forward voluntarily as penitents and in their reluctance to do so even when coerced. Their attitudes had what might be called a strong sociological foundation in that the Church's current situation no longer corresponded to that which had initially shaped the penitential structures and institution. Sin and repentance had come to be seen in individual terms and largely in terms of law and legal process, but the structures and institution had been oriented to making the community whole by restoring lost members.

Individuals sought ways to handle the anxiety and guilt that were intensified by increased legislation but instead were offered institutional structures intended to reintegrate them into a community that was no longer a part of their experience. The outdated system served more to induce guilt than to reduce it, for it gave the impression that those unwilling to enter penance were left in their sins. Rejection of pastoral "experiments"[56] meant that the inherent contradictions would continue to unfold and pastoral ineffectiveness would hold the field.

Even as people lost touch with the eucharist as the sacrament of reconciliation and failed to see how canonical penance could assist them in day-to-day living, they found some measure of consolation in other ritual forms of ecclesial penance: penance for the dying, the institution of the *conversi*, and Lenten penance. These outgrowths of ancient penance retained their vitality even after the order of penitents had withered.

Penance for the Dying
By the end of the period of ancient penance, penance for the dying, once considered an extraordinary form of an exceptional institution for emergency situations, had come to be its most common form. Cyprian had authorized the reconciliation of dying penitent apostates, as had fourth-century Rome, though with reservations on its value (Letter 30, 8). Though Ambrose complained about those who postponed penance until the end (*De paenitentia* 2, 10, 11) and Augustine questioned its value (Sermo 393), canon 13 of the Council of Nicaea had insisted that the dying should not be deprived of the Church's communion. Those who were in danger of death, then, and had not yet received penance often demanded and were given it. If necessary, they were at once reconciled through the laying on of hands and/or the reception of the eucharist.[57] Likewise, those who were already penitents were reconciled.

Reconciliation was often granted simply by giving the eucharist. The imposition of the hand in reconciliation restored the *ius communicationis*, the peace of the Church and the eucharist. In emergencies, the ritual imposition of the hand in penance and reconciliation could be omitted and the eucharist given as sign of communion and welcome, a vestige of the older practice, when participation in the eucharistic gathering had signed conversion and reconciliation, and the older view that penance, like initiation, admitted individuals to that gathering.

Because of the heavy lifelong responsibilities that went with it, young people were forbidden to enter penance. While the definition of young undoubtedly varied, those under 30 or 35 were usually not allowed to become penitents.[58] In view of the life expectancy at the time, we can presume that even penance for the dying was often given reluctantly, if at all. Perhaps the most curious penitential prayer extant is one found in the *Liber Ordinum* for a seriously ill young person. "We dare not impose the yoke of penance because of youthful age and uncertain commitment," the priest prayed. And so viaticum was given without penance or reconciliation![59]

Communion was not withdrawn from those who recovered. What should we do, Cyprian had asked (Letter 55, 13), suffocate them since they were supposed to have died? However, by the sixth century not only were people required by Spanish church law to receive penance as a "last sacrament,"[60] those who recovered had to spend the usual time as penitents.[61] (This no-win situation led many who began to feel better before the priest arrived to refuse to admit him!) They were not, however, to receive the laying on of the hand during this time,[62] a fact that supports the contention that the regular, repeated blessing given the penitents prior to reconciliation functioned as an exorcism. Those who had already received the Spirit did not need these exorcisms but only to make satisfaction, though many ignored these requirements.

Penitents who died without reconciliation were generally still remembered in the eucharist.[63] Like catechumens who died before baptism, they were in some degree of communion. The Gelasian mass formulary for those who had asked for penance but died without it prayed that they "might not lose the fruit of penance which the will desired but mortality prevented."[64] (A rubric indicates that if a person had asked for penance but could not speak when the priest arrived, some sign would be sufficient for the priest to proceed to reconcile.)[65] The general Roman practice from the time of Leo, however, was not to name in liturgical prayer a person who had died without being reconciled to the Church, a practice maintained in the 1917 Code of Canon Law (canons 1240–1241).

The early ritual forms of deathbed penance are unknown to us, apart from the gesture of imposing the hand. Presumably, there was a prayer for forgiveness and probably an assurance to the dying person that the Church's peace and communion were restored. Our oldest ritual for reconciling a penitent at death is in the Gelasian, inserted into the Holy Thursday public reconciliation of penitents.[66] There is no rubric regarding imposing the hand, and the first three prayers would be appropriate for any reconciliation; the second, in fact, calls the Lord's attention to how much the person has already suffered in penance. Only the fourth prayer fits the deathroom situation, asking the merciful God who opens to those who knock not to leave out one whose life is ending. A final prayer has the heading: "Prayers after reconciliation or after (s)he has communicated."

There is, however, a further liturgical symbol of which we have evidence. Just as anointing with the oil of the sick or with chrism became common in the reconciliation of apostates and heretics late in the ancient period, so the oil of holy reconciliation was used to reconcile the dying.[67] As confirmation and the reconciliation of heretics were frequently confused—fused into one rite from the viewpoint of our understanding and distinctions—so there was a close relationship between penance for the dying and the anointing of the sick as a last rite, with anointing functionally equivalent to the imposition of the hand.

A later and more elaborate Visigothic rite made use of sackcloth and ashes. It presumes that other people are present. Several prayers are used, including Psalm 50 and the Lord's Prayer. A rubric indicates that the individual should be suspended from communion for a time, but that in danger of death, the priest may proceed with the remaining prayers and then give the eucharist.[68] The details fit the description of Saint Isidore of Seville receiving penance before his death in 636 (PL 81: 30ff), our earliest evidence of penance as a deathbed ritual and devotional practice for those not guilty of sins requiring the canonical discipline or not subject to that discipline.

By the end of the ancient period, when few were entering the order of penitents, most people did hope to receive penance before death. The ritual (generally tonsure, sackcloth and ashes, reconciliation, and communion) abbreviated the canonical process, retained liturgical features of the entry into and exit from penance, but omitted the central element, the doing of penance, which had reformed the individual as a converted Christian. Faustus of Riez and others continued to question its value (Letter 5). Caesarius of Arles warned that "sudden penance" (*poenitentia subitanea*) was useless without repentance (Sermo 256), but he acknowledged that everyone wanted to receive it and encouraged them to do so (Sermo 60, 4). Even clerics, forbidden to enter public penance, could have it.[69]

An outgrowth of the canonical institution, this death ritual remained prominent as the institution itself declined. It is also the only clear instance in the ancient period of something approaching private sacramental penance. Originally an exceptional form for emergencies, it eventually became common and popular, reaching more people than had the institution, the only indication of a pastoral adaptation of canonical penance to make it more accessible.

81

A community ministry and liturgy for living out conversion accommodated itself to the situation of the dying penitent or sinner, and as that ministry and liturgy grew inflexible and was more and more ignored, its extraordinary form became ordinary. As a consequence, however, receiving penance as a ritual act became increasingly more common than doing penance as a conversion process. Penance was becoming a thing given by the clergy rather than a reality lived by the faithful, as Christianity in much of the West became a religion of birth and routine rather than one of adult conversion and catechumenal formation in faith. This shift in attitude and practice, when rationalized in the medieval scholastics' reflection on their sacramental experience, became the acknowledgment and exercise of the confessor's power of the keys.

In general, penance for the dying in the ancient period suggests caution in typing ancient penance as public. There were clearly varying degrees of publicity. Moreover, the status and popularity of deathbed penance near the end of the ancient period show that its original significance had been lost and that it had become a devotional exercise for the pious—not unlike what happened with private confession near the end of the Counter-Reformation period. Aspects of this devotional penance continued into the Middle Ages (see, for example, the descriptions of Francis of Assisi's death) and modern times (the combined rituals of penance, anointing, and viaticum).

The Conversi
Monasticism and canonical penance (in part parallel responses to the Church's changing social situation and efforts to maintain aspects of the old Church in a new setting) grew closer together, as is seen in the changing character of the group known as the *conversi*.[70] This term was used from the fifth century, particularly in Spain and Gaul, for those who voluntarily became penitents, but it was also used in monastic rules for those who entered monastic life. Getting religion after living a sinful life and

entering religion, whatever one's previous life had been, were both conversion, almost as though the person was only then becoming Christian. The canonical expectations of penitents made them quasi-monks. The term *religionis habitum assumere* became synonymous with "to become a penitent" (e.g., Caesarius of Arles, Sermo 56) and those who for reasons of piety entered penance were as much models and heroes as those who entered monasteries.

Initially, clerics guilty of sins subject to the formal discipline were treated no differently than laypersons.[71] As the clericalizing tendency grew, this changed, presumably to protect clerics from the infamy of public penance. By 313, clerics were not permitted to become penitents in Rome; Optatus and Augustine in north Africa regarded this as a point of doctrine since public penance would dishonor their ordination. Soon, degradation to the lay state was regarded as the equivalent of public penance. Since penance was coming to be seen as punishment, a double punishment was not imposed. Sinful clerics were, in fact, treated as lapsed penitents, allowed to do penance privately but without reconciliation. Leo I (d. 461), for example, called for a *privata secessio*, perhaps to a monastery, for doing penance, though the eucharist was not denied.[72]

From the fifth century, religious were treated similarly and not allowed to become public penitents. They were dealt with as lapsed penitents if their sins were subject to the canonical discipline and could be expelled from the monastery. Entry into religious life was regarded as a second baptism, much as the penitential system had earlier been regarded as a *secunda paenitentia*. Religious life was itself *exomologesis* and a substitute—a praiseworthy one!—for the ecclesiastical institution. Its starting point was a conversion from among the layfolk (*conversio ex laicis*), just as the institution was a conversion from sin. Its ritual beginning was the *benedictio paenitentiae*, the blessing of conversion, and those who bound themselves to this penitential way of life were the *converti* or *conversi*. It is, in fact, difficult in this period to distinguish a penitential ordo from a rite for religious profession, because of the binding character of the vows taken by both penitents and religious. Descriptions of the lives of the *conversi* are practically identical to the lives of both religious and penitents. Some of the *converti* remained in their communities, much like members of secular institutes, and some were associated with monasteries, like the lay brothers and lay sisters of later times.[73]

Innocent I had earlier indicated that penance could be done for light sins as well as for grave ones, though church discipline did not require it.[74] Since accumulated light sins were then regarded as equivalent to grave sin, an order of penitents that did not carry with it the stigma of the canonical system was undoubtedly attractive. While the majority of Christians did not take this route, the pious and many widows and widowers and elderly people did. The self-righteous character of canonical penance, sharply distinguishing between sinners and saints, eventually led to sinners avoiding it and saints entering it! Some apparently did so out of piety or as a way of preparing for death in serious illness or old age. Sometimes, it was a postulancy or prelude to monastic life or clerical ordination. Still others probably chose it because it was somewhat easier than canonical penance and was praised rather than looked down on.

But was this really penance? To ask an anachronistic question, can this (and the earlier permitting of penance without reconciliation to a recidivist) be regarded as a form of the sacrament? In the sixth and seventh centuries, there was a clear intervention of Church authority for those who became *conversi*.[75] The individual sought and received the Church's blessing and was regarded as being in the peace of the Church, even though there was no formal reconciliation by the bishop, no more than when a presbyter or deacon or acolyte reconciled the dying by giving the eucharist. If nothing else, such historical cases suggest caution in attempting to draw a clear, continuous line of development from New Testament times to our own—or in being too quick to distinguish what is sacrament from what is not.

Lenten Penance

Lent's origins and development raise similar questions. Though it began as a baptismal season, it became a penitential preparation for paschal communion and the only form of official penance, apart from penance for the dying, for the majority of people. It was, in fact, the earliest form of repeatable penance, one that abandoned the questionable distinction between saints and excommunicated sinners and provided a challenge and support for ongoing conversion.

In the second century, a two-day fast preceded the Easter Eucharist.[76] In Rome, a three-week period of preparation was added to this.[77] Because baptism was linked with Easter from early times,[78] the period was oriented toward preparing the elect for baptism. It included fasting, prayer, exorcisms, and special assemblies to complete their preparation for Easter initiation. Even before the organization of the catechumenate, members of the community had prayed and fasted with those preparing for baptism (Justin, First Apology 61, 2). Before the end of the fourth century, according to Leo, the period of preparation had been extended to the six weeks before the paschal fast, beginning on Quadragesima Sunday and lasting through Holy Thursday (Sermon 39, 2–3). It was clearly regarded as a time for the entire community—many of whom were only nominal believers—to journey with the chosen catechumens toward Easter, atone for their own failures to be faithful to their baptismal *sacramentum*, and have their sins removed (Leo, Sermon 39, 2–3; Sermon 42, 1), all in order to be ready to receive new members.

By the fifth century, most of those entering the catechumenate in Rome were infants or children. There was little or no training for the few adults involved; those who did apply for baptism before the beginning of Lent had to accomplish in a few short weeks of intense doctrinal and moral catechesis and formation what had previously been done over two or three years. The scrutinies and other elements of initiation became little more than ritual formalities, first shifted from Sundays to weekdays and then detached altogether from the eucharist. Becoming a catechumen was more a ritual than a step taken in faith. The catechumenate as a whole basically deteriorated. The structure of Lent was necessarily affected and its baptismal character began to be lost.

The development of the order of penitents probably parallels that of the catechumenate. The emergence of the canonical order of penitents to parallel catechumenal formation meant that those penitents who had completed their period of penance began, at this time, their final purification and were given special attention.[79] In the fifth century, however, if episcopal complaints are to be believed, entry into the order of penitents was becoming as much a ritual formality as entry into the catechumenate, with little evidence of sincerity and minimal change in life-style. The conversion and reformation that should have been happening throughout the assigned period of penance now had to take place in condensed form during Lent. Exorcisms and fasting were emphasized; ritual and ascetical practices substituted for living a converted life. Daily Lenten liturgy and the daily blessing of penitents were attempts to provide concentrated formation.

By the fifth century, Lent in Rome was a six-week period beginning on Quadragesima Sunday and lasting until Holy Thursday. On the first day of the fast, the Monday after Quadragesima Sunday,[80] the penitents who would be reconciled on Holy Thursday were solemnly received. Each day they, like the catechumens, were to be exorcised. With the relaxation of the penance discipline and permission for penitents to remain present for the eucharist, this blessing took place after the postcommunion prayer of the Mass on weekdays during the time of penance. There was a prayer over the penitents, followed by the individual laying on of hands in blessing while the penitents knelt. Then, the congregation stood with bowed heads while the bishop, hands extended, blessed all the people. On the last day of Lent (what we call Holy Thursday) before the paschal celebration began, the penitents were reconciled. Then the community, whole and healed, was ready to celebrate the Easter sacrament.

As the baptismal character of Lent was forgotten, its conversion character changed and the community followed the penitents rather than leading the catechumens. Near the beginning of the fifth century, Innocent I mentioned that many of those not subject to the canonical discipline joined the penitents during this time (Letter 25, 10), an early indication that penance was already replacing baptism as the Lenten focus. According to Canon 80 of the *Statuta ecclesiae antiqua*, these people received the same laying on of hands as the penitents. (Clerics, of course, by this time could not.)

The shift from a season of baptismal purification to one of penitential purification seems to have taken place gradually and without difficulty. During the late fifth and the sixth centuries, the three weeks preceding Lent (Septuagesima, Sexagesima, and Quinquagesima Sundays) grew in importance as a pre-Lent. Lenten fasting as an ascetic exercise was increasingly emphasized but largely disengaged from the prayer and service to others' needs with which it had earlier been linked. Together the three had been evidence that a genuine conversion was reshaping an individual's life. Now fasting was interpreted as an ascetic means of satisfaction and a ritual atonement to God for sin. The word penance itself lost its original meaning of conversion and began to take on the connotations of difficulty, sacrifice, and penalty. The fifth-century Lenten order of penitents was probably already primarily ritualistic and ascetic. With adult initiation a rarity, the Lenten season had lost its baptismal character and its orientation to the paschal celebration (which was itself reduced from the triduum to Easter Sunday and from *pascha* to resurrection as eschatological festivity was historicized) and become self-contained as a season of penance.

The Wednesday and Friday fast-days before Quadragesima came to be considered as an introduction to Lent, probably by the early sixth century. By the seventh century they were part of Lent, making it a period of forty days of fast.[81] The Gelasian Sacramentary calls the Wednesday of Quinquagesima week the *caput ieiunii*, the beginning of the fast, for Lent and fasting had become synonymous. Later termed Ash Wednesday because of the symbol that replaced the imposition of hands, it became the day for receiving penitents.

Lent grew in importance as the order of penitents declined. Vocations to the order of penitents almost disappeared from the sixth century on, but the ranks of ceremonial penitents steadily increased. By the tenth century, all Christians were expected to become Lenten penitents.[82] The penance of Lent with its rituals became the only official penance other than the death ritual for most people from the time of canonical penance's decline until the emergence and general use of a new form of penance. In time, as communion became infrequent, Lent's only clear connection with the paschal mystery was that it was a season of penitential purification to prepare for Easter communion. Everyone was expected to make confession before or during Lent.

NOTES

1. In the East, for example, Basil of Caesarea listed long periods of penance but insisted that quality was more important than quantity. He suggested that his lists be used as guidelines and that bishops evaluate each case, lengthening or shortening the penance as circumstances suggested. See Letter 188, 2; 217, 54, 74 (PG 32: 671, 795, 804).

2. Samuel Leuchli does not make an altogether convincing case for the explanation that his title discloses in advance: *Power and Sexuality* (Philadelphia: Temple University Press, 1972), but his

theory coupling clerical prerogatives and restrictions on sexuality is intriguing. An appendix (pp. 126–135) gives the canons. Elvira's legislation, though embarrassing at points, is not altogether atypical. It shows that the history of our understanding and practice cannot be rewritten to provide an unambiguous and always edifying tradition.

3. See CCL 148 for texts; see also *Les Statuta Ecclesiae Antiqua,* Charles Munier, ed. (Bibliotheque de l'Institut de Droit Canonique de l'Université de Strasbourg, 5; Paris: Presses Universitaires de France, 1960). For an analysis of Leo's teaching and influence, see Peter J. Riga, "Penance in St. Leo the Great," *Église et Théologie* 5 (1974) 5–32.

4. For a synopsis, see A.-M. La Bonnardiere, "Pénitence et réconciliation des pénitents d'après saint Augustin," *Revue des Études Augustiniennes* 13 (1967) 31–53, 249–283; 14 (1968) 181–204. See also Marie-François Berrouard, "Pénitence de tous les jours selon saint Augustin," *Lumière et Vie* 13, No. 70 (November-December, 1964), pp. 51–74.

Augustine's writings, particularly his sermons, give pause to those who exaggerate the fervor and enthusiasm of the ancient Church. He complained, for example, that many who had entered the Church had done so without undergoing real conversion, that Church membership was regarded as guaranteeing salvation, that entering penance was postponed as long as possible, and that many entering it regarded it as a formality and refused to change their lives.

5. Cf. Ambrose, *De paenitentia* 2, 10, 95. I am not aware of a claim that penance, like baptism, impresses a character on the individual, but there is a similar outlook in the insistence on a single penance—or, rather, on a single reconciliation, since recidivists were sometimes permitted to enter penance without hope of reconciliation.

6. For examples of such legislation, see Poschmann, *Penance,* pp. 104–109.

7. This is a modern problem; the distinction of seven separate sacramental signs came only after the disintegration of initiation and the corresponding dissolution of community and sacramental cohesiveness. Moreover, Cyprian and others rejected the efficacy of initiatory rites performed outside the Church, since

they could not see how those who had left the Church could claim to give the Spirit that was the bond of its unity. Even when rebaptism came to be almost universally rejected, the efficacy of the rites of heretics and schismatics for giving the Spirit remained in question. As the West identified the giving of the Spirit with a particular ritual gesture—the laying on of hands or anointing after baptism—that gesture was repeated in receiving those baptized outside the Church.

8. Canon 8 (Mansi 2: 472).

9. Letter 1, 2, *ad Himerium* (PL 13: 1133), addressed to the Spanish bishops regarding Arians, and Letter *ad episcopos Africae*, 5 (PL 13: 1159–1160). His statement that this is the universal custom of East and West is probably exaggerated.

10. *Contra luciferianos* 6 (PL 23: 160).

11. See, for example, *De baptismo* 2, 7, 11 (CSEL 51:186).

12. *De baptismo* 3, 16, 21 (CSEL 51: 213). Though the context is the reconciliation of apostates and heretics, the statement is general.

13. *De baptismo* 5, 20, 28 (CSEL 51: 285–286); 3, 16, 21 (CSEL 51: 212); 5, 23, 33 (CSEL 51: 290); *Sermo* 269, 2 (PL 38: 1235–1236).

14. Letter 2, *ad Victricium* (PL 20: 475).

15. Letter 24, 3, *ad Alexandrum* (PL 20: 550–551): "we receive them through the imposition of hands, under the likeness of penance and the sanctification of the Holy Spirit."

16. Letter 159, 6–7, *ad Nicetam* (PL 54: 1138–1139); Letter 166, 2, *ad Neonem* (PL 54: 1194); Letter 117, 18, *ad Rusticum* (PL 54: 1209).

17. Letter *ad Eutherium*, 3 (PL 69: 18). Penitential elements (abjuration of heresy) continued to mark reception of a baptized person into the Church in modern times. It is still customary for adults received into the Church to make a first confession prior to confirmation and communion, although reception into the Church's communion and reconciliation to the Church are the same theological reality.

18. Letter 67, *ad Quiricum* (PL 77: 1205–1206). See also Joseph Coppens, *L'imposition des mains*, p. 377, for references indicating which oil was used. The substitution of anointing for the laying on

of hands seems to have begun in the East and was influenced by viewing sin as a disease, with the anointing with the oil of the sick understood as a prayer for healing. The use of chrism probably emphasized the restored gift of the baptismal Spirit and its use here perhaps parallels the developing independence of confirmation from baptism.

19. See Arles II, canons 17, 26 (Mansi 7: 880–881); the seventh-century Spanish *Liber Ordinum* (ed. M. Férotin; Paris: Librairie de Firmin-Didot, 1904), XXXVII, 102; Isidore of Seville, *De ecclesiasticis officiis* II, 25, 9 (PL 83: 822)—in II, 27 he refers to confirmation; Hildephonsus of Toledo, *De cognitione baptismi* 121 (PL 96: 121), who explains the importance of the imposition of hands in 128 (PL 96: 164–165).

20. "... inasmuch as baptism is only administered once, while the Sacrament of Penance is administered repeatedly, and as almost every baptized person comes to be in a position for requiring this latter Sacrament, for which no other can be substituted, this sacrament becomes practically the *most important means of grace.*" Adolph Harnack, *History of Dogma* 6 (New York: Dover, 1961), p. 243.

21. Cf. the prayer from 1 Clement 60:1–4, cited above, p. 20f.

22. The supposition is that the structures of penance began to have literary counterparts at the same time as free prayer gave way to formula in the eucharist and for some of the same reasons. For factors affecting eucharist, see Allan Bouley, *From Freedom to Formula: The Evolution of the Eucharistic Prayer from Oral Improvisation to Written Texts* (Washington, D.C.: Catholic University of America Press, 1981), especially pp. 159–215.

23. *Sacramentarium Gelasianum*, I, xvi; I, xxxviii; *Liber Sacramentorum Romanae Aeclesiae Ordinis Anni Circuli*, ed. L. C. Mohlberg (Rome: Herder, 1960), pp. 17–18, 55–58.

24. Council of Arles III, canon 24 (Mansi 9:18); *Vita Hilarii* 13, 16 (PL 50:1233). Cf. *Praedestinatus* 3, 8 (PL 53:644).

25. The third- and fourth-century Church probably singled out those who had completed their period of penance and were preparing for reconciliation, much as it did the elect among the catechumens. By the fifth century, however, with the collapse of the catechumenal structures, entry into the order of penitents

(if it took place liturgically) was largely a formality and the order of penitents was primarily a Lenten reality as was what survived of the catechumenate. Cf. below, p. 85.

26. *Historia Ecclesiastica*, VII, 16; PG 67: 1459; *A Select Library of Nicene and Post-Nicene Fathers of the Christian Church* (Second Series; P. Schaff and H. Wace, eds.; New York: Christian Literature Company, 1890) 2: 386–387.

27. See Jungmann, *Die lateinischen Bussriten*, pp. 35–38.

28. *Liber Sacramentorum*, I, xv (Mohlberg, pp. 17–18). The fifth prayer in the Gelasian is of Gallican origin. The old Gelasian Sacramentary has these prayers after Sexagesima, but this was not their original place. The seventh-century addition of Ash Wednesday and the days that followed probably caused the displacement. See below, p. 88. The rubric, as presently found in the Gelasian, mentions seclusion (in a monastery), but this too represents a later discipline.

29. For example, "For seven years let them as penitents receive the laying on of hands from the priests. . . . They should not be upset to bow down before God if they were not afraid to deny God." Felix III, Letter 13, 3, 6 [*Epistolae Romanorum Pontificum Genuinae*, ed. Andreas Thiel (Brunsberg: Peter, 1868) I:263–264].

30. Letter 149, 16 (CSEL 44:363); Sermon 232, 7, 8 (PL 38:1111).

31. Hippo, canon 30 (Mansi 3:923); cf. Carthage III, canon 32 (Mansi 3:885) and see also Jerome, Letter 77, 4 (PL 22:692).

32. Leo the Great, Letter 167, 19 (PL 54:1209): "they can be cleansed by fastings and the imposition of hands." He is responding to a question regarding what to do with those baptized as infants but raised by pagans and now seeking to come into the Church. He adds that if they are guilty of idol worship, murder, or fornication, "they should not be admitted to communion except through public penance." Clerics could not receive the imposition of hands; see, for example, Jerome, *Contra luciferianos* 5 (PL 23: 159); Leo the Great, Letter 167, *ad Rusticum*; Carthage VI, canon II (Mansi 3: 970). The imposition of hands in penance on clerics was regarded as an insult to the Spirit that they had already definitively received. This supports the interpretation that the blessing of penitents functioned as an exorcism and a consecration to a specific way of life and that the reconciliation

involved the Spirit in a special way. The later tradition in the sacrament of the sick of anointing the priest's hands on the backs rather than the palms is perhaps a vestige of the ancient prohibition.

33. In 506, the Council of Agde required penitents to receive this blessing [Canon 15 (Mansi 8:327)] and reserved it to the bishop [Canon 44 (Mansi 8: 332)]. See also the Council of Toledo (589), Canon 11 (Mansi 9: 995); *Statuta Ecclesiae Antiquae*, Canon 80 (PL 56:886).

34. Felix, for example, commands that no one is to reconcile "a penitent or one who is under the priest's hand" without authorization. Letter 13, 6 (Thiel, p. 265). Similarly, in Letter 13, 4, 7 (Thiel, p. 264) he states that communion may be restored to youthful penitents "after they have remained under the imposition of hands for a while."

35. *Die lateinischen Bussriten*, pp. 21–25.

36. *Sermo* 232, 8; cf. *De civitate Dei* xv, 20, 4. Augustine apparently ignores the "order of penitents" but often alludes to the "place of penitents."

37. *Sermo Guelferbytanus* (Sermon 213), 16, 2 (quoted by La Bonnardière, "Pénitence et réconciliation," p. 198):

". . . if this was said to Peter as an individual, then only Peter did it. He died and left the scene, so who binds, who looses? I dare to say that we ourselves have those same keys. Should I go on to say that we bind and we loose? Yes, and you yourselves bind and you yourselves loose! For whoever is bound is kept isolated from your company and the person who is separated from your company is bound by you. And when reconciled that person is loosed by you, for it is by you that God is beseeched on the individual's behalf."

This is Augustine's only allusion to the assembly's role in reconciliation, but it is a powerful one.

38. Synod of Hippo (393), Canon 30 (Mansi 3: 923); Third Synod of Carthage (397), Canon 32 (Mansi 3: 885). For a further study, see the essay of Franz Dölger, "*Ante absidem*. Der Platz der Büssers beim Akte der Rekonziliation," in *Antike und Christentum*, v. 6 (Münster in Westfalen: Aschendorffsche, 1950), pp. 196–201.

39. Letter 25, 7, 10 (PL 20: 559).

40. See Ambrose, Letter 20, 26 (PL 16: 1022): "the day on which the Lord handed himself over for us is the day on which penance is relaxed in the Church."

41. *Liber ordinum,* ed. Férotin, col. 200ff.

42. Later, when penance's link with baptism had been forgotten and confession was regarded as a means of purification and preparation for communion, this was understood instead in connection with paschal communion.

43. Letter 77, 4 (To Oceanus); PL 22: 692. The letter was written in 400, shortly after Fabiola's death.

44. See below, p. 78.

45. "Archidiaconi Romani sermones tres de reconciliandis paenitentibus," *Corpus Christianorum,* Series Latina, v. 9. (Turnhout and Paris: Brepols, 1957), pp. 355–363. These sermons were at one time attributed to Augustine. For commentary, see François Bussini, "L'intervention de l'assemblée des fidèles au moment de la réconciliation des pénitents d'après les trois 'postulationes' d'un archidiacre romain du Ve–VIe siècle," *Revue des Sciences Religieuses* 41 (1967), 29–38; "L'intervention de l'évêque dans la réconciliation des pénitents d'après les trois postulationes d'un archidiacre romain du Ve–VIe siècle," *Revue des Sciences Religieuses* 42 (1968), 326–338. See also Michel Coune and Robert Gantoy, "Une 'postulation diaconale' pour la réconciliation des pénitents," *Paroisse et Liturgie* 49 (1967), 365–373, for contemporary implications. An English commentary, heavily dependent on Bussini and somewhat difficult to follow, is written by Peter Riga, "The Roman Liturgical Rite and Prayers of Reconciliation of the Fifth Century," *American Ecclesiastical Review* 167 (1973), 196–207.

46. *Contra luciferianos* 5 (PL 23: 159).

47. The archdeacon's first sermon, for example, compares the penitents to Lazarus called forth from the dead by Christ and the bishop to the disciples who freed him from the shroud; see *De reconciliandis penitentibus,* I, 9–10 (CCL 9: 357). Augustine had frequently used this comparison, referring it to the imposition of hands; see La Bonnardière, "Pénitence et réconciliation des pénitents d'après saint Augustin," pp. 192–198. Augustine's ac-

commodated use of scripture for homiletic purposes became the base for the scholastics' (generally unsuccessful) attempt to deal systematically with the interaction of personal repentance and priestly intervention.

48. The Gelasian rite, which is the base of the rites found in the medieval pontificals, will be discussed in the next chapter.

49. *De reconciliandis penitentibus*, III, 3.

50. See Juan Antonio Gracia, "La eucaristia como purificacion y perdon de los pecados en los textos liturgicos primitivos," *Phase* 7 (1967) 65–77, for a survey of the prayers over the gifts in the Leonine Sacramentary, and Rinaldo Falsini, *I postcommuni del Sacramentario Leoniano* (Roma: 1964), for a thorough study of the postcommunions of the Leonine. The two scholars conclude independently that in the late sixth century the eucharist was the sacrament of reconciliation for those not subject to the canonical discipline. The situation is even clearer in the East; see Louis Ligier, "Pénitence et eucharistie en Orient: théologie sur une interférence de prières et de rites," *Orientalia Christiana Periodica* 29 (1963) 5–78. Of particular interest is the West Syrian liturgy; see Brian Gogan, "Penance Rites of the West Syrian Liturgy: Some Liturgical and Theological Implications," *Irish Theological Quarterly* 42 (1975) 182–196. For general discussion of the historical relationship of eucharist and penance, see especially D. A. Tanghe, "L'eucharistie pour la rémission des péchés," *Irenikon* 34 (1961) 165–181; J. M. R. Tillard, "Pénitence et Eucharistie," *Maison Dieu* 90 (1967) 103–131; and John J. Quinn, "The Lord's Supper and Forgiveness of Sin," *Worship* 42 (1968) 281–291.

51. See Optatus of Milevus, *De schismate Donatistarum* 2, 20 (PL 11: 975). See also 1, 24 and 2, 25; *Contra Parmen.* 2, 25.

52. Socrates, *Historia Ecclesiastica* 6, 21.

53. As in other large churches, the supervision of the penitents required a good deal of time and made it necessary for the bishop to entrust the responsibility to a presbyter. Such a ministry existed at Constantinople from the mid-third century until about 391, when Nectarius abolished it because of scandals which had arisen. People were then left to their consciences on taking communion and so a precedent existed for Chrysostom's advice, though he recommends taking counsel first. Such counseling was by no means a private celebration of the sacrament; the

counseling was recommended, not required, and it did not lead to reconciliation without public *exomologesis*.

54. Ep. 1, 5 (PL 13: 1130–1131).

55. *Penance*, p. 123.

56. Canon 2 of Toledo III (589) condemns the repeated penance that had apparently become common in parts of Spain. This appears to be our earliest mention of repeated penance in the West.

57. See, for example, *Statuta ecclesiae antiqua*, canon 76. Canon 12 of the Eleventh Synod of Toledo (675) also stated that "penance received through the imposition of hands" was sufficient for reconciliation" (Mansi 11: 144).

58. J. de Chellinck, "Iuuentus, grauitas, senectus," *Studia mediaeualia in honorem R.-J. Martin* (Bruges: 1948), pp. 40–44, cited by Marie-François Berrouard, "La pénitence publique durant les six premiers siècles: Histoire et Sociologie," *Maison-Dieu* 118 (1974) 126. Cf. Cyrille Vogel, *La discipline pénitentielle en Gaule des origines à la fin du vii siècle* (Paris: Letouzey et Ané, 1952), pp. 117–118.

59. *Liber Ordinum*, ed. Férotin, "Item Oratio Viatica Super Infirmum Iuvenem," col. 86–87. The heavy obligations and nonrepeatable character of canonical penance created this reluctance.

60. Cf. canon 9 of the Synod of Barcelona; Isidore of Seville, *De ecclesiasticis officiis*, 2, 17, 6. By Isidore's time, even clerics were permitted to receive it as a death ritual.

61. Synod of Gerona (517), canon 9 (Mansi 8: 550), regarding someone who receives the blessing of penance and reconciliation by means of viaticum; Synod of Barcelona (540), canon 8 (Mansi 9:110); *Statuta ecclesiae antiqua*, canon 21, 78.

62. Canon 78 of the *Statuta ecclesiae antiqua* is an exception to the apparent rule, for it states: "they are not to think themselves loosed (*absolutos*) without the imposition of the hand."

63. *Statuta ecclesiae antiqua*, canon 49. Burial inscriptions often witness to the individual's status as penitent. See Cyrille Vogel, "La discipline pénitentielle dans les inscriptions paléochrétiennes," *Rivista di Archeologia Cristiana* 42 (1966) 317–325.

64. *Liber Sacramentorum,* ed. Mohlberg; XCVIII, "Orationes ad Missa pro Defunctis Cuius Desiderantibus Penitenciam et Minimum Consecutus," 1658–1661 (p. 242). A similar, though less complete, formulary is found in the Veronense; see *Sacramentarium Veronense,* ed. L. C. Mohlberg; *Rerum Ecclesiarum Documenta, Series Major, Fontes,* 1 (Romae: Herder, 1956) XXXIII, "Super Defunctos," 1141–1146 (pp. 144–145).

65. *Liber Sacramentorum,* III, CXVIII, ed. Mohlberg, 1657 (p. 242). Cf. *Statuta ecclesiae antiqua,* canon 20, and Leo I, Letter 108, 5 (PL 54: 1013).

66. *Liber Sacramentorum,* ed. Mohlberg, XXXVIII, "Reconciliatio Paenitentis ad Mortem," 364–368 (pp. 58–59).

67. The sixth-century "Life of Tresanus" describes how Tresanus, after acknowledging his sins, received the *oleum sanctae reconciliationis* before death. For this and other references to such anointing see Jungmann, *Die lateinische Bussriten,* pp. 150–151, and Paulus Galtier, "Imposition des mains," *Dictionnaire de Théologie Catholique* (A. Vacant, E. Mangenot, and E. Amann, eds.; Paris: Éditions Letouzey et Ané) 7: 1397ff.

68. *Liber Ordinum,* ed. M. Férotin, XXX, "Ordo Penitentie," col. 87–92.

69. First Synod of Orange, canon 4; Second Synod of Arles, canon 21: "penance is not to be denied to clerics who wish it." For a fuller discussion, see Cyrille Vogel, "La *paenitentia in extremis* chez saint Cesaire évêque d'Arles (503–542)," *Studia Patristica* 5 (1962) 416–423. Caesarius emphasized that receiving such penance guaranteed nothing. Those who felt unable to enter the order of penitents had to prepare for it by personal conversion and amendment.

70. The classic study is that of P. Galtier, "Pénitents et 'Converti': De la pénitence latine à la pénitence celtique," *Revue d'Histoire Ecclésiastique* 33 (1937) 5–26, 277–305. But see also Cyrille Vogel, *La discipline pénitentielle,* pp. 128–138, 170–174.

71. Cyprian speaks of a presbyter's penance in Letter 64, 1 and of a bishop's in Letter 65, 1, though it is questionable whether the formal institution is being referred to. In Letter 67, 6 a penitent bishop is restored to communion as a layperson. Canon 76 of Elvira restores a penitent deacon to communion if he does pen-

ance voluntarily, but degrades him to the lay state if he waits to be denounced.

72. Letter 167, inq. 2 (PL 54: 1203).

73. The *Liber Ordinum* does distinguish the two in its rituals; see pp. 82–85 and Férotin's notes on the "Ordo conversorum conversarumque." The medieval orders of penance (e.g., the Franciscan) are more formal organizations of the *conversi*. See Alfonso Pompei, "Il movimento penitenziale nei secoli XII–XIII," *Collectanea Franciscana* 43 (1973) 9–40, for a general discussion.

74. Letter 25, 7, 10 (PL 20: 559).

75. Galtier, "Pénitents et 'Convertis,' " p. 286.

76. See, for example, Tertullian, *De ieiunio*, 13–14; Hippolytus, *Apostolic Tradition*, 20, 33; cf. Didache 7, 4.

77. Socrates, *Historia ecclesiastica* 5, 22, and Sozamen, *Historia ecclesiastica* 7, 19. But see also Antoine Chavasse, "La structure du carême," *La Maison Dieu* 31 (1952) 82–84.

78. This connection may have begun at the time of Tertullian (see his *De baptismo* 19), but see also Thomas Talley, "Liturgical Time in the Ancient Church: The State of Research" in *Liturgical Time* (Wiebe Vos and Geoffrey Wainwright, eds.; Rotterdam: Liturgical Ecumenical Center Trust, 1982), pp. 36–37, for other views.

79. Parallels with initiation suggest that a distinction was probably made between those beginning penance and those ready for reconciliation. So far as initiation is concerned, a special preparation for baptism goes as far back as the Didache. Hippolytus clearly distinguishes between the catechumens and those ready for baptism (Apostolic Tradition 20). The latter, during their final purification, were to be exorcised daily—probably for a week—and we later find a similar practice for the penitents throughout Lent.

80. The Gelasian rubric, which follows the prayers, states that the penitent is to be received on the Wednesday that begins Lent and to be excluded until reconciliation on Holy Thursday [*Liber Sacramentorum*, Mohlberg, ed., I, XVI (p. 18)]. However, when the Roman Lent began on Sunday rather than on Ash Wednesday, the reception of penitents had been on the first

Monday of Lent, as the stational church, the first prayer of the Mass, and the lectionary readings for that day suggest. See Jungmann, *Die lateinischen Bussriten*, pp. 48–51.

81. For a study of the changing computations of the forty days and of the relationship of Lent and the paschal celebration, see Patrick Regan, "The Three Days and the Forty Days," *Worship* 54 (1980) 2–18.

82. Jungmann contends that once the whole community entered penance for Lent the prayer over the penitents gradually coalesced with the blessing of the people and became the prayer over the people. See his *Die lateinischen Bussriten*, pp. 15–20, 38–44, and "*Oratio super populum* und altchristliche Büsserseg-nung," *Ephemerides Liturgicae* 52 (1938) 77–96.

Chapter Four

Pastoral Adaptation in the Middle Ages

The barbarian invasions of the second half of the fifth century and the waves of converts that flooded the Church as entire tribes were initiated into Christianity created a massive pastoral problem. How were these people, little more than baptized pagans, to be integrated into the Church and to learn Christian ways?

The catechumenate could not do it. It had declined in importance in areas where Christianity was strong since few adults were being baptized; the baptism ritual, not initiation, had become the focus in making Christians. In any case, the catechumenate structures could not have coped, for they worked best to introduce small groups into a closely knit community.

Nor could the canonical institution, which had reformed Christians, solve the problem. It too presupposed a vibrant community life and small groups of people receiving special attention as they were reintroduced into a full sharing in that life. By this time even those raised in the Church avoided it like the plague.

Church officials, however, clung to it and made only a few superficial pastoral adaptations. The prominence of exhortations to penance in papal correspondence, conciliar decrees, and sermons is perhaps the surest sign that the institution was no longer a vital force in people's lives.

For all practical purposes, canonical penance was a dead letter during the sixth and seventh centuries. In Gaul, it was generally ignored, leading some bishops to bend the rules. In Rome, it was almost nonexistent except for the death ritual and Lenten ceremonial penance. In England and Ireland, canonical penance seems either never to have been established or to have become defunct and almost forgotten by the time Theodore arrived at the end of the seventh century.

Developments were taking place in Gaul, however, that indicated some pastoral adaptation and helped prepare the way for the work of the Celtic missionaries. Caesarius of Arles (501–542) distinguished minute sins calling only for personal repentance from capital crimes requiring public penance. His comments, however, show that the original reason for public penance had been forgotten; he says that while satisfaction for such sins could be made alone and secretly the prayers of others are *helpful* (Sermo 261). The focus had now almost totally shifted from the well-being of the community and the reintegration of penitent sinners to enabling sinners to make satisfaction for their sins and experience forgiveness. The ministry was less and less perceived as a community ministry—the ministry of the community to penitent sinners with the goal of restoring the integrity of the community—and instead regarded as an individual ministry of the priest or spiritual expert for the sinner who sought healing.

There is evidence that Caesarius of Arles permitted at least one repetition of public penance and also allowed those guilty of grave sins but reluctant to enter the order of penitents to do penance privately. Then, after a time, they could return to the eucharist. In the seventh century, individuals alienated from the canonical system could go privately to a priest and do the assigned penance under his supervision. Then, after obtaining forgiveness through their penance, they presented themselves to the bishop for reconciliation. Though reconciliation could not substitute for penitential works, confession and doing penance were now linked together as the cause or source of forgiveness and were detached from the community and reconciliation to it. Reconciliation was coming to be regarded as no more than a public declaration that forgiveness had been obtained.[1] *Confessio* and *paenitentia* were together the cause of the forgiveness that reconciliation acknowledged. As the focus and goal shifted from reconciliation to forgiveness, the way was prepared in the Church of Gaul for the monastic penance that the Celtic missionaries would introduce. This opening may, in fact, have been due to the early influence of such missionaries who, by the beginning of the seventh century, were at work on the continent.

Though outgrowths of the canonical institution survived throughout the Middle Ages, their response to the pastoral challenge was inadequate. Resourceful Celtic and Anglo-Saxon monks tried to meet the pastoral needs of unformed and uninformed Christians with a practice they had found helpful—confession. They extended this to the laity surrounding their monasteries and began a process that eventually occasioned a new development—tariff penance.

ORIGIN AND DEVELOPMENT OF TARIFF PENANCE
The complex development that is crucial to understanding the crisis of penance in our times is that associated with the work of the Irish or Celtic monks during the sixth through the ninth centuries. They are usually credited with originating and popularizing the form of the sacrament that we know best: the reconciliation of an individual through private confession and absolution. They developed this form, it is said, to replace the ancient or canonical penance that had come to be practically ignored because it no longer met people's basic religious needs.

Contrary to this frequently accepted but overly simplified view of the origins of medieval private penance and our modern form of the sacrament, the Irish monks were neither the originators of private penance nor directly responsible for its development in the Western Church. As we distinguished canonical penance as a phase and form within the developing institution of ancient penance, so

102

we must mark off developments within the medieval Church: the origin of Irish monastic penance and its extension to the laity, its popularization on the continent by Celtic and Anglo-Saxon missionaries, the reaction of Church officials, and the establishment of private penance. Monastic or Celtic penance differed significantly from the later, officially recognized, medieval form of private penance: both had the distinctive tariff or tax exacted as satisfaction for sin,[2] but Celtic monastic penance lacked a ritual marking the Church's acceptance of the penitent's conversion. Its absence influenced the direction of Western spirituality and is a factor impeding the implementation of the 1973 Rite of Penance.[3]

Celtic or Monastic Penance
The Celtic and Anglo-Saxon churches faced a serious pastoral problem. Little Christian formation had taken place as whole tribes were converted and baptized. How were these baptized pagans to be made into Christians and helped to modify their behavior to meet what was expected of Christians? A second pastoral need, endemic to the Celtic and Anglo-Saxon cultures and also to the various Teutonic tribes on the continent, was fear and anxiety regarding the supernatural. This expressed itself in a preoccupation with demons and fairies and the like and in a concern to be purified from whatever might provoke the hostility of supernatural powers and beings, even including God. The Christian gospel proclaimed redemption and salvation. Could it provide tangible reassurance, a means of purification, liberation, and protection?

Canonical penance could not do this. It was apparently never established in the British Isles or at least never took hold enough to become familiar, though its existence was known. Perhaps the peculiar ecclesiastical organization of the Celtic Church, where the abbot's role largely overshadowed the bishop's, helps to explain why, but the canonical structures would have been of little value in any case. Though canonical penance had tangible ritual elements, they focused primarily on communal living and their nonrepeatable character kept them from providing ongoing reassurance and protection.

To meet these needs, the monks began to extend to the lay populace surrounding their monasteries a practice that had already proven valuable to them in their spiritual growth—counseling with a spiritual director.[4] This was probably borrowed from Eastern monasticism, though it took on a special character in the Celtic context.[5] The most striking element of ancient penance was absent: the assembled community—supporting and interceding for the person during the time of penance and then, when the reformation has taken place, seeking and providing the context for reconciliation by the bishop. This, together with the lack of a ritual of reconciliation, indicates that Celtic monastic penance was not private performance of canonical penance.

Since monastic penance had no official exclusion of penitents, an authoritative reconciliation was unnecessary, but the absence of an expressed relationship to the community distinguished it not only from canonical penance but also from the various signs of forgiveness and communal acceptance of those not subject to canonical penance. Public reconciliation was ruled out because monks were not subject to the canonical discipline—their whole life was *exomologesis.* Private reconciliation had existed only for the dying. The only similarity to the current canonical discipline was in the link, on the one hand, of *confessio* and *paenitentia* and, on the other, of *paenitentia* and forgiveness. God's forgiveness was obtained through prayer and penance, an understanding largely inspired by Origen and Chrysostom.

Nor were Celtic and Eastern monastic penance the same, though the Celtic monks had borrowed from the East. Monastic penance was originally individual and nonliturgical: advice from one monk to another on how to follow the path of repentance and do *paenitentia* privately,

104

since the canonical format was unavailable. Without formal excommunication, formal reconciliation was not strictly necessary, but in the fifth and sixth centuries Eastern monasticism did add a communal and liturgical dimension. It did so by linking this noncanonical penance to the community liturgy of the hours and eucharistic liturgy and theology. Prayers and actions acknowledging sinfulness and pleading for forgiveness gave a communal liturgical dimension to the private *confessio*. Reconciliatory prayers gave a communal liturgical dimension to the individual's *paenitentia* by giving ritual expression to its goal— reconciliation to and in the community.

In this way Eastern monastic penance was kept within the context of communal worship, as was likewise the case in the West in the Rule of Saint Benedict. This did not happen in the Celtic situation where the penitential process, though it probably included prayer, was decidedly aliturgical. Celtic monasticism thus seems to have copied the Eastern monastic practice at an early stage of its development before it had advanced beyond simple spiritual direction and been integrated within the monastic liturgy.

The rarity of ritual formularies raises the question of whether Celtic penance was ever actually more than spiritual direction, counseling, or a means of maintaining monastic discipline and extending it to the laity. Perhaps the more individualistic spirit and more eremitical way of life of the Celtic monks made the prayer of reconciliation within communal worship seem unimportant or impractical. Perhaps the Latin liturgy was itself already unintelligible; certainly the sense of being a worshipping community was fading. More likely, a communal ritual simply had little cultural meaning.

Several characteristics of Celtic culture either affected and shaped the emerging monastic penance or at least resonated deeply with it. Arthur Mirgeler notes a Celtic and Teutonic instinct as powerful as the bond of the clan: "the drive of the individual to make a name for himself by his deeds and his steadfastness in face of danger."[6] It seemed natural enough, then, for the penitent to be left alone to achieve forgiveness. The desire to prove one's ability and worth through heroic deeds and suffering undoubtedly influenced the severe types of *paenitentia* that were characteristic of Celtic penance, including exile, pilgrimage, fasting, nocturnal singing, and even more bizarre forms.[7]

The secular legal system was another factor.[8] Satisfaction, regulated by tariffs (taxes or fines) and commutations (lesser, substitute penalties), had to be made for crimes, and this led to the human relationship with God being seen largely in legal and commercial terms. Eastern spiritual directors had prescribed specific penitential practices for particular sins by analogy with medical science: as diseases are healed by their opposites, so a particular vice is cured by the contrary virtue. But the Celtic monastic tariffs, like those of secular law, were more punitive than medicinal, penalties to satisfy for sins or even the price to be paid to God (or sometimes the clergy) for having sinned. Heavy penances and attempts to measure sin and expiation led to penance being regarded as a punishment. The sense of God's all-powerful mercy came close to disappearing. Performing the assigned satisfaction obtained forgiveness.

Secular law also provided for composition, a money payment or fine to satisfy for crime. The monastic penitentials (guides for confessors, containing lists of sins and appropriate penances) only rarely allowed a money payment or the hiring of a proxy to do one's penance.[9] They did, however, provide for commutations of sentences. These were substitute penalties, generally easier and more lenient, that took age, health, and occupation into account: shorter but more intense fasts, repeated prayers, kneeling on stones, keeping arms outstretched during prayer, genuflecting repeatedly, and the like. Commutations became more common in the later penitentials to temper excess severity. Their use (and abuse) helped provoke the ninth-century continental reaction to the penitentials. They are also the origin of indulgences.[10]

Cultural influence is also seen in sins with which the penitentials were concerned. Keening, for example, was forbidden. Often, however, the monks compromised with residual paganism rather than eliminating it. The *Kyrie* substituted for funeral songs and the *Pater noster* for magical formulas. Oaths were to be taken in churches rather than in pagan shrines.

The penitentials often contrast a pre-Christian and a Christian way of life, seeking to wean people away from remnants of their pagan superstitions and ways of life as had once been done in the catechumenate. Thus, the monastic penitential system, extended to half-converted layfolk, functioned something like a catechumenate but in a spirit far removed from the catechumenate's communal orientation and atmosphere. The Celtic system is a kind of limited catechumenate where the catechumen is neither confronted nor supported by the Christian community, except in the person of the catechist-confessor, and admitted to eucharist without baptism. The confessor took the place of the community at entry to, and during, penance, and there was no formal reconciliation to the community (the structural parallel to baptism) before the penitent was again allowed to receive communion. The situation was much the same in Anglo-Saxon England, where parallels between Eastern and monastic penance made it easy for Theodore, once an Eastern monk, to accept the penitential practices of the Anglo-Saxon church. There, too, the penitent seems to have had the right to return to communion as a result of performing penance.

Though most authors assume there was some form of ritual of return or absolution in the Celtic and Anglo-Saxon confession,[11] we have no evidence of it. It is clear, however, that in the Celtic and Anglo-Saxon Churches a repeated private confession did become common and served to express sinners' repentance. As lay people close to monasteries sought advice and help, monks used the customary monastic confession for guidance and penitential practices for help. But the monastic forms had developed in groups already following the path of penance and sincerely seeking a deepened conversion. When they were extended to a nominally Christian population whose motives were primarily fear and superstition, they could hardly fulfill their original purpose. Confession may have begun as a form of spiritual guidance and advice, but it was soon practiced for its own sake, as were penitential practices. Without a rite of reconciliation, both were so individualized as to have lost almost all reference to the worshipping community beyond the juridical right to receive the eucharist—something that was itself increasingly rare and difficult to recognize as communal worship. Penitent sinners had little support beyond the confessor's advice on how to do penance.

The Irish Missionaries
Irish missionaries began working on the continent near the end of the sixth century. They planted and propagated the system to which they were accustomed and found that the direction taken by the old canonical system of penance in Gaul had prepared a soil in which monastic penance could easily take root and grow. The focus, for example, on the dispositions of the penitent and on the penitent's efforts to achieve forgiveness had led to seeing both *confessio* and *paenitentia* as the sources of forgiveness. Such a climate was certainly congenial enough to the monastic efforts and what the missionaries offered quickly became popular. Clear evidence of popularity is offered by the profusion of Frankish penitentials in the eighth and ninth centuries. The Penitential of Columban, originating in Ireland at the end of the sixth century, had contained tariff penances for layfolk as well as monks, but continental compilations, though modeled on Columban's slender volume, were even more obviously intended for pastoral rather than monastic use.

Historians and commentators often state that Celtic penance brought no revolutionary change but merely extended the role the priest had already attained in the canonical system and added new forms of expiation. They then conclude that the monastic practice was readily accepted and that it increased the frequency of penance, which was disappearing in its canonical form.[12] It is true, so far as *confessio* and *paenitentia* are concerned, that the monk was doing no more than the priest was then doing in the official system in southern Gaul. Both were only receiving the confession and assigning the penance, since official reconciliation was reserved to the bishop. The canonical system, however, did provide for an official acceptance of the penitent by the Church, in the person of the bishop, on the completion of the penance under the priest's supervision. There is no evidence that this existed in the monastic practice. Its absence suggests that Irish monastic penance did have a novel character.

The public ceremony whereby an individual had entered penance in the ancient system had been a *confessio*, in the sense of praising a merciful God for bringing the sinner to a desire for conversion. In the Celtic tariff system, this became a specification of the past sinful behavior that made reform necessary. What there was of prayer largely evolved out of the intercessory element of the old *berakah*. In ancient penance, the *paenitentia* itself had been a time of reforming the penitent's life through true conversion. In the Celtic setting, this became expiation and punishment as the price for having sinned. There was a parallel with the canonical system, but there was also a significant reinterpretation, though in line with developments in the continental canonical system.

But the monastic system was not a private administration of canonical penance, with the phases of penance privatized and reinterpreted and the monk (presbyter or not) substituting for the bishop. The true novelty of the monastic system was that it lacked the ritual of reconciliation that the canonical system reserved to the bishop and restricted to once in a lifetime. Nor did the Irish and Anglo-Saxon missionaries on the continent introduce a private ritual of reconciliation. When Theodulf of Orléans lists advantages of confession to a priest over confession to God, such a ritual is not one of them.[13] Boniface's homilies refer to the penitent's self-purgation by confession to the priest and performance of the assigned penance, but mentions no ritual of reconciliation.[14]

If we are to presume, as does Poschmann, that there must have been such an absolution, then we should also presume that the women who served as spiritual directors (and thus as confessors) to monks and the abbesses who heard their subjects' confessions had the right to give it. However, the questions posed by Celtic penance go beyond women's role in ministry. The absence of an official and authoritative acceptance of the penitent need not mean that such confession was not sacrament—in the later sense of the term—but it certainly raises basic questions regarding the criteria of sacrament and the basic nature of the sacrament of penance. The evaluation of Celtic penance is thus an important test case in the development of the doctrine and theology of penance and the limits of adaptation and development.[15]

Reaction and Compromise

So far as the people were concerned, monastic penance seemed much like the canonical system that preachers urged them to enter. Both systems required severe mortification and made harsh demands; in both, *confessio* and *paenitentia* obtained God's forgiveness. The monastic system, however, was much more practical. It was private: social stigma could be avoided. It had no further consequences: penitents could return to a normal way of life. It was repeatable: sinners could turn to it again and again to be purified of their sins and freed from guilt and anxiety.

Church officials, on the other hand, reacted against the Irish innovation as it grew popular in the eighth and ninth centuries. As Irish monasticism expanded, native Gallic monasticism declined. As monastic penance became popular, the ranks of the already unpopular canonical order of penitents became even smaller. As monastic and priestly confessors gathered followers around them, the position of the bishops was threatened. The bishops in synod saw the fundamental problem as contempt for ancient law: an abundance of sinners but no public penitents.[16] The monks were offering a novelty that, though popular, went contrary to the canons and bypassed the bishop. Church authority and penance practice were in conflict.

Carolingian reform councils attempted to revive canonical penance and to outlaw the penitentials. Councils at Tours[17] and Rheims (813)[18] and later at Paris in 829[19] and Mainz in 847[20] spoke out against the Celtic experiment. They harshly criticized the penitentials for laxity, particularly in matters relating to sex and marriage (penance could be done for adultery again and again), for inconsistency and lack of agreement, for failure to recognize the public or criminal character of certain sins, and for abuses in redemptions and commutations. (The classicism of the Carolingian reformation was undoubtedly also a factor; the untutored Latin of the penitentials could hardly command respect from those who saw themselves as the heirs of the Roman rhetoricians!) Synods outlawed the penitentials (Chalon) or ordered them to be burned (Paris) or at the least required the local bishop to select and approve only one (Tours). The penitentials might better have been criticized for tending to reduce penance to external mechanical acts that automatically guaranteed grace, but, despite the efforts to outlaw them, they continued in use. They had become valuable guides for confessors who needed to know how much penance a given sin was worth.

As a compromise, the synod of Chalon-sur-Saône in 813 approved Theodulf's option of confession either to God or to priests but only for sins not subject to the canonical discipline.[21] They considered it safer and more useful,

111

however, to confess to the priest to learn how to purify oneself. Crimes were still to be submitted to the canonical system for excommunication, public penance, and public reconciliation by the bishop.

Late ninth-century writers speak as though the traditional institution was flourishing, but it is doubtful that the Carolingian Reformation revived it to any great extent, even with secular intervention and support.[22] Jonas of Orléans' (d. 843) characterization of public canonical penance as "rare in the Church today"[23] was probably still true at the end of the century. Fewer sins were subject to public discipline than in the fourth and fifth centuries, since the canonical discipline now applied only to *public* crimes, but the attempt to restore it maintained and sometimes enhanced the old severity.

The Carolingian penitential discipline was still out of touch with the laity's everyday life. Though the bishops had reacted against a monastic initiative, their efforts to enforce the ancient canons actually seem aimed at monasticizing the lay population. Because of this intolerable severity, commutations and redemptions were grudgingly conceded, and other substitutes for the public penance came to be accepted: pilgrimage, entry into a monastery, flagellation.

Eventually, there was a more far-reaching compromise: public penance according to the traditional system was to be done for grave sins publicly known, while private penance sufficed for grave sins that were not publicly known.[24] Notoriety was the significant factor, for the penance (satisfaction or expiation) was to be the same in both cases. The concession was more a face-saving maneuver than anything else, however, since the canonical discipline was practically a dead letter. Commutations and redemptions made private penance easier to bear and its secret character certainly made it more attractive than the canonical system that, in the West, meant public embarrassment. The provision for nonpublic penance and reconciliation of the dying in canonical penance had been an emergency adaptation of the usual procedures; the Carolingian compromise was the first official recognition of private penance as an ordinary form of ecclesiastical penance, as official and canonical as public penance.

THE OPERATION OF PRIVATE PENANCE

In one sense, the Carolingian compromise led to merging two traditions (ancient canonical penance and monastic private penance) or patterns (Mediterranean and Irish),[25] but the compromise of public penance for grave sins publicly known and private penance in other cases was an unstable one. The private penance that eventually won was spiritually in the tradition of Celtic monasticism, even though it was ritually related to canonical penance.

The private penance initially approved was neither the Celtic system nor modern confession. There was a reconciliation rite, but usually not until after the penance had been performed. The structural phases of public penance were maintained in private penance at first, with reconciliation added to the monastic confession-penance to keep the parallel. Nevertheless, an added reconciliation rite had little effect on a popular understanding shaped by the Celtic system.

If private confession was merely useful and led to nothing different than simply imposing penance on oneself, it would be little more attractive than the outmoded canonical form. Private ecclesiastical penance had to include the same benefit as public penance or it would have been no different from the monastic form. Thus private and public penance dealt with the same sins and had the same outcome: an expression of restoration to the Church's eucharist. (The disintegration of the liturgical community—the lack of a sense of community and active participation—meant that this was no longer restoration to an active role in the eucharistic assembly but rather, as in the performance of monastic penance, the rarely-exercised right to receive communion.) The confessor's priestly ordination now became important: it was a link to the Church postponing the next logical step from monastic penance, the dropping of the ecclesiastical middleman.

Priest-confessors still needed guidelines to impose penance. Collections of ancient canons and decrees came to replace the outlawed Celtic penitentials. To one such collection, made by Halitgar (d. 830) about 817, was attached a penitential that he put forth as completely reliable for the heirs of the Romans, since, he claimed, it was obtained from a Roman church archive. This pseudo-Roman penitential is clearly based on Frankish predecessors of the Celtic type, but its ritual gives us a picture of "how penitents are to be received, judged, or reconciled."[26]

Confessors are first warned to fast with their penitents for at least one day.[27] (Confessors are to be priests, though in an emergency a deacon may receive a penitent for satisfaction or communion.[28]) The confessor goes aside to pray, seeking God's mercy and assistance for himself and the penitent. The confessor then advises the sinner and assigns the penance (fasting) by which sins are redeemed. If the person is unable to fast, an offering is to be made for the poor or for ransoming captives or for the service of the altar. The confessor is told, however, to be compassionate and lenient with the poor and with servants. Psalms are prayed and several prayers asking God's mercy for the sinner. The hand is imposed and another prayer asks for forgiveness.

Penitents seem still expected to return for solemn reconciliation in Holy Week, as in the earlier procedure in Gaul, where the penitent was supervised by the priest and then presented to the bishop for reconciliation. Confession and reconciliation eventually came to be joined together—because of the pastoral difficulty of getting those accustomed to the monastic procedure to return for a reconciliation that seemed superfluous—but it is difficult to determine just when this happened. Canon 31 of the *Statuta quaedam*[29] says that when it is difficult to get penitents to return for the reconciliation they should be reconciled at once. These statutes were once attributed to Boniface, but they are no earlier than the Carolingian reformation and probably date from near the end of the ninth century, since experience was showing that the penitents could not be expected to return.

According to Vogel and Elze, the rite for confession at the beginning of Lent in the Romano-Germanic Pontifical[30] is part of the rites for public penitents. It uses two of the Gelasian reconciliation prayers but still warns the penitent to return for the Holy Thursday reconciliation. The rite was long, including not only conversation (the confessor is advised to adapt himself and his advice to the penitent) but also the seven penitential psalms and numerous other prayers and psalms. A Mass followed, and at its end ashes and a hairshirt were put on the penitent who was then excommunicated until the Holy Thursday reconciliation. Only if the penitent was unable to return or the priest was unable to persuade the person to return was he to reconcile at once.[31]

The tariff ritual in the Romano-Germanic Pontifical (c. 950) is the first sure indication of an immediate reconciliation.[32] This ritual for private sacramental penance contains many elements identical to those in the rite for public penitents. As in the pseudo-Roman penitential's rite, the confessor goes aside to pray and then returns to the penitent. After praying over the person, the confessor asks whether the Lord's Prayer and Creed are known and then questions concerning faith in the Trinity, the resurrection and last judgment, and willingness to forgive others. After more questions concerning the penitent's status, there are several prayers and psalms and then confession of sins follows in response to the priest's questions. If the penitent is willing to reform, the priest indicates how much penance should be done and yet how merciful God is. He asks, "Do you believe that through confession and sincere correction your sins are forgiven by God?" and after the response assigns the penance. Other questions and prayers follow, including one by the penitent. The priest then accepts the prostrate penitent. Several prayers follow and then a Mass.

Such a ritual took some time. Cyrille Vogel estimates that the medieval penitential ordo took about twenty to thirty minutes for each penitent[33] and, as noted, a Mass frequently followed. While dialogue was a part of the rite (or at least questions by the confessor and answers by the penitent), much of the time was taken up by psalms and prayers read (in Latin) by the priest. Such a ritual was clearly not intended for everyday use by large numbers of people.

The Mass that followed the penance ritual and the Masses that penitents were often required to have said as a commutation of more severe penances had a further influence in promoting absolute ordination (ordination without relationship to a specific community) and the private Mass (Mass without a congregation). The religious state was transformed as monks became priests and said Mass (sometimes as many as twenty a day), thereby enriching their monasteries. While personal devotion and the desire for clerical prestige were undoubtedly factors, a less edifying motive was more influential: simple greed, which expressed itself as well in the stipend or stole fee that the confessor expected for hearing confession and imposing penance.[34]

Confession was liturgically enriched by having reconciliation follow, but its primary purpose, assigning penitential practices to expiate sins, was initially unchanged. As time went on, however, the amount of penance to be performed decreased and confession's importance increased. More sins could be submitted than in the canonical public system, so adding up all the required penances would have made their performance in one lifetime difficult. The confessor was advised to take the penitent's abilities into account, not to impose too much penance, or to substitute prayer or almsgiving for fasting.[35] The shame, humiliation, and self-punishment that were seen as freeing a person from sin's consequences were being transferred from the penance to the confession. Not only is this evident in the early medieval rituals, but from the eighth and ninth centuries confession became the name for the entire procedure. By the twelfth century, this confession, once the means of assigning the tariffs that expiated sin, had itself become the essence of expiation and absolution always followed immediately.[36]

After the transition to private penance, penitents were not excluded from the Church community but only from receiving communion. Nevertheless, the traditional notion of reconciliation was kept, with reconciliation and the renewed right to receive communion granted through the priest's prayer for forgiveness. (Several such prayers are provided in the rituals. At first, only a few prayers mentioned the exercise of a special ministry or authority, but these references became more frequent as time passed.) Confession and correction were still regarded as the source of the remission of sins; in the Romano-Germanic Pontifical, for example, the confessor is told:

"You ought to warn [the penitent] not to despair. God is merciful and forgives all sins if only one reforms. And say that just as water washes everything, so penance purges the sins of those who receive it sincerely. The person who becomes the child of the devil by sinning can become the child of God by doing penance; the one who ought to go to hell can [instead] enter paradise."

However, private ecclesiastical penance did not completely eliminate monastic penance. Private confession and penance without ecclesiastical reconciliation were still evident in the eighth century and survived into the fourteenth as lay confession.[37] Precedent could be found in James 5:16 and in the role of the assembly and of spiritual directors in ancient penance, but lay confession probably originated from the monastic custom. As confession took on an obligatory character during the Carolingian Refor-

117

mation period, grave sins were confessed to the priests, who were considered more qualified to impose the necessary satisfaction, but lesser sins were still often confessed to other members of the laity or unordained monks. In the tenth and eleventh centuries, as confession became a means of expiation and satisfaction, even grave sins were confessed to lay persons if no priest was available.[38]

Twelfth- and thirteenth-century theologians heightened the value of contrition, regarding confession as an exterior signs of contrition, but they also emphasized absolution. Confession came to be seen theologically in relation to absolution and as necessary for it. Thomas, for example, saw absolution as an essential element of the sacrament (the exercise of the power of the keys), but still considered lay confession an incomplete sacrament—if no priest is available—since the penitent's acts are likewise sacramentally essential. Scotus was the first to question the legitimacy and value of lay confession, on the grounds that absolution is the essence of the sacrament, and Scotist juridicism was largely responsible for its abandonment. The Counter-Reformation's emphasis on ministerial power was the final blow, and the only vestige to survive was the confession by religious to their superiors of infractions against the rule.

COMMUNAL FORMS OF PENANCE
Official penance took a variety of forms in the Middle Ages. Writers of the period often distinguish "solemn," "public," and "private" or "secret" penance.[39] Ancient canonical penance, revived to some extent by the Carolingian reform councils, maintained a shadowy existence, though its extraordinary character is seen in the name *paenitentia solemnis*. Another remnant of canonical penance, the Lenten season, became an ordinary part of the liturgical calendar for all Christians. Pilgrimage was a form of public penance marked by liturgical ceremony. The medieval general absolutions, given during liturgical celebra-

tions, were also a significant communal expression of conversion and forgiveness.

Paenitentia Solemnis *and Lent*

The medieval liturgy of solemn penance had its origins in the fifth- and sixth-century Roman liturgy. Our oldest formulary, however, is in the old Gelasian manuscript. Though based on earlier Roman sources, this was written from the mid- to late-eighth century, when the Church in Gaul was attempting to revive the canonical system. From this time on, the rites for expelling the public penitents at the beginning of Lent and reconciling them on Holy Thursday became increasingly solemn and dramatic even as they fell into disuse. The same basic shape survived through the Middle Ages, however, reaching its final form in the sixteenth- and seventeenth-century Roman Pontificals. (It is important to keep in mind that the most important sources of Western liturgy date from the sixth and seventh centuries and later, a time when initiation no longer occurred during adulthood and when liturgical documents are more and more detached from actuality.)

According to the Gelasian rubric, at the beginning of the Lenten fast (which, by this time, was the Wednesday before Quadragesima Sunday) the penitent was clothed with the penitential garb, the hairshirt, prayed over, and remanded to a special place until the Holy Thursday reconciliation. (During the Middle Ages, when this form of penance was rare, the penitent often was incarcerated in a monastery for Lent—hardly public!—and there is no evidence of communal aid or support.) The five prayers over the penitents that precede the Gelasian rubric frequently reappear in the medieval rites, with the first four still in the Pontifical of Urban VIII (1645) for Ash Wednesday and the fifth in its rite of reconciliation.[40] A second ordo for imposing penance, at the very end of the Gelasian, contains a request to the congregation for prayers for the penitent and alludes to baptism.[41]

119

On Holy Thursday, penitents left the place of penance to be presented in the bosom of the Church.[42] While they lay prostrate, the deacon made a presentation asking the bishop to reconcile them.[43] The bishop preached and then reconciled the penitents by praying over them.[44] While the Gelasian gives no rubric for the imposition of hands either on Ash Wednesday or on Holy Thursday, the seventh-century Lateran ordo has it at the beginning of Lent,[45] several later sources mention it,[46] and the Gelasian's final prayer for reconciliation suggests that it did take place:

"Kind creator and merciful recreator of the human race: you, O God, have redeemed by the blood of your only Son our humanness pulled down from immortality by the devil's envy. Give life, then, to this person who certainly does not want to die to you; receive back one who is now on the right path, one whom you did not abandon though wandered away. Let your servant's tears and sighs move you to loving compassion. Heal the wounds! Stretch forth your saving hand to the one who lies before [you], lest your Church suffer the loss of any member of its body, lest your flock be damaged and diminished, lest the enemy rejoice in the perdition of one of your family, lest the second death take possession of one who was reborn in the saving font. It is to you, Lord, that we pour out our suppliant prayer and weeping hearts. Spare the one who confesses to you so that by your mercy (s)he may not incur sentence at the judgment to come. May (s)he not know the terror of darkness nor that which shrieks in the flames, but now returned to the path of righteousness from the way of error may (s)he never again be hurt by new wounds. Rather, let that endure untouched and be everlasting in him/her which your grace has granted and your mercy has reshaped. Through [Christ our Lord]."[47]

Though the reform efforts of the eighth and ninth centuries probably did not succeed in reviving the canonical discipline and liturgy to any great extent, the restoration of public penance was a literary success. The rites underwent development and modification, were lengthened considerably, and were embellished with elaborate and dramatic symbolism. The more than 25 ordines of the Roman type that survive from the period between the ninth and fourteenth centuries[48] suggest that there were more churchmen with imagination and literary creativity than with the abilities to persuade people to become public penitents, since there is little evidence that these liturgies were used.

From the tenth century the giving of ashes, previously a secondary and supplementary symbol, replaced the laying on of hands for entry into penance and even those who were not public penitents received them.[49] The substitution was apparently almost complete by the tenth and eleventh centuries, for the Ordo of Arezzo is a rare witness to an imposition of hands when penance is received.[50] What was lost as a tactile symbol was more than compensated for verbally, however, as the litanies and the seven penitential psalms, a popular Gallican devotion, were frequently inserted into the rituals of both public and private penance after the Carolingian Reformation.[51] After receiving hairshirt and ashes, penitents were "excommunicated"—symbolically expelled from the Church as Adam had been expelled from Paradise, the bishop driving them out, swinging his staff, while the choir sang the antiphon, "In the sweat of your brow. . . ."[52]

The Holy Thursday reconciliation rites underwent even more development. Ordo L ("Ordo Romanus Antiquus"), which forms a significant part of the Romano-Germanic Pontifical—both are from the mid-tenth century—expanded on the simple Gelasian rite.[53] The ceremony took place in the church atrium, but there was no scrutiny of the penitents and part of the archdeacon's address had become rubrics and a prayer by the bishop. The bishop said the antiphon, "Come, children, hear me, and I will teach you the fear of the Lord." All knelt for prayer and then stood ("Flectamus genua" . . . "Levate"). The bishop repeated the antiphon, "Come, come, children," and the kneeling and standing took place again. The bishop repeated the antiphon a third time, "Come, come, come, children." The choir began Psalm 33, "I will bless the Lord," during which the penitents were literally handed over ("manuatim") by the parish priests to the archdeacon and by him to the bishop who restored them to the Church. All, including the bishop and clergy, were prostrate for the litany. After several verses and responses came the prayers for reconciliation (sixteen are provided!), three plural formulas of absolution, three in the singular, a sprinkling with holy water, and an incensing.[54] "Rise up, you who sleep," the bishop said, "rise up from the dead and Christ will give you light." The penitents stood, were warned not to sin again, and the ceremony concluded.

The so-called Pontifical of Poitiers, from the late tenth century, expanded the Gelasian material even more.[55] After the bishop had examined the penitents in the church vestibule, they were brought into the church for the morning office and a penitential Mass presided over by a presbyter. A deacon read a special sermon to the penitents after the gospel of that Mass. All then proceeded to another church, where the bishop was to celebrate Mass for those to be baptized. After the gospel of that Mass, the deacon, using the Gelasian text, addressed the bishop, who stood in the ambo, while the penitents were prostrate. After the bishop's response, the Litany of the Saints was sung with special intercessions for the penitents. While the bishop said the prayers for reconciliation over the prostrate penitents, priests touched them whenever the penitents were mentioned.[56] They rose reconciled and the Mass continued, after which they were invited to dine with the bishop.

A modified version of the rite found in Ordo L and the Pontificale Romano-Germanicum is in the Pontificals of Aix and Arles and Besançon,[57] the Roman Pontifical of the twelfth century,[58] the Pontifical of the Roman Curia of the thirteenth century,[59] and the Pontifical of Durandus, which is from the end of the thirteenth century. Durandus incorporated several features from earlier modifications and added contributions of his own, following his usual tendency to verbalize the meaning of gestures.[60] By Durandus's time, these Lenten rites were probably used only for the most notorious sinners, if even then.

From the twelfth century on, the term *paenitentia solemnis* indicates the extraordinary character of these rites, first in contrast with private penance and then later with public penance (pilgrimage). While the ancient laws and regulations continued to be repeated—including the prohibition of repetition and the imposition of lifelong penalties—this form of penance had lost most of its significance once private penance was introduced. It became so rare as to have no real place in the life of the Church, even if it did retain a place in liturgical books.

The season with which penance was associated did, however, have an increasingly prominent place in Church life, though its original connection with baptism had been lost. By the tenth century, all Christians were expected to become penitents for Lent. They were ceremonially enrolled by receiving ashes on Ash Wednesday. The strict fast imposed by law from the fifth century on began to relax somewhat in the ninth, but fasting remained the dominant characteristic of the season. In line with other changes, fasting became less the external expression of interior conversion and more the means of purifying oneself and repaying God for one's sins. The season was no longer a time for spiritual renewal in order to live more fully the Easter mystery of redemption but rather a time for purification to prepare for the customary (and later obligatory) annual communion.

As private penance in the form of confession became officially acceptable, it too was linked with Lent as a particularly reliable form of purification. Thus, the medieval rituals for private penance not only frequently retained vestiges of their origin in rituals for the dying but also incorporated such characteristically Lenten features as the seven penitential psalms. Rubrics indicated that confession was to be made and an assigned penance accepted during the week before Lent, on Ash Wednesday, or during the first week of Lent.[61] In twelfth-century England, the three days before Ash Wednesday came to be called Shrovetide, for confessors then wrote ("shrove") in the penance registers the names of those who had made their confessions.[62]

The ancient ritual gesture of laying hands on penitents underwent a metamorphosis as the experience and understanding of penance changed. Imposition of ashes came to substitute for it at the beginning of penance. At reconciliation, as the bishop prayed, a priest touched the penitents or helped them stand up. Beginning in the tenth century, the laying on of hands was deemphasized as public penance continued to decline and was replaced by private penance. There were some fine absolution prayers, generally expressing verbally what the imposition of hands said ritually, but gesture was giving way to words. The gestures retained became less personal and more allegorical than symbolic—indicative, for example, of an abstract emotional state rather than of relationship to community. Even the prayers changed somewhat in tone, becoming increasingly juridical. Purification, forgiveness, and restoration to grace were the focus, with little or no mention of Spirit, eucharist, or Church community. As the indicative formula of absolution became common, the imposition of hands lost its significance and disappeared.

Pilgrimage

While pilgrimage was a rich element of Christian piety as early as the time of Egeria (and a laudable outlet for curiosity and the sightseeing urge!), the Celtic monks supplemented it with the idea of exile from one's homeland. This punitive element from Celtic culture added a stronger penitential dimension. *Peregrinatio* is frequently prescribed in the penitentials as the remedy for the less scandalous public sins of the laity and the particularly scandalous sins of the clergy—the latter, not subject to solemn public penance, were thus removed from the scene—or as a commutation of other penalties.

Rome was a particular attraction for pilgrim-penitents, for to receive penance from the pope was regarded as especially beneficial. One who had already received penance could also expect an indulgent lightening of the penalty. Dimissorial letters from one's own bishop came to be required, however, in order to protect his rights.[63]

That pilgrimage was a form of public penance is evident not only from the penitentials and canonical decrees but also from the sacramentaries and rituals. The Gelasian contains a votive mass "for setting out on a journey" and two prayers "for those making a journey," but other medieval ordines provided for the blessing of the pilgrim's staff and garb at the church door, with the priest's prayer that the pilgrim-penitent "merit in this world to receive remission of all sins and in the future world the company of all the saints."[64]

The Crusades and many of the medieval indulgences were closely aligned with this penitential practice. So too were many of the medieval vagrancy laws, issued to prevent abuses of the pilgrim status. Canon law regarding wandering clerics *(vagi)* may also have its root here. Particularly during times of plague many of these pilgrims, wandering in groups, adopted another popular substitute for solemn penance—flagellation. These flagellants, who sought thus to appease divine anger and end the plague, instead were often an important cause of its spread.

General Absolutions
Though by no means as elaborate a ritual as solemn penance, general absolutions were a recognized communal penitential liturgy from the ninth to the fourteenth century.[65] This rite was generally in the context of another liturgy, particularly the eucharist. It centered on the Word (scriptures and sermon) and consisted of an examination

125

of conscience, a general confession, and an absolution given collectively to those who wished it.

The most dramatic of these general absolutions was the outgrowth of canonical penance linked with Lent and obligatory Easter communion. Those who were not official penitents received ashes at the beginning of Lent and an absolution during Holy Week. In most areas the Holy Week absolution was on Holy Thursday. Thus, Bishop Gilbert of Limerick (d. 1139) speaks of an absolution "from lesser [sins] at the beginning of the fast [and] from criminal ones at the Lord's Supper."[66] Several sources have the bishop use the Gelasian prayers to absolve the congregation on Holy Thursday prior to the service for reconciling the public penitents.[67] In other areas, a similar general absolution was given on Wednesday of Holy Week or on Good Friday, with the Mozarabic "indulgentia" rite for unofficial penitents on Good Friday the most spectacular.[68] The import of this absolution can be seen from one example: on Holy Thursday of 1020, Pope Benedict VIII, in Bamberg, Germany, absolved the entire congregation, using the same formula as he had used earlier for the public penitents.

Another, more common example occurred after the confiteor of the Mass as the ninth-century Gallican apologiae became a general confession and absolution.[69] Several fourteenth- and fifteenth-century German missals, for example, give an indicative formula of absolution almost identical to that which came to be used in the Ritual of 1614. Even earlier, from about 1000, a rite of general confession and absolution developed after the sermon, similar to the clerical prayers at the foot of the altar. This was a highly valued ritual used on major feasts and communion days. After proclaiming the Word, the preacher invited the people to lift their hands as a sign of repentance and to make a confession of sinfulness. Then he gave absolution and forgiveness.[70] A confiteor and absolution also became a part of the Liturgy of the Hours, being used at Prime and Compline from the tenth and eleventh centuries.[71]

Other examples include the absolution of soldiers before battle, the sick and dying, those who were to be granted indulgences, congregations on special feasts, and communities of religious. In effect, these were communal celebrations of penance with general absolution.

Later scholastic theologians, for whom these were only a marginal problem, regarded the absolutions as sacramentals rather than the sacrament and thus of value only for venial sins. Several factors influenced their judgment: the gradual focus on the individual format of the sacrament, the more precise distinction of venial and mortal sin, the emphasis on the power of the keys, and the use of the concepts of matter and form in sacramental theology. Their major argument was that these general absolutions lacked an indicative formula stating the exercise of the power of the keys. They were apparently unaware that such formulas had been used and that the indicative formula was itself a late development even in private penance.

Although many historians of penance have ignored this general absolution, it does appear to have functioned in the same way as private penance: as a sign of ecclesial forgiveness for those sins not subject to solemn penance. Though tariff penance could be repeated, it hardly became frequent, since its liturgy was long and elaborate and its penances still severe and frequently costly. From the viewpoint of the historian of liturgy, these rites are the resumption of the interrupted Western development of penitential liturgy: communal prayers for forgiveness and reconciliation, like those in the East that complemented private confession and the assignment of private penances, which signified the sinners' part in the Church assembled for eucharist. They expressed in a communal setting what private penance did less obviously—

restoration to the eucharistic assembly, the sacrament of humanity's reconciliation to God.

NOTES

1. Eloi of Noyon, hom. 4, hom. 11; Gregory of Tours, hom. 26.

2. There are traces of a similar outlook in southern Gaul prior to the influence of Celtic missionaries, who are generally credited with popularizing the notion of a specific penance or penalty levied to satisfy for particular sins. The graduated *epitimies* of the East are the probable source. A. Boudinhon used the term tariff in the late nineteenth century to characterize Celtic penance.

3. See my "The Absence of a Ritual of Reconciliation in Celtic Penance," published in *The Journey of Western Spirituality* (A. W. Sadler, ed.; Chico, CA: Scholars Press, 1981), pp. 79–105, for references to both primary and secondary sources.

4. Cf. *Dialogus Egberti*, cited by Watkins, *History of Penance*, p. 636. The *Penitentialis Vinniani*, our oldest Western manual, already had penances for the laity, suggesting that the system was used with the laity very early.

5. Celtic monasticism seems to have been largely based on customs originating in Eastern (especially Egyptian and West Syrian) monasticism and entered the British Isles through the monastic foundations of southern Gaul. Parallels with Eastern monastic penance include: (1) the special role of monks in administering penance to laypeople; (2) classification of sins, detailed confession, and penitential exercises assigned in proportion to the sins confessed; (3) the absence of canonical penance for monks; (4) public *confessio* and *paenitentia* imposed by the abbot on a monk guilty of a sin belonging to the canonical discipline; (5) public *confessio* and *paenitentia* for infractions of the rule; (6) private *confessio* by a monk guilty of a capital sin to another monk (not necessarily a priest) and the performance of *paenitentia* on his advice.

For the spirit of Eastern monastic penance and the role of the confessor, see H. Dörries, "The Place of Confession in Ancient Monasticism," *Studia Patristica* 5 [*Texte und Untersuchungen* 80] (1962) 284–308, and Thomas Merton, "The Spiritual Father in the Desert Tradition" in *Contemplation in a World of Action* (Garden City, N.Y.: Doubleday Image, 1973), pp. 282–305.

128

Celtic monasticism's link with the East through southern Gaul also explains the occasional references to the continental canonical system in Celtic penitential literature and the similarities between the two systems, particularly in the evaluation of sins and the penances assigned.

6. *Mutations of Western Christianity* (Notre Dame, Indiana: University of Notre Dame Press, 1964), p. 68.

7. J. T. McNeill, "Folk Paganism in the Penitentials," *Journal of Religion* 13 (1933) 450–466. McNeill also claims indications in pagan Celtic culture of a "spiritual guide" akin to the later Christian "soul friend" or "confessor."

8. See Thomas P. Oakley, *English Penitential Discipline and Anglo-Saxon Law* (New York: Columbia University Press, 1923). See also his "Celtic Penance: Its Sources, Affiliations, and Influence," *Irish Ecclesiastical Record* 52 (1938) 147–164, 581–601, and "Cultural Affiliations of Early Ireland in the Penitentials," *Speculum* 8 (1933) 489–500.

9. The earliest penitentials are from the British Isles and probably originated among the British in Wales in the sixth century, though our oldest and most complete penitentials are from the Irish. Irish missionaries brought the system to the Anglo-Saxons and Irish and Anglo-Saxon missionaries brought them to the continent. The later Frankish penitentials are derived from Irish and Anglo-Saxon sources.

For texts of the penitentials, see Ludwig Bieler, ed., *The Irish Penitentials* (Dublin: Irish Institute for Advanced Studies, 1963); J. T. McNeill and H. M. Gamer, *Medieval Handbooks of Penance* (New York: Columbia University Press, 1938); H. J. Schmitz, *Die Bussbücher und die Bussdisciplin der Kirche* (Mainz: F. Kirchheim, 1883); F. W. H. Wasserschleben, *Die Bussordnungen der abendländischen Kirche* (Halle: Verlag Graeger, 1851; reprinted; Graz: Akademische Druck- u. Verlagsanstalt, 1958). See also Allen J. Frantzen, *The Literature of Penance in Anglo-Saxon England* (New Brunswick, N.J.: Rutgers University Press, 1983).

10. For a study of the commutation system, see Cyrille Vogel, "Composition légale et commutations dans le système de la pénitence tarifée," *Revue du Droit Canonique* 8 (1958) 289–318; 9 (1959): 1–38, 341–359. See especially pp. 30–34 for the influence

of penitential redemptions on the development of the private Mass and the understanding of the Mass as a good work.

11. E.g., Poschmann, *Penance*, p. 144, note 63.

12. Watkins, for example, regards canon eight of the synod at Chalon-sur-Saône (which he dates between 639 and 654) as evidence of official approval. See his *History of Penance*, p. 626. The text, however, could as easily refer to the priest's role in the canonical system as the monk's role in Celtic penance.

13. *Capitulare*, I, c. 30 (PL 105:200).

14. Sermo 3 (PL 89: 849); Sermo 4, 5–6 (PL 89: 851); Sermo 8 (PL 89: 858–859).

15. The absence of an official ecclesial acceptance of the penitent raises significant questions for sacramental theology and an understanding of Western spirituality. Mentioning such questions here is far from anachronistic, even though sacrament is a later theological concept. These questions concern the very essence or *substantia* of the sacrament of penance—the constant theme found in every historical form, whether then articulated as such or not—and the Church's place in the sinner's relationship to God and salvation.

To show conversion to be ecclesial, penitents' repentance must be shown to the Church, but how is the Church's response to be known? While absolution formulas in the modern sense of an indicative judgment are a late Western development and are still rare in the East, canonical penance, presided over by the bishop, clearly contained the Church's authoritative prayer for the penitents' forgiveness, granting them reconciliation with the Church. There is no evidence that such a prayer concluded the Celtic penance process and, even if it did, it was not voiced by the bishop—at the time, the only qualified official—nor by the bishop's occasional delegate, the presbyter (or deacon), and so cannot be considered authoritative, particularly if disobediently used to return serious sinners to communion. In that case, if Celtic penance is considered sacramental, the priest's judgment cannot be the basic criterion of sacramentality and it must rather be the penitent's confession, which may be made, in need, to any Church member. As the ecclesial sense disappears in the late Middle Ages, however, Protestant Reformers concluded that confession may be made directly to God without ecclesial mediation.

What, then, of the sacrament—and where is the sacrament? Such perennial questions were implicit in the Celtic penance experience and are explicit in current discussions of the sacramentality of the penitential celebration.

16. Chalon-sur-Saône, canon 25 (Mansi 14: 98).

17. Canon 22 (Mansi 14: 86).

18. Canon 12 (Mansi 14: 78).

19. Canon 32 (Mansi 14: 559).

20. Canon 31 (Mansi 14: 911).

21. Canon 38 (Mansi 14: 101). Theodulf said that sins could be remitted either by ecclesiastical or private penance, with the latter either received from a priest or self-imposed. Confession and the assignment of penance was thus regarded as useful though not necessary. See his *Capitulare*, II (PL 105: 215).

22. For a general study of the Carolingian reform of penance, see Antonius Babiak, "Doctrina poenitentialis et administratio sacramenti poenitentiae tempore reformationis carolingiae," *Apolinaris* 30 (1957) 444–469, 31 (1958) 118–138.

23. *De institutione laicali* 1, 10 (PL 106: 138–139).

24. Canon 26 of Arles (Mansi 14: 62); Canon 31 of Rheims (Mansi 14: 80). Hrabanus Maurus in 840 also distinguished between public penance for public sins and private penance for private sins; see the preface to *Poenitentium Liber* (PL 112: 1400).

25. Cf. Monika Hellwig, *Sign of Reconciliation and Conversion* (Wilmington, Delaware: Michael Glazier, 1982), Chapter 4, and Ladislas Orsy, *The Evolving Church and the Sacrament of Penance* (Denville, N.J.: Dimension Books, 1978), especially pp. 44ff.

26. For the text, see Wasserschleben, *Die Bussordnungen*, pp. 360–364. Wasserschleben gives texts from several tariff ordos. Though there are many similarities among them, the lack of critical texts and precise chronology makes it impossible to establish relationships or trace development.

27. Fasting combined with prayer had been so frequently prescribed in the penitentials that *paenitere* in medieval Latin came

to mean "to fast." Thus, the one who imposed penance as well as the one who received it had to fast.

28. For the medieval deacon's role in penance, see Georg Gramer, "Zur Geschichte der Diakonenbeicht im Mittelalter," in *Festgabe Alois Knöpfler* (Freiburg im Breisgau, 1917), pp. 159–176.

29. Mansi 13: 386.

30. XCIX, 44–73 [Cyrille Vogel and Reinhard Elze, *Le Pontifical Romano-Germanique du Dixieme Siècle* (Studi e Testi, 227; Vatican City: Biblioteca Apostolica Vaticana, 1963) pp. 14–21] See also Ordo L, XVIII, 1–44 [Michel Andrieu, *Les Ordines Romani du Haut Moyen Âge* (Louvain: Spicilegium Sacrum Lovaniense Administration, 1961) 5: 108–124]

31. XCIX, 44 (Vogel—Elze, *Le Pontifical Romano-Germanique*, p. 14) and Ordo L, 2–3 (Andrieu, *Ordines Romani* 5: 108). See also Pseudo-Alcuin, *De divinis officiis*, XIII (PL 101: 1192).

32. CXXXVI (Vogel-Elze, *Le Pontifical Romano-Germanique*, pp. 234–245).

33. *Le Pécheur et la Pénitence au Moyen Âge* (Paris: Éditions du Cerf, 1969), p. 21.

34. Cyrille Vogel, "Une mutation cultuelle inexpliquée: Le passage de l'eucharistie communautaire a la messe privée," *Revue des Sciences Religieuses* 54 (1980) 230–250. For examples of penitential Mass formularies, see *Liber Sacramentorum*, I, 39 (Mohlberg, no. 57); Romano-Germanic Pontifical, CXXXVII, CXLVI (Vogel-Elze, *Le Pontifical Romano-Germanique*, II, pp. 245, 277–278; *Liber Ordinum*, ed. Férotin, col. 351–359). Charles Borromeo still considered the practice acceptable in the sixteenth century.

Fees or gifts were infrequent in the ancient period, when conversion was the goal of the sacramental process, but the tariff system lent itself to such abuse. The Penitential of Columban (*Poenitentiale Columbani*, 19) directed the penitent to give a banquet for the confessor. As the sacrament became a ritual means of pardon, the voluntary *Beichtgeld* (penance money) or *Beichtpfennig* (penance penny) was increasingly common. An eighth- or ninth-century homily against confessors' greed (attributed to Maximus of Turin in the fifth-century) is in PL 57: 493–496. For a biased (though factually accurate) account, see Henry Charles Lea, *A History of Auricular Confession and Indulgences in the Latin*

Church (reprint, New York: Greenwood, 1968) 1: 404–411 and 2: 142–145.

35. E.g., Romano-Germanic Pontifical, CXXXVI, 18, 20 (Vogel-Elze, *Le Pontifical Romano-Germanique,* p. 241).

36. See, for example, "De vera et falsa paenitentia," 10 (PL 40: 1122). Peter the Chanter (d. 1197) states explicitly that "oral confession is the essence of expiation" ["Verbum abbreviatum," 143 (PL 205: 342)].

37. The classic study is that of Amédée Teetaert, *La Confession aux Laïques dans l'Église Latine* (Paris: Gabalda, 1926).

38. Epics describe knights dying in battle making their confessions to their horses or swords if no human being is available and eating a flower or dirt if the eucharist is not available for viaticum!

39. This continued throughout the period, though by the late Middle Ages solemn penance was quite rare. Robert of Flamborough's penitential, written just before Lateran IV, states: "There are three kinds of penance: public penance with liturgical solemnity; public penance with no solemnity, and private penance." See his *Liber poenitentialis* (Francis Firth, ed.; Toronto: Pontifical Institute of Medieval Studies, 1971), p. 205.

40. *Liber Sacramentorum,* I, XV, ed. Mohlberg, nos. 78–82, pp. 17–18. See above, pp. 69f. The Gelasian of the eighth century (e.g., the Sacramentary of Angoulême) keeps the ordo for reception of penitents and makes only minor revisions in the reconciliation ordo. See *Le sacramentaire gelasien d'Angoulême* (Angoulême: Societé Historique et Archéologique, 1918), Ordo agentibus publicam penitentiam, XLVIII, 271–275 (pp. 17–18); Ad reconciliationem poenitentium, XCVIII, 598–603 (pp. 36–37). Cf. also Orationes super poenitentem, XCIX, 604–606 (pp. 37–38); Item missa ad reconciliandum poenitentem, C, 607–617 (pp. 38–39); Reconciliatio poenitentis ad mortem, CI, 618–621 (p. 39). The Gelasian rite is also the basis of the rite found in Ordo L and the Romano-Germanic Pontifical. For a detailed study of penance in the pontifical, see Wolfgang Lentzen-Deis, *Busse als Bekenntnisvollzug. Versuch einer Erhellung der sakramentalen Bekehrung anhand der Bussliturgie des alten Pontificale Romanum* (Freiburg im Breisgau: Herder, 1968).

41. *Liber Sacramentorum*, III, CVII (ed. Mohlberg, nos. 1701–1704, p. 248).

42. For the Gelasian rites, see *Liber Sacramentorum*, I, XXXVIII, ed. Mohlberg, nos. 352–363, pp. 56–58. The Gelasian uses the singular throughout.

43. The deacon's address, with some changes and modifications, is found in the medieval rites, in the seventeenth-century Roman Pontifical (where part becomes a set of verses and responses), and in the 1973 *Rite of Penance* (Appendix II, 13).

44. The three prayers from the Old Gelasian are also in Urban VIII's Pontifical, together with two prayers from the Gelasian's ordo for deathbed penance (*Liber Sacramentorum*, XXXVIII, Mohlberg, ed., nos. 364–365, p. 58).

45. *Bernhardi Cardinalis et Lateranensis Ecclesiae Prioris Ordo Officiorum Ecclesiae Lateranensis* (ed. L. Fischer; Historische Forschungen und Quellen, 2/3; Munich: 1916).

46. The Penitential of Halitgar, similar to the Gelasian, has it for the private reception of a penitent, though it is not mentioned in the Holy Thursday liturgy (Wasserschleben, *Die Bussordnungen*, p. 363). Canon 76 of the Synod of Meaux-Paris ordered it at the beginning of Lent (Mansi 14: 840). Hinomar of Rheims (c. 857) called for it [*Capitula* III, I (PL 125: 793)], as did Benedict the Levite in referring to both reception and reconciliation and to the sacramentary prayers [*Benedicti Capitularum Collectio* 1, 116 (PL 97: 715)].

47. *Liber Sacramentorum*, I, XXXVIII, ed. Mohlberg, nos. 358–359, p. 57. Variations of the prayer appear in numerous later rituals, including the 1973 *Rite of Penance* (Appendix II, 13).

48. The number is given by Jungmann, *Die lateinischen Bussriten*, p. 87.

49. See *Ordo Romanus Antiquus* (c. 950): Ordo L, XVIII, 45; Andrieu, *Les Ordines Romani* 5: 124. In the eleventh century, all the clergy and people were to receive ashes; cf. Jungmann, *Die lateinischen Bussriten*, p. 60.

50. See *North Italian Services of the Eleventh Century*, C. Lambot, ed. (London: Henry Bradshaw Society, 1931), p. 40. Though

this is a ritual for private penance, it is clearly modeled on that for public penance.

51. Jungmann, *Die lateinischen Bussriten*, p. 79.

52. This is found in several rituals, including the seventeenth-century Roman Pontifical. See, for example, Ordo L, XVIII, 43–44 (Andrieu, *Les ordines romani* 5: 123–124).

53. Ordo L, XXV, 24–59 (Andrieu, *Les ordines romani* 5: 192–207); *Le Pontifical romano-germanique du dixieme siècle*, XCIX, 224–251 [C. Vogel and R. Elze, eds. (Vatican City: Biblioteca Apostolica Vaticana, 1963), 2: 59–67].

54. Though there is no rubric regarding the imposition of hands the prayers contain many tactile images. One, for example, reads:

"O God, you have mercifully lifted up the world which was trapped in the pit of sin. O God, you commanded lepers and those trapped by other diseases to be cleansed by the judgment of the priests. O God, by the imposition of your hand you have in the past driven out illnesses of soul and body and have commanded your disciples and their successors to perform the same work. Hear our prayers for these servants of yours . . . and *substitute the hand of your compassion for our hand so that by the imposition of our hand and your assistance* the grace of the Holy Spirit may be poured out on them, the remission of sins may be granted them, the penalties owed for their crimes may be lightened, and the benefits of your gifts may be more abundantly conferred."

Ordo L, XXV, 49 (Andrieu, *Les ordines romani* 5: 201); Pontificale Romano-Germanicum, XCIX, 243 (Vogel-Elze, 2: 65). This prayer is not in the twelfth-century Pontifical. The following prayer (not in the Romano-Germanic Pontifical) strongly emphasizes the role of the Holy Spirit [Ordo L, XXV, 50 (Andrieu, *Les ordines romani* 5: 201)] and the next, based on the Gelasian (nos. 358–359) and found in many medieval ordos, calls on God to "stretch out your hand of kindness to those prostrate here," [Ordo L, XXV, 51 (Andrieu, *Les ordines romani* 5: 202–203)] Pontificale Romano-Germanicum, XCIX, 245 (Vogel–Elze 2: 64–65). This prayer is also in the twelfth-century Pontifical; XXXA, 20 (*Le Pontifical Romain au Moyen-Âge* (ed. Michel Andrieu; Vatican City: Biblioteca Apostolica Vaticana, 1938) 1: 217–218].

55. *Il cosiddetto Pontificale di Poitiers*, VI, no. 204–324 (ed. Aldo Martini; Roma: Herder, 1979), pp. 139–186.

56. The Pontifical of Rheims (c. 845–882) first has a touch on the head and then, where earlier rites had the imposition of the hand, a long prayer by the bishop who faces the penitents and uses an indicative absolution formula. The rubric then directs the bishop to take the penitent's hand and help him or her to rise. See Jungmann, *Die lateinischen Bussriten*, p. 91. He gives several other examples of touching and assistance to rise. Though the tenth-century Ordo of Evreux refers to the laying on of the hand—"I, a sinner and unworthy bishop, confirming this absolution by hand, mouth, and heart . . . "—it was apparently not used; cf. Jungmann, *Die lateinischen Bussriten*, p. 224. The eleventh-century Ordo of Arezzo has the gesture in receiving the penitent but at reconciliation uses the stole instead (Jungmann, *Die lateinischen Bussriten*, pp. 194–195, and cf. pp. 219, 227, 250, 276, 284).

57. In the Pontificals of Aix and Arles, priests examine the penitents individually beforehand; in that of Besançon, the archdeacon and archpriests conduct the scrutiny in the presence of the bishop. There are other minor differences.

58. XXX, 3–26 [*Le Pontifical Romain* (Andrieu, ed.) 1: 215–219].

59. The Holy Thursday reconciliation rite appears only in an appendix to some manuscripts of the Avignon period, although it is mentioned in the Holy Thursday rite; Appendix III, 4 [*Le Pontifical Romain* (Andrieu, ed.) 2: 579 and cf. pp. 455 and 542]

60. III, II, 7–44 [*Le Pontifical Romain au Moyen-Âge* (Andrieu, ed.) 3: 559–569]. Jungmann, *Die lateinischen Bussriten*, p. 98, notes that Durandus combined and enlarged Ordo L and the Ordo of Aix. While Patrizi's *Pontificalis Liber* (1485), which is otherwise based on Durandus's text, omitted the rites of public penance since they were no longer in actual use, the official Pontificals of Clement VIII (1595 or 1596) and Urban VIII (1645) restored them almost as they were found in Durandus. They will be described in Chapter 6.

61. See, for example, Theodulf, *Capitulare* I, 36 (PL 105: 203); Egbert, *Dialogus* 16, 4 (Mansi 12: 488); Synod of Chalon-sur-Saône, canon 8 (Mansi 10: 1191); Burchard, *Decretum* 19, 1–2 (PL 140: 949). The early ninth-century decree *Praemonere debet*, fre-

quently found in subsequent service books [e.g., Romano-Germanic Pontifical, XCIX, 44 (Vogel-Elze, 2: 14)], gave the instruction: "Each priest is to advise those accustomed to confess to him that they should renew their confession at the beginning of the fast." Regino of Prüm (d. 915) had only a vague sense of the earlier baptismal character:

"Priests are to instruct the people subject to them that each one conscious of having been struck by the deathbearing wound of sin should, on the Wednesday before Quadragesima, hurry to the lifegiving mother Church. . . . Not only those who have done something deadly but also all who recognize having soiled by the stain of sin the immaculate tunic of Christ received in baptism should hurry to their own priest [i.e., pastor] and with purity of mind confess all their transgressions and with diligence accept and with care perform whatever the priest commands as though spoken by the mouth of almighty God." (*De synodalibus causis* I, 292)

What was at first customary and then a matter of local law became a universal regulation at Lateran IV in 1215.

62. As confession became a prerequisite for communion and confession was to be made to one's *sacerdos proprius* (generally the pastor), a record was kept of those who had fulfilled the requirement. Those permitted to confess to an order-priest received from him an indication that the confession had been made and gave it to the pastor.

63. See, for example, R. A. Aroustam, "Penitential Pilgrimages to Rome in the Early Middle Ages," *Archivum Historiae Pontificiae* 13 (1975) 65–83.

64 As usual, the Pontifical of Durandus is the most elaborate. In II, XXXI [*Le Pontifical Romain* (Andrieu, ed.) 3: 543–545], he provides blessings for those setting out, and in II, XXXII [*Le Pontifical Romain* (Andrieu, ed.) 3: 545–546[, he provides an office for those returning from pilgrimage.

65. Anton Eppacher, "Die Generalabsolution. Ihre Geschichte (9.–14. Jahrhundert) und die gegenwärtige Problematik im Zusammenhang mit den gemeinsamen Bussfeiern," *Zeitschrift für katholische Theologie* 90 (1968) 296–308, 385–421. The article summarizes his 1967 Innsbruck dissertation. The term absolution,

first used for the final blessing in a liturgical service, takes on the meaning of pardon or remission after the ninth century.

66. *Liber de statu ecclesiae* (PL 159: 1002). As an example of formularies used, in the fifteenth-century Sarum Missal an absolution before the imposition of ashes parallels the Holy Thursday absolution; see *The Sarum Missal*, ed. J. Wickham Legg (Oxford: Clarendon Press, 1916), p. 50.

67. See Jungmann, *Die lateinischen Bussriten*, pp. 276ff.

68. A mid-ninth-century Milanese preface suggests that a public service was held for the people on Wednesday of Holy Week and for the penitents on Holy Thursday; see Pietro Borella, "La Confessione al Mercoledi Santo," *Rivista Liturgica* 49 (1962) 244–250. For the Good Friday "indulgentia" liturgy of the Mozarabic rite, which appears to precede the reconciliation of penitents, see *Liber Ordinum*, ed. Férotin, col. 199–204.

69. For a study of the eucharistic apologiae, see Adrien Nocent, "Les Apologies dans la célébration eucharistique" *in Liturgie et Rémission des Péchés*, pp. 179–196. Closely related are the prayers in the *libelli precum*, popular in the Carolingian era, which may have been used to prepare for tariff penance. For a representative collection, see PL 101:1383–1416.

70. The raising of hands was, at least from the ninth century, a sign of the desire to receive absolution. A twelfth-century text introduces the customary *confiteor* formula with the invitation: "My brothers and dear sisters, lift your hands and hearts to God and confess your sins, saying: I confess. . . . " For this and other references to the gesture, see Jungmann, *Die lateinischen Bussriten*, p. 279, note 160.

71. For the relationship between forgiveness and the Liturgy of the Hours, see V. Fiala, "Die Sündenvergebung und das lateinische Stundengebet," in *Liturgie et Rémission des Péchés*, pp. 97–114.

Chapter Five

The Origins of Modern Confession

The ninth-century Carolingian reformation and the sixteenth-century Counter-Reformation are both key periods when crucial changes took place quickly. However, both were preceded by long periods of slow development. From the sixth through the eighth centuries, the dominant form of ecclesial penance, canonical penance, slowly declined in importance, with no official replacement in most areas until the ninth and tenth centuries. From then on, private penance took its place alongside other forms of ecclesial penance and confession became increasingly prominent. From the thirteenth through the fifteenth centuries, private penance steadily grew in importance and other forms of ecclesial penance declined in the estimation of theologians. By the eve of the Reformation, little was left of the once-varied symbolic language of conversion other than confession and absolution.

Medieval tariff penance looked much like modern confession once the penitent's confession of sins and reconciliation by the priest had been joined together, but there were significant differences in understanding. Before we can speak of modern confession, three sets of developments had to take place:

1. The ritual had to evolve to the point where confession absorbed satisfaction and the absolution was considered to have a causal role in the forgiveness of sins; 2. Theological understanding had to attain precision in relating the personal and ecclesial factors to one another and in determining the sacramental essentials; 3. Canonical regulation

and popular understanding had to give the ritual primacy in the forgiveness of all sins committed after baptism, generally as preparation for communion.

MEDIEVAL CONFESSION AND ABSOLUTION

Satisfaction as the means of purification from sins and liberation from guilt was primary in the tariff system but gave way to confession for several reasons. The possibility of repeating penance lessened its significance. More frequent confession of more sins made it necessary to limit the length of penances and to provide other means of expiation, such as indulgences and Masses. For the penance ritual to assure the penitent of forgiveness and be a consoling experience, it had to be self-contained, and so contrition and confession themselves came to be regarded as expiation and the power of the keys to remit sin was emphasized.

Though tariff penance emphasized complete confession in order to determine satisfaction, confession remained secondary until reception as a penitent and reconciliation were joined together in a single ceremony and satisfaction was postponed. Then the impression was given that the essentials were completed and pardon had been obtained. By the end of the twelfth century, the period of satisfaction had been so shortened that it had effectively been absorbed within the confession. In the first half of the century, the authoritative assignment of the tariff penance for expiating sin was still given a great deal of weight. It began to appear too severe and too rigidly regimented, however, coming as it did after the authoritative grant of pardon. Bishops accordingly granted indulgences freely and advised their priests to adapt the tariffs. In the second half of the century, the penitentials gradually disappeared. Oral confession then came to be regarded as the essential means of expiation, because of the shame and humiliation that accompanied it, and our modern system began to appear.

Confession no longer implied grave sin, however, or certainly not sins so grave as those that had earlier necessitated entry into the order of penitents. The category of sins needing to be confessed in order to be worthy of receiving communion steadily broadened. Throughout the early Middle Ages, both frequency and fullness of confession became increasingly important as the effort was made to enforce more frequent communion and encourage proper preparation. (Of course, the broader understanding of the sins from which one had to be freed before communion could also be used to justify not receiving communion.) By the tenth century, confession three times a year was recommended: in preparation for communion at Christmas, Easter, and Pentecost. The tariff system, naturally enough, encouraged detailed confession and an outlook that saw complete confession and the performance of the assigned penances as the path to complete purification.[1] Yet since the majority of people could hardly confess privately on a regular basis, general absolution was usually given at Mass on communion days.

Private confession and absolution as the means to prepare for a worthy communion grew in importance, as confession rather than satisfaction became self-purgation and priestly absolution became purification.[2] Confession's value had become linked with the confessor's priestly ordination and, naturally enough, the importance of absolution grew with that of confession. Originally, *absolutio* had been a concluding blessing in any liturgy. From the Carolingian Reformation onward, because of its emphasis on the need for an official ecclesiastical declaration of forgiveness and on the power of the keys, *absolutio* began to take on the meaning of pardon or remission, indicating that the period of penance had been completed. The variety of forms of absolution found in rituals from the eighth through the fifteenth centuries shows the changing evaluation.

The literary formulas developed out of the sacerdotal prayer that had accompanied the laying on of the hand in the ancient reconciliation rite, but as they became more direct, the imposition of hands disappeared. The sacerdotal gesture and prayer, because of its own origins, had been a *berakah* in action, praising a merciful and compassionate God while asking for divine mercy. The petitionary elements of the prayer expanded as the relationship between God and humanity was differently conceived. As a consequence, the intercessory element became uppermost,[3] with the element of praise expressed primarily through the address, though the preface form continued in occasional use, particularly in public ordos.[4] The reconciliation rite, centered on this gesture and prayer, was thus regarded as the Church's authoritative intercession for the repentant sinner—which God hears and grants.

From the ninth century on, in the aftermath of the reaction against Celtic penance and the attempt to restore canonical penance, the authoritative character of the prayer received increased attention. "Absolutions," at first the concluding blessing and then the indication that satisfaction had been made, began to declare pardon or remission. References to the priest and to the petrine authority are increasingly frequent in the prayers. The "absolution" thus became either the *supplicatory* prayer, whereby the priest addressed God directly and asked forgiveness for the sinner, or the *optative* prayer, whereby he addressed the penitent, speaking of God in the third person and expressing the desire for the penitent's forgiveness.[5] From the tenth and eleventh centuries, when reconciliation was definitively joined to confession, an *indicative* formula of absolution came into use, generally in conjunction with one or both of the other forms, and by the late-twelfth century, it was commonly used. Through it, the priest addressed the penitent, and granted pardon.

The two ancient roles of spiritual counselor and community official were thus combined in the person of the priest-confessor. Formulas not only often referred to the apostolic authority of Peter and Paul but also, with a direct statement in the first person singular, necessarily emphasized the judicial element. The wider use of this formula, paralleling that used in baptism, helped to provide a liturgical base for the scholastic discussions of the power of the keys, and we find the thirteenth-century scholastics arguing that the indicative formula is the more appropriate. Because of their eventual consensus on the judicial role of the priest, after the mid-thirteenth century only the indicative formula was regarded as sacramental in the western Church. This form then played a crucial role in Scotus' theology; it led him to see absolution as the essence of the sacrament, with the absolution formula having the meaning of "I administer to you the sacrament of absolution." Lay confession consequently declined, though Thomas had been able to see confession of venial sins to a lay person—and even of mortal sins in necessity—as sacrament, though incomplete.[6]

Repeating penance had been in part a response to Celtic and Teutonic insecurity and anxiety, but simply to leave the individual to expiate sins alone was unlikely to be reassuring. Nor did emphasis on contrition and absorption of satisfaction within oral confession promote confidence, since the depth of contrition and the completeness of the penitent's confession became crucial to purification from sin. If the ritual was to console and offer the penitent assurance of forgiveness, only one element of that ritual could promote such confidence: absolution as the priestly exercise of the power of the keys. Modern confession, then, began to appear in the twelfth century as the ritual combination of confession and absolution finally displaced *confessio-paenitentia* as the central factor in receiving divine forgiveness. The next step was for Lateran IV (1215) to oblige all who had attained the use of reason to make an annual confession to their own priest. The modern system was complete after the fifteenth century, when confession and absolution were regarded as the only normal form of the sacrament.

143

The Theological Problematic

Liturgical development culminated in combining confession and reconciliation (the latter as priestly absolution). Then theological issues came to the fore, with the major problem being that of establishing the functions and effects of contrition and absolution in relation to one another.

The interrelation of the personal and ecclesial (subjective and objective) elements of the penitential process became a problem for several reasons. Conversion was reduced from a way of living in community to individual repentance and a private ritual. Orientation shifted from reconciliation to forgiveness. Both priest and penitent concentrated on the penitent's interior dispositions. Absolution had to be reinterpreted once confession and absolution were combined and satisfaction postponed. An indicative form of absolution became more common, since it better expressed the new understanding of absolution. Finally, scriptures used in an accommodated sense by patristic writers came to be understood literally. (Ambrose, Augustine, and Gregory had used the raising of Lazarus and the healing of the lepers to explain the role of Church officials. Ninth-century writers used the same examples to uphold the power of the keys, as did some liturgical texts.) Since interior contrition was now emphasized rather than external penitential works, satisfaction could no longer be regarded as the cause of forgiveness. Yet assigning satisfaction to be performed after the absolution implied that all punishment was not remitted by the absolution. How, then, did the penitent's contrition, confession, and satisfaction relate to the priestly absolution? What obtained divine pardon? What did God pardon? And when was that pardon received?

Twelfth-century theologians initially found it difficult to treat penance within their newly developed category of sacrament. It did not seem to fit their definition (the visible sign or form of invisible grace), since there was no obvious sign of presence as there was in the eucharist.

144

However, the controversies that occupied the schoolmen from Abelard to Aquinas and after are beyond the scope of our study, except insofar as they affect the liturgy of penance.[7]

Scholastic theologians analyzed their experience of the sacrament. They did not know how it had been shaped nor were they aware of alternatives. Their conclusions made their restricted experience normative and established it as the ordinary way to symbolize postbaptismal repentance. They were concerned, for example, with determining when forgiveness was received and providing the penitent with the assurance that sins were indeed forgiven.[8] Where ancient penance, even in its late canonical form, had focused on the community's health and wholeness and provided the means for reconciling penitents to the community, medieval penance focused instead on the individual's guilt and anxiety about salvation and provided the means for receiving the forgiveness that would alleviate guilt and anxiety. The shift recast questions on gauging sincerity of conversion before reconciliation, especially as interior dispositions were given higher priority than reshaping external behavior. Questions and concerns paralleling those in eucharistic theology became paramount; it was essential to determine when and how forgiveness is received and, because of the framework of scholastic thought, to state its precise conditions and causes.

Abelard (d. 1142) saw contrition as the decisive factor, largely because he took literally both scripture and the patristic accommodated use of scripture. Sorrow for sin out of love for God made the penitent; this, rather than *doing* penance, obtained divine pardon. Confession (which had largely absorbed the element of satisfaction) was secondary to contrition. Confession to the priest and the performance of the assigned penance were necessary because of God's command, but contrition embraced them both. Though he was almost alone among the scholastics in remembering that loosing restored peace with the

Church, Abelard regarded the power of the keys as having no effect on guilt. Lombard (d. 1160) similarly saw confession (and satisfaction) as the payment of debt, but did not see the power of the keys as forgiving sins.

Other scholastics (e.g., Hugh of St. Victor and Richard of St. Victor) emphasized the power of the keys as effective in removing guilt, not knowing the rabbinic meaning of binding and loosing and understanding it as forgiveness of sins. They distinguished the aftereffects of sin as hardheartedness (removed by contrition) and damnation (removed by absolution) or as liability to expiation (removed by God and the priest) and liability to damnation (removed by God because of contrition but on the condition of subsequent absolution). The need to provide sinners with the assurance of forgiveness led them to link repentance with absolution and, in the case of William of Auvergne (d. 1249), Bonaventure (d. 1274), and others, to distinguish attrition and contrition as types of repentance. Thus, for example, Bonaventure saw confession and absolution disposing a person to become contrite, with that contrition the cause of guilt's remission.

Aquinas (d. 1274) best managed a balanced synthesis of the personal and ecclesiastical factors while giving absolution, the expression of the Church's involvement, a causal role in the remission of sin. Like Lombard, he distinguished between penance as a virtue and penance as a sacrament and also distinguished the parts of the sacrament.[9] For Aquinas, the parts of the sacrament were the penitent's acts (contrition, confession, and satisfaction signifying interior penance) as the matter of the sacrament and the priest's absolution as the form. While the penitent's acts are sacramental signs and the absolution is dominant in its efficacy, matter and form act as a single cause. There is thus an intrinsic causal relationship between contrition and the power of the keys. (Using nonscholastic language, we might say that matter and form are human events in which the Spirit becomes evident as the means of discerning and experiencing salvation in community.) Thomas thus unites the personal and ecclesiastical factors in a manner almost unknown since the time of Cyprian, but this had little pastoral influence.

So far as sacramental justification is concerned, Thomas distinguished between the infusion of grace, conversion (the movement away from sin toward God: contrition and faith), and the remission of sin, though without separating them. Here there is reciprocal causality: grace is the formal, efficient, and final cause of conversion and the remission of sin; conversion and remission of sin are the material causes of grace and dispose the individual to receive it. Thus the sacrament disposes the individual for grace, and so far as the infusion of grace and forgiveness of sins is concerned, absolution serves as the instrumental cause.

There are two possibilities for the relationship between contrition and absolution, then, since absolution both produces contrition and requires contrition for its efficacy: either the remission of sins takes place before absolution because of contrition (which can happen, although contrition is motivated and oriented toward the absolution that will be received) or forgiveness coincides with absolution. In the latter case, using the terms somewhat differently than his predecessors, Thomas regarded attrition as the beginning of contrition and a remote disposition for grace and explained that the grace of the sacrament matures attrition into contrition, changing a remote disposition into a proximate one. Thus, for him there is only one means of justification, whether in the sacrament or outside it, and that is genuine conversion, faith, and contrition, with the ecclesial dimension of conversion expressed through the absolution or the desire for it.

Today we might say that the all-embracing grace of reconciliation received in and through the Church is the correlate of personal conversion. Still, it is clear that Aquinas united the personal and ecclesial dimensions more closely than had been customary for centuries. Later scholastics, however, exploiting ambiguities in Thomas's theology, usually understood this as an extrinsic relationship. Was the sacrament a dispositive cause of grace or a direct cause of it? What distinguishes attrition from contrition? What degree of attrition is necessary for sacramental justification?

The late medieval tendency was to see the sacrament as the direct cause of grace, distinguish attrition from contrition on the basis that contrition is motivated by love of God above all things while attrition is motivated by self-love (fear of punishment and desire for happiness), and regard attrition as sufficient for justification in the sacrament. The latter position was largely due to the influence of Duns Scotus, who regarded contrition, confession, and satisfaction as necessary conditions for the sacrament, but not parts of it. For him, there were two separate means of justification: penance, which is contrition motivated by love of God above all things, and the exercise of the power of the keys by absolution, where attrition suffices. This was also the base of the Nominalist position, which likewise saw absolution as the sacrament, with the penitent's acts necessary conditions for its effective operation.

These scholastic discussions affected both the liturgy and practice of penance. As the schoolmen moved away from Thomas's synthesis, the acts of the penitent became progressively less important. While sincere contrition, full confession, and satisfaction were required, they were necessary *conditions* for the efficacy of the absolution—the essence of the sacrament—and not themselves causes of forgiveness and grace. The tendency from the fourteenth century on was to abbreviate the sacramental ritual, omitting elements that, according to Thomas, helped attrition become contrition, and concentrate on the absolution, efficacious in itself as the direct cause of forgiveness. The ritual expression of the Church's judgment came close to replacing personal conversion in late medieval theology. Popular understanding went even further, sometimes verging on a quasi-magical view.

Lateran IV and the End of Medieval Penance

The transition from medieval to modern penance began with Lateran Council IV in 1215, for its legislation marked the beginning of a new official outlook, one that concentrated on individual auricular confession and priestly absolution as the means to further postbaptismal conversion and be cleansed of sin. During the three centuries preceding the council, private confession had come to be adopted almost universally and other forms of the sacrament received less attention. Canonical pronouncements had given confession official status and urged its use. Scholastic theologians had deepened and clarified insights into the nature and workings of the sacrament. The ritual combination of confession and absolution had effectively replaced *confessio-paenitentia* as the cause of forgiveness. The early twelfth-century *Decretum* of Gratian had recognized that there were well-founded arguments for either confession to the priest or personal contrition and satisfaction, but changing circumstances in the decades immediately preceding the Council—particularly the growing threat of Albigensianism—led to a new outlook that considered private auricular confession and priestly absolution a touchstone of loyalty to the Church and the obligatory means of ecclesiastical forgiveness. This became law at Lateran IV.

Chapter 21 of the decrees of Lateran IV (DS 812) obliged all who had reached the age of discretion to make an oral and secret annual confession of all their sins to their own priest and to receive communion at Easter.[10] About 20 years before, Alan of Lille had recommended auricular confession even by those unaware of sin so that they might be purified of sins that they had forgotten and show respect for the rules of the Church.[11] Lateran IV made such confession compulsory, though most scholastics (and all modern commentators) saw this binding only those conscious of mortal sin, an interpretation tacitly approved by Trent and incorporated into the 1983 Code of Canon Law. The obligation, as asserted by Lateran IV, is an ecclesiastical one, although many subsequent theologians have held the opinion that the Council had implicitly settled the debate on whether the obligation to confession was from divine law.[12] The age of discretion was not specified and opinions covered a wide range, though fourteen, the age for marriage, was probably what the Council had in mind.[13] The requirement that the confessor inquire into the circumstances of the sins was particularly significant, for this reinforced the tendency developing throughout the Middle Ages to make the confession a detailed or integral confession.

The abundance and type of vernacular penitential literature in the thirteenth and fourteenth centuries raise the question of whether Lateran IV's prescription was willingly accepted.[14] Its sanctions—denial of a funeral and Christian burial and the threat of hell—led to compliance, yet the majority of people went no more often than they were obliged. The frequent use of interrogations by confessors suggest that lay people either came unwillingly or with little understanding. Perhaps its most important effect on our time was reinforcing the medieval association of confession with communion, for at the end of the Middle Ages few other than religious confessed except as preparation for the infrequent communion, the antecedent of the later devotional confession.

TARIFF PENANCE AND POPULAR PIETY

Monastic penance as popularized in Europe by Celtic and Anglo-Saxon monks was a dead end in the historical development of the structures of sacramental penance, but it occasioned the Carolingian compromise. This eventually led to privatizing postbaptismal conversion into the Church community and, after some rearrangement, the modern ritual of the sacrament. More important, monastic penance influenced popular piety and thus transformed sacramental experience far beyond what could be explained by structural differences. The Western system became aliturgical as well as private throughout, with little or no attention given to community worship. It is not surprising, then, that it helped shape an individualized piety preoccupied with sin, where individuals were largely left to their own resources to deal with guilt, overcome sin, be converted, and find salvation. While Christians had always had to face the fact of sin both as individuals and as community, it was rare that they were unable to see past sin to a broader perspective. Certainly canonical penance had been situated in the broader perspective of salvation experienced in community. Monastic penance, however, helped shape a spirituality where one element, the acknowledgment of guilt, became the focal point. Sin and its avoidance became the dominant preoccupation of such a spirituality. An introspective guilt was intensified by the need to ferret out such past sins to be freed (absolved) from them and their consequences.[15]

Similarly, humiliating and punishing oneself now made it possible to avoid divine punishment hereafter. Despite the penitentials' claim that *paenitentia* was medicinal, the punitive character was uppermost in experience.[16] An earlier age had seen *paenitentia* as the substitution of Christian for pagan attitudes and ways, but the individualized nonliturgical character of the tariff system led it to lose sight of the probationary and medicinal function. The principle of "contraria contrariis sanantur" was held to verbally, but it is difficult to see how the various means of satisfaction contributed to rehabilitation or the reconstruction of personality.

For the most part, individuals were left on their own. The absence of a ritual of reconciliation in Celtic penance accentuated isolation, despite the intention of bringing a semipagan laity closer to being a Christian community. All other features of monastic penance aside, this is the clearest sign that it was no longer the Church that obtained sinners' restoration to the community of salvation by interceding for them, cooperating with their efforts to be converted, and then sharing with them the fullness of the Holy Spirit dwelling in the faithful. The penitents obtained forgiveness for themselves through self-humiliation in confession and prayer and mortification in penance. Then they had the juridical right to return to eucharistic communion—a right, however, that was rarely made use of. The priest's prayer did little to link the penitent to the Christian community. As the priest lent an ear to penitents seeking to deal with their guilt, so he offered advice on the means to expiate sin. In both situations, however, penitents were largely left on their own. Conversion was a matter of individual achievement.

The corresponding spirituality was one appropriate to individuals seeking to save their souls by avoiding sin and satisfying for sin. It was an introspective spirituality where the individual accomplished whatever was accomplished, aided by externals supplied by the Church as a means of grace to compensate for individual limitations. Law, with its system of requirements and requitals, became the measure of the human relationship with a demanding God. Sin and guilt, on the one hand, and virtue and merit, on the other, were similarly quantifiable.

The radical individualization of what had earlier been clearly related to communal liturgy moved people away from an awareness of Church community. This had already been weakened in the West by a changing conception of sin and forgiveness and a reinterpretation of the elements of canonical penance. The tie to the Church through the priest was tenuous. There was little or nothing to prevent this from being eliminated as well, with the penitent left entirely self-sufficient, since it had been the penitent's *paenitentia* that obtained forgiveness. The priest's only value in the Celtic system had been his presumed expertise in matters spiritual, including his judgment on how best to satisfy for sin. It is no wonder that the Carolingian reformation reacted against a development that moved people away from the Church and its pastors.

The official reaction to the Celtic experiment kept the last tie to the Church community from being eliminated. It did so by linking the penitent's *confessio* and *paenitentia* to the solemn ritual of reconciliation, then later by privatizing that ritual, and finally, in modern confession, by putting the element of satisfaction subsequent to reconciliation in the form of priestly absolution. This was admittedly a compression, reordering, and reinterpretation of the structural phases of canonical and ancient penance as well as a privatizing of them, but it did maintain them and with a discernible, though weakened, link to the Church through granting the priest faculties that authorized him to exercise the power of the keys on behalf of the bishop of the local Church.

Yet the climate of popular piety and spirituality had already been shaped. Later theology might appeal to an abstract power of the keys exercised by the Church through absolution, but penitents, trained to look inward to gauge repentance and to themselves to expiate guilt, found it difficult to think themselves into a sense of community that was clearly absent. The pastoral response was then twofold: the development of commutations and redemptions into indulgences and the elaboration of intellectual theories on the relationship between what the penitent felt and what absolution did. Times would come, however, when large numbers of Christians would reject such compromises—vociferously in the early sixteenth century, quietly in the latter half of the twentieth.

Efforts to condemn the Celtic practice and to reintroduce canonical penance succeeded only in adding a formula of absolution paralleling (but not equivalent to) the canonical system's reconciliation in and to the community. The ritual and experience and corresponding spirituality were not, however, greatly affected. While the modern theology of penance could not begin to develop until absolution was joined to the *confessio*, the medieval (and modern) spirituality of the sacrament had been established in its general lines prior to that development.

By the thirteenth century, penance was almost totally a private act. An earlier repentance and desire for conversion had become guilt and remorse—probably because of the detachment from community that left the penitent without support and encouragement. Ecclesiastical penance still functioned as a means of formation, but its social function was not so much oriented toward maintaining and strengthening the Church's holiness as it was toward maintaining discipline and strengthening hierarchical control. Its orientation to the individual became one of consolation rather than of assistance and support in conversion. The late Middle Ages found it difficult to integrate these functions of discipline and consolation, probably because both had been detached from an orientation toward community. Only the appeal to an abstract and nonempirical power of the keys (interpreted in legal terms) maintained the semblance of a relation to Church community.

The penitentials' influence is nowhere as evident as in the attitudes shaped regarding the knowledge and confession of sin. Their attention to differentiating and cataloging sins ensured that action and not attitude would be the prime category. The quantifying mentality shaped by the tariff system helped create habits of introspection and standards for assigning responsibility that made a scientific moral theology possible. But this was often at the cost of seeing humanity as basically and helplessly sinful. The richness of conversion was debased into an understanding of an amendment of life, with perseverance until death. An emphasis on an integral confession or complete enumeration of sins was another consequence. Many of the questions asked in the medieval confession were rooted in the penitentials.

The cost of such a situation was high, both financially—the stipend—and psychologically. Sin became the prime paradigm through which the Christian life was viewed. Though popular spirituality centered on sin and redemption, sin was uppermost. Penance itself came to be defined as consisting of the vow to avoid sin, the act of confessing sin, and the act of satisfying for sin.[17] The seven steps of penance—knowledge of self, repentance, sorrow, oral confession, mortification of the flesh, correction and satisfaction by works, perseverance—gave little attention to the experience of redemption that had earlier motivated conversion as transformation into a member of the community of salvation.[18]

The notion of satisfaction that the monks had offered as a way of dealing with sin and guilt was itself perhaps the greatest obstacle to penance as a means of consolation. Penance itself contained possibilities for serious sin—if all sins were not confessed so that satisfaction could be assigned or if satisfaction was not performed adequately. Invalid confessions and satisfaction not done in the state of grace had to be repeated.

The introspection encouraged by the system and the tendency to place individuals on their own gave contrition almost total causal effectiveness in medieval theology. As a consequence, the scholastics found it difficult to explain the priest's role. Did he simply declare that forgiveness had been attained? Did he simply remove the temporal punishment deserved? Or did he forgive sins directly? The failure to see the intimate relationship between conversion and reintegration into the community left theologians asking whether contrition or absolution was the more important and answers varied. This controversy, and that over contrition and attrition, had a base in the earlier understanding of penitents returning to communion through performing their *paenitentia*.

Medieval spirituality (and much of modern) was monastically derived. Perhaps there is more than a loose connection between this continuing clericalization of the Church and a tendency to see laity as second-class citizens whose only hope is to live as much like monks as possible, with the Ten Commandments as their rule. Celtic penance may have been a dead end in the development of penance structures, but its influence on spirituality has been far-reaching. We can see what happens when the Church's liturgy is poorly or wrongly celebrated for a long enough time as well as the results of introducing a reformed liturgy without considering what popular piety will make of it.

PENANCE ON THE EVE OF THE REFORMATION

By the late thirteenth century, private confession was, for all practical purposes, the only survivor of the rich and varied sacramental forms with which the Church had earlier supported postbaptismal conversion. Scholastic theologians had concluded that the sacrament existed only where there was a clear judicial exercise of the power of the keys. The penance of Lent, pilgrimage, and general absolutions were therefore regarded as sacramentals and sharply distinguished from the sacrament. Solemn penance, though recognized as an authentic form of the sacrament, was too rarely used to affect theology. The late medieval form of penance had thus been canonized by theologians and it was the only adequate means for obtaining the forgiveness of mortal sins. Lateran IV had made it mandatory and the few developments that took place in later centuries only secured its hold on the Christian imagination. There was hardly any other way for the average individual to experience personally the reality of justification.

Developments were primarily in theology, canon law, and popular piety.[19] Abuses, though rampant, were not quietly tolerated. Synodal regulations and literature for confessors in the period between Lateran IV and Trent show the attempt to root them out: to provide competent confessors, eliminate charging for absolution or requiring penitents to purchase Masses from the confessor as their penance, prevent solicitation (attempts to seduce penitents), overcome superstitious understandings of the working of absolution and indulgences. Canonical regulations and popular penitential literature show the attempt to increase frequency of confession beyond the minimum required by Lateran IV. For the most part, however, both attempts were unsuccessful. The Counter-Reformation had to repeat the prohibition of abuses, and before Trent confession was generally no more than once a year, usually during Lent.[20]

Changes in ritual were due to the continuing influence of the factors that had promoted private confession and were in turn reinforced by it: the tendency toward individualism, the emphasis on judgment and the priestly power of the keys, the theological distinction of sins and detailed confession, the absorption of satisfaction within oral confession. The continued disintegration of the liturgical community likewise had its effect on both ritual and attitude. This is seen particularly in heightened clericalism and increased lay passivity, a fixation on theological essentials and canonical validity leading to an increasingly routine and mechanical performances of the ritual, and a continued diminishment of all symbols but the verbal ones.

The liturgical formalities in the late Middle Ages were simple. The priest was seated in an open place in the church and the penitent usually knelt in front of him (or, if a woman, to the side) as a sign of humility and contrition. The preliminaries were quickly gotten through: a greeting, ascertaining the penitent's status,[21] and encouraging a complete and confident confession.[22] The penitent made the sign of the cross, if that had not already been done, and began the confession of sins, usually with a general confession, the *confiteor*. Confessors were usually told not to interrupt with questions unless necessary. Penitents were expected to be both complete and succinct.[23] The penitent completed the prayer of general confession (the second part of the *confiteor*) and frequently added a statement of sorrow for sins that might have been forgotten. The confessor asked any necessary questions,[24] advised the penitent, determined whether the penitent was properly disposed for absolution, imposed a penance, and then absolved.[25] The penitent gave an alms, asked the priest's prayers, and left.

Though the etiquette of confession emphasized proper deference toward the priest who exercised the power of the keys, this, like other formalities, ensured that the penitent felt that guilt was removed and sins forgiven. In his detailed study, *Sin and Confession on the Eve of the Reformation*, Tentler sees the correlated functions of discipline and consolation in late medieval penance and correctly indicates that the reformers reacted against what they perceived as primarily disciplinary and thereby anxiety-producing. But he fails, in my opinion, to recognize that this double function was primarily the product of a shift from Church reconciliation to individual forgiveness. In other words, whatever might be said of the theology and practice of penance in its late medieval form, its primary purpose and motivation was for individuals to obtain forgiveness—to be freed from sin, guilt, and the threat of divine punishment—and to be sure that they stood in God's grace. It functioned, therefore, as a means of justification and, while it was undoubtedly hedged about with disciplinary requirements that were at times burdensome (and sometimes resisted), it was intended and perceived as a source, primarily, of forgiveness and, secondarily, of grace.

Late medieval penance, then, stressed the therapeutic element, purification, to remove sin and eliminate the debt of eternal punishment incurred by mortal sin, both of which kept the sinner from God's favor. Other means, indulgences in particular, were necessary to deal with the temporal punishment due to sin,[26] but in both cases the primary concern was to enable the individual to be assured of God's forgiveness and grace. Since this purification was no longer seen in the context of a living and growing relationship with God and reconciliation with the

Church, the penitential system was no longer functioning as a means of formation and continuing conversion in the fullest sense. Apart from the power of the keys entrusted to the priest by ordination in apostolic succession, it had little or no ecclesial meaning. Penance, in both theology and practice, was geared toward the individual's forgiveness. What little liturgy remained was intended to help the individual experience that forgiveness.

The penitential experience can be correlated with the Christ images that emerged in the Middle Ages and became traditional by the sixteenth and seventeenth centuries.[27] On the one side was the imaginative contemplation and portrayal of the historical sufferings of Christ, with the emotions that came from realizing that these were due to sin. To intensify the anxiety arising from guilt there was, on the other side, the Christ who would be judge at death. It is no wonder, even apart from other cultural influences, that the *dies irae* was feared, that the Christian life became an *ars moriendi* and that a funeral spirituality was prevalent.

The situation was complicated intellectually by fuzzy theology, religious ignorance, and superstition. The penitential experience itself was affected by individualization and legal enforcement. It is therefore impossible to paint a simple picture of the penitential system on the eve of the Reformation. Tentler shows its complexity by indicating that though its critics and defenders were dealing with the same system, they were doing so out of vastly different social and psychological experiences of it.[28]

The system's requirements for forgiveness—sufficient sorrow, full confession, and willingness to perform the assigned satisfaction—could be criticized as semi-Pelagian because of their emphasis on human action, effort, accomplishment, and merit, but from the viewpoint of its defenders it was human weakness that stood to gain from submission to the power of the keys. Though an *ex opere operato* theology of the absolution formula and emphasis on jurisdiction and the like might look magical to some, others could point to the sincere faith, effort, and involvement that were required for the penitent's forgiveness. In many respects, the bewildering maze of distinctions of sins, circumstances, jurisdiction, reservation, and casuistry made the system a mass of legalism and ritualism, but the system also focused on the conscience of the individual and the individual's realization of guilt, desire for forgiveness, and purpose of amendment. Did the system promote laxity, encourage sin by assuring forgiveness? Its defenders could point to how it carefully delineated obligations and responsibilities. Was it a rigid system that created fear and scrupulosity? Others experienced it as a source of forgiveness and reassurance. It could be criticized as a means of clerical domination and tyranny, but the tyrants were themselves subject to the system.

Martin Luther and Ignatius Loyola are perhaps symbols of the two parties to the debate, examples of its complexity, and indications of how the opposing groups came out of vastly different experiences of the system. Neither can be classified simply as a critic or a defender of the system. Martin Luther had experienced the torment of the penitential discipline as an Augustinian, but he could never bring himself to reject the sacrament totally. Ignatius Loyola experienced its reassurance and consolation, but he could also levelheadedly call for the elimination of superstitions and abuses.

Several liturgical factors entered into this ambivalent experience. A discussion of them may be helpful in understanding the late medieval situation and evaluating and interpreting the Tridentine decrees.

By the end of the Middle Ages, the symbolic language of penance had become extremely limited. For all practical purposes it had been reduced to individual auricular confession and priestly absolution, as the element of satisfaction had steadily diminished in importance. The narrowed focus had not developed all at once. Conversion as a process lived out in community had telescoped. Due in part to a moralizing tendency resulting from changing initiation practice, conversion had ceased to be the comprehensive foundation of the Christian life and became a change in the individual's behavior. The lived reality was reduced to a ritual symbol. Rather than being a life process symbolized in communal worship, conversion had become a ritual intended to bring about transformation in a quasi-magical way. Individualizing and clericalizing tendencies had contributed to isolating the ritual from community life and worship. Because of all this, individual confession and absolution had become the primary, if not the only, symbol of postbaptismal conversion.

In addition, baptism was little appreciated in the late Middle Ages. Infant baptism, done privately, meant that not even baptism, let alone initiation, was an ordinary part of the Christian experience. It is not surprising, then, that confession could later be regarded by Harnack as the central symbol and means of justification in Catholicism. Likewise significant is what had happened to the eucharist. Unintelligible language, incomprehensible rites and ceremonies, passive attendance, and infrequent communion meant that the forgiveness of sins was largely an independent reality apart from reconciliation to God in the community.

The philosophical and theological trends, cultural developments (including the individualistic humanism of the incipient Renaissance), and an almost aliturgical experience of the officially stressed but infrequently approached sacrament had all contributed to the creation of a situation where the Protestant reformers would reject the penitential system of individual auricular confession to receive priestly absolution and Trent would reaffirm not only its value but also its necessity. Both, however, were motivated by a common concern: to assure individuals of God's forgiveness and grace. Neither party to the controversy was aware of the historical importance of reconciliation to the Church or of the communal significance of the sacrament. It is understandable, then, that the reformers eliminated the ecclesiastical middleman to enable sinners to go directly to God and that the Council of Trent appealed to a juridical priestly power. In any case, the late medieval penitential format and experience was fixed, in modern confession, as a primary component of Catholic religious life into the twentieth century.

NOTES

1. However, this was not universal. The late ninth-century Spanish Church gave the penitent the option to make a full confession or simply to make the statement of having sinned, seeing both as rooted in tradition. See Gonzalo Martinez Diez, "Un tratado visigotico sobre la penitencia," *Hispania Sacra* 19 (1966) 89–98, especially p. 91. Penance was admission to the eucharist, the sacrament of reconciliation. For context in Spanish practice, see Joseph M. McCarthy, "The Pastoral Practice of the Sacraments of Cleansing in the Legislation of the Visigothic Church." *Classical Folia* 24 (1970) 177–186, and Gonzalo Martinez Diez, "Algunos aspectos de la penitencia en la iglesia visigodomozárabe," *Miscelanea Comillas* 49 (1968) 5–19. An extensive study, which I have not been able to examine, is that of D. Borobio, *La penitencia en la iglesia hispanica del siglo IV al VII* (Bilbao: 1978).

2. Alcuin spoke of the necessity of confession before each communion; see *De psalmorum usu*, II, 9 (PL 101: 499). In some medieval versions of the *confiteor*, communion without previous confession was a point of accusation; see Jungmann, *Die lateinischen Bussriten*, p. 173. For a thorough study, see Peter Browe, "Die Kommunionvorbereitung im Mittelalter," *Zeitschrift für katholischen Theologie* 56 (1932) 375–415.

3. Leo I had spoken of the "supplicationes sacerdotum" in Letter 108, *ad Theodorum* (PL 54: 1011).

4. For the meaning of confession as worship and praise, see Jean Leclercq, "Confession and Praise of God," *Worship* 42 (1968) 169–176. This was not totally forgotten in the Middle Ages; see his "Confession et louange de Dieu chez saint Bernard," *La Vie Spirituelle* 120 (1969) 588–605.

162

5. Jungmann, *Die lateinischen Bussriten,* p. 202, note 147, distinguishes the types of absolutions. The term absolution was, of course, used in a wider sense before the eleventh century. The term deprecatory has generally been used for the absolution prayer addressed to God, but the English connotations of the word suggest that supplicatory is more appropriate. For examples of the various forms and their eventual combination, see Jungmann, *Die lateinischen Bussriten,* pp. 201–237, especially pp. 223–230.

6. See *Summa Theologiae,* Suppl., q. 8, a. 2 (on confessing mortal sins) and a. 3 (on confessing venial sins).

7. For summary histories see Vorgrimler, *Busse und Krankensalbung,* pp. 114–153, whose extensive bibliography supplements that of Poschmann, *Penance and the Anointing of the Sick,* pp. 155–193. See especially Paul Anciaux, *La théologie de pénitence au XIIe siècle* (Louvain: Publications Universitaires de Louvain, 1948). Unfortunately, most histories, these included, fail to relate the development of theological reflection to collateral institutional developments in discipline, liturgy, and popular understanding.

8. For a summary of this theological discussion in the twelfth and thirteenth centuries, see Robert Hancock and Robert Williams, "The Scholastic Debate on the Essential Moment of Forgiveness," *Resonance* 1 (1965) 63–74.

9. Lombard had tried to combine Abelard's position on contrition with the Victorines' emphasis on the efficacy of the power of the keys by distinguishing the virtue and sacrament of penance. He held that the virtue did not exist only in the sacrament but was rather coextensive with the Christian life. While he thus partially recovered a fundamental biblical and Augustinian insight, failing to appreciate baptism meant that his view of penance (as a virtue) was in practice restricted to contrition. He had also tried to overcome the dichotomy between contrition and confession by speaking of the penitent's outward acts as signs of the interior contrition that was the cause of forgiveness. The Aristotelian concepts of matter and form were, however, difficult to apply to penance, and the problem of relationship to absolution remained.

10. This is the base of the obligation stated in Canon 906 of the 1917 *Codex Iuris Canonici* and in Canon 989 of the 1983 Code,

although the latter specifies that only mortal sins must be confessed; cf. also Canon 988. Lateran IV did not establish anything new—it ratified existing regulations and determined when the obligation had to be fulfilled—but it did serve as a base for a steadily increasing emphasis on individual auricular confession and priestly absolution to the point of practically eliminating any interest in other means of forgiveness.

Lateran IV required confession to one's own priest (usually the pastor). Confession to another priest without permission meant that the absolution was invalid because the priest lacked jurisdiction.

11. For the antecedents, see T. J. van Balen, "Das Sakrament der Beichte um die Wende des 13. Jahrhunderts," *Studia Moralia* 6 (1968) 295–350.

12. Pierre M. Gy, "Le precepte de la confession annuelle et la necessité de la confession," *Revue des Sciences Philosophiques et Théologiques* 63 (1979) 529–547.

13. Pierre M. Gy, "Les bases de la pénitence moderne," *Maison Dieu* 117 (1974) 79. See also Peter Browe, "Die Kinderbeichte im Mittelalter," *Theologie und Glaube* 25 (1933) 689–701, Richard L. De Molen, "Childhood and the Sacraments in the Sixteenth Century," *Archiv für Reformationsgeschichte* 66 (1975) 49–71, and W. La Due, "The Age of Reason Re-Examined: The Sacraments of Marriage and Confession," *Living Light* 11 (1974) 564–571. Thomas proposed 10 to 12 as the proper age. The tendency in the late Middle Ages was to see the Lateran obligation binding around 12 to 14, although in some places children confessed—frequently without being given absolution—from the age of 7 or 8. But see also John A. Hardon, "First Confession: An Historical and Theological Analysis," *Eglise et Théologie* 3 (1972) 69–110, who argues, unconvincingly, that early and frequent confession, even of venial sins, existed from patristic times.

14. See Jean Charles Payen, "La pénitence dans le contexte culturel des XIIe et XIIIe siècles," *Revue des Sciences Philosophiques et Théologiques* 61 (1977) 399–428.

15. The special type of fascination sex held for celibate monks is prominent in the penitentials and comes to dominate the Celtic Christian outlook. When the *Liber Angeli* (late seventh or early eighth century) names the nonordained orders of the church,

they are the virgins, the legitimately married, and the penitents—those who keep the sexual rules and those who have broken them! For the quotation (used in a different context), see Kate Dooley, "From Penance to Confession: The Celtic Contribution," *Bijdragen* 43 (1982) 394, note 24.

16. See especially John T. McNeill, "Medicine for Sin as Prescribed in the Penitentials," *Church History* 1 (1932) 14–26. Cf. Oakley, *English Penitential Discipline*, p. 43.

17. See, for example, Richard of Saint Victor, *De potestate ligandi et solvendi*, 5 in *Textes Philosophiques du Moyen Âge* (Paris: 1955) 15: 83.

18. See, for example, Bernard of Clairvaux, Sermons on Diverse Topics, 40, in *Sancti Bernardi Opera*, Jean Leclercq and Henri Rochais, eds. (Rome: 1957) 6 234–243. See also Nicholas of Clairvaux, Sermo 58 (PL 144: 831–833).

19. Only in the late Middle Ages, with the extensive development of penitential literature, do we begin to have some understanding of how penance functioned in the life of the average person. Besides theological and canonical literature, confessors had summas (lengthy and detailed discussion of the sacrament and cases of conscience) and manuals (less learned and more practical handbooks). Clergy and laity had an abundant devotional literature. Thomas N. Tentler, who provides a thorough analysis of the literature in his *Sin and Confession on the Eve of the Reformation* (Princeton: Princeton University Press, 1977), notes that this literature, taken as a whole, was popular, practical, cautious, and its quantity obviously due to the invention of printing (see especially pp. 28–53).

20. For the frequency of confession, see Peter Browe, "Die Pflichtbeichte im Mittelalter," *Zeitschrift für katholische Theologie* 57 (1933) 335–383, especially pp. 342–347; see also Tentler, *Sin and Confession*, pp. 70–82, and the sources he cites. Though the Tridentine decrees primarily reflect doctrinal concerns, the penance decree suggests that Lateran IV's requirement was customarily linked with Lent; cf. DS 1683, 1708.

21. Because of the requirement that penitents confess to their own priest and because of restrictions on jurisdiction, the priest had to know whether he could absolve the penitent. He also needed to know something of the penitent's profession, social

and marital status, and religious knowledge in order to ask the necessary questions and to offer suitable advice.

22. Manuals for confessors frequently expanded on this and thereby implied what their authors saw as the qualities of good confessors. See Tentler, *Sin and Confession*, pp. 84–85, 95–104. Although the liturgical formulas were abbreviated by this time, the confessor's encouragement drew on the content of earlier prayers: assurance that God forgives the repentant, examples of divine mercy from the scriptures, the power of Christ's passion.

23. Scholastic theologians and authors of confession manuals often listed the qualities of good confessions. See, for example, Thomas Aquinas, *Summa Theologiae*, Suppl., q. 9, a. 4. All agreed that completeness was essential. A thorough, methodical, and diligent examination of conscience was to precede the confession. The penitent was to be frank and honest in the confession itself. To ensure completeness, the confessor was advised not to interrupt or show surprise or displeasure. Even the followers of Scotus, who saw the essence of the sacrament in the absolution and denied that the confession was part of the sacrament, emphasized the need for completeness. Many manuals recognized the danger of scrupulosity and cautioned against it. The emphasis on completeness ("integral confession") seems to parallel the requirement in the ancient period that conversion be complete or at least well underway before reconciliation was granted and the tariff requirement that the debts due to one's sins be satisfied before readmission to eucharistic communion. As penance becomes a matter of ritual and the confession becomes the means of expiation, a complete confession is crucial for achieving purgation and scrupulosity increases.

24. The need for detail, the basis for such questioning, was rooted in tariff penance and its penitentials. Manuals generally recommended discretion as well as investigation, but it is difficult to determine what the actual practice was. Most manuals called for thorough questioning to assure completeness of confession and an accurate understanding of the case on the confessor's part. For examples of detailed enumeration and questioning, see Pierre Michaud-Quantin, "Deux formulaires pour la confession du milieu du XIIIe siècle," *Recherches de Théologie Ancienne et Médiévale* 31 (1964) 43–62.

25. Some manuals placed the absolution before the assignment of penance. Manuals likewise disagreed whether the confessor should impose his hand during the absolution. Most considered the gesture unnecessary. Tentler, *Sin and Confession*, pp. 281–294, gives a sampling of absolution formulas (all indicative by this period) and discusses how absolution was understood. The tendency from the thirteenth century on was to make the indicative absolution formula clearer and shorter to emphasize the causal role of the exercise of the power of the keys and to assure the penitent of forgiveness. Contemporary literature frequently recommended that the confessor omit any superfluous prayers or phrases that might dilute the penitent's confidence or distract from the central reality of the *ex opere operato* operation of the sacramental absolution.

26. The concept of the temporal punishment due to sin was a product of the earlier scholastic disputes on the relations between contrition and absolution and on what the exercise of the power of the keys accomplished. The eventual consensus was that the sacrament removed the debt of eternal punishment. The assigned penitential works were seen as implying that some debt still remained to be paid, though the amount was undoubtedly lessened by more intense contrition. The concept is thus the residue of the ancient insistence on complete conversion and the tariff requirement of satisfaction. For an assessment of Trent's dogmatic commitment in relation to current concerns, see Peter J. Beer, "Trent's Temporal Punishment and Today's Renewal of Penance," *Theological Studies* 35 (1974) 467–481.

27. I have borrowed this correlation from Robert E. McNally, "The Counter-Reformation's Views of Sin and Penance," *Thought* 52 (1977) 155–158.

28. *Sin and Confession*, pp. 364–365.

Chapter Six

Modern Penance and the Counter-Reformation

The medieval penitential experience contained within itself the seeds of a bitter controversy regarding the requirements and ministers of ecclesial forgiveness. This controversy grew through the late Middle Ages, with Marsilius of Padua (d. c. 1343), John Wyclif (d. 1384), and Jan Hus (d. 1415) particularly prominent, and ended in the Protestant reformers' rejection of individual auricular confession and absolution. To the fathers of the Council of Trent, the problem and solution were as obvious as these had been to the bishops of the Carolingian reform councils. The problem was contempt for ancient tradition and rejection of the Church's official structures. The solution was to eliminate abuses, reaffirm the value of the official procedures, and encourage their use.

A new epoch in the history of penance thus began in the sixteenth century, for the purified and simplified medieval ritual of individual auricular confession and priestly absolution provided by the Tridentine reform remained the sole official form of the sacrament throughout the post-Tridentine era. Not until the scholarly rediscoveries and pastoral reforms of the twentieth century would alternatives be known or imagined.

THE TRIDENTINE RESPONSE

By attacking indulgences, Luther put the entire medieval penitential system into question. As he further applied the principle of justification by grace through faith, he considered the sacrament of penance legitimate only to the extent that it proclaimed the gospel's promise of grace and encouraged the sinner to trust fully in divine forgiveness. This, the reformers concluded, was not the case in penance as they knew it. Contrition, confession, and satisfaction were, to Luther's mind, Church inventions and not gospel consolation. Full or integral confession of all mortal sins received particularly harsh criticism: it was a torment to the penitent, an irritation to the confessor, a waste of time for both, a sign of a lack of confidence in divine mercy, and, in the final analysis, impossible. The judicial character of absolution he likewise objected to: the power of the keys and priestly absolution was the ministry of proclaiming the gospel of forgiveness. The individuals's confident faith that sins were forgiven and grace granted by God was essential to an evangelical confession.

Trent gave little attention to areas of agreement between Protestants and Catholics. It did not, for example, deny a link between confident faith and sacramental efficacy—several bishops defended a position on this that was basically the same as Luther's.[1] The council was primarily concerned with answering attacks on the current Catholic practice of private confession and priestly absolution. However, both parties to the dispute were largely unaware of actual historical evidence: Protestant reformers claimed that Lateran IV had invented private confession; Trent and the Counter-Reformation asserted that the late medieval system of penance had existed from the beginning.

Trent's formulation of its teaching on integral confession and on absolution as judgment was conditioned by its mistaken understanding of history (that the late medieval form of penance had existed from the beginning), its failure to take Eastern practice into account (where a different understanding both of integrity and the nature of absolution had changed little through the centuries), and the perceived need to defend the current system against the reformers. Situating Trent's teaching in the context of the history of penance, both Eastern and Western as well as in its immediate historical context, can lead to a reformulation that preserves the Tridentine dogmatic affirmations while compensating for their limitations. As an earlier age had required full reform—or at least clear evidence that it was well underway—so, in the late Middle Ages, once penitential works were practically absorbed within the confession, full confession was the prerequisite for ecclesial forgiveness. Such confession showed the penitent's transparency before the Lord, the sincerity and completeness of personal conversion, and enabled Church representatives to gauge the penitent's conversion and assist it by prescribing appropriate remedies for sin and ways to undo the harm done. Likewise, the Church's ability to bind and loose had taken the shape of excluding the serious sinner from the eucharist by legal regulation and of readmitting by priestly absolution after authenticating conversion.

Trent's dogmatic definition is in continuity with the practice and understanding of the ancient Church, but it was stated in terms of a much narrowed and restricted sacramental expression. However Trent's definition is reformulated, there is no doubt that it insisted that the Church had a stake in its members' repentance and therefore the right and responsibility to direct the penitent in the process of conversion that leads to forgiveness. It is likewise clear that Trent saw the Church exercising that right and fulfilling that responsibility through the current penitential system.[2]

Essential—*iure divino*—to that system was an integral individual auricular confession before absolution (canon 7; DS 1701) through which sinners manifested their consciences, reviewing or recounting[3] their mortal sins. Trent gave no clear answers on what constituted integrity, what mortal sins had to be submitted, or what circumstances required (or excused from) integral confession. It did, however, clearly state that the individual's conversion had to become ecclesially visible for it to be complete and defended the current form of penitential discipline and liturgy as in accord with Christ's will for his Church. Yet it

170

did not establish as Catholic dogma that the sacrament of penance was limited to this form of ecclesial visibility.

The council characterized penance as analogous to court judgment (canon 9 [DS 1709] and cf. DS 1685) and thus showed the need for the priest to know the case set before him by the penitent. Trent did not explain the meaning of this judgment beyond stating that it is more than proclaiming the gospel or declaring that sins are already forgiven and that it is an exercise of a real power of pardoning received from Christ—efficacious and creative (canons 9 and 10; DS 1709–1710). But, beyond affirming the legitimacy of the current form—it could not envision alternatives—Trent did not indicate the precise limits within which that judgment could be exercised.

The two most obvious characteristics of medieval penance, confession and absolution, were rejected by the reformers in their current form. Both—again, in their current form—were reaffirmed by Trent as consistent with what Christ intended for the Church. Trent did not, however, rule out other forms, past or future. Its primary concern was to respond to the reformers' rejection by insisting that the sinful Christian's conversion had to be visible in the Church and that the Church's authoritative response to that conversion was a real factor in divine forgiveness. Abuses and superstitions had to be eliminated, but the central features of the current expression of the sacrament—individual confession and priestly absolution—had to be maintained.

IMMOBILITY AND INDIVIDUALIZATION
The Tridentine decrees were, of course, interpreted in a much narrower and more legalistic manner at the time and subsequently. Though major abuses and superstitions were eventually done away with, the liturgy of penance was frozen in its late medieval state—what we call modern penance or confession—for four centuries. Clarifying doctrine and providing a standard ritual eliminated some of the less pleasant aspects of the late medieval format,

171

but what remained of the medieval liturgy of penance continued to be affected by individualism and depersonalization in the post-Tridentine period. The few proposals for reform put forward in the centuries following Trent were generally ignored or condemned.

The Tridentine Ritual

At its final session on December 4, 1563, the Council of Trent entrusted to the pope the task of liturgical reform. That commission began to be fulfilled when Pius V issued the reformed *Breviarium Romanum* (1568) and *Missale Romanum* (1570). Under Clement VIII, the *Pontificale Romanum* (1596) and *Caeremoniale Episcoporum* (1600) were published. It was not, however, until the pontificate of Paul V that the *Rituale Romanum*, which contained the rite of penance (Titulus III), was published.

Cardinal Julius Santorio had begun work on the *Rituale Sacramentorum Romanum* under Gregory XIII and continued until his death in 1602, depending heavily on Alberto Castellani's *Liber sacerdotalis* (1523), which had been approved by Leo X. In 1612, Paul V appointed a commission to revise and complete Santorio's work and the *Rituale Romanum* was finally promulgated on June 17, 1614. Though its use was recommended rather than mandatory, local rituals followed it closely and so its *ordo ministrandi sacramentum poenitentiae* was the base for the rite of penance used throughout the post-Tridentine Western Church.

Solemn Penance

Though sixteenth-century handbooks for priests (*Sacerdotale*) still spoke of triple penance (*paenitentia solemnis, paenitentia publica* or pilgrimage, and *paenitentia secreta* or private confession), solemn penance was rarely, if ever, used. Patrizi had omitted its ritual from his 1485 *Liber Sacerdotalis*, but it was restored in Clement VIII's Pontifical almost as it had been in Durandus's. It consisted of the expulsion of public penitents from the church on Ash Wednesday and their reconciliation on Holy Thursday.

On Ash Wednesday morning, those to receive solemn penance gather at the cathedral, simply dressed, barefoot, and with downcast faces. Their names are recorded and the penitentiary (the priest delegated for that function) assigns their penances, after which they go outside. When the bishop and clergy have taken their places in the middle of the church, the penitents return and prostrate themselves before the bishop seated between the two choirs of clergy. Ashes are put on their heads with the words: "Remember, mortal, that you are dust and that to dust you will return. Do penance that you may have eternal life." Holy water is sprinkled on them. Sackcloth is blessed with a prayer and holy water and then placed over the heads of the penitents while the bishop says: "With the Lord there is mercy and with God redemption, for [God] comes to the help of fallen mortals not only with the grace of baptism and confirmation but also with the medicine of penance so that the human spirit may be restored with eternal life."

An antiphon and the seven penitential psalms are said; the antiphon is repeated and the litany of the saints and first three Gelasian prayers follow. In his sermon, the bishop explains how the penitents are to be expelled from the church as Adam was driven out of paradise. After the sermon, he takes a penitent by the hand and all of them, holding hands and with lighted candles, are led out of the church, while the bishop says: "Behold, today you are expelled from the threshold of holy mother Church because of your sins and crimes, just as Adam the first human was driven out of paradise because of his transgression." The choir meanwhile sings the antiphon "In the sweat of your brow. . . . " The penitents stand outside the church, while the bishop, in the doorway, warns them not to despair of God's mercy but rather by fasting, prayer, pilgrimage, almsgiving, and other good works to come to the fruit of penance. They may then return on Holy Thursday but are not to enter the church in the meantime. The church door is then closed in their faces.

On Holy Thursday, the bishop and clergy pray the penitential psalms and the litany of the saints. The penitents are prostrate outside the church with unlighted candles. Twice during the litany, two subdeacons with lighted candles go to the penitents, say an encouraging antiphon, and then extinguish their candles. Near the end of the litany, the deacon goes to the penitents with a large lighted candle and lights their candles. Then, after the litany, the bishop takes his seat in the middle of the church with the clergy arranged in facing choirs on either side of the doorway. The archdeacon, standing in the doorway, reads the address to the bishop. The bishop goes to the doorway and exhorts the penitents. The "Come, children" antiphon is sung three times, with the penitents kneeling each time it is sung and then standing as it ends. During the antiphon and following psalm the penitents reenter the church and kneel before the bishop. The archdeacon completes the address, after which the bishop asks him whether the penitents are worthy of reconciliation. He responds, the penitents stand, the bishop takes one by the hand and then, as they hold hands, leads them to his seat in the middle of the church.

Standing there, with the penitents kneeling, he begins an antiphon and then prays:

"May almighty God absolve you from every bond of sins, that you may have eternal life and live. Through our Lord Jesus Christ, your Son, who lives and reigns in the unity of the Holy Spirit, God, for ever and ever."

He then sings the introductory dialogue and preface:

"It is truly right and just, our duty and salvation, that we always and everywhere give you thanks, holy Lord, Father almighty, eternal God, through Christ our Lord. You, almighty Father, willed him to be born ineffably to pay

174

to you, the eternal Father, the debt of Adam, to destroy our death by his own, to bear our wounds in his body, to wash away our stains by his blood, so that we who were felled by the envy of the ancient enemy might be raised up by his compassion. We humbly beg and beseech you through him, Lord: deign to hear us who are unworthy to pray for our own transgressions as we pray for those of others. And so, most merciful Lord, in your accustomed tenderness call back your servants whose crimes have separated them from you. You did not despise the humiliation of wicked Achab but wrote off the vengeance due. You heard the weeping Peter and later gave him the keys of the heavenly kingdom. You promised the rewards of that kingdom to the penitent thief. And so, most merciful Lord, mercifully regather those for whom we pour out prayer. Bring them back to the bosom of your Church so that the enemy may not be strong enough to conquer them. May the Son, co-equal with you, reconcile them to you, free them from every evil deed, and admit them to the feast of your most holy Supper. May he so restore them by his Flesh and Blood that after this life he may lead them to the heavenly kingdom."

Antiphons, psalms, and prayers follow and then the absolution:

"The Lord Jesus Christ deigned to purge the sins of the whole world by giving himself. To his disciples he said, 'Whatever you bind on earth will be bound in heaven and whatever you loose on earth will be loosed in heaven.' He willed me, though unworthy, to be a minister in their number. Through the intercession of Mary the Mother of God and holy Michael the archangel and holy Peter the apostle, to whom was given the power of binding and loosing, and all the saints, by the intervention of his holy blood poured out for the remission of sins may he absolve you, through my ministry, from all your sins, whether by thought or speech or deed done negligently. May he lead you, set free from the bonds of sins, to the kingdom of heaven."

175

The bishop sprinkles the penitents with holy water, incenses them, gives an indulgence, and concludes by blessing them.

These ceremonies were retained in the corrected edition of the Pontifical of Urban VIII (1645), though the extent to which they were used in succeeding centuries, if at all, is undocumented.

Private Confession
The 1614 *Rituale Romanum's* rite for private confession, with its 25 regulations, is quite simple. The sacrament is stated to be instituted by Christ for the restoration to grace of those who have sinned after baptism and its matter (remotely, sins; proximately, the contrition, confession, and satisfaction of the penitent), form (the absolution), and minister (the priest) are stated (1). The role of the minister as judge as well as physician (2)—the former is more prominent—and his need for spiritual (3), canonical (4), and doctrinal knowledge (5) are stated, and then the ordo for ministering the sacrament is given.

This ordo is structurally much the same as the form common in the late fourteenth century.[4] Though it contains elements of prayer, the focus overall is on the priest's role as judge and the penitent's role—passive, except for the actual confession—is not given much attention. The priest is advised to begin, if possible, with private prayer for God's help in his ministry (6). The confession is ordinarily to be heard in the church, in an open place (7) in a confessional with a screen between the confessor and penitent[5] (8), with the priest vested with surplice and purple stole (9). If necessary, the penitent is to be warned to approach humbly. The penitent kneels and makes the sign of the cross (10). The confessor then inquires about the penitent's status, the time since the last confession and the completeness of that confession, the performance of the penance, and whether an examination of conscience has been made (11). Should the confessor learn that the penitent is under censure or guilty of a reserved sin, he is

176

forbidden to absolve without obtaining the necessary faculties (12). Should the confessor realize that the penitent is lacking in basic religious knowledge, he is to give the necessary instruction (13).

The penitent begins with a general confession (e.g., the *Confiteor*) in Latin or the vernacular and then makes a proper and complete confession, with the priest helping as needed (14). The priest may ask about number, species, and circumstances of sins if the penitent is not explicit enough (15), but should be cautious and prudent, asking no unnecessary questions (16). Then, taking into account both the sins and the condition of the penitent, he offers counsel and supports the penitent's contrition and amendment (17). He imposes a penance to assist the penitent in renewal, to remedy the penitent's weakness, and to punish for the sins committed (18); for example, almsgiving, fasting, and more frequent confession and communion (19).[6]

Confessors are neither to ask for nor to accept money for themselves (20) and are not allowed to impose open penance for secret sins (21). Situations calling for the postponement or refusal of absolution are noted (22), though if the danger of death exists, absolution is given at once (23). If confession is physically impossible, signs or knowledge that the penitent wants to confess are sufficient for giving absolution (24). The confessor is also advised to be cautious in imposing penance on the sick (25).

Chapter Two gives the form of absolution:

"May almighty God have mercy on you, forgive you your sins, and bring you to everlasting life. (The priest raises his hand and extends it toward the penitent[7] while saying the following and makes the sign of the cross while naming the Trinity:) May the almighty and merciful Lord grant you pardon, absolution, and remission of your sins.[8] May our Lord Jesus Christ absolve you: and I by his authority absolve you from every bond of excommunication [suspension] and interdict, insofar as I can and you need it.

And finally[9] I absolve you from your sins, in the name of the Father, and of the Son, and of the Holy Spirit. Amen"[10]

Following the absolution was a prayer—the *Passio*—for the penitent that, like the *Misereatur* and *Indulgentiam*, could be omitted in "more frequent and shorter confessions."

"May the passion of our Lord Jesus Christ, the merits of the blessed Virgin Mary and all the saints, whatever good you do and evil you endure, be to you for the remission of sins, the increase of grace, and the reward of everlasting life. Amen."[11]

Chapter Three gives the rite for absolving from excommunication in the external forum and Chapter Four the rite for absolving an excommunicated person who has died with some sign of contrition. Chapter Five has the rite for absolving from suspension or interdict and for dispensing from an irregularity.

The 1614 *ordo ministrandi sacramentum poenitentiae* stands in a strange relationship to the medieval ordos that preceded it. In one respect, it is the final phase of the medieval development and canonizes the late medieval format of the sacrament. In it we see the full flowering of both individualism and clericalism: the sacrament is a clear judgment rendered by the priest to the individual penitent who has just confessed and passively receives the verdict. The only vestiges of an ecclesial and communal dimension were the unstructured opening dialogue, the recommendation of the *confiteor*, the optional *passio* prayer (which adverted to the communion of saints), and the necessity of ecclesiastical jurisdiction for valid absolution.

In another respect, however, the 1614 ritual contrasts sharply with the medieval penance ordos, for it is quick, efficient, and almost aliturgical. Where they had been rich in scriptural allusions and filled with reminders of God's mercy to the sinner, the 1614 ritual wasted no time with these remnants of the *berakah* and *exomologesis*. It simply has the penitent express contrition, make confession, and be willing to make satisfaction, and then the priest gives absolution. In this, the 1614 ritual is much more in continuity with medieval theology than it is with medieval liturgy. Almost every element of praise and prayer is absent. The few that remained diminished still further in the following years, due largely to liturgical minimalism and concern for canonical validity, until the liturgy was effectively reduced to confession and absolution.

The character of the ritual is understandable enough in context. The reformers' denial of the priestly exercise of the power of the keys required the fathers of Trent and the post-Tridentine Church to emphasize it, intensifying the medieval preoccupation with that dimension of the sacrament. The climate of the times prevented them from likewise emphasizing facets of earlier theology and liturgy that the reformers had *not* denied. Neither Trent nor the framers of the ritual intended to minimize the dimensions of prayer and worship. Their intentions were to make clear the Catholic faith commitment regarding penance, indicate precisely the rights and responsibilities of both penitent and priest, and eliminate any likely possibilities of abuses or superstitions. That the cultic dimension gave way almost completely to the therapeutic and judicial was, in part, a logical consequence of the developments of scholastic theology. It was likewise almost inevitable in an era when worship and sacraments had come to be seen as things done by the priest for the people.

Succeeding centuries would further streamline the liturgy of penance. As penitents learned the rudiments of the scholastic distinction of sins and the significance of confessing according to number, species, and circumstances, there was less need for questioning and dialogue. As pastors and teachers were concerned that penitents meet all the theological requirements, the general confession—the ritual suggested the *confiteor* prayer—frequently became a statement that the penitent was sorry for the sins confessed and for all past sins. An act of contrition modeled on the scholastic description of the contrite attitude was then recited during the absolution. The act of satisfaction generally became a prayer recited before leaving the church to ensure that it would be performed. As confessions became more frequent and more numerous, confessors were frequently content to use only the essential form of absolution. The Latin prayers were, in any case, unintelligible to most penitents. With the act of contrition prayed during the absolution, the proper dispositions for a penitent thus coincided, at least verbally, with the priest's absolution. The final phase of these developments was the practice common in the 1960s of having penitents recite the act of contrition before entering the confessional so that they could listen to the vernacular absolution. The last vestige of prayer then disappeared from the rite and the final form of modern penance bore almost no resemblance to worship.

The Post-Tridentine Era

The century following the close of the Council of Trent, though it was an age of reform, is generally termed the Counter-Reformation, because Catholic thought and practice were overwhelmingly determined by the need to respond to the Protestant threat. Yet both Catholic and Protestant were the product of late medievalism and the piety of both parties was shaped in large measure by tariff penance. Religious individualism was a major component of this heritage and, even though Trent had demanded that Christians acknowledge the Church's role in their relationship with God, individualistic views of sin and repentance necessarily dominated the Counter-Reformation. The key to Church reform was seen as the reform of the Church's members and the means whereby individuals reformed was the sacrament of penance.

Reformation and Counter-Reformation were alike not only in their common medieval inheritance but also in a common motivation: to Christianize a population that had scarcely heard the gospel, let alone undergone conversion.[12] Their methods and means differed, of course. The characteristically Catholic procedure was to revitalize the sacraments; confession and communion were the primary focus. Encouraging frequent communion met with little success, but Catholics were so successful in promoting confession that it became a key element of the Counter-Reformation. Like the Irish monks before them, the seventeenth-century missionaries in France, for example, saw confession as an important tool for converting baptized pagans into Christians by ridding them of sinful ways.

The Counter-Reformation thus continued the late medieval fixation on confession as purification, but with greater energy, focus, and organization. The individual's life, brought into question by inevitable death, was recognized as marred by sin, weakness, and failure even where there was no grave offense against God. But the generic recognition of this fact was not enough. The specific shape of sin in each person's life had to be seen if it was to be overcome. Regular, even daily, examination of conscience followed by an act of contrition was required if self-knowledge was to develop. Frequent confession was necessary in order to be freed from these faults. The Counter-Reformation thus established as a staple of Catholic piety frequent regular confession not only of mortal sins but also of venial. Thus, the seventeenth-century parish missions first spent time teaching the basic prayers—a clear sign of how far from Christian the people were—and then a method for examining conscience, preaching a fear of God that would lead people to individual general confession as a beginning of fervent religious practice.

The Counter-Reformation did not, however, merely continue the medieval view of confession as a therapeutic means of purification from sin and liberation from guilt. It supplemented this with an ascetic element that, though acknowledged in medieval times, had received less attention: confession as a means of sanctification. Over the centuries, the sacrament had ceased to focus on reconciling sinners to the community of salvation and had become instead the source of forgiveness and grace for individuals. In the perspective shaped by tariff penance (and particularly by its Celtic monastic form), the primary motivation was purification and liberation so as to be right with God. The Counter-Reformation altered this significantly by also seeing confession as the means to grow in holiness and come closer to God.

Two key practices, then, became characteristic of Counter-Reformation spirituality and sharply set it off from the piety of the previous age: frequent confession and a relatively more frequent communion.[13] Though confession and communion had already been linked in medieval piety, communion had been rare for centuries and the equally infrequent confession was a means of purification in preparation for communion. While the majority of Catholics probably did perform Easter duties at the time of the Counter-Reformation, the fact that sanctions were still threatened shows that many people did so under duress; many received communion only then.

As the Counter-Reformation took on the task of restoring Christians to an active role in the eucharistic assembly—a goal it did not achieve—the traditional means of readmitting sinners and the traditional sign of full membership were given new prominence. While regular attendance at the (somewhat) reformed mass and more frequent communion were still passive means of participation, they did begin a movement away from medieval liturgical decadence.[14] With more frequent communion came more frequent confession, for the practice of confession as preparation for communion had long been established. The sacrament of postbaptismal conversion was, admittedly, recognized only in the form of individual confession and absolution, but giving it wider scope in the process of justification and sanctification made possible a balance that had been lacking in the Middle Ages.

The balance was not, however, easily maintained and was soon threatened by Jansenism. Renaissance humanism had made late medieval individualists introspective, and they tended to become scrupulous puritans when they took on high religious standards. The moral rigorism and ecclesiastical antiquarianism of Jansenism idealized early Church practice and sought to return to it. Thus, Antoine Arnauld in his *De la fréquente communion* (1643) denied the existence of private confession in the ancient Church and condemned the subsequent relaxation of discipline. He cited the long periods of penance that were required by the ancient Church as an argument for strict contritionism[15] and delaying absolution until the confessor was satisfied that the person was sincerely repentant. He recommended abstaining from communion as a supernatural fast and mortification.

Most of Arnauld's opponents responded by denying that canonical penance was sacramental, but moral rigorism and an exaggerated respect for the eucharist that made confession more basic and frequent than communion was not confined to Jansenists. We find it even in saints such as Charles Borromeo and Francis de Sales.[16] It stood for centuries as a counterforce impeding the Tridentine efforts at liturgical reforms, particularly at encouraging frequent communion.

However, Jansenism promoted its own program of reform. The 1786 Synod of Pistoia in northern Italy, partially inspired by Febronianism and Jansenism, proposed reestablishing the canonical order of penitents, delaying absolution until perfect contrition had been attained and satisfaction made, and reforming laws on reserved sins and jurisdiction. It also questioned the value of indulgences and overly frequent confession. Such proposals were condemned by Pius VI as, at the least, "false, rash, and offensive to pious ears" (DS 2634–2645).

One short-lived attempt to expand and develop the shape of the sacrament was made in Germany in the period of the Aufklärung (Enlightenment).[17] While late seventeenth-century Catholics who advocated reform risked being labeled Protestant or Jansenist, the movement for liturgical reform in Germany in the latter half of the eighteenth century and the first half of the nineteenth century was entirely different in inspiration and orientation. However, it met the same fate. One set of proposals suggested restoring something of the ancient public and communal character of the sacrament by having a common preparation and confession, whether with private confession included or with a common absolution. Others proposed both private and communal forms of the sacrament. But even the moderate proposal of a common preparation for private confessions was considered dangerous and Protestant. Post-Tridentine Catholicism was still too unstable and insecure to face the full task of reform. Indeed, in *Mirari vos* (1832), Gregory XVI denied that the Church ever needed reform.

REDISCOVERY AND REFORM

The notion of the Church as "stabilis et immota,"[18] long the ideal of post-Tridentine Catholicism, began to be shaken by the historical studies of the late nineteenth century and the reform movements which they spawned. Reformation polemics and Renaissance interest in the past had stimulated historical scholarship and led to a critical and systematic study of the scriptures and the fathers of the Church and the development of positive theology. Robert Bellarmine, among others, had used historical sources, though without a sense of development or an attempt to account for differences.

Francisco Suarez and most post-Tridentine theologians had little interest in history as such, even though the question of the origins of penance was a major issue for the first time. Research into the patristic era had meant the publication of many ancient rituals, for example, but most Catholic theologians regarded canonical penance and medieval *paenitentia solemnis* as merely ceremonial enhancements or canonical penalties, with no bearing on the

184

sacrament of penance itself, which they identified with its late medieval format.

When Arnauld in the seventeenth century denied the existence of private penance in the ancient period and called for a return to ancient canonical penance, his opponents simply denied that canonical penance was sacramental. Jean Morin, one of the first to investigate the history of penance thoroughly, challenged this view, agreeing that public penance was sacramental but also arguing that private penance had existed in the ancient period.[19] In general, the use of history was not at all what would today be termed scientific, for it had no sense of development. Not until the nineteenth century did the historical sciences begin to develop, and when they did they were generally regarded suspiciously by Catholic theologians as a probable threat. Möhler and others of the Tübingen school were among the few exceptions.

Nineteenth-century historians often revived the Jansenist notion that penance in the early Church had always been rigorous, with leniency and laxity gradually developing. Thus, Adolph von Harnack argued that the penitential discipline had shifted in the direction of leniency as the Church came to be regarded as an institution assuring salvation, with its officeholders having special powers to forgive sins. Since historical studies and the use of the historical-critical method appeared to threaten the Church's power structure and its image as stable and unchanging, they were suspect, and Catholics who used such methods were considered Modernist. Thus, when the origins of penance came to be a highly debated issue at the beginning of the twentieth century, parties to the debate tended to divide along Catholic-Protestant lines. Pius X upheld a literalist understanding of the institution of penance by Christ in condemning Modernist errors (DS 3446–3447) and Catholic theologians, careful not to be associated with Modernism, remained suspicious of historians and regarded their data as unimportant. They continued to insist that the ancient evidence showed only that there had been a supplementary canonical penalty and ceremony and that private penance had always existed.

Xiberta's 1922 thesis on ancient penance[20] began a new phase of development, because it carefully documented and incontrovertibly established that penance in the ancient Church had indeed been social and communal in character and oriented toward the reconciliation of repentant sinners with the Church and thereby with God. Though most theologians initially rejected or ignored Xiberta's study, they were eventually forced to take history seriously.[21] Thus, Paulus Galtier's 1923 *De paenitentia* incorporated much historical data and recognized the sacramentality of ancient public penance while still arguing for the simultaneous existence of a private form. That element continued to be debated through the 1930s and 1940s, particularly between Galtier and Bernhard Poschmann, with the latter initially almost alone among Catholic theologians in arguing for the Celtic origins of private penance.[22]

On the pastoral level, confessional practice had been affected by Pius X's encouragement of frequent, even daily, communion[23] and his rejection of the practice of prohibiting children from communion.[24] Both infrequent communion and the postponement of first communion were regarded as the lingering effects of Jansenism, though they might more accurately be described as the lasting consequence of medieval liturgical decadence and disintegration. From the time of Pius X, full eucharistic participation began to increase in frequency among Catholics and frequency of confession increased as well, probably reaching its peak in the early 1950s. (The controversy over whether first confession should precede first communion also had its origin in the change in initiation practice that Pius X introduced by permitting earlier communion.)

Various factors influenced the growing frequency of confession. A major one, of course, was frequent communion, because confession was regarded as the therapeutic sacrament, the sacrament of forgiveness, purification, and liberation in preparation for communion—a pale shadow of the ancient means for restoring errant Christians to the eucharistic assembly. Pius X stated that freedom from mortal sin was all that was absolutely required for eucharistic communion and encouraged frequent communion. He tempered the Jansenist insistence that a person must also be free from all attachment to venial sin and again rejected the strict contritionist requirement of a pure love of God before receiving communion. But Jansenist influences remained to reinforce the medieval association of confession with communion. The encouragement to prepare properly for communion usually included the recommendation to confess frequently, and as communion became more frequent, so did confession.

Understanding sin as something apart from the person, as a stain or defilement, made confession of venial sins a common practice. This, and regarding mortal sin as easily committed, encouraged frequent confession. Sin regarded as a violation of order or as an act contrary to law promoted a view of confession as purification or the source of strength against sin.

Closely related to this view was understanding the sacrament as not only a source of forgiveness but also a source of grace and a means for growing in holiness. Confession was thus regarded as a psychological and ascetic practice for rooting out defects, receiving grace, and growing in virtue. Though the sacrament could not substitute for personal repentance, it did offer a reliable support to compensate for personal weakness. Imperfect contrition was sufficient for forgiveness in confession, though perfect contrition was required apart from the sacramental ritual. An understanding of sacrament and grace that isolated both from life regarded the sacrament as the sure means for receiving grace. This attitude encouraged more frequent confession as the *ex opere operato* understanding of sacramental efficacy, originally intended to give reassurance if presiders were unworthy, became instead a mechanical guarantee.

Devotional confession, the practice of receiving the sacrament regularly as an act of piety, thus became common, even for those who found it necessary to confess again sins from the past in order to have *"matter"* for the sacrament.[25] Closely associated with this was a conception of penance as an external means of salvation, giving grace *ex opere operato* to those who did not hinder it, a sacramental understanding based on the operation of infant baptism. This ran the risk of making confession a ritual replacement for personal repentance or, at the least, a supplement to an individual's imperfect contrition. The power of the priest's absolution was thus looked at apart from the acts of the penitent.

Neither Pius X nor those who supported his efforts foresaw the eventual effects of eucharistic experience on penitential experience, but the effects did begin to be felt.[26] The practice of devotional confession began to be questioned in German-speaking countries in the 1930s and came under strong criticism in the 1940s. This provoked Pius XII's defense of the ascetic practice in *Mystici corporis* in 1943. By it, he asserts, "genuine self-knowledge grows, Christian humility develops, bad habits are corrected, spiritual neglect and lukewarmness are countered, the conscience is purified, the will is strengthened, healthy self-control is gained, and an increase of grace is obtained by the very fact the sacrament is received." His statement summarizes the motives for frequent devotional confession, and it was during his pontificate that confession became most frequent.[27] His language in *Mystici corporis*, *Mediator Dei, Menti nostrae,* and elsewhere accentuated the role of penance as a means of cleansing and purification.

Pius XII's encouragement of the liturgical movement in *Mediator Dei* (1947) gave new impetus to work already underway. By this time, the movement began to move beyond academic studies and pastoral revitalization, recognizing that full liturgical renewal could not take place without liturgical reforms. So far as penance is concerned, academic studies showed the need for reform by providing a contrast with current practice. They were also resources for reform and renewal.

Scripture studies gave important data for understanding sin, conversion, and forgiveness or reconciliation and a foundation for the major theological emphases that had been developing: the ecclesial dimension of sin and penance, redemption as God's reconciling activity in history. Though the revival of biblical studies gave a new context for the theology of penance, historical studies were undoubtedly the greatest single inspiration and foundation for reform. Ancient penance attracted the most attention, since the ecclesial and communal character of that system showed how far penance had come from its origins, but the entire history not only showed the sacrament's past flexibility but also suggested possibilities for contemporary adaptation. Trent, however, seemed to have blocked further development, and so it too was the object of intense scrutiny.

The Eastern Churches also attracted interest. East and West had followed noticeably divergent paths since the patristic age, particularly because of different views of Church and sin. Though the development of Eastern penance has not been as thoroughly studied as the Western, its history and the practice of the Orthodox, who have largely escaped Latinization, provoked some rethinking.[28]

The contemporary human sciences contributed to developments in moral theology centering on the understanding of sin (particularly its social dimension), the gradation of sin and the frequency of mortal sin, and the relationship between sin and conversion. In systematic theology, developments in ecclesiology and sacramentology reinforced the rediscovery of the ecclesial dimension of penance by relating the sacrament to the Church's mission and the Christian's everyday life and by providing a

189

clearer understanding of the sacraments as acts of community worship. Interest in questions of doctrinal development and hermeneutics was likewise influential.

The rediscovery of forgotten theological truths,[29] and particularly the realization of the social and ecclesial character of ancient penance and its nature as reconciliation with the Church, had its effect not only in theology but also in pastoral practice and in proposals for reform that recognized the indispensable role of reconciliation with the Church. The grassroots origin of the modern communal celebration, the major pastoral innovation, is particularly interesting since this celebration is one of the few instances in recent history of such an innovation eventually receiving official approval and the only emergence of a completely new form of penance in a millennium.

The communal celebration of penance began in the 1950s and, like other historical forms of the sacrament, emerged in response to pastoral needs. It was apparently first used in either France or Belgium to prepare children for first confession and then used with adults, particularly during Lent, but did not attract a great deal of attention until it came into common use in the Netherlands and there achieved a quasi-official status. Controversy soon followed, because there the service was often associated with delaying first confession until after first communion. (In 1964, for example, the bishop of Roermond authorized a phased introduction of children to the sacrament by means of communal celebrations.)

In the Netherlands, the service came to take the form of a celebration with general absolution without previous individual confession. The difference between the Dutch and French services goes much deeper than this, however, since many variations of both types developed; for example, celebrations with individual confession and individual absolution, individual confession and communal absolution, communal confession and communal absolution, and communal confession and no formal absolution but rather a prayer for forgiveness. The divergence involves, on the one hand, situating private penance within a communal setting and, on the other, clearly distinguishing private penance from communal penance.

Providing opportunity for private penance within a communal celebration—the French confession service—became popular in parishes and received little opposition from theologians or Church officials. However, experience led to some criticism. It was difficult to obtain enough confessors to make the service practical, the framework of the service encouraged haste and impersonality, and it seemed to some an ambiguous compromise between private and communal penance.

Experience thus led to greater emphasis on the fully communal form of celebration with communal confession and communal absolution—the Dutch penance service. This too was popular, but apparent conflicts with Tridentine dogma led to controversy among theologians and opposition from Church officials. A variant of this, the penitential celebration (a service with communal confession and a priestly prayer for forgiveness rather than absolution), raised serious theological questions regarding the nature and criteria of sacramentality.

Though the fully communal celebration is identified with the Dutch pastoral setting, the Dutch bishops did not encourage the use of general absolution. What they recommended was the penitential celebration and, where the groups were small enough to make it practical, services with individual confession. They insisted on private confession of mortal sins as an inner requirement of conversion and advised priests not to preach on the sacramentality of the penitential celebration, since it was still a matter of theological controversy.[30] General absolution was frequently used, however, but usually as a by-product of penitential celebrations rather than, as in other countries, because of dissatisfaction with the confession service. In mission countries, the 1944 Instruction of the

Sacred Penitentiary on the use of general absolution in emergencies was officially extended to situations where, for example, large numbers of people wished to receive the sacrament before major feasts.[31]

Other episcopal conferences also gave official approval to liturgical services including private confessions (e.g., the Canadian in 1966, the French in 1967, the Italian in 1970), as did individual bishops. The most extensive statement was that of the Swiss bishops, who recognized three principal means of forgiveness: personal conversion and penance, the foundation of all forms; communal penitential celebrations; and the sacrament in the full sense, with confession and absolution, required in the case of grave sin.[32] The 1972 Pastoral Norms on general absolution (to be examined in the next chapter) significantly changed the situation by expanding the existing opportunities for general absolution and stating clearly the restrictions on the practice.

While most pastoral efforts and reform proposals centered on communal celebrations, private penance was not forgotten. The need for instruction and catechesis was emphasized and attention was called to the vestiges of an ecclesial sense that still existed in the 1614 ritual of penance. What was most emphasized, however, was what was most distinctive about private penance, though obscured by a routinized and mechanical practice: the clear expression of the personal dimension of repentance and conversion. This was developed by giving more time to the dialogue between confessor and penitent and calling for a change in attitude by both confessor and penitent. The personal character of the individual encounter with the priest and Christ was highlighted by several suggestions: developing the negligible prayer and worship dimensions through shared prayer and scripture, making the assigned penance an act of service rather than a recited prayer, and changing the place of celebration to a pleasant room rather than the dark confessional.

The rediscovery of the social and ecclesial character of the sacrament of penance thus led to many reform proposals and pastoral initiatives intended to express more clearly the nature and effects of the sacrament. The major features of the new orientation that took shape in the 1950s and 1960s were not only the result of academic discovery but also a response to specific pastoral needs:

1. The need to give attention to the social and ecclesial dimensions of sin and penance and the involvement of the Church in the conversion process; 2. The need for an atmosphere of shared prayer and worship; 3. The need to express both the personal and communal dimensions of the sacrament, preferably through a variety of forms corresponding to the situation and the needs of the penitents; 4. The need to relate the sacrament and its ritual celebration to everyday life and to the other sacraments, especially baptism and eucharist.

The liturgical renewal was preparing the way for a major shift in Catholic attitudes toward penance.

NOTES

1. See Harry McSorley, "Luther and Trent on the Faith Needed for the Sacrament of Penance," *Concilium* 61 (1971): 89–98. See also H. Fagerberg and Hans Jorissen, "Penance and Confession," in G. W. Forell and J. F. McCue, eds., *Confessing One Faith: A Joint Commentary on the Augsburg Confession by Lutheran and Catholic Theologians* (Minneapolis, Minn.: Augsburg, 1982), pp. 234–261, and Hans Jorissen, "Does the Teaching of the 'Confessio Augustana' about Repentance Stand in the Way of Its Recognition by the Catholic Church?" in Joseph A. Burgess, ed., *The Role of the Augsburg Confession: Catholic and Lutheran Views* (Philadelphia: Fortress, 1980), pp. 101–121.

2. Crucial questions in contemporary theology and practice revolve around the interpretation of the Tridentine decrees, but the Tridentine teaching seems more convincing, significant, and open to continued development when interpreted within the horizon of penance as communal reconciliation than within the more restricted one of penance as individual forgiveness.

The literature is understandably extensive; hardly any serious work on penance ignores the questions posed by Trent. For an examination of the literature immediately preceding the 1973 *Rite of Penance*, see my "A Decade of Discussion on the Reform of Penance, 1963–1973: Theological Analysis and Critique" (unpublished S.T.D. dissertation; Catholic University of America, 1976). For a thorough analysis coming to different conclusions on the Tridentine statements, see Hans-Peter Arendt, *Busssakrament and Einzelbeichte: Die tridentinishchen Lehraussagen über das Sündenbekenntnis und ihre Verbindlichkeit für die Reform des Busssakramentes* (Freiburg: Herder, 1973).

For varying perspectives, see also Zoltan Alszeghy and Mauricio Flick, "La dottrina tridentina sulla necessità della confessione," *Magistero e Morale* (Bologna: Edizioni Dehoniana, 1970), pp. 103–192; Hubert Jedin, "La nécessité de la confession privée selon le concile de Trente," *Maison Dieu* 104 (1970) 88–115; Carl J. Peter, "Integral Confession and the Council of Trent," *Concilium* 61 (1971) 88–109. For the meaning of "ius divinum," see Carl J. Peter, "Dimensions of *Jus Divinum* in Roman Catholic Theology," *Theological Studies* 34 (1973) 227–250, and the literature he cites.

3. Trent used "recenseri" (DS 1680)—review, recall, narrate—though late scholastic thought patterns came to think of this as a detailed enumeration.

4. See above, pp. 157–158.

5. In the Middle Ages, confessions were at first received in the priest's home and then in the church, with the priest seated before the altar and the penitent kneeling to one side. The confessional with its screen was introduced in some places in the fifteenth century, and Charles Borromeo required it in his diocese to prevent both solicitation and the possibility of the priest being accused of it. The 1614 ritual prescribed the screen, and later decrees made it mandatory for hearing women's confessions. Though the 1973 Rite of Penance did not mention confessionals, the 1983 Code of Canon Law requires that confessionals with screens be available for those who wish to use them (Canon 964, 2). For a history of the confessional, see Wilhelm Schlombs, *Die Entwicklung des Beichtstuhls in der katholischen Kirche* (Düsseldorf: L. Schwann, 1965).

The 1952 *editio typica*, where penance is *Titulus* IV, has, as no. 9, a regulation on the place for hearing the confessions of the sick, increasing subsequent numbers by one.

6. Assigning prayers developed later as the satisfaction became increasingly lenient and it was feared that the penance would not be performed if it could not be done before leaving the church. See Petrus J. Schellens, *De satisfactione sacramentali, quatenus est problema pastorale* (Rome: Analecta Dehoniana, 1964), especially pp. 35–39, 52.

7. Though the rite fails to proclaim the Word, lacks any expression of the paschal mystery or the role of the Spirit and the Church, and has barely a vestige of the ancient praise of an "almighty and merciful Lord," it does restore a semblance of the laying on of the hand, the raising of the priest's hand. However, requiring a screen between confessor and penitent made it invisible to the penitent.

8. The *misereatur* and *indulgentiam* had originally been reconciliation prayers—"supplicatory absolutions"—and appear in various forms in many sources. See, for example, the *misereatur* in the *Poenitentiale Valicellanum II* (Wasserschleben, *Die Bussordnungen*, p. 555) and in the *Pontificale Romano-Germanicum XCIX*, 51 (Vogel-Elze, *Pontifical Romano-Germanique*, p. 17).

9. In the 1614 edition "finally" (*deinde*) was a rubric. In subsequent editions, the word was printed in black ink and came to be regarded as part of the text. In the *Rituale* of Santorio the rubric had read: "Deinde producens signum crucis super poenitentem subiungat. . . ." ("Then, making the sign of the cross over the penitent, he adds. . . . "

10. The absolution formula is almost identical to Santorio's, although the differences are significant. His initial absolution from excommunication concluded: "and I restore you to the unity and communion of the faithful and to the holy sacraments of the Church." In Santorio's ritual the "Amen" following the *misereatur*, the *indulgentiam*, and the absolution were to be spoken by the penitent. The impression is that the 1614 ritual edited out anything that would detract from the role of the priest, including the ecclesial context and the active participation of the penitent in the liturgical elements. The title, *ordo ministrandi sacramentum*

poenitentiae (service for ministering the sacrament of penance), itself presupposed lay passivity. In later centuries, the Counter-Reformation emphasis on ministerial authority led to an even more passive penitent and an emphasis on the juridical and therapeutic character of the absolution that almost totally excluded the elements of cult and worship.

11. Some form of this prayer was known to Aquinas, who stated that the phrase "may whatever good you do be to you for the remission of sins," which some priests used, turned subsequent good works into part of the sacramental penance *vi clavium;* see *Quodlibet* 3, art. 28. In its present form, the prayer is similar to the Sarum Pontifical's blessing after absolution, which may come from John the Chanter (d. 1191), and to that found in the Sarum Manual, which was first printed in 1497. It was perhaps inspired by medieval prayers for restoration to the altar and the sacraments, which in turn may derive from the final prayer over the penitent in the Gelasian. See J. H. Crehan, "The Prayer after Absolution," *Clergy Review* 48 (1963) 95–101, especially pp. 100–101. The prayer was in the *Rituale* of Santorio and, in somewhat different form, in the *Liber sacerdotalis* of Castellani. A similar prayer was used as the absolution (concluding blessing) in the *Poenitentiale Valicellanum II* (Wasserschleben, *Die Bussordnungen*, pp. 556–557.

12. See Jean Delumeau, *Catholicism between Luther and Voltaire: A New View of the Counter-Reformation* (Philadelphia: Westminster, 1977).

13. Robert E. McNally suggests that three elements of architecture prominent in the Jesuit churches of the time show Trent's influence: the pulpit, the confessional, and the extended altar rail. He sees the latter two as the most concrete expressions of Counter-Reformation piety. See his "The Counter-Reformation's Views of Sin and Penance," pp. 151–166, especially p. 162.

14. Confraternities and other organizations frequently required monthly confession and communion of their members, leading to the custom of monthly corporate communion Sundays for various groups. The introduction of the solemn first communion ceremony, which was common by 1750, was likewise a means of increasing regard for communion and making it more frequent. Though there was apparently a steady increase in frequency of

communion (and likewise of confession), it was not until the twentieth century that the average churchgoer became a frequent communicant.

15. The post-Tridentine attrition-contrition controversy is continuous with the thirteenth-century discussion in that both were concerned with a question of justification: the disposition required of the penitent in the sacrament in the context of a private ritual combining confession and absolution and deemphasizing satisfaction. However, the post-Tridentine view, influenced by Scotus, generally distinguished attrition and contrition on the basis of psychological motive rather than the relationship to grace and intensity. Much of the discussion centered on the interpretation of Trent's statement that "imperfect contrition" or "attrition" disposed the sinner to receive grace in the sacrament (DS 1678). The position of Michael Baius and the Jansenists, that sorrow motivated by fear is useless and immoral, was condemned in 1567. In 1667, the Holy Office recognized attritionism as the more widely accepted position but ordered both parties not to defame opponents nor to attach theological censures to opposing views; see DS 2070. Attritionism here is not the "gallows repentance" that Luther rejected—that was a servile fear still attached to sin—nor is either position contritionism in the medieval sense. The post-Tridentine controversy was due to an inadequate integration of the personal and ecclesial factors of justification.

16. See, for example, *Introduction to the Devout Life*, 1, 21. Following Trent, Charles Borromeo (d. 1584) had tried to restore the ancient penitential discipline in Milan and his instructions for confessors were still being reprinted in France a century later.

17. See Leonard Swidler, *Aufklärung Catholicism, 1780–1850: Liturgical and Other Reforms in the Catholic Aufklärung* (AAR Studies in Religion, 17; Missoula, Montana: Scholars Press, 1978), especially pp. 35–37. Most of the liturgical reforms sought by the Catholic Aufklärung, though rejected and condemned at the time, have been implemented since Vatican II.

18. Pius IX, "Iam vos omnes," September 13, 1868; DS 2997.

19. *Commentarius historicus de disciplina in administratione sacramenti Poenitentiae* (1651).

20. Bartholome F. Xiberta, *Clavis ecclesiae: De ordine absolutionis sacramentalis ad reconciliationem cum ecclesia* (Rome: Collegium Sancti Alberti, 1922).

21. Rahner notes the reactions in his "Penance as an Additional Act of Reconciliation with the Church," *Theological Investigations* 10 (New York: Herder and Herder, 1973) 125–128.

22. Particularly important are his *Paenitentia Secunda [Die abendländische Kirchenbusse im Ausgang des christlichen Altertums* and *Die abendländische Kirchenbusse im frühen Mittelalter]* (Bonn: Peter Hanstein Verlag, 1940) and *Der Ablass im Licht der Bussgeschichte* (Bonn: Peter Hanstein Verlag, 1948). By the ninth edition of his *De paenitentia: Tractatus dogmatico-historicus* (Rome: Pontifica Universitas Gregoriana, 1956), Galtier had begun to respect Poschmann's methodology, though not his conclusions.

23. "Sacra tridentina synodus," *Acta Sanctae Sedis* 38 (1905) 400–406. Though the Council of Trent had encouraged those present at Mass to receive communion, few had responded. The influence of Jansenism ensured that few Catholics considered themselves properly disposed for frequent communion. Pius's decree insisted that anyone in a state of grace and with the right intention could receive communion frequently, even daily. However, reference to the confessor's advice reinforced the prevalent association of confession with communion; it was not repeated in the 1917 Code of Canon Law (Canon 863).

24. "Quam singulari," *Acta Apostolicae Sedis* 2 (1910) 577–583. The decree presumes that confession and absolution is permitted to such children and will continue to precede first communion, but rejects the view that greater maturity is required for communion than for confession. What is required is the ability to distinguish the eucharist from ordinary bread and to approach it with the proper devotion. The age of discretion for satisfying the Lateran IV precept is set at "about the seventh year, more or less." The decree forbids denying children either confession and absolution or communion and witnesses to the prominent role of the confessor in the Counter-Reformation Church, since he permitted or refused access to the eucharist.

25. Devotional confession (regular confession as an act of piety, with the content either venial sins or mortal sins already confessed and forgiven) is an outgrowth of the medieval use of

confession as a means of purification before communion. It differs from the early monastic manifestation of conscience and later spiritual direction in its association with the sacrament. Cf. Catherine Dooley, "Development of the Practice of Devotional Confession," *Questions Liturgiques* (1983) 89–117. For a thorough study of the interrelation between confession and communion, see Louis Braeckmans, *Confession et Communion au Moyen-Âge et au Concile de Trente* (Gembloux: Duculot, 1971).

26. One of the few who apparently realized that regular communion would mean a drop-off in confessions was F. M. de Zueleta, a religious educator. For an apparent parallel between the forces against which Pius X worked and those that today charge a lost sense of sin, see Linda Gaupin, "More Frequent Communion, Less Frequent Confession," *Living Light* 20 (1984) 254–260.

27. *Acta Apostolicae Sedis* 35 (1943) 192–248, especially paragraph 86, p. 235. As we saw in the last chapter, the notion of the ritual's automatic effectiveness is a post-twelfth-century development, though scholastic theology always emphasized the need for the proper dispositions in order to receive and benefit from the grace.

For the modern debate, see Felix Funke, *Christliche Existenz zwischen Sünde und Rechtfertigung. Das Problem der Andachtsbeichte in der modernen Theologie* (Mainz: Grünewald, 1969), and Joseph Meyer-Schene, *Die häufige Beichte. Studie zur Literatur der letzten Jahrzehnte* (Vienna: Verlag der Herz-Jesu-Priester, 1968), and cf. John F. Dedek, "The Theology of Devotional Confession," *Proceedings of the Catholic Theological Society of America* 22 (1967) 215–222. The Rite of Penance admits the usefulness of confessing venial sins but fails to cite *Mystici corporis* and explicitly rejects frequent confession as a ritual repetition or psychological exercise, although it does encourage "frequent and careful use" of the sacrament (RP 7b). Cf. Eliseo Ruffini, "La prassi della 'confessione frequente di devozione.' Dalla teologia degli anni trenta all Novus Ordo Paenitentiae," *Scuola Cattolica* 104 (1976) 307–338. Pope John Paul II, however, has quoted Pius XII on frequent devotional confession and presents a similar outlook; see, for example, *L'Osservatore Romano* [English edition], October 8, 1979, p. 4, and *Reconciliation and Penance*: Post-Synodal Apostolic Exhortation (Vatican City: Libreria Editrice Vaticana, 1984), especially pp. 128–130.

28. In the East, without the sharp Western distinction between mortal and venial sin, the sentiment of sin remained more a matter of the heart than a juridical concept. Lesser offenses (regarded as expressions of human frailty) were not subject to canonical penance; completeness of confession and the confessor's role were thus understood differently. Eastern emphasis on the action of the Spirit in the sacrament also contrasted with Western juridicism in a manner reminiscent of the differing perspectives of the Johannine and Matthaean communities and ensured both a strong sense of community and a rich liturgical expression. The East maintained a much more vibrant and less juridical relationship between penance and eucharist as well as a variety of forms for the sacrament. See James Douglas, "The Sacrament of Penance in Present-Day Orthodoxy," *Diakonia* 4 (1969) 211–226; David Kirk, "Penance in the Eastern Churches," *Worship* 40 (1966) 148–155; Franz Nikolasch, "The Sacrament of Penance: Learning from the East," *Concilium* 61 (1971) 65–75; Nicholas P. Smiar, "Notes on Byzantine Penance," *Resonance* 2 (1966): 97–105; 6and articles in *Busse und Beichte*, Ernst C. Suttner, ed. (Drittes Regensburger Ökumenisches Symposium; Regensburg: Pustet, 1972) and *Liturgie et Rémission des Péchés* (Rome: Edizioni Liturgiche, 1975). For Eastern influences on the RP, see Jacob Vellian, "The New Rite of Reconciliation: Understanding Its Newness from Eastern Tradition," *Ephemerides Liturgicae* 91 (1977) 377–381. Apart from Eastern studies, ecumenical considerations had little influence on penance theology.

29. See Karl Rahner, "Forgotten Truths Concerning the Sacrament of Penance," *Theological Investigations* 2 (Baltimore: Helicon, 1963) 135–174. The essay was originally published in 1953. Rahner's careful systematic studies of elements of the early history of penance have been collected and translated in *Theological Investigations* 15 (New York: Crossroad, 1982). Rahner's methodology has been studied by Giles Pater, "Karl Rahner's Historico-Theological Studies on Penance: The Retrieval of Forgotten Truths" (unpublished Ph. D. dissertation; University of Notre Dame, 1977), to whom I am indebted for data and insight on the historiography of penance.

30. The pastoral letter of the Dutch bishops, dated March 16, 1965, is available in English in William Freburger, *Repent and Believe* (Notre Dame, Ind.: Ave Maria Press, 1972), pp. 91–96.

31. The permission granted to the bishops of Papua-New Guinea on July 17, 1966 was the first and was the reference for subsequent requests. See "A Request and a Reply," *Teaching All Nations* 4 (1967) 432–434, and C. van der Geest, "Die Generalabsolution in Papua-New Guinea," *Liturgisches Jahrbuch* 21 (1971) 174–176.

32. November 5, 1970; *Documentation Catholique* 68 (1971) 110–123. For a survey of such statements, see Philippe Rouillard, "L'enseignement du magistère sur le sacrement de la pénitence de 1964 à 1974," *Ephemerides Liturgicae* 89 (1975) 177–193.

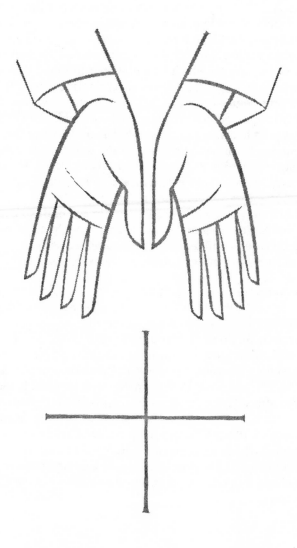

Part Two: The Revised Rites

Postbaptismal conversion's varied forms over the centuries and its many shapes in most periods of history make the modern era look impoverished in comparison. For centuries, the Church rarely needed an official channel for authenticating such conversion and valued the many informal means by which its members continued their conversion. In the Middle Ages, several forms were official in varying degrees. By the end of that era, however, the only form of official ecclesial penance that had any vitality was private confession. For the four centuries of the Counter-Reformation that remained the sole symbolic language for expressing postbaptismal conversion. The unchanging and all but mechanical character of private confession as a therapeutic means of purification and growth in virtue is almost a mirror image of the life of the Counter-Reformation Church, which sought security in rigidity, self-confidence through repeated self-purgation, and strength through introspective exercises.

At Vatican II, the Church underwent a *revision de vie* and its present Rite of Penance symbolizes the path of conversion and renewal that it has, somewhat hesitatingly, chosen to take. To understand that rite, it is first necessary to realize what kind of reform was sought and recognize the tensions that accompanied its preparation and publication. The ambivalence and ambiguity that mark it and later affect its use can then be acknowledged as the consequence of an inability to break away completely from the mentality of the Counter-Reformation. The doctrinal and theological foundations of the Rite of Penance will be explored and its liturgical rites will be examined before we evaluate it in relation to tradition and contemporary needs.

Chapter Seven

The Reform of Penance

Church reform movements grow out of a prophetic sense of responding to pastoral needs in new and more effective ways. Pope John XXIII's decision to convoke an ecumenical council came from such a vision. Vatican II's pastoral thrust was clear from start to finish, not only in calling for liturgical reform but also in situating that reform within the Church's pastoral mission. Other concerns entered in, of course, and sometimes interfered with the pastoral one. Nevertheless, the council provided the foundation for the liturgy, law, and pastoral practice that has come after it.[1]

The call for penance reform at the council seems almost an afterthought, with little indication of crisis or pressing pastoral needs. Yet penance, which became a center of controversy during the preparation of the new rite, remains such today.

VATICAN COUNCIL II
Though the Constitution on the Sacred Liturgy called for the reform of the rites and formulas of penance to express the sacrament's nature and effect more clearly, it gave no specific guidelines for the reform (*Sacrosanctum concilium*, 72). Penance reform was not mentioned in early drafts or in the final text of the Preparatory Commission, but the text presented to the bishops when the council opened called for clearer expression of the sacrament's effect.[2] The eventual conciliar mandate, together with related comments on penance and the general principles established for liturgical reform, are the primary criteria for under-

standing and evaluating the Rite of Penance (RP). They are likewise the key to assessing implementation and disciplinary regulation of the RP.

The chapter on the sacraments was discussed on November 6–7, 1962, but little was said about penance. Some bishops considered the call for reform too general and wanted a statement of what was to be reformed, with clear limits.[3] Specifics mentioned were faculties for confessors[4] and a simple rite with a shorter absolution formula.[5] A more significant set of interventions asked that the reform express more clearly the nature of the sacrament, particularly the social and communal character of both sin and penance as in the public reconciliation of ancient penance.[6] The only major innovation suggested was by a spokesman for the bishops of Colombia who "timidly" proposed authorizing general absolution without previous confession in certain cases.[7]

When the final text of Chapter Three was presented to the Forty-Eighth General Congregation, a declaration gave the official sense of article 72 (formerly 56):

"Among the rites to be reformed, an important one would seem to be the imposition of the hand, which, according to Saint Cyprian, was the sign of the reconciliation and communion with the Church that is restored in penance— necessary because the living bond with the Church had been destroyed by sin. It signified reconciliation through the Holy Spirit, as its retention in the Roman Pontifical in the rite for reconciling an apostate [shows]. The imposition of the hand is, of course, called for in the Ritual, though in a modified form: 'Then, with his right hand lifted toward the penitent, he says . . . ' The Ambrosian Ritual even more clearly states: 'with his right hand lifted and extended over the head of the penitent.' The rubric should therefore be revised so that this rite would be recognized as the imposition of the hand, even if there is no physical contact. Among other things, the words 'from every bond of excommunication' should be revised. They are not needed for an absolution from censures in the canonical sense, and they are almost always superfluous. In ancient times the sacramental formula by which the penitent was restored to 'communion' in the Body also absolved him."[8]

A further official interpretation by Archbishop Hallinan of Atlanta indicated that the added reference to the "nature" of the sacrament referred to the social and ecclesial character, as had been requested.[9]

Council documents say little on penance but do affirm the sacrament's social and ecclesial nature by linking reconciliation with God and reconciliation with the Church. The Constitution on the Church links them in relating the sacraments to the priestly community of the Church and hints at the sacrament's place in the Church's wider pastoral mission:

"Those who approach the sacrament of penance obtain from God's mercy pardon for the offenses committed against him and are, at the same time, reconciled with the Church which they have wounded by sinning and which has been working for their conversion by charity, example, and prayers." (*Lumen gentium,* 11)

The same link is made in the Decree on the Ministry and Life of Priests (*Presbyterorum ordinis,* 5).

The Liturgy Constitution suggested that the context for this sacrament of reconciliation is the Church's mission to call people to faith and conversion and continue to call believers to faith and penance, seeing liturgical reform as part of the Church's ministry to the world as well as to its own members (*Sacrosanctum concilium,* 9). In speaking of Lent and penitential practices, the council mentioned the social consequences of sin, the Church's role, and the responsibility to pray for sinners (*Sacrosanctum concilium,* 109), and in calling for the reform of Lenten discipline, the council insisted that such penance should be external and social as well as internal and individual (*Sacrosanctum con-*

cilium, 110).[10] Other statements also affirmed the value of penance for developing the Christian life, an application of the earlier general statement on the sacraments' role in nourishing, strengthening, and developing faith,[11] with their power drawn from the paschal mystery of the passion, death, and resurrection of Christ (*Sacrosanctum concilium*, 61). The sacraments are Christ's priestly acts "through his Spirit," with all "bound up with the eucharist and directed toward it" (*Presbyterorum ordinis*, 5). The role of the bishop in the celebration of the sacraments was emphasized.[12]

The pastoral thrust of the council, stated in its opening "Message to Humanity,"[13] inspired liturgical reform as one dimension of a response to the challenges presented by the modern world (*Sacrosanctum concilium*, 1). The immediate goal was to make the texts and rites clear enough for people to understand them easily and take part in them "fully, actively, and as a community" (*Sacrosanctum concilium*, 21). Theological, historical, and pastoral investigations would ensure effectiveness and continuity with tradition, with necessary innovations growing out of existing forms (*Sacrosanctum concilium*, 23), and the involvement of experts and bishops from around the world would facilitate the work of revision (*Sacrosanctum concilium*, 25).

Other general principles to guide reform included the affirmation of scripture's value and place in celebrations (*Sacrosanctum concilium*, 24, 35) and the clear statement that, so far as possible, communal celebrations were always to be preferred to individual and "quasi-private" celebrations (*Sacrosanctum concilium*, 26–27). Rites were to be clear and intelligible (*Sacrosanctum concilium*, 34), so that the sacramental signs could nourish, strengthen, and express faith (*Sacrosanctum concilium*, 59). Likewise, the rites were to be adapted to present-day pastoral needs as these vary from culture to culture (*Sacrosanctum concilium*, 27–40, 62).

When the Constitution on the Liturgy was promulgated on December 4, 1963—400 years to the day from the Council of Trent's last session and its call for liturgical reform—the general lines of reform had been laid down. The work of revision and implementation began immediately, yet it was 10 years before Pope Paul VI officially promulgated the *Ordo Paenitentiae*, the last of the reformed sacramental rites. Those 10 years, tumultuous in many ways, were spent, so far as penance reform is concerned, in drafting the new ritual and in initiating some preliminary reforms. They were also a time of creative ferment, as theologians and pastoral writers dealt extensively with the subject of penance.[14]

PREPARING THE NEW RITUAL

That it took 10 years to prepare the revised penance ritual was primarily due to theological and doctrinal issues, although political and personal tensions cannot be totally discounted. There was, for example, a tension between the Counter-Reformation perspective rigidly adhering to Trent's authoritative pronouncements and a perspective more sensitive to pastoral needs in the context of the broader tradition. The strain between these two perspectives, already apparent before the council, increased during the reform and remained even after the promulgation of the new rite.

Coetus 23bis (De Rituali, III), responsible to the Consilium or Commission for Implementing the Constitution on the Liturgy, prepared the penance ordo. There were, however, two completely different committees: the first, from 1966 through 1969, the second, in 1972 and 1973, with a two-and-a-half-year hiatus due to the issues and tensions that resulted from the first committee's work. The work of these committees should be correlated with the initial penance reforms that will be discussed in the next section, but it is impossible to do so as long as the materials remain under the pontifical secret.[15]

The first committee was established on December 2, 1966, and was chaired by J. Lecuyer, C.S.Sp., a Lateran professor who served as consultant to the Congregation for the Doctrine of the Faith and was a specialist on the priesthood and diaconate. Franz Heggen of Roermond, the Netherlands, well known as an advocate of communal celebrations, served as secretary until replaced in 1967 by Franz Nikolasch of Salzburg, Austria.[16] Other members of the group were Zoltan Alszeghy, S.J., of the Gregorian University; Paul Anciaux of Malines, Belgium; C. Florestan of Madrid, Spain; Alfons Kirchgässner of Frankfurt, Germany; Louis Ligier, S.J., of the Pontifical Oriental Institute; Karl Rahner, S.J., of Münster, Germany; and Cyrille Vogel of Strasbourg, France.

These distinguished scholars first met on February 8–9, 1967, in Rome and prepared a preliminary work plan according to the general guidelines laid down by the council. Their initial report, submitted by Lecuyer on March 31, 1967, was Schema 222, the first on penance. Initial discussion dealt only with the reform of the existing rite, since members disagreed on the committee's competence to propose communal celebrations. Topics included place, vestments, posture, dialogue, the addition of prayer to the rite, and the revision of the absolution formula. The report submitted to the consilium proposed including communal celebrations as part of the committee's work, with the topic of general absolution without previous individual confession to be studied as well. The consilium approved the plan on April 13, 1967, but objected to the suggestion that a variety of absolution formulas be provided from which the confessor could choose.

The consilium's comments and votes were considered at the committee's second meeting in Rome on May 10–11, 1967. The major aspects of the committee's work were now outlined: renewal of the current rite and establishment of a communal rite. The initial task would be to compile relevant data and particularly to study the general absolution question. Schema 251 (De Paenitentia, 2), dated

October 15, 1967, contained a report on communal absolution by Kirchgässner and a summary history by Vogel. After another meeting in December 1967 and the circulation of schemata to a wider circle of experts,[17] a report dated March 16, 1968, was prepared for submission to the April 1968 meeting of the consilium.[18]

This 57-page document reported on the committee's work, indicated criteria proposed as norms for the revision, outlined and documented what the committee members saw as the scholarly consensus on the sacrament's historical development in West and East, and gave specific reform proposals for both individual and communal celebrations. The committee not only proposed a common absolution after individual confessions in communal celebrations but also general absolution without previous individual confession when, in the judgment of the bishops, individual confessions could not be heard in the appropriate atmosphere and with the proper dignity. This proposal was supported by documentation on Eastern practice that Ligier, an Oriental expert, supplied; by a collection of 48 previous Roman indults gathered from the curial archives by Nikolasch; and by a survey of the common teaching of theologians on the subject. The draft rites included four absolution formulas from which either the consilium or national episcopal conferences could choose: an optative formula from the ancient Holy Thursday reconciliation rite,[19] a totally new declarative formula,[20] an abbreviation of the current official formula,[21] and a deprecative formula from the Gelasian Sacramentary.[22]

Summarizing points from the council and their own research, the members of the committee outlined four major criteria for the reform: to express more clearly: 1. The nature of sin as an offense against both God and the Church; 2. Simultaneous reconciliation with God and the Church; 3. The whole Church collaborating with the sinner's effort at conversion through its charity, example, and prayers; 4. The value of the sacrament of penance in fostering the Christian life.

The consilium accepted this report, responded to the questions put to it by the committee, and suggested some minor changes in the proposed rites. The consilium agreed that the present rite had to be revised to comply with the four proposed criteria and that a reformed rite needed to express the communal dimension by providing for a communal celebration and for a celebration with general absolution when that was permitted.[23]

The committee discussed the consilium's responses at a meeting in Senonches, France, on July 4–7, 1968.[24] In Constance, September 3–8, 1968, the members of the committee worked on an introduction to the rites that would provide a theological, pastoral, and canonical foundation. This document[25] was further critiqued and then redrafted[26] and submitted to the consilium at its October 17 meeting. The consilium asked the committee to complete its work by autumn of 1969 and to submit a report on the advisability of a variety of absolution formulas at that time.

The absolution formula was apparently a matter of contention between the consilium and the committee and within the consilium itself, where votes were almost equally divided. The consultants had amended somewhat each of the first three formulas that the committee had proposed and eliminated the fourth.[27] At its April 1967 meeting, the consilium, almost without discussion, had narrowly turned down the proposal to provide several formulas from which the confessor could choose. The following April, when the committee again proposed several formulas (but this time for episcopal conferences to choose from), the consilium had amended and approved one formula[28] but gave no response to the two alternates. The question was presented to the consilium again at the October 1968 meeting, but the procedural question of reopening the matter dominated the discussion. A narrow vote (17 to 15) decided that the question would be discussed again at the November 1969 meeting. The report that the consilium had requested was submitted.[29] In it, the committee analyzed the arguments pro and con as they had been made in the consilium and in the committee meetings and recommended alternatives on the basis of historical precedent, Eastern practice, and pastoral and theological advantages.

On May 8, 1969, the consilium was dissolved and the Congregation of Rites was divided into the Congregation for Divine Worship and the Congregation for Saints' Causes. As a consequence, the matter was now presented to a special commission of the new Congregation for Divine Worship, where it was discussed in an atmosphere of tension and irritability. In the end, it was narrowly decided to allow for more than one formula. Even the questions of communal celebrations and general absolution had not provoked such bitter disagreement.

The committee finished its work at the end of 1969 and submitted its final report and draft.[30] What action the Congregation for Divine Worship took on the completed draft rite is unclear, but the new rite did not appear in early 1970 as expected. The Congregation for the Doctrine of the Faith, which was responsible for evaluating the orthodoxy of proposed rites, apparently took exception to the liberal provisions for general absolution. Sensitive doctrinal issues were involved, most notably Trent's requirement of integral confession and emphasis on the judicial character of absolution. The congregation's position on these issues prevented the promulgation of the rite as it had been prepared; it insisted, for example, that the Tridentine formula of absolution had to be used.[31]

A long silence followed. Rite after rite was released, and nothing was heard about the rite of penance. Tension apparently grew between the Congregation for Divine Worship and the Congregation for the Doctrine of the Faith. Then, in late 1971, after two years with no word, the publication of a detailed commentary on the draft rite, evaluating it in a positive fashion, indirectly raised the question of what had happened to it.[32] A few months later, on

June 16, 1972, the Congregation for the Doctrine of the Faith issued its Pastoral Norms on general absolution.[33] These norms responded disapprovingly to the doctrinal questions raised by the draft, the growing practice of using general absolution, and the approval of the practice by several national hierarchies.

The norms did timidly expand opportunities for using general absolution but also set boundaries for reform. Now that the fate of the draft had been decided, work on another proposal could begin. Within the month, a new work group was appointed to complete the preparation of the new rite. None of the members of the first committee served on the second. The members of the second committee, though not as well known academically, were more pastorally oriented. The new group was headed by P. Jounel of Paris, with Franco Sottocornola, S.X., of Parma, Italy, serving as secretary. Other members were Antonio Gracia of Zaragoza, Spain, P. Visentin, O.S.B., of Padua, Italy; Hans Bernhard Meyer, S.J., of Innsbruck, Austria; Kevin Donovan, S.J., of London; and G. Pasqualetti, I.M.C., of the Congregation for Divine Worship.

Sottocornola says that the work of the new group was to adapt the earlier draft to conform to the Pastoral Norms, complete the introduction in the style of the other new rites, and enrich the rites themselves.[34] He reports that their work was made easier by the cumulative experience of preparing new rituals and by the decision (presumably made by the Congregation for the Doctrine of the Faith) to provide only one absolution formula that would contain the current indicative formula. Eliminating this controversy, as well as resolving questions on general absolution, led to quick progress, but the draft produced bore little resemblance to the final work of the first committee. (The most obvious structural change was the addition of the Celebration of the Word in the rite for reconciling individuals.) This draft was submitted to the consultors of the Congregation for Divine Worship in early November and to the plenary session of the Congregation on November 22. After another revision because of the comments received, the draft was again submitted.[35]

This draft of November 30, 1972, was circulated to the Congregation for the Doctrine of the Faith, the Apostolic Penitentiary, the Congregation for the Sacraments, the Congregation of the Clergy, and the Congregation for the Evangelization of Peoples. Conflicts over jurisdiction and personal likes and dislikes complicated the process. Over 300 suggested amendments led to further changes. As a compromise, both penance and reconciliation were used to refer to the sacrament. The Lord's Prayer was replaced by an act of contrition in the individual rite and the "I absolve you" formula was retained. The consultors of the Congregation for Divine Worship discussed the draft again in early March 1973. The Congregation for the Doctrine of the Faith had issued an extensive critique on February 7, 1973, with detailed criticisms and corrections and these were incorporated. After receiving approval from the Congregation for Divine Worship and a special joint session of representatives of the various offices involved, the draft was submitted to the presidents of episcopal conferences and other experts. The divergence between those rigidly adhering to the Tridentine perspective and those pastorally more sensitive to the broader tradition became even more apparent as evaluations were sought from outside Rome, but the Congregation for the Doctrine of the Faith generally had the final say.[36] On November 29, Pope Paul approved the final text, and on December 2, the Congregation for Divine Worship promulgated it.[37]

INITIAL REFORMS

The first general reform relevant to penance was that initiated by the Apostolic Constitution *Paenitemini* of February 17, 1966.[38] This reform of the Church's penitential discipline, authorizing episcopal conferences to regulate the discipline for their own territories, was far-reaching in intent but extremely restricted in influence. Its goal was to let Christ's call to conversion be heard and answered

215

more clearly and effectively in the everyday life of modern Christians, with emphasis on the social dimension of conversion, penance's link with the world's progress. The gift of *metanoia* or conversion, first received in baptism, is a gift restored and strengthened through the sacrament of penance, the document said, but ways must be found to express it in everyday forms. Self-restraint expressed in fasting and abstinence has been a traditional way of doing so and remains a way in which the people of richer nations can help those who are poorer with what they have denied to themselves, but new means of linking penance and everyday life must be found.

This reform emphasized doing penance because of social responsibility rather than obligation; more importantly, it tried to restore the realization that the Christian life has a penitential orientation because it is ongoing conversion. *Paenitemini* related this continuing *metanoia* both to baptism and to penance and viewed its expression in everyday life from a social and ecclesial perspective. Though much of the late medieval and post-Tridentine understanding of mortification and self-denial was kept, penitential practices were presented more as elements of social action than individualistic asceticism. In retrospect, a successful revitalization of the virtue of penance would have provided rich soil in which the reformed rite of penance could have put down strong roots. Unfortunately, though the U.S. bishops and some other episcopal conferences tried to highlight *Paenitemini*'s significance, it was generally regarded as no more than a relaxation of Church discipline on fasting and abstinence.

The reform of indulgences, by the Apostolic Constitution *Indulgentiarum doctrina* of January 1, 1967,[39] is less directly related to penance reform. Indulgence grants originated out of the commutations and redemptions of tariff penance. Though a weak and barely recognizable residue of the rich resource of intercessory prayer that had supported and encouraged members of the ancient order of penitents, they had helped humanize the long and harsh tariff penances. Ignorance of their historical origins and super-stitious abuses in late medieval practice had made them the occasion for the controversies that led to the Protestant Reformation. So closely were they linked with the experience of justification in the sacrament of penance that an attack on them led quickly to questioning the entire penitential system.

Although *Indulgentiarum doctrina* does not break entirely free from a legalistic and commercial outlook—it still speaks of making "satisfaction" to remove the "temporal punishment due to sin"—it does adopt perspectives that serve as correctives. It emphasizes social and ecclesial dimensions of sin and conversion, Christ's redemption as the context and foundation for Christian conversion, reconciliation as the goal of conversion, and the Church's cooperation with those seeking conversion. Emphasizing indulgences' social and ecclesial dimension and orientation and clearly stating their subordinate relationship to other means of sanctification and purification—the Mass and sacraments, works of piety, penance, and charity—offers a doctrinal foundation for revitalizing and finding new expressions of ecclesial assistance to those undergoing conversion.[40]

Much more significant than the reform of penitential practices or indulgences was the gradual development of an entirely new experience of liturgy as the activity of the Church gathered to respond to God's Word. The pattern of giving a place to the liturgy of the Word in sacramental celebrations and of associating other sacramental celebrations with the eucharist had a major influence on penance reform. Because of this experience, the 1973 RP gives heavier emphasis to the value of communal celebrations than did the 1968 draft of a reformed ritual. The transformation of the old prayers at the foot of the altar into a communal penitential rite in the 1969 Order of Mass also had a significant effect, intended or not, for it made it possible to express repentance in a context totally new to most people—that of community worship—and began to fulfill, for many people, the function previously served by regular devotional confession. Its effect on penance praxis (together with prayers of the faithful, offertory procession, sign of peace, and other new liturgical symbols) should not be underestimated.

Another minor reform, from the Congregation for Religious on December 8, 1970, allowed for a less frequent celebration of the sacrament by religious and thus showed Church officials' changing understanding of the nature and purpose of the sacrament and the conditions for its proper celebration.[41] Documents on the subject of first confession and first communion, though relevant to the topic of penance, had no effect on the eventual liturgical reform. Although these documents were generally interpreted and implemented as requiring children to make a first confession before first communion, they actually only insisted that children could not be required to postpone first confession until after first communion. As applied in practice, however, these documents maintained the liturgical incongruity of ritually reconciling children to a community into which they were not yet fully initiated and regarding a symbol of conversion as a rite of passage.[42]

Of the reforms preliminary to the new rite that have been mentioned, only one, *Paenitemini*, is of real significance, and it went almost unnoticed, seen more as a disciplinary concession than as an attempt to revitalize everyday penance. A similar reaction to pastoral liturgical experiments resulted in the promulgation of Pastoral Norms on June 16, 1972, by the Congregation for the Doctrine of the Faith.[43] This conclusion to the long silence regarding the fate of the proposed new ritual for penance also determined the final shape of the ritual.

The Pastoral Norms responded not only to pastoral difficulties but also to frequently proposed theological theories regarding communal celebrations of the sacrament and the growing practice of general absolution that was regarded approvingly by several episcopal conferences.

The Tridentine discipline was reaffirmed: "Individual and integral confession and absolution remain the single ordinary way whereby the faithful reconcile themselves with God and the Church, unless physical or moral impossibility excuses from this confession" (Norm I).[44]

The norms did, however, expand the opportunity for general absolution: not only the emergency situation (e.g., danger of death) when there is no time for individual confessions (Norm II), but also any situation in which a "grave need" legitimates general absolution (Norm III). As an example of such grave need, the document mentioned a large gathering of penitents and an insufficient number of confessors to hear individual confessions properly within an appropriate time, with the result that penitents, without any fault of their own, would be deprived of sacramental grace or holy communion for a long time. While priests are not to neglect this ministry for other duties (Norm IV), the bishop can specify circumstances that call for general absolution and priests may give such absolution when another grave necessity arises, consulting the bishop beforehand, if possible, or informing him afterward (Norm V). Penitents are to be properly disposed; this includes the intention to confess grave sins within a subsequent or suitable time (Norm VI), if possible before receiving general absolution again, and certainly within a year, if possible (Norm VII). In a tone reminiscent of the old warnings against postponing penance till the end, priests are told to instruct people not to postpone confession of mortal sin with the expectation of receiving general absolution (Norm VIII); they are to ensure that everyone has the opportunity for private confession at least once a year (Norm IX).

The document spoke of liturgical celebrations and communal penitential rites as "very useful" for preparing for a more fruitful confession and amendment of life, but it insisted that these not be confused with sacramental confession and absolution. When these celebrations include individual confession, each penitent is to receive absolution individually. When general absolution is used, it must be kept altogether distinct from the celebration of Mass (Norm X).

A penitent who has received general absolution is to remove any cause of scandal before receiving communion (Norm XI). The document also insists on the value of frequent devotional confession and warns against any practice that would keep individual confession for grave sins or discourage penitents from devotional confession (Norm XII). The last norm declares general absolutions beyond these limits to be "grave abuses" (Norm XIII) and the document concludes with the statement that the norms were approved "in a special way" by Pope Paul VI.

The Pastoral Norms were not welcomed. Although commentators noted that the opportunity for general absolution had been broadened, they raised questions regarding the adequacy of the norms and their theological underpinnings, even while agreeing that most communities were not yet ready for a regular use of general absolution.[45] Critics called attention to an attitude that set individual and communal forms in opposition to each other, a narrow understanding of sacramentality that restricted it to judicial absolution, and a failure to address the need for a more credible rite for the sacrament. Karl Rahner noted that the dispositions of the penitents were more significant than the sacrament's judicial character so far as forgiveness was concerned and suggested that pastors say nothing about the sacramentality of a celebration, preaching instead that God's forgiveness is present for the truly repentant—whether in sacramental form or not. Rahner was, in fact, unable to understand how a celebration by a repentant community with an authoritative ministerial prayer could not be sacramental.[46]

Other critics found the norms completely inadequate, based on a nonviable concept of sin and an outmoded theology unaware of the current pastoral situation.[47] Still others regarded the norms as actually harmful and non-pastoral or, at best, irrelevant to the present situation.[48] Interestingly, the norms came in for a good deal of theological criticism even from those who agreed with the disciplinary position established.

The norms were not uniformly implemented.[49] Many bishops declared that situations calling for general absolution did not exist in their dioceses. In Africa, Asia, and Latin America, bishops authorized such celebrations. In Europe, Belgian, French, and Swiss hierachies concluded that the conditions required existed. In North America, some Canadian and U.S. bishops did likewise,[50] but the majority were cautious.

In summary, the Pastoral Norms issued by the Congregation for the Doctrine of the Faith represented a rejection of positions taken by the framers of the draft rite. While the value of communal celebrations was grudgingly conceded, the traditional format of individual confession and absolution was maintained as the most desirable mode of celebration, the possibility of general absolution was expanded somewhat but only for circumstances of grave need, a collective absolution after individual confessions was ruled out, and sacramentality was recognized only where a judicial absolution was given. In general, the norms appear motivated by a view that private and communal forms are in competition and general use of communal forms would be detrimental to the Tridentine discipline. As the last word of higher authority, these norms were to guide the final preparation of the new Rite of Penance and to be reinvoked in the 1983 Code of Canon Law.

THE RITE OF PENANCE

Though the reformed ritual was promulgated before the tenth anniversary of the Constitution on the Liturgy, the Latin *editio typica* was not published until February 7, 1974.[51] The English translation, prepared by the International Committee on English in the Liturgy and approved by the National Conference of Catholic Bishops, was submitted to the Holy See on March 4, 1975, confirmed on March 11, 1975, and published later that year, with implementation set for February 27, 1977.

There was ample time to prepare.[52] Workshops informed priests of the orientations of the new rite and prepared them to minister more effectively. Articles, talks, workshops, and homilies similarly prepared the laity. Whether because of lessons painfully learned in implementing eucharistic reforms or because of confession's previous prominence in Catholic life, preparations for implementing the RP were handled carefully. Reconciliation rooms were set up for reconciling individuals and participation aids were printed. In some places, communal services were held for the first time. A sincere effort was made to communicate what underlay the changed settings and forms of the sacramental rites, and there was some measure of success.

The RP was generally well received. Though the final rite placed more restrictions on general absolution than the first committee's draft had, it did, overall, improve on it. The introduction was pastorally and theologically far better, largely as a result of experience gained from the production and implementation of other new rituals, and the rites themselves were richer and more original, particularly because the Word was given greater prominence.

Later Developments

By the time the RP was published, the crisis of penance was a major concern. Initial evaluations of the new ritual were cautiously optimistic, but a sharp decline in confessions was apparent. Some observers saw this decline as regression, signaling the loss of the sense of sin and penance, and a few even blamed the liturgical changes initiated by Vatican II. Others, however, saw the decline as the correction of a previous overemphasis.

The limited opening given communal celebrations in the Pastoral Norms and the RP was immediately utilized by several national hierarchies. Services with general absolution were celebrated more frequently. Tensions also became more common, particularly when such celebrations were publicized, because the tensions that had become apparent during the preparation of the RP had not been resolved. Interventions followed: papal comments on general absolution, individual confession, and first confession, especially to bishops making *ad limina* visits, and exhortations on the sacrament;[53] declarations regarding the delay of first confession;[54] and official reprimands of bishops using or allowing general absolution too liberally.[55]

Curial officials often seemed to regard communal celebrations as competing with individual confession. They were concerned over less frequent confession, the loss of the sense of sin, the increasing use of general absolution in communal celebrations, the tendency to postpone first confession, and, in general, changing attitudes toward clerical authority symbolized by changing practices in this, Catholics' most intimate contact with the official Church.

The proposed U.S. national pastoral letter on penance was a moderate expression of such concerns. Initially mandated in May 1979, it took the form of a letter to priests and another to the laity, neither of which was issued. The draft of the first letter saw the crisis largely as an eroded sense of sin. This sense of sin had to be restored, authentic Christian norms had to be studied, and the RP had to be given wider scope. Completed by September 1980, but unable to be acted on until November 1981 because of conference rules, the draft was sent to individual bishops to use or adapt as a letter to their priests.[56] When reconciliation was announced as the topic for the 1983 Synod of Bishops, the proposed letter to the laity was postponed.

Ten years after the RP was issued, the tensions that surrounded the preparation of the RP came to the surface in the new Code of Canon Law and the 1983 Synod of Bishops. Both were indications that the rough transition from Counter-Reformation penance to new forms was far from complete.

The new Code was intended to reform Church law to conform with Vatican II, but the canons on penance (Canons 959–997) at some points contrast with council documents and postconciliar reforms. Regulations concerning the minister (Canons 965–986), especially on faculties, are much simplified, but several others are actually regressions. The convoluted definition of the sacrament (Canon 959), for example, manages to avoid the mention of both Christ and the Spirit and fails to refer to God's mercy; conciliar influence is seen only in noting reconciliation with God and the Church. Only twice in the 39 canons is the scriptural and conciliar term reconciliation used (Canons 959 and 960); the terminology is otherwise almost invariably the preconciliar confession. Communal celebrations are adverted to only by the restrictions placed on general absolution.

In general, the Code modifies the direction set by rescripts in the 1960s, the 1972 Pastoral Norms, and the 1973 RP and prefers the standard of the 1944 Instruction of the Sacred Penitentiary, where the primary criterion was not pastoral benefit but the impossibility of observing the Tridentine norm. It seems even more concerned with restricting general absolution than were the Pastoral Norms. Changes from the wording of parallel passages in the RP and changes required in the RP by the Code often revert to a passive individualism.[57] There is, overall, a thin veneer of Vatican II and a barely modified Counter-Reformation outlook.

The 1983 Synod of Bishops was also marked by tension and ambivalence. The preparatory document on the Synod topic, "Reconciliation and Penance in the Mission of the Church," though placing the sacrament in the broad context of the Church's life and mission in the world, contained many indications of the Counter-Reformation out-

224

look: a negative assessment of the world, personalization and socialization as contrasting tendencies, little appreciation of communal celebrations and the universal priesthood, an individualistic understanding of the sacrament's nature and effect, little reference to the liturgy, and an emphasis on the priest as minister, the judicial character of absolution, and the need for complete and individual confession.[58]

The report prepared for the Synod by the International Theological Commission had a historical consciousness lacking in the preparatory document and, in general, a more balanced and optimistic view.[59] Still, the historical knowledge seems more legal and theological than liturgical; the authors quickly conclude that penitential celebrations cannot be sacramental and that general absolution must be restricted to "extraordinary situations of emergency"—again, a return to the standard of the 1944 Instruction. The late medieval Western form of penance canonized by Trent seems to be regarded as ending possible development; both history and sacramentality seem measured by the categories of post-Tridentine manual sacramentology. Though there is some ecumenical sensitivity, the witness of Eastern Christians and separated Western Christians is ignored. There are inconsistencies and contradictions, due either to disagreements within the International Theological Commission or requirements by outside authorities.

Similar inconsistencies and contradictions marked the meetings of the Synod, but there they clearly expressed disagreements among the participants. Pope John Paul hinted at these difficulties and tensions in his closing address.[60] Press reports and published interventions give the impression that disagreement was largely between curial officials and diocesan bishops. Participants concurred on the Church's responsibility to seek reconciliation in society and among its members, but dissatisfaction with current discipline and trends showed itself as bishops complained about restrictions on general absolution, the requirement of subsequent confession, and a general prejudice against communal celebrations. The presentations of curial officials, particularly Cardinals Ratzinger (Congregation for the Doctrine of the Faith) and Oddi (Congregation of the Clergy), based more on the Counter-Reformation understanding of penance than on that of Vatican II and the RP, typified the object of criticism.

The same understanding remained prominent in Pope John Paul II's postsynodal exhortation, *Reconciliatio et Paenitentia*, issued December 2, 1984. In contrast with his usual approach to social issues, he speaks cautiously of social sin and the Church's role in society. It is as though sacramental piety requires privacy and isolated individualism, with social action and calls to it only loosely connected. He implicitly rebukes Synod participants who spoke of the values of communal celebration, especially those who called for fewer restrictions on general absolution and those who called for the Church to make greater efforts to reach out to those alienated from the Church. Defects in catechesis on penance and reconciliation are prominent among the differences in opinion and option that are mentioned as divisive in the Church. The points that are emphasized are those most prominent in the teaching of Trent: individual confession and the priestly ministry of absolution. Vatican II's focal themes, reconciliation with the Church and the sacrament's social and ecclesial nature and effects, are put into the background. Other orientations of the RP are also neglected. The community's presence seems relatively unimportant, if not superfluous, with the communal celebration regarded as ceremonial enhancement and the form with general absolution warned against. Inconsistencies and internal contradictions show the difficulty of integrating social consciousness and personal piety and seem to derive from a perceived need to maintain an institutional model of Church.

Ambivalence and tension are to be expected in a time of transition such as ours. Nevertheless, the main lines of

226

the reform called for at Vatican II and fleshed out in the RP remain clear.

Contents of the Ritual
The outlook of the Rite of Penance extends beyond sacramental reconciliation to include—by intention, though not in fact—all the ways a penitent Church ritualizes conversion and reconciliation. Nevertheless, the title gives no indication that it looks beyond rites to the Church's overall ministry of challenging to conversion and promoting reconciliation. Likewise, the premises stated in the Introduction are not as visionary as the *Rite of Christian Initiation of Adults* nor as broadly ministerial as the *Pastoral Care of the Sick*, primarily because the RP represents a compromise between divergent perspectives.

The Rite of Penance consists of an introduction, four chapters, and three appendices. The Introduction describes the Church's understanding of penance and the ministry of penance (RP 1–11) and its celebration (RP 12–40). Chapter I gives the rite for reconciling individual penitents (RP 41–47); Chapter II, the rite for reconciling several penitents with individual confession and absolution (RP 48–59); Chapter III, the rite for reconciling several penitents with general confession and absolution (RP 60–66). Chapter IV contains various texts for use in the celebrations (RP 67–214). The first appendix provides formulas for absolving from censure and irregularities. The second appendix contains regulations for penitential celebrations (1–4) and nine models for such celebrations (5–71). The third appendix is a model examination of conscience.

The Introduction to the RP is, except for the "General Instruction" of the Roman Missal, the most developed of all the introductions to the reformed liturgies. It was also the first to detail the theology underlying the new rite, though not with an eye to deciding theological controversies or interpreting historical facts. It intended to synthesize traditional doctrine, theology, and practice as set out by the Council of Trent and nuanced by Vatican II. As a rule, it reflected contemporary theological consensus, but the spiritual renewal of the Church and its members was its major purpose, not resolving theological questions.[61]

However, biblical and patristic language and outlook do not always harmonize well with those of the Middle Ages and Trent. Reconciliation and a notion of penance still somewhat regarded as purification, for example, do not fit well together. Primacy is given to reconciliation—reconciliation with God through the Church justifies and sanctifies the sinner—but other terms, the lack of clear consensus in the Church, and controverted questions show the tentative nature of the reform and the need for cultural adaptation and ongoing efforts.

Still, changes in terminology do significantly reorient awareness. The most important is that the RP speaks of reconciliation rather than forgiveness of sins. Though the word "penance" (i.e., conversion) is the title of the new ritual and frequently appears as the name of the sacrament in the Introduction, the sacrament is primarily understood as the sacrament not of conversion but of reconciliation with God and Church. The implementing decree begins by speaking of reconciliation, each of the doctrinal sections of the Introduction has "reconciliation" in its title, and in each of the chapters the rites are rites of reconciliation. Confession, which has been the common term for the sacrament for centuries, is, except for RP 7b (and, possibly, RP 10b), used only to refer to the part of the sacrament, not to the sacrament itself.

Penance emphasizes the human side of the mystery, striving after God's gift of conversion, while reconciliation brings out the double element of God's initiative, offering pardon, and the human response, receiving pardon and expressing love by conversion. Reconciliation also puts greater emphasis on the social and ecclesial dimension of the sacrament as well as on the reciprocity of the encounter between God and people and among people. Penance has had a more individualistic and negative tone, though its proper meaning is conversion and reconciliation does depend on conversion. Sincere conversion and experienced reconciliation are, in fact, the dominant concerns of the RP, not purification and individual forgiveness.

Nuances of connotation and persistence of habit ensure that all three terms will continue to be used. The RP seems to prefer reconciliation when it means only the completion of the sacrament, while using penance in a more inclusive fashion as "conversion," though the words are frequently interchangeable. "Confession," a means of self-purgation and purification, is no longer used metonymously for the sacrament, a radical reorientation. More important than word usage, however, is the fact that reconciliation is the major theme of the Introduction, the atmosphere for ritual celebration, and the context and perspective for understanding the sacrament.

The first two sections of the Introduction synthesize the doctrinal and theological underpinnings by speaking of reconciliation in the history of salvation (RP 1–2) and in the Church (RP 3–7). The third section regards reconciliation as the basis for understanding the Church's ministry in this sacrament (RP 8–11). The sacrament of penance is called the sacrament of reconciliation, but so are baptism and eucharist (especially RP 2, 4, 5). In reality, the whole Church is the place of reconciliation between God and humanity (especially RP 4, 8). This presentation of the Church as reconciled and reconciling community is basic (RP 1–5, 18). It orients the understanding of redemption and God's action in the sacraments, it establishes the rhythm of celebration, and it integrates liturgy and life.

Understanding and appreciating the RP requires approaching it from the perspective of the Church's broad tradition rather than from the perspective of past personal experience of private confession. In effect, the RP provides a variety of sacramental and nonsacramental penitential liturgies for different situations. Three sacramental rites are provided: the first, for reconciling individual penitents; the second, for reconciling several penitents with individual confession and absolution; and the third, for reconciling several penitents with general confession and absolution. The three are complementary, each with distinct values for penitents and communities in different situations.

The first rite can, at first, seem no more than an embellishment of the familiar confession. However, the two celebrations for reconciling a group of penitents are clearly more. They are new official rituals—the first new forms of penance in a millennium. The RP sees them as standard and model forms of ecclesial worship, the appropriate form whenever a group of penitents seek reconciliation: "When a number of penitents assemble at the same time to receive sacramental reconciliation, it is fitting that they be prepared for the sacrament by a celebration of the word of God" (RP 22). This goes well beyond the 1972 Pastoral Norms' reluctant recognition of the value or usefulness of communal celebrations.

Though the second rite, like the French confession service, can initially be considered a new, communal setting for the familiar private confession, the third rite, much like the Dutch penance service, clearly distinguishes private and communal penance by providing a fully communal form for ritualizing conversion and reconciliation. This third rite is the model rite in the RP,[62] for it shows what is new in the RP and most radically different from what we have been accustomed to: the sacrament's nature and effect as radically social and ecclesial.

In the late 1950s and early 1960s, the communal celebration of penance with general confession and general absolution apparently grew out of experience with the penitential celebration and the French confession service. Promoting the development were a desire to complete the penitential celebration with the grant of reconciliation and a dissatisfaction with the haste and impersonal routine that accompanied the confession service. Both factors were closely connected with the growing realization that private confession and communal penance have distinct values. Inclusion in the RP fulfilled the conciliar mandate to give full expression to the social and ecclesial character of the sacrament and responded to growing pastoral needs.

Its position alongside the other rites makes it appear ordinary enough, but regulations restrict it to extraordinary situations. Precedents were centuries removed from the current pastoral situation: the ritual of reconciliation of canonical penance and the medieval general absolutions.[63] In the minds of Church officials and many theologians, the Tridentine statement that integral confession and priestly absolution were necessary *jure divino* took precedence over such historical data. Yet Trent's acknowledgment that the Church cannot change the *substantia* of the sacraments suggests that the essentials of penance cannot simply be identified with the late medieval form. Trent recognized exceptions to the requirement because of physical impossibility and later theology admitted that other obstacles could make complete confession morally impossible, but the only recent precedents were the wartime permissions to give general absolution when death threatened and individual confessions were physically impossible because of numbers. However, such emergencies were not really a precedent because what was then envisioned was an act of contrition and absolution, not a complete liturgy celebrated by the assembled faithful.

Critics have pointed out not only the doctrinal obstacles posed by Trent but also the pastoral loss of personal dialogue between penitent and priest. If time restrictions reduce this to a minimum in the confession service, the use of general absolution in the penance service eliminates it altogether. Though the criticism is legitimate, the conclusion to be drawn is not that the fully communal liturgy should not be used. Rather, it is that this rite, like the individual rite, realizes certain values clearly and presents others more obscurely.[64] The individual rite emphasizes

the personal character of conversion, individual responsibility, and the deepening of spiritual life through dialogue
with the confessor. The second rite assists formation of
conscience in community, allows reconciliation with others to be experienced as the condition of reconciliation
with God, and attempts to balance the personal and communal elements. The third rite permits a more frequent
celebration than would otherwise be possible and, most
important, shows the need of true conversion as a permanent dimension of the Christian life by making repentance superior to self-accusation. Penitential celebrations
maintain this awareness of gospel demands and the spirit
of continual conversion. The question then is which values are able to be realized in specific situations and which
values are more important in a given situation for particular penitents.

Rather than an emergency form of the sacrament for people in imminent danger of death, the third rite in the RP is
a fully developed sacramental liturgy wherein penitents
responding to God's Word ritualize their conversion to
the Church and seek reconciliation. It is internally coherent and its structure is complete. It more thoroughly expresses the council's guiding principles for reform than do
the other rites. Placed alongside the other rites, it seems
ordinary enough, even though present regulations restrict
it to situations where the sacrament could either not be
properly celebrated in another form or not be celebrated at
all. Because of its setting, the absolution given here might
better be termed public or communal, because of the connotations of emergency and imminent death attached to
general absolution.

Such situations are considered extraordinary, but, as in
the case of canonical penance's provision for the dying,
extending the sacrament into an extraordinary situation
shows how it is understood. Here, sinners present themselves to the assembled Church as repentant and the
Church realizes itself as a reconciling community by receiving them back. Sincere repentance or conversion is

232

the major condition for reconciliation. A new epoch in the history of penance begins. Focus on sincere conversion continues the recent emphasis on individual contrition, but expression in a community context revives the ancient tradition. As the medieval postponement of satisfaction until after confession showed satisfaction to be secondary, this postponement of confession shows that accusation is secondary to sincere conversion and genuine reconciliation.[65]

From this perspective, the second rite is more than a new setting for private confession and the first rite is more than an embellishment of private confession. Both are approximations, in varying community situations, of a sacrament social and ecclesial in its nature and effects and thus fully celebrated only in full community. In structure, both parallel the third form. This structure, itself very different from the Tridentine form, particularly in celebrating the Word, likewise expresses what is new in the RP and fundamentally reorients penance. In each rite, the Church's activity is primary.

The second rite, by putting traditional private confession and absolution within a liturgy, could appear to be only an updated setting for private confession or a helpful way to prepare for confession, but it is more than that. It does introduce people to communal celebrations by putting the familiar rite into a new context, but its restoration of the ecclesial sense and the experience it offers of prayer, worship, and the place and power of the Word are too basic to allow it to be considered as anything less than a new form of the sacrament. Pope Paul VI, in fact, considered it the preferable and normal sacramental form for our times for these reasons.[66] Its place and form in the reformed liturgy of penance is described in RP 22–30, a model celebration is given in RP 48–59, and alternate texts are provided in RP 94–100, 202–214. A large lectionary is included (RP 101–201) and the penitential celebrations in Appendix II are also proposed as models.

Despite the retention of what the Constitution on the Liturgy calls the less preferable quasi-private format of celebration, the first rite still expresses several of the basic principles of the liturgical reform and also emphasizes the personal encounter and transformation that are essential to conversion and reconciliation. Even as an abbreviation of the full sacramental celebration it shows that sacramental ritual requires:

1. Personal interaction and dialogue if it is to be sacrament of the encounter with God in Christ.
2. Fullness of vital content rather than detachment from life: a celebration of what is being lived.
3. Community as its only intelligible context rather than isolation from others.
4. The impassioned warmth of prayer and worship rather than the cold objectivity of legal procedures.

This rite also presupposes that the goal of the sacrament of penance is not forgiveness of sins but reconciliation with Church and God and that conversion is first lived out in community by the penitent, with celebration being the prayerful though private ritual reliving of what has been taking place. It seems long and complex in comparison with the pre-Vatican II format, but this is because it expresses, in muted fashion, the basic orientations of the conciliar reform.

The penitential celebration, regarded as nonsacramental, differs from the other forms in lacking the single expression of community found in all three sacramental rites, the proclamation of reconciliation, but its value is that it ritualizes conversion more fully and shows that the Church is always penitent. Developed in the 1950s as a scripture service to prepare people for confession, it came to have a special value in forming penitents by providing the ritual ecclesial setting wherein authentic Christian conversion could take shape and mature, a value noted in RP 36–37 (cf. Appendix II, 1). Though penance (conversion) is ritualized in the other sacramental celebrations, it has fuller ritual expression here in order to support and deepen it

234

and show that penance is more than an occasional purgative but rather a vital part of being Christian. The penitential celebration promotes both "conversion of life and purification of heart" (RP 37), extending penance into everyday life both by shaping behavior and forming the attitudes that are the base of a contrition that goes beyond emotion. It is a crucial—though largely ignored—part of the reform, because only with the revitalization of the virtue of penance and the realization that the sacramental ritual recapitulates life experience can the new rites have hope of success.

Recognizing that the Church itself is penitent can be a major factor in building Christian community and restoring penance to a place in the life of the Church. The most significant ministry that can be offered the converting sinner is the acceptance, encouragement, and support that comes from being part of a converting community. This is symbolized more clearly in the penitential celebration than in any of the other liturgies of penance because here the assembly as a whole—including its presider—manifests repentance and seeks renewal.

The penitential celebration of the Word calling us to conversion not only offers the Church's support but also proclaims the renewal and freedom from sin that is ours in Christ, that is, in the Church. The efficacy of God's Word means that this power is realized and drawn on in the very proclamation and that the penitential celebration is therefore not completely extrinsic to the sacrament. Whether in preparing people for subsequent confession or in forming children and catechumens or in sustaining Christians' lifelong conversion, the penitential celebration has an intrinsic value, particularly in the community's celebration of Lent (RP 40b; Appendix II, 5). Its importance is underlined by the fact that Appendix II of the RP provides several model celebrations for different seasons (Lent [5–19] and Advent [20–24]), on different themes (sin and conversion [25–30],[67] the prodigal's return [31–36], the beatitudes [37–42]), and for different types of groups (children [43–53], young people [54–61], the sick [62–73]).

The RP's only mention of children comes in connection with the penitential celebration. RP 37 indicates its value in forming children's conscience about sin and redemption in Christ. Careful preparation and planning, with their participation, is especially important (Appendix II, 2, 3, 44, 54). Appendix II (43–53) provides a model celebration for younger children (including those who have not yet shared in the sacrament) and there is one for young people (54–61). In view of the energy expended on the question of the relative order of first confession and first communion in recent years, it is interesting that the RP ignores the issue and, except in these celebrations, presumes adult celebrants of conversion and reconciliation. That is not unexpected in a ritual, since, from a liturgical and theological perspective, it is incongruous to speak of conversion and reconciliation when initiation is barely underway. From such a perspective, penance has been used in recent centuries as an ersatz confirmation, a ritual completion of baptism as initiates are brought into the eucharistic assembly.[68]

Though adaptation for the sake of pastoral effectiveness has been a basic principle of liturgical reform, there has been little effort to adapt the RP to differing cultural situations.[69] Where there has been adaptation, it has often been to avoid implementing the RP. The RP offers more freedom for adaptation than most rituals (RP 38–40) and explicitly states that "pastoral need" may dictate omitting or shortening some parts (RP 21), but it also explicitly calls for enlarging on the elements to make the celebration more "rich and fruitful" (RP 40a). Pastoral need may call for shortening, but it may more likely call for further development. Celebration must meet penitents' real needs and, especially at the present time of transition, respect their sensitivities, but the need for omitting or adding any element must be measured by the importance of the element's relationship to the sacrament, not personal convenience or taste.

Episcopal conferences may adapt the RP, establishing disciplinary regulations and composing new texts (RP 38). Diocesan bishops regulate penance within their dioceses, including adaptations permitted by the national conference and general absolution within the limits of law (RP 39). Priests may adapt the rites to the concrete circumstances of the penitents (RP 40). This includes shortening or enlarging parts (RP 40a), but they must keep the essential structure and the entire form of absolution. (Only when the penitent is in imminent danger of death may the priest use only the "essential words" of the absolution formula in the rite for reconciling individuals—RP 21—or the emergency form of the communal rite—RP 64–65.) In general, the freedom for adaptation is intended to make the celebration richer and more effective; it cannot be invoked to justify the minimal, meager, routine celebration that has been characteristic in the past. Another point of adaptation is the responsibility of parish priests to provide and plan occasional communal celebrations or penitential celebrations throughout the year, particularly during Lent (RP 40b). They are advised to have others assist in the planning and preparation so that the service will be more effective.

Pastoral benefit is always the major consideration, but adequate assessment and response to needs requires sound knowledge of the sacrament and familiarity with the structure, style, and modes of celebration. Neither pressures of time nor numbers and wishes of penitents justify abuses in any celebration. They call instead for a revision of priorities or attitudes or discipline. The major pastoral need, however, is for understanding and appreciation of the RP's orientations. Failure to internalize its theological foundations and be comfortable with its liturgical dynamics make it impossible for a priest to preside properly or catechize adequately and for a penitent to benefit most effectively from the celebration.

1. Pope John Paul II made this clear regarding the interpretation of the 1983 Code of Canon Law: the council, not previous law, is the primary base for interpretation and subsequent law is intended to be in complete conformity with the council. See his January 26, 1984, address to the Roman Rota, *Origins* 13 (1984) 583–585, especially p. 584.

2. *Schema de liturgia,* 56; this became article 72 in the final text. The schemata and records of conciliar deliberations are in the *Acta Synodalia Sacrosancti Concilii Oecumenici Vaticani II* (Romae: Typis Polyglottis Vaticanis, 1962–). The *Acta* do not indicate how article 56 came to be added to the schema that was completed on July 23, 1962, and presented when the council opened on October 11, but the January 16, 1962, report of the central commission in charge of preparation indicates an initial interest only in simplifying canonical regulations on faculties. See *Preparatory Reports: Second Vatican Council* (Philadelphia: Westminister, 1965), p. 54.

3. *Congregatio Generalis* XIII, November 6; *Congregatio Generalis* XIV, November 7; *Acta* 1, part 2, pp. 164, 180, 343, 348, 380.

4. Ibid., pp. 170, 358, 364.

5. Ibid., pp. 168, 320, 346, 385.

6. Ibid., pp. 174–175, 188, 377.

7. Ibid., pp. 178–179. A quick written response insisted there should be no such change; see ibid., p. 362.

8. *Acta* 2, part 2, pp. 558–559.

9. Ibid., p. 567.

10. *Ad gentes,* 36 and *Optatam totius,* 2 also mention works of penance and mortification.

11. *Presbyterorum ordinis,* 13, 18; *Christus dominus,* 30. Cf. *Sacrosanctum concilium,* 59.

12. *Presbyterorum ordinis,* 5; *Christus dominus,* 15. *Lumen gentium,* 26 mentions the bishops' role as moderators of the penitential discipline.

13. *The Documents of Vatican II*, edited by Walter M. Abbott (New York: Herder and Herder, 1966), pp. 3–4.

14. I have analyzed this literature as a means of assessing the RP's relationship to contemporary theology; see "A Decade of Discussion on the Reform of Penance." For shorter surveys of the theological literature, see Gabriel M. Coless, "The Sacrament of Penance: Creative Ferment," *Worship* 47 (1973) 463–472; Charles E. Curran, "The Sacrament of Penance Today" in his *Contemporary Problems in Moral Theology* (Notre Dame, Ind.: Fides, 1970), pp. 1–96; Felix Funke, "Survey of Published Writings on Confession over the Past Ten Years," *Concilium* 61 (1971) 120–132. For a theological analysis of the renewal, see *The Renewal of the Sacrament of Penance* (Committee Report; Catholic Theological Society of America, 1975).

15. The committee's records have not been published nor have their reports and drafts. I have examined some of these; it is possible to piece together a general picture of the committee's progress from these documents, official announcements, and articles published by members of the committees. See especially Julio Jimenez, "Reformas en el rito de la penitencia," *Teologia y Vida* 9 (1968) 135–146; Juan Antonio Gracia, "Historia de la reforma del nuevo ritual," *Phase* 14 (1974) 11–22; Carlo Braga, "Il nuovo 'Ordo Paenitentiae,' " *Ephemerides Liturgicae* 89 (1975) 165–176; and Pelagio Visentin, "Il nuovo 'ordo paenitentiae': Genesi-valutazione-potenzialità," in *La celebrazione della penitenza cristiana* (Turin: Marietti, 1981), pp. 64–78.

16. This was apparently due to Heggen's advocacy of communal celebrations. By 1966, two of his books on penance were in their third edition and had been translated into several languages. For English translations, see *Confession and the Service of Penance* (Notre Dame, Ind.: University of Notre Dame Press, 1967) and *Children and Confession* (London: Sheed and Ward, 1969). See also "The Service of Penance: A Description and Appreciation of Some Models," *Concilium* 61 (1971) 134–154. Other works by members of the committees are noted in the bibliography.

17. Schema 265 (De Paenitentia, 3), undated; Schema 267 (De Paenitentia, 4), January 25, 1968; Schema 272 (De Paenitentia, 5), February 17, 1968.

18. Schema 279 (De Paenitentia, 6) is dated March 16, 1968. A second and final draft (Schema 279bis; De Paenitentia, 6bis) is dated April 22, 1968, and there is an addendum of May 11, 1968.

19. "By his self-giving our Lord Jesus Christ has set the whole world free and given his disciples power to forgive sins. By the grace of the Holy Spirit and my ministry may he absolve you from your sins and restore you to complete unity with the Church. He lives and reigns forever and ever."

The formula condenses the absolution in the Roman Pontifical's Holy Thursday reconciliation rite. See also *Pontificale Romano-Germanicum*, XCIX, 246; Vogel-Elze, II, p. 65.

20. "Our Lord Jesus Christ, who redeemed the world by his passion and resurrection, by the grace of the Holy Spirit absolves you from your sins and fully restores you to peace with the Church. He lives and reigns forever and ever."

The formula, a new text drawn from various traditional sources, follows the declarative model often found in Eastern liturgies.

21. "May our Lord Jesus Christ absolve you and by his authority I absolve you from your sins in the name of the Father and of the Son and of the Holy Spirit."

At the priest's discretion, the traditional "Passio" prayer could be added. The committee felt that, with minor changes, the "Passio" prayer would be sufficient but was unwilling to abandon completely the formula in use.

22. "We ask you, Lord, to grant your servant the fitting fruit of penitence so that by obtaining pardon for what he/she has done he/she may be restored blameless to your holy Church, from whose wholeness he/she has strayed by sinning. [We ask this] through Christ our Lord."

This prayer from the Gelasian (n. 357; Mohlberg, *Liber Sacramentorum*, p. 57) is also in the Roman Pontifical's Holy Thursday rite. The committee acknowledged that vernacular translations would have to avoid the implication of canonical excommunication.

23. See *Notitiae* 4 (1968) 183.

24. Schema 297 (De Paenitentia, 7), dated July 2, 1968.

25. Schema 312 (De Paenitentia, 8), dated September 28, 1968.

26. Schema 318 (De Paenitentia, 9), dated October 7, 1968.

27. The first formula was amended to read: "Our Lord Jesus Christ has offered himself for us to the Father in sacrifice and given his Church power to forgive sins. By the grace of the Holy Spirit may he absolve you from your sins and restore you to complete peace with the Church. He lives and reigns forever and ever."

The second was amended as follows: "Our Lord Jesus Christ, who redeemed the world by his passion and resurrection, by the grace of the Holy Spirit through my ministry forgives your sins and restores you to the full life of the Church. He lives and reigns forever and ever."

The third: "Our Lord Jesus Christ forgives your sins by my ministry and fully restores you to the Church's peace. He lives and reigns with the Father and the Holy Spirit forever and ever."

28. "In the name of our Lord Jesus Christ and in the power of the Holy Spirit I absolve you from your sins and restore you completely to peace with the Church."

29. The committee had met at Douvres-La-Delevrande, France, July 15–19, and in Luxembourg, September 9–14. Its report went through several drafts: Schema 350 (De Paenitentia, 10), dated September 23, 1969; Schema 356 (De Paenitentia, 11), dated October 30, 1969; Schema 356bis (De Paenitentia, 11 bis), with the same date.

30. Schema 361 (De Paenitentia, 12), dated January 31, 1970. This contained a report of the committee's work, the criteria for the reform, a survey of the history of penance, a description of the revised rites, particular problems encountered, and the text of the proposed rite.

31. In a statement of July 9, 1970, according to Visentin, "Il nuovo 'ordo paenitentiae,' " p. 65.

32. José Luis Larrabe, "Renovacion posconciliar del sacramento de la penitencia," *Phase* 11 (1971) 459–478. Larrabe comments on Schema 318 of October 7, 1968.

33. These will be discussed in more detail below, pp. 218ff.

34. Franco Sottocornola, *A Look at the New Rite of Penance* (Washington, D.C.: United States Catholic Conference, 1975), p. 2; "Les nouveaux rites de la pénitence. Commentaire," *Questions*

Liturgiques 55 (1974) 95. Though both Sottocornola and Gracia were on the second committee and knew something of what had happened to the work of the first, Gracia's article is much more revealing.

35. Schema 386 (De Paenitentia, 13), dated October 20, 1972, exists in two forms. Schema 387 (De Paenitentia, 14), together with an appendix containing plans for penitential celebrations, is dated November 30, 1972. Two more appendices, dated December 1, 1972, and February 14, 1973, were later added.

36. I have not been able to examine the February 1973 document. It is mentioned by Visentin, "Il nuovo 'Ordo Paeniten-tiae,' " p. 68. Schema 420 (De Paenitentia, 15) is dated April 3, 1973. Schema 423 (De Paenitentia, 16) is dated July 17, 1973. It is unclear how the various schemata relate to the process of consultation.

37. The final form of the new rite is Schema 427 (De Paenitentia, 17) dated December 2, 1973.

38. *Acta Apostolicae Sedis* 58 (1966) 177–198; excerpts may be found in *Documents on the Liturgy, 1963–1979* (Collegeville, Minn.: Liturgical Press, 1982), pp. 936–943 (DOL 358, nos. 3017–3030). "Paenitemini" is cited twice in the RP: (1) deeper love and commitment is the goal of penance ("Paenitemini," p. 179; RP 5); (2) on the nature of repentance as *metanoia* ("Paenitem-ini," p. 179; RP 6a). The general perspectives of "Paenitemini" and the RP parallel each other closely.

39. *Acta Apostolicae Sedis* 59 (1967) 5–24; *Documents on the Liturgy*, pp. 995–1009 (DOL 386, nos. 3155–3187). See also *Enchiridion Indulgentiarum: Normae et Concessiones* (Rome: Typis Polyglottis Vaticanis, 1968) and cf. *Documents on the Liturgy*, pp. 1011–1015 (DOL 390, nos. 3193–3228), for the norms on indulgences. The 1983 Code of Canon Law has six canons on indulgences (992–997).

40. *Indulgentiarum doctrina* is open to the position, developed by Poschmann and Rahner as a result of their historical studies, that indulgences are signs of the Church's intercessory prayer rather than jurisdictional grants from a treasury of merits. See Karl Rahner, "On the Official Teaching of the Church Today on the Subject of Indulgences," *Theological Investigations* 10 (New York: Herder and Herder, 1973) 166–198. The recasting of the

object of old controversy helps clear the way for finding effective ways to express such intercession and assistance; indulgence grants measured by days and years (now eliminated) had been a pious fiction since the demise of tariff penance. For some suggestions, see Peter J. Beer, "What Price Indulgences? Trent and Today," *Theological Studies* 39 (1978) 526–535.

For further consideration of the theology of indulgences, see Charles Journet, "Théologie des indulgences," *Nova et Vetera* 4 (1966) 81–111, or *Teologia delle indulgenze* (Rome: Ancora, 1966).

41. "Dum canonicarum legum recognitio," *Acta Apostolicae Sedis* 63 (1971) 318–319; *Documents on the Liturgy*, pp. 947–948 (DOL 360, nos. 3032–3037). While stressing the value of the sacrament, the norms gave religious greater freedom in choosing confessors by no longer requiring special jurisdiction for hearing the confessions of women religious and required less frequent confession: twice a month rather than weekly. The reasons given for frequent confession are based on those given in *Mystici corporis*.

42. Curial documents are in *Documents on the Liturgy*, pp. 985–991 (DOL 379–382, nos. 3141–3151).

43. "Sacramentum paenitentiae: Normae pastorales circa absolutionem sacramentalem generali modo impertiendam," *Acta Apostolicae Sedis* 64 (1972) 510–514. The English text is in *Documents on the Liturgy*, pp. 948–951 (DOL 361, nos. 3038–3051). These norms are cited nine times in the RP:
1. The need for confessors to be prepared to exercise their ministry (PN 12; RP 10b); 2. The conditions for general absolution (PN 3; RP 31); 3. In special circumstances, the possibility of imparting general absolution outside the cases specified by the bishop (PN 5; RP 32); 4. The requirement that people be informed during the celebration of the conditions (PN 6, 11; RP 33); 5. Subsequent confession of grave sins required (PN 7, 8; RP 34); 6. Homily and instruction on requirement of subsequent confession of grave sins (PN 6; RP 35a); 7. Penitential celebrations are not to be confused with celebrations of the sacrament (PN 10; RP 36); 8. The value of penitential celebrations (PN 10; RP 36); 9. Bishops' conferences are to determine the conditions for general absolution (NP 5; RP 39).
The number of citations indicates the major influence of the Pastoral Norms on the 1973 RP.

44. The first norm appears aimed directly at the draft rite, which stated: "Although individual confession of all grave sins to the competent minister is ordinarily required for obtaining sacramental absolution, there are circumstances in which some generic or general confession of sins or even some sign of internal repentance is sufficient."

45. See, for example, Francis J. Buckley, "Recent Developments in the Sacrament of Penance," *Communio* 1 (1974) 83–98; Karl Lehmann, "General Absolution—Private Confession," *Communio* [International Catholic Review] 1 (1972) 319–322; Carl J. Peter, "The New Norms for Communal Penance: Will They Help?" *Worship* 47 (1973) 2–10; John R. Sheets, "Communal Penance and Private Confession: The New Directives," *Communio* 1 (1974) 99–102.

46. "Bussandacht und Einzelbeichte. Anmerkungen zum Römischen Erlass über das Busssakrament," *Stimmen der Zeit* 190 (1972) 363–372, especially pp. 370–371.

47. For example, Ladislas M. Orsy, "Communal Penance: Some Preliminary Questions on Sin and Sacrament," *Worship* 47 (1973) 338–345; Edward Quinn, "Home Thoughts on Penance," *Month* 233, 2nd N.S. 5 (1972) 369–371.

48. John Gallen, "General Sacramental Absolution: Pastoral Remarks on Pastoral Norms," *Theological Studies* 34 (1973) 114–121; Robert Hovda, *Living Worship*, October 1972.

49. See, for example, Monique Brulin, "Orientations pastorales de la pénitence dans divers pays," *La Maison Dieu* 117 (1974) 38–62.

50. For the bishop of Juneau's rationale, see Francis T. Hurley, "Communal Absolution—Anatomy of a Decision," *America* 127 (1972) 203–206.

51. Congregation for Divine Worship, Decree "Reconciliationem inter Deum et homines," AAS 66 (1974) 172–173; *Notitiae* 10 (1974) 42–43; *Documents on the Liturgy*, pp. 955–956 (DOL 367, nos. 3063–3065); Sacra Congregatio pro Cultu Divino, *Rituale Romanum . . . Ordo Paenitentiae* (Editio typica; Rome: Typis Polyglottis Vaticanis, 1974).

Though the ritual was promulgated by the Congregation for Divine Worship, the decree also bears the signature of Cardinal Villot, the Papal Secretary of State, the first liturgical document to do so, perhaps because the congregation lacked a president at the time. A reference to the "special mandate" of the pope, also unusual, is perhaps due to earlier opposition to liturgical reforms.

English-language commentaries on the RP include J. D. Crichton, *The Ministry of Reconciliation* (London: Geoffrey Chapman, 1974); Ralph Keifer and Frederick R. McManus, *The Rite of Penance: Commentaries*, v. 1 (Washington, D.C.: The Liturgical Conference, 1975). For a historical and theological study of penance in light of the RP's orientations, see Monika Hellwig, *Sign of Reconciliation and Conversion*. Richard Gula gives valuable pastoral suggestions in *To Walk Together Again: The Sacrament of Reconciliation* (New York: Paulist Press, 1984) and Doris Donnelly offers a helpful "workbook," *Putting Forgiveness into Practice* (Allen, Texas: Argus Communications, 1982). For assessments, see also Edward K. Braxton, "The New Rite of Reconciliation in American Culture," *Chicago Studies* 15 (1976) 185–198, and William Marrevee, "New Order of Penance: Is It Adequate?" *Église et Théologie* 7 (1976) 119–137.

52. This was not the case worldwide. The Italian translation, for example, was approved on March 7, 1974, and implemented on April 21, 1974. For a survey of implementation and statements issued by European episcopal conferences, see Philippe Rouillard, "Indicazioni teologico-pastorali sul rito della penitenza negli interventi delle conferenze episcopali" in *La celebrazione della penitenza cristiana* (Turin: Marietti, 1981), pp. 112–122.

53. Paul VI's initial enthusiasm seems to have given way to a desire to rein in those putting the RP to full use. Numerous homilies and addresses can be found in *L'Osservatore Romano*, *Notitiae*, and other places. Some of the more important papal remarks on general absolution are in *Documents on the Liturgy*, for example, of Paul VI, DOL 363, 376, 378, and of John Paul II, DOL 75, 192, 291; see also John Paul II's encyclical "Redemptor hominis," 20 (DOL 191, no. 1331), and *Reconciliatio et Paenitentia*: On Reconciliation and Penance in the Mission of the Church Today (Vatican City: Libreria Editrice Vaticana, 1984). I have examined the latter document in more detail in *Worship* 59 (1985) 98–116.

54. April 30, 1976 letter of the Congregation for Sacraments and Divine Worship and the Congregation for the Clergy [*Documents*

on the Liturgy, pp. 986–988 (DOL 380)]; March 31, 1977 letter "In quibusdam ecclesiae partibus" of the Congregation for Sacraments and Divine Worship and the Congregation for the Clergy [*Documents on the Liturgy*, pp. 988–990 (DOL 381)]; May 20, 1977 reply of the Congregation for Sacraments and Divine Worship and the Congregation for the Clergy [*Documents on the Liturgy*, pp. 990–991 (DOL 382)]

55. In the United States, use of general absolution in Memphis and Newark occasioned the January 14, 1977, letter of the Congregation for the Doctrine of the Faith [see *Documents on the Liturgy*, pp. 978–979 (DOL 375)] and the January 20, 1978, reply to a query [see Documents on the Liturgy, pp. 980–981 (DOL 377)]. There were similar cases in England. The language of the RP, like that in previous documents, implies that the situation it describes is an *example* of the grave necessity that allows for general absolution. Bishop Dozier of Memphis, among others, determined in accordance with RP 39 that the situation with which he was presented was another extraordinary situation where individual confession was morally impossible. The Roman reaction seems to indicate the curial view that despite theological consensus and existing regulations only physical impossibility excuses from observance of the Tridentine requirement.

56. See "Celebrating the Sacrament of Penance" (Lenten pastoral letter of Bishop Frank Harrison of Syracuse to priests), *Origins* 10 (1981) 632–635; "Celebrating the Sacrament of Reconciliation" (pastoral letter of the bishops to Texas to priests), *Origins* 11 (1982) 489–495.

57. For example, canon 960 and RP 31; canon 961, 1 and RP 31; canon 961, 2 and RP 32, 39, and 40; canon 962 and RP 33; canon 964 and RP 12 and 38.

58. *Origins* 11 (1982) 565–580. For a more detailed study of the Synod, see my "Church Authority and the Sacrament of Penance: The Synod of Bishops," *Worship* 58 (1984) 194–214.

59. "Penance and Reconciliation," *Origins* 13 (1984) 513–524. There are several points of confusion in this text, generally due to missing words or phrases. Cardinal Ratzinger did not release the report until long after the Synod.

60. *Origins* 13 (1983) 376. For presentations and statements from the Synod, see *Origins* 13 (1983), nos. 18–22. Several of these were also published in *Living Light* 20 (1984) 219–247 and in *Penance and Reconciliation in the Mission of the Church* (Washington, D.C.: National Conference of Catholic Bishops, 1984).

61. The importance of the introduction was underlined by a letter of the Congregation of the Doctrine of the Faith to Cardinal Marty, president of the French episcopal conference, on June 3, 1974. The letter insisted on "an *integral and faithful* translation" of the introduction in all vernacular editions. The congregation went on to say: "This text in fact provides doctrinal and disciplinary principles that apply to the whole Church. It therefore stands as the obligatory reference point and provides a clear setting for adaptations that the various conferences of bishops judge to be necessary." See *Documents on the Liturgy*, p. 971 (DOL 370, no. 3114).

The introduction is divided into six parts:
1. The Mystery of Reconciliation in the History of Salvation (RP 1–2); 2. The Reconciliation of Penitents in the Church's Life (RP 3–7); 3. Offices and Ministries in the Reconciliation of Penitents (RP 8–11); 4. The Celebration of the Sacrament of Penance (RP 12–35); 5. Penitential Celebrations (RP 36–37); 6. Adaptations of the Rite to Various Regions and Circumstances (RP 38–40).
The first two parts, which are primarily doctrinal and theological, will be discussed in Chapter 8 and the remainder, together with the rites themselves, will be examined in Chapter 9.

62. J. D. Crichton sees it as the model rite not only because of its clear expression of the conciliar understanding of the sacrament's nature and purpose but also because in it the general pattern of sacramental reform is clearest: liturgy is an act of the Church; the Word is proclaimed; the rite is visible; the people as a community can participate. See *The Ministry of Reconciliation*, pp. 11–12. McManus likewise sees it as the clearest expression of the Liturgy Constitution's desire to bring out "the public and communal features of every liturgical celebration." See Keifer and McManus, *The Rite of Penance: Commentaries*, v. 1, p. 61. Similar statements are found in most commentaries.

63. In addition to works such as Eppacher's, which have already been cited, see Joseph A. Jungmann, "The Question of General Absolution," *Teaching All Nations* 4 (1967) 426–431. José Ramos-

Regidor, " 'Reconciliation' in the Primitive Church and Its Lessons for Theology and Pastoral Practice Today," *Concilium* 61 (1971) 76–88, also suggests how ancient forms provide precedent for meeting current pastoral needs. While the council mandated a reformed liturgy that maintained continuity with recent practice, it also insisted that tradition could not be restricted to the recent past. For a discussion of conflict between the RP (which allows for absolution after a generic common confession in certain situations) and a literal or fundamentalist interpretation of Trent, see Angelo Amato, "Il concilio di Trento e il nuovo 'ordo paenitentiae': Alcune considerazioni a proposito della legittimazione dogmatica dei nuovi riti di riconciliazione," *Ephemerides Liturgicae* 89 (1975) 282–293.

64. For the complementary character of the three rites and their respective values as seen by a member of the drafting commission, see Franco Sottocornola, "Les nouveaux rites," pp. 128–129.

65. The first epoch was that of penance; the second, that of confession; the third will be that of reconciliation. For a more extended discussion, see Sottocornola, "Les nouveaux rites," pp. 109–113, 128.

66. See, for example, *Documents on the Liturgy*, p. 970 (DOL 369, no. 3112). For a similar, more detailed evaluation regarding the second rite as the ideal sacramental form, see Charles E. Miller, "The Best of Three Rites," *Homiletic and Pastoral Review* 78, No. 3 (December 1977), pp. 55–58.

67. This celebration is unique in that all three readings are from the gospels.

68. Though the RP ignores the controversy over first confession, canon 914 mentions first communion prior to confession, seemingly requiring more of children than of adults, who are required to confess only when conscious of grave sin. Canonists may have to wrestle with this, but the basic principle that the sacrament is required before eucharist only for those conscious of grave sin holds, and few theologians consider a child of seven capable of mortal sin. Law presently requires that children be prepared for both sacraments; however, they cannot be required to receive penance as a condition of receiving communion. The current fragmented and unrealistic situation of law and practice is

the consequence of a centuries-long toleration of a disintegrated sacrament of initiation. Disintegration obscured the intrinsic logic and interrelation of sacramental celebrations and led to their being shuffled like cards, able to be done in practically any order.

Children do require help to develop an awareness of sin and their need for forgiveness, but how this is furthered simply by private confession is unclear. The RP's suggestion on the value of penitential celebrations in this regard would seem to recommend a progressive formation in conversion and repentance, proceeding from the penitential celebration to a communal celebration with group absolution, then to the communal celebration with individual confession, and finally to the individual rite.

69. For a communal confession in Africa, see Baudouin Waterkeyn, "The Sacrament of Forgiveness Celebrated in Living Christian Communities," *Lumen Vitae* 37 (1982) 191–194.

Chapter Eight

Theological Foundations

The Introduction to the RP begins by showing that the mystery of reconciliation is key to perceiving God's work in our world and understanding redemption, conversion, and the sacraments (RP 1–2). This mystery gives focus to the Church's mission and ministry. Though initiation (baptism and eucharist) is the primary sacramental experience of reconciliation, the mystery is powerfully present in the Church's reconciliation of penitents (RP 3–7). In line with the conciliar mandate, the social and ecclesial character has first place in the understanding and manner of celebrating the sacrament.

RECONCILIATION AND SALVATION

RP 1–2 sketch the pattern of humanity's reconciliation to God. God always takes the initiative, as is clearest in Jesus, who shows divine compassion by calling people to conversion and welcoming sinners. His cure of the sick signs his power to forgive sin. However, obedient love for God and compassionate kindness for people is most evident in the Paschal Mystery of his dying and rising. This again made humanity one with God and released the power of the Spirit to enliven the Church, its work and worship, its preaching, and its sacraments, especially the eucharist, which show Christ's victory. In baptism, we die with Christ to sin and rise with him to live for God. In the eucharist, his saving power is present to forgive sin and unite us in the Spirit. In the ministry exercised in the sacrament of penance, divine grace is renewed in those who have sinned. But by speaking of "reconciliation" rather than the "forgiveness of sins," the RP reorients our understanding of redemption, conversion, and the sacraments.

Redemption
The mystery of redemption is the obvious context or horizon for understanding the sacrament of reconciliation, since faith in Christ as redeemer enables believers to recognize and deal with sin and guilt. Redemption, a commercial metaphor, is only one way of expressing what has happened to us in Christ: we have been bought back, returned to God's ownership after being in another's possession. The RP proposes another scriptural model: redemption as reconciliation. The RP is not always consistent, sometimes reverting back to something like the Celtic legal model, but personal relationships provide the basic metaphor, and reconciliation after estrangement is its primary model for understanding the salvation that is ours in Christ.

Studies of sacramental history have shown the primacy of reconciliation in ancient penance, but it was probably the recent "sociological transformation of the Christian mind"[1] that called attention to the corporate character of Christian faith, enabled us to see history differently, and made it possible to retrieve this forgotten truth. Nineteenth- and twentieth-century historical studies and twentieth-century theological reflections prepared the way for this rediscovery, and recent catechetical literature and popular works of spirituality have helped to disseminate it. Conciliar documents and postconciliar reforms gave it official status. Now we are more inclined to speak of sin and penance in terms of a relationship of friendship with God (cf. RP 5, 7) rather than a relationship to legal norms. We recognize the sacraments as manifesting Christ's actions in the Church and enabling us to share his relationship to the Father.

The rediscovery is both profoundly biblical and theologically useful. It reveals how various areas of doctrine interrelate (e.g., Christology, ecclesiology, sacramentology, eschatology, and ethics). It emphasizes and reintegrates the personal and ecclesial dimensions of the sacrament of penance. In particular, it integrates the personalist perspective of sacramental theology and the communal emphasis of ecclesiology. It has affinities to widely shared perspectives within contemporary culture, even if, in other situations, it is strongly countercultural.

By basing itself on a personal and relational view of sin, this approach to redemption and the sacrament of penance situates the believer within the history of salvation and a historic community. This releases the individual from an isolation where sin and salvation were matters between the soul and the Creator. Redemption is shown to have a covenant structure and the individual's relationship to God and the individual's relationship to his or her neighbor are no longer in separate compartments. Reconciliation with others then becomes the sacrament of reconciliation with God, the personal and communal dimensions of sin and penance are balanced, and the sacrament is situated in close relationship to the Church's mission and the Christian's everyday life.

Reconciliation can, of course, be no more than a fad word, a synonym for understandings formerly conveyed by confession or penance. A one-sided understanding of reconciliation, emphasizing only the social dimension, can also flatten it out and almost eliminate the personal relationship with God.[2] Despite the dangers and occasional regressions, redemption is understood as reconciliation in the RP. Baptism is presented as the paradigmatic experience of reconciliation through Christ's Paschal Mystery (RP 1, 2, 7b). The season of Lent is regarded as a special time for a community experience of conversion and reconciliation with God as its goal (RP 13, 40b). The new emphasis on the Word of God is based on this understanding (RP 17, 22, 24, 36–37). The purpose of the sacrament is presented as deeper love and friendship and reconciliation with God and the Church (RP 5 and passim). Absolution is understood as reconciliation: it is the sign by which God grants salvation and renews the broken covenant (RP 6d). The formulas of absolution explicitly recall and proclaim the history of salvation as the mystery of our being reconciled to God in Christ (RP 46, 62). Reconciliation is, in fact, the constant theme of the RP.

Conversion

The mystery of reconciliation is, at the same time, the mystery of conversion: conversion is for the sake of reconciliation as well as a consequence of it. Just as the divine and human elements and contributions cannot be isolated from one another in salvation history, the same occurs in the mystery of conversion and reconciliation; divine initiative and human response are inseparable. *Metanoia* or conversion is, in fact, a process in which the penitent is so deeply and personally engaged as a human and a Christian—though a sinful one—that the personal involvement and response contribute to the constitution of the sacrament. The acts of the penitent are parts of the sacrament (RP 6).

Process should perhaps be underlined. History suggests that a major root of the current crisis is that penance, once a long process of conversion, collapsed, folded into itself like an accordion, and was reduced to a ritual. The RP extends it out again as a characteristic dimension of the Christian life (RP 4, 6a, 7, 20). Just as God's dealings with humanity have a history, so do God's workings in the life of the individual. Ancient penance showed greater sophistication in this regard than later forms, because its framers knew that neither divine grace nor the human response to it can be realized in a moment. God reaches through time into an individual's life and the individual responds over time. Those who entered the order of penitents were not expected to have undergone conversion but only to have the willingness to be converted. Its liturgy and discipline assisted them in hearing the divine call and responding to it.

Its structures helped them to grow and mature as converting Christians.

Scriptural and historical studies substantiate the process character of conversion, but the most significant factor in the modern rediscovery is probably moral theologians' use of psychology to develop a more authentic and realistic understanding of sin and penance. Sin understood as an individual, objective, and impersonal act supports a mechancial, legal, and formal understanding of penance. This grew under the influence of the penitentials, with their attempted precision in differentiating sins, and was reinforced by late medieval scholasticism, with its distinctions and categories. The post-Tridentine preoccupation with integral confession and judgment sharpened the view of sin as an individual isolated act, with the sincerest of Christians frequently and subtly excommunicated by the manualists' understanding of mortal sin. Ecclesial forgiveness then became a ritual event. Modern psychology, with its stress on the complexity of human decision making, has led moral theologians to emphasize the subjective and psychological aspects of sin and conversion and thus to diminish the importance of a single act in establishing an orientation either toward or away from God. Contemporary theology is consequently more inclined to view conversion as a process rather than a decision and the opposite of sin as faith rather than morally correct behavior.

There are obvious implications for the theology and practice of penance in terms of the dispositions expected of the penitent, what the penitent is expected to do, how the Church assists penitents, and the general relationship of the sacrament to the everyday life situation of the penitent and the Church. But only through an emphasis on the social and ecclesial dimensions of sin and conversion can a fundamental option approach avoid the danger of overpsychologizing and making the whole matter purely human and totally subjective. Most contemporary theologians adopting this approach do, in fact, avoid that danger more successfully than did past theologians preoccupied with the psychology of contrition.

However, moral theologians offer few practical suggestions for organizing penitential discipline and liturgy to structure and support the process of conversion. The same is true of the RP itself. While it understands conversion as a process, it suggests no structured support other than repeated use of the rites, especially the penitential celebrations.

The RP's understanding of sin likewise reflects contemporary theological developments. The initial emphasis on salvation history situates sin in a covenant and religious context (RP 1). The human goal is seen as likeness to Christ rather than conformity to a set of laws (RP 6a, 15) and conversion is thus far more radical than a mere change in belief or behavior.

By seeing sin more as an attitude or power than an act, the RP emphasizes the relational character. It does this too when it challenges penitents to compare their lives with the example and commandments of Christ and then pray for forgiveness (RP 15) and when it makes conforming ourselves to Christ and being more attentive to the Spirit the purpose of frequent celebration (RP 7b). By asking about the "fundamental orientation of life," the RP's examination of conscience also helps situate sin in a perspective going beyond individual acts.[3] While the RP maintains a distinction of sins, its descriptive definitions speak of relationships. Grave sin is a withdrawing from the communion of love with God; venial sin is a matter of human weakness, a failure to attain the full freedom of God's children (RP 7). By speaking of grave rather than mortal sin, the RP avoids connotations of that term that tend to identify it with particular actions.

The RP does not adopt a particular theology of sin—the fundamental option theory, for example—though it is certainly open to it. Like Trent, it defines sin in terms of relationships, effects, and consequences rather than as specific acts. Its nuanced distinction of grave and venial sin and its view of the Christian life as penitential (and thus a matter of continual conversion) likewise run counter to a view that limits sin to particular actions contrary to legal norms.

Metanoia or conversion is thus more readily seen as a movement or process toward full union with the Father, through Christ, in the power of the Holy Spirit active in the Church. While the emphasis on the ecclesial context of conversion limits the danger of psychologizing and individualism, the personal character of conversion is at the same time brought out more radically than by a view that would confine it to the mere matter of making a decision or changing a behavior. The complexity of the mystery of conversion embraces the divine initiative and the free human response that is both interior transformation and a reshaping of relationships.

Word and Sacraments
A scripturally derived theology of the Word is basic if conversion is to be a religious event rather than merely a moral or ethical change in behavior; it is God who calls us to conversion, not we as individuals who decide to make changes in our behavior. Christ, the Incarnate Word, as the sacrament of God's presence in the world, is the light letting us see our sinfulness and the power overcoming it. The Word of God reveals human sinfulness, calls people to conversion, encourages trust in divine mercy, and reveals the true nature of conversion and penance (RP 17, 22, 24).

Proclaiming the Word in every ritual form of the sacrament counters subjective piety and the neosemi-Pelagianism that came to prevail in the late medieval format of the sacrament. It shifts the focus from the sinner's deeds to the reconciling power of God in Christ. Considering the foundational character of the proclamation of the Word in establishing the setting and thrust of the liturgy of reconciliation (RP 24), the fact that it is considered optional in the rite for reconciling individuals (RP 43) is indeed strange and inconsistent.

Christians first hear and respond to the Word as they are initiated into the Christian community. Initiation starts the continuing conversion that is the life of discipleship and the way to become a personal instance of Jesus' Easter victory over sin. It provides an experience of Church that is essential for understanding and appreciating penance. Initiation establishes the Christian's union with Christ. Penance, in its various forms, reactualizes or strengthens this union throughout life. The goal of both is the fullness of likeness and union that comes in the kingdom, an eschatological goal sacramentally anticipated.

Baptism and penance have been closely paralleled in their historical evolution, not only in the coordination of the order of catechumens and the order of penitents but also in their eventual fate. The Easter Mystery receded into the background in both sacraments. Both became privatized rituals. Both were juridicized, with baptism obligatory for removing original sin and penance the means for escaping divine retributive justice for personal sins. The sense that reconciliation to God is a sharing in Christ's Easter victory transforming the community of his disciples was, for all practical purposes, lost in both sacraments.

Restoring penance's paschal character is a major factor in reform. The power of the keys given to Peter (Mt 16:19) is first exercised in preaching baptismal forgiveness and continues in calling people to conversion and in celebrating penance (RP 1). Baptism, eucharist, and penance are closely interrelated as sacramental sharing in Christ's victory (RP 2), with penance flowing out of baptism (RP 7) and expressing and renewing the paschal mystery (RP 19, 44, 54, 57) that is complete in the eucharist (RP 2, 6).

The eucharist is presented as the primary sacrament of reconciliation (RP 2) and the penitential elements of the Mass are noted (RP 4). While this was also stated at Trent, for centuries the Western Church has not maintained a close relationship between the eucharist and the remission of sins, except for the Jansenistic use of confession as preparation for communion.[4] The RP, basing itself on *Eucharisticum mysterium* 35,[5] sees the eucharist expressing and celebrating the continual conversion begun at baptism and completing the special conversion of penance (RP 6). Penance is no longer simply preparation for eucharist and becomes a sacrament in its own right. It is closely related to baptism, out of which it flows and which it renews, and to eucharist, to which it restores sinners and which completes it. However, what is primary is not ritual but the Christian life itself, intrinsically penitential and a continuous liberation from sin and transformation into Christ.

RECONCILIATION AND THE CHURCH

As the vision and vital expression of the Church is the central issue in initiation, so the self-realization of the Church as a reconciled and reconciling community is central to the renewal of penance. The Introduction situates its discussion of the sacrament of penance within this context by indicating the nature of the Church as penitent (RP 3), the place of penance in the Church's life and liturgy (RP 4), and the integral relationship of reconciliation with God and reconciliation with the Church (RP 5).

The Penitent Church

Presenting reconciliation as an ecclesial reality requires seeing the Church itself as penitent (RP 3; cf. *Lumen gentium*, 8). The Church is holy—purified and made holy by Christ to bring truth and grace to all—but it still needs purification and must constantly work at repentance and renewal.

This theme, though deeply rooted in patristic tradition, was practically forgotten until retrieved at the council.[6] Instead, the Church was thought of as something irreformable and perfect, apart from its sinful members. The role of this theme in the renewal of penance is still largely unexplored, but it is certainly critical to appreciating the central convictions of ancient penance. There the Church did penance with the repentant sinners, recognizing its own complicity through failure to encourage and support, and penance liturgy was as much for the community as for penitents. Today, a Church of penitent sinners is still a penitent Church, and only that adequately explains the ecclesial dimension of sin, conversion, and penance and the significance of penitential practices and Lent.

The theme of the penitent Church is also crucial to appreciating communal celebrations. The gathering of the faithful shows that the Church is conscious of its sin and convinced that it needs to be converted. This gathering *is* the Church. Though the Church excludes sinful members from full participation in its eucharistic assemblies, here it gathers as a community of sinners seeking to be reconciled with God and renewed. The Church usually admits sin only when it is historically distant or esoterically abstract—the medieval persecution of Jews and "witches," the prosecution of Galileo, the sixteenth-century abuses that precipitated the Reformation, the early twentieth-century decrees of the Pontifical Biblical Commission—but when it confesses its present sinfulness, it shows that it lives only by God's purifying grace. Only a converting community, one that recognizes and struggles to overcome the collective sin that has taken root in it, knows how to welcome and work with penitent sinners. A disincarnate, transcendent, and perfect institution, standing apart from its members, may channel an abstract forgiveness and grace, but it is unlikely to be a community that supports conversion and promotes reconciliation.

A reconciled and reconciling community is affected by every celebration of the sacrament. As each sinful member is reconciled, the Church is renewed and made whole again, not only when it gathers as a community to follow the path of repentance but also when an individual is reconciled (RP 3, 7, 11). Ancient rituals showed this plainly when the community and even the bishop identified with penitents so that they might share the redemption received from Christ. However, not only the acknowledgment of communal sinfulness, but even the very existence of such a sacrament in the Church witnesses to Christ's redeeming action. As an individual or group is reconciled, the community is made whole and holy, reconciled to itself and thus to the God victorious over sin in Jesus.

Only the community that seeks reconciliation is a reconciling community, but the community that reconciles is reconciled. For such a community, every celebration of penance not only reconciles penitent sinners with God and the Church but also reconciles and reintegrates the Church, making it whole once again. While RP 3 implies that the Church is sinful only in its members, other sections state explicitly that the community's life is wounded by sin (RP 7) and that in each celebration "the Church continually renews itself" (RP 11). As in the documents of Vatican II, so in the RP: the Church itself is both holy and sinful.

Many aspects of this theme are still virgin territory. What happens to the Church in the sacrament? How does the Church pursue and express conversion and reconciliation? What effect does the realization of its own sin have on the way the Church ritualizes acceptance of sinful members? How does its understanding of the nature of its eucharistic assembly and everyday life change when it realizes that *it* needs purification and must constantly seek repentance and renewal? Can it so readily condemn and exclude as it has sometimes done? Trying to answer such questions may well determine the future of the Church and the sacrament of penance.

Penance in the Church's Life and Liturgy
Continual repentance is shown in many ways (RP 4). The People of God endure difficulties, they do works of mercy and charity, they make the effort to conform to Christ's Gospel. The Church itself becomes a sign of conversion when the faithful confess their sinfulness and seek pardon of God and their brothers and sisters in penitential ser-

vices, the proclamation of the Word, prayer, and the penitential elements of the eucharist. In the sacrament of penance, they obtain pardon from God for their sins and are at the same time reconciled with the Church, which they have harmed by their sins and which works for their conversion by charity, example, and prayer.

The place of penance in the Church's life and liturgy is plain once we recognize and express the social and ecclesial dimensions of sin and penance. Such a rediscovery has been prompted by the biblical-patristic movement in recent theology, the conciliar renovation of ecclesiology, and the new consciousness of ecclesial coresponsibility, as well as by the contemporary sense of solidarity and interdependence in politics and economics and in society at large. All these have aided a realization of the social dimensions of Catholic dogma and the theology of penance in particular.

There are, of course, many approaches to developing and understanding this social dimension. While the RP speaks of sin's social effects (e.g., RP 5), the major approach taken in both the Introduction and the rites is theological and liturgical: sin shows infidelity to one's baptismal pledge as a member of the covenant community, and penance reconciles the person with that community. This approach requires a strong scriptural, ecclesiological, and sacramental foundation. It also needs strong trinitarian and eschatological underpinnings—the latter contextualizes the judicial element of the sacrament—and should emphasize the role of the Spirit and salvation history. The RP does bring out the trinitarian emphasis (RP 5, 6d, 9a, 10c, 19), but the eschatological character—service to the kingdom—is weak (e.g., RP 7), probably because of a residual preoccupation with the Tridentine requirements, and needs further development.

The theological and sacramental approach avoids the dangers of an overly sociological, anthropological, or ethical orientation. It also lessens the previous overemphasis on the judicial element by putting Christian morality in a God-centered and personal perspective, recognizing that the opposite of sin is not morality but faith. It is, however, difficult to communicate such a perspective pastorally. Without an extensive reformation of attitudes, including a living experience of Church community and an evangelization and ecclesialization of conscience, the general thrust of this approach will seem almost pointless to people who see the sacrament as a way of getting rid of their sins. As in the Carolingian reform, it is hard to introduce a ritual that goes counter to prevailing spirituality. Only as the vision of a renewing and reforming Church, such as is found in the *Rite of Christian Initiation of Adults*, takes flesh will a renewed penance rite be able to be fully implemented.

Appreciating the ecclesial dimension is key to understanding both ancient penance and the contemporary situation. While its loss is easily linked with the rise of medieval tariff penance, that system could develop only in a setting that so prized individualism and subjective piety as to adulterate the Church and its liturgy. Liturgy then maintained and fostered individualism and subjectivism, isolating penitents from any visible or psychological involvement with the community and letting them relate only to the priest, himself without any evident aid from or connection with the community. Only as we come again to see the community aspect of sin, the priesthood of the whole community, and a penitential way of life as a sign and witness for the community's continual conversion will we be ready to benefit fully from the RP.

The Church is not only a sign of conversion but also the universal sacrament of salvation (cf. *Lumen gentium*, 9). Sins are Christians' failure to respond to Christ's call to holiness, their infidelity to their baptismal pledge as members of the covenant community, and obstacles to the Church's mission of signing salvation to all the world. The ecclesial dimension receives closest attention in RP 5.

Sin and penance are first seen in relation to God: sin offends God by breaking asunder the love relationship that committed us to God. The purpose of penance, then, is a deeper love and a total commitment on our part. While the trinitarian nature of the return is noted, the social and ecclesial character of sin and reconciliation is more absorbing. The Christian's sin and holiness affect other Christians and the Church as a whole. Penance consequently always involves reconciliation with those who have been harmed by our sins. Sin is social (e.g., people cooperate in committing injustice) and so people should also help one another do penance. Liberated from sin by Christ's grace, they can then work together with all people of goodwill for justice and peace in the world.

The sacrament's thrust toward social action helps reintegrate the liturgy and life of penance and to situate the Church's sacramental ministry within its mission to the world. While the council and *Paenitemini* had already stressed the link between penitential practices and social action, this is the first correlation of the sacrament and work for justice in an official document. RP 7 does this even more forcefully by stating: "in order that this sacrament of healing may truly achieve its purpose among Christ's faithful, it must take root in their whole lives and move them to a more faithful service of God and neighbor."

Penance as a reconciling force in the Church's life and society is new to people more accustomed to seeing its focus as inward guilt and its effect as forgiveness and wholeness. For them, reconciliation with oneself is a sign of reconciliation with God. Such views have often led those concerned with social justice to regard the sacrament as pointless.[7] The RP is a warning to those who too sharply differentiate sacramental celebration from secular life and the Church's mission from social justice. Both Church and Christians find salvation only in the midst of worldly affairs.

At the 1971 Synod of Bishops, Archbishop Greégoire spoke of the liturgy's inherent potential for conscience formation and education in social justice. He claimed that, particularly among the young, it is not so much the consciousness of sin that is in question as a concept of sin not rooted in the gospels, a concept that restricts sin to certain areas (especially sex) and prevents people from assuming responsibilities in line with the gospel's demands. He saw the Church's problem here as one structurally rooted in its institutions and intensified by a practice of the sacrament of penance that was inadequate to the social dimensions of Christian responsibility. He criticized current practice for emphasizing confession and humiliation, neglecting conversion, reparation, and the correction of intolerable situations, and for doing too little serious conscience formation. He was convinced that communal celebrations would more adequately educate for Christian responsibility, particularly in the area of social justice.[8]

Discussions at the 1983 Synod of Bishops began by situating the sacrament of penance in this context of the Church's ministry of reconciliation in society. Despite weaknesses in the preliminary document and in the study paper prepared by the International Theological Commission and the persistence of Counter-Reformation attitudes in curial officials, the Synod discussions marked a major step forward in integrating sacramental liturgy, pastoral ministry, and Church mission and life. The sacramental clericalism that reappeared in the 1983 Code as a restriction on communal celebrations was prominent in curial interventions at the Synod and notably absent in those by pastoral bishops.

The strong emphasis on the ecclesial dimension of penance in the new rites (even that for reconciling an individual) can eventually help alleviate this problem of formation. Communal and penitential celebrations are the most appropriate context for experiencing it, but even they must be properly structured and celebrated if reconciliation is to go beyond a purely intellectual realization or an individualistic experience of forgiveness.

Only an individualistic misinterpretation of the Christian faith could regard reconciliation with oneself—that is, the forgiveness of one's sins—as the ultimate sign of reconciliation with God. This view of the sacrament is an understandable consequence of the early medieval effort to relieve individuals of anxiety and guilt and the scholastic emphasis on contrition and the corresponding theory that interior penitence mediated divine forgiveness. Nevertheless, it is increasingly untenable as we realize that work for peace and justice is a constituent element of the gospel for our time. It can no longer be enough for the sinner to feel forgiveness by God; penitents must experience and strive for reconciliation with their brothers and sisters as sign of reconciliation with God. Only then does the sacramental symbol present an experience of the reality that it proposes as ultimate goal.

Reconciliation with God and Church
A clear sign of the rediscovery of the ecclesial dimension of penance has been the widespread acceptance among theologians that reconciliation with the Church is the *res et sacramentum* of penance—that the sacrament is, in other words, the taking back of the sinner into the Church as symbol of divine acceptance. In scholastic theological discussion, *sacramentum* referred to the liturgical action (viewed as matter and form). This visible activity led one into the invisible happening, which, though open to experience, led one still further. The intermediate symbolic reality, *res et sacramentum*, was thus the means to encounter the transcendent reality, the *res sacramenti*, which was beyond direct experience. Scholastic theology, reflecting on an individualistic and increasingly aliturgical experience of penance as forgiveness of sins, had difficulty relating the penitent's and priest's parts, but Trent regarded the activities of both as making up the *sacramentum*. Generally, interior conversion was regarded as the *res et sacra-*

265

mentum, with contrition required apart from absolution and attrition sufficing with absolution. This was regarded as the means whereby the transcendent reality of divine forgiveness, the *res sacramenti,* realized itself within human experience.

The movement away from the earlier scholastic position that interior penance is the mediatory symbolic reality began with the publication of Xiberta's *Clavis Ecclesiae* in 1922. His study of patristic writings concluded that the fathers understood reconciliation with the Church to be primary. Despite strong initial opposition, his contention came to receive support from biblical and historical studies and dogmatic syntheses giving new insight into the ecclesial character of all the sacraments.

This concept, like all ideas, has important practical consequences as well as significance for understanding the sacrament. Are sin and penance realities that simply affect the individual and the individual's relationship with God? Is the social and ecclesial dimension a mere corollary? What are we to experience in the sacrament as sign of the grace of reconciliation with God? Is it interior conversion and contrition (the medieval and Counter-Reformation view) or actual reconciliation with others (the biblical and patristic view)?

An important step was taken when Vatican Council II, in its Constitution on the Church, paralleled reconciliation with the Church and reconciliation with God (*Lumen gentium, 11*). As is usual in such documents, the council did not rule on theological theories, even though by this time almost all Catholic theologians who held that reconciliation with the Church is an effect of penance regarded it as the *res et sacramentum.*[9] The council thus left unresolved the question whether it is divine pardon that restores the penitent to full membership in the Church or restoration to full membership that enables pardon. Still, the council without debate and matter of factly expressed what theologians only a few decades before had reacted against vehemently.[10]

By stating that in the sacrament of penance there is always reconciliation with the Church, the council implicitly affirmed the ecclesial aspect of all sins and encouraged a development of moral teaching and conscience formation to sensitize people to it. It also affirms that the Church's action in the sacrament goes beyond absolution—the Church is involved in the whole conversion process—and thus implicitly encourages the development of structures to express the Church's assistance. It also implies that the whole Church, not just priest and penitent, is involved in the entire sacramental process and that diverse ministries need expression in the conversion process and liturgical celebration.

The social consequences of the sacrament are viewed differently if reconciliation with the Church, rather than contrition, is the sacramental sign and the first and most immediate consequence of the sacrament. Our understanding of the Church also affects this. If, for example, the Church is regarded primarily as an external and juridical organization of those who hold the same faith, then belonging to the Church or not belonging to it has no essential significance for relationship with God. Exclusion (or excommunication) and reconciliation can only refer to the Church's this-wordly discipline. However, if the Church is regarded as the community-Body of Christ and the sacrament of salvation, then a return to peace with the Church is a return to peace with God, since the Church is a sacrament of communion with God. Views on the Church's mission are also involved. Not only is there an intrinsically social character to human sinfulness and the sacrament's action and purpose, but the celebration of the sacrament is part of the Church's mission and orients that mission to a social finality, the formation of community.

The RP does regard reconciliation with the Church as an effect of the sacrament (e.g., RP 4, 5, 31) and tries to express this in its rituals (e.g., RP 203–204) to fulfill the conciliar mandate. While the RP, like the Constitution on the Church, takes no stand on disputed theological questions, the overall emphasis given to reconciliation with the Church suggests that the RP favors seeing it as the *res et sacramentum*. The Latin of RP 2 is clearer: the English translation parallels reconciliation with God and the renewal of grace, but the Latin sees reconciliation with God flowing from and consequent on the renewal of grace. Reconciliation with the Church, symbolized through the imposition of hands, is restoration to the community in which the Spirit of Jesus is active (e.g., RP 5, 6d, 9a, 19, 24) and thus the penitent's reinsertion into the Paschal Mystery (RP 1, 2, 7, 19). The broken covenant is remade because the penitent is once more restored to the covenant-community (cf. RP 5, 6d). Reconciliation with the Church thus renews grace, from which follows reconciliation with God. The RP thus seems open to the interpretation that reconciliation with the Church is the symbolic reality and the immediate effect of the sacrament.

While this theory of the *res et sacramentum* helps to explain the role of the ordained ministry and the need for jurisdictional faculties and largely resolves the attrition-contrition controversies, it does leave other theological questions unanswered. How are canonical excommunication and mortal sin related, since both exclude an individual from participating in the Church's assemblies? Is the person who sins venially excluded from the Church and reconciled to it, or would it be better in this case to speak of the penitent Church accepting and identifying itself with sinners? How does sin damage one's relationship to the Church? Can we speak of reconciliation in a therapeutic or devotional confession? Such questions may not seem liturgically relevant, but they do recommend some caution lest reconciliation become no more than a synonym for confession. They have a liturgical relevance in that the answers to them have implications for the form, style, and frequency of celebration.

Neither absolution formula mentions reconciliation with the Church. They express the Church's ministerial and mediatory role in the remission of sin (RP 46, 62) and indicate that reconciliation flows from the Father's mercy. They show the connection between reconciliation and Christ's Paschal Mystery, emphasize the role of the Holy Spirit in the remission of sins, and point up the ecclesial aspect of the sacrament by referring to the Church's ministerial role (see RP 19), but they do not speak of reconciliation with the Church. However, when the formula is combined with the gesture of the imposition of hands, as it should be, this is clearly expressed. Gesture always precedes words, and absolution formulas have historically put into words what the imposition of hands does. The gesture is a sign of solidarity, of sharing the Spirit of Christ's community-Body, and the immediate experience should be one of ecclesial acceptance and welcome through the ministerial representative presiding over its worship.

This last remark on the gesture that accompanies the formula of absolution illustrates the difficulty of theologizing without reference to rites or studying a ritual while making use only of formularies—a recurring difficulty in the historiography of penance. The *lex orandi* takes concrete shape only within the liturgical assembly, not in the texts or rubrics of a ritual. At the same time, theological reflection affects ritual and such reflection, on the basis of current sacramental experience and without comprehension of history, can further distort.

SACRAMENTAL CONVERSION AND RECONCILIATION
Ancient penance (and to some extent, medieval), emphasized the penitents' activity, a conversion of heart prepared for and expressed by a special way of life. However, we know little about organization and support offered. Writers spoke hesitantly of the exceptional remedy for a seriously irregular way of life and only mentioned fea-

tures already familiar to observant nonparticipants—penitential practices, community prayer, blessings. Canonical legislation assumed these traditions and said little about pastoral provisions. In time, the elements of the conversion process that writers did refer to were little more than ceremonial. As this reduction to ritual continued and theologians reflected on its results—with little knowledge of origins—the phases of the penitent's conversion came to be called the penitent's acts: contrition, confession, and satisfaction.

The Thomistic synthesis regarded the penitent's acts as parts of the sacrament and the Council of Trent spoke of them as the quasi-matter of the sacrament, though with little realization of their original ecclesial character. Continued theological reflection, with little attention to the quality of liturgical expression, led gradually to further liturgical impoverishment. Priests and penitents concentrated on the essentials—contrition, confession, satisfaction, absolution—until, in our own times, these were practically reduced to ritual forms, with little or no realization of their relationship to a life process of conversion. Not only was the ecclesial context lost, the personal and cultic dimensions came likewise to be almost totally absent except for verbal ritual. What was important was that the penitent make an act of sincere contrition and a complete confession and say the penance assigned by the priest who gave absolution to forgive the sins. The liturgy of penance was reduced to the bare bones, much like a Mass reduced to the essentials of consecration and communion. Though there were still acts to perform, penitents were, for all practical purposes, passive recipients of priestly ministration.

Passivity resulted from many factors: the reduction to ritual, the clericalization of ritual (including emphasis on the power of the keys), stress on the *ex opere operato* efficacy of ritual, and reaction to Protestant reformers and Jansenism. The need today, underlined in the RP, is to emphasize again the penitents' activity as a sacramental role as well as the Church's involvement in the process of conversion that leads to reconciliation. RP 6 discusses the acts of the penitent as parts of the sacrament (traditional since the thirteenth century), situating each in the context of total conversion and indicating that absolution, the expression on the Church's part of reconciliation, presupposes that the penitent is converted, once more aligned with the Christian community's way of life.

To emphasize the ecclesial and cultic character of these acts, they are first spoken of as parts of the sacramental ritual, but the discussion indicates that what is ritualized flows from personal life and activity. For example, though the order of the ritual has been rearranged in modern penance—it is further revised when general absolution is used in communal celebrations—the RP's discussion follows the more logical and true-to-life pattern of ancient penance. Conversion involves sorrow for sin and the intent to lead a new life (inner conversion), but it also requires external expression and manifestation, referred to here as confession to the Church and satisfaction and amendment of life. After penitents ritualize their conversion by celebrating the liturgy of penance, the priest responds by proclaiming reconciliation: pardon is granted by God through the Church working by the priest's ministry.

Penitents are active in celebrating the sacrament, but how they understand and experience their activity largely depends on how they understand the process of sanctification. Individualistic spirituality sees the sacrament as spiritual hygiene—the penitent's acts ritually prepare for purification through priestly absolution. Penitents then are essentially passive; their acts are little more than conditions for the priest's action. A more inclusive spirituality sees these acts as ritual expressions of personal conversion lived out in community. The RP shows this by referring to penitents as members of the faithful (RP 2, 4), members of the Church (RP 3), disciples of Christ (RP 6), as well as sinners (RP 3, 5 and passim) and penitents (RP 6 and passim).[11]

The atmosphere and style of liturgical celebration, as well as catechesis and preaching, affect penitents' understanding and experience. While the RP stresses the personal, ecclesial, and sacramental character of the acts of the penitent, who is cocelebrant (RP 11), it also stresses the pastoral character of the confessor's ministry (RP 10). The presider's style, particularly in the reconciliation of an individual penitent where the presider is the only minister, generally sets the tone. A more relaxed and less rigoristic and juridical approach on his part enables penitents to sense an atmosphere of acceptance where they are treated in an individual, personal, and reverential manner.

A recurring problem in the history of penance, intimately related to each past crisis as well as to the current one, is the need to balance the personal and social or ecclesial dimensions of the sacrament. Individuals often seek forgiveness—the removal of obstacles to union with God and Church—so it is important that penance reform link forgiveness and reconciliation, balancing personal and communal dimensions of sacrament and celebration. Liturgical reform must make clear that personal conversion has an essentially social function in a community moving through history toward the kingdom of God. Simply providing communal forms of celebration is not enough. Christian life and liturgy must be intimately linked by realizing that penance is neither a thing nor a momentary ritual experience but rather part of personal and community history.

Recognizing that the parts of the sacrament are not only acts of the penitent but phases of conversion correlates the ecclesial and personal dimensions, avoids the piecemeal approach of past descriptions of the penitent's acts, and underlines that these are aspects of penitents' lives, not merely things ritually said or done. The ecclesial dimension shows that these acts are where the penitent's personal expression of conversion and the Church's ministry intersect. Thus, the focus is more on a new way of life than on past sin, situating the requirement of complete or integral confession within a new perspective and evoking praise and thanksgiving in response to the God who grants grace and renewal.[12]

The first and lasting conversion through which we are made Christian in the sacraments of initiation is both personal and ecclesial. So too is the second conversion, which is ritualized in the sacrament of penance. It consists of phases or processes, likewise both personal and ecclesial: experiencing guilt and repentance (contrition), expressing guilt and repentance (confession), and rebuilding one's life (act of penance or satisfaction). This conversion is ritualized in the sacramental liturgy and leads to the ritual of reconciliation with the Church.

Contrition

In its ministry of reconciliation, the Church confronts the sinful Christian and brings the person to a recognition of culpability. In modern times, this challenge has generally been through legal statements, either internalized by the individual or brought to consciousness through a printed or verbalized examination of conscience. While such pointed reminders of specific areas of responsibility always have some value for the insensitive or irresponsible person, they do not exhaust the Church's ministerial ability.

If the Church's ministry in calling people to conversion is to be fully effective, it must help them discover sin and culpability for themselves.[13] An examination of conscience reviewing a code of obligations—as though sins were no more than isolated points of disorder in an otherwise orderly life—cannot do this. It lets us see where we have failed to correspond with the pattern, but other areas will go unnoticed. It is better to begin, like the Ignatian method, with gratitude for God's gifts—particularly Christ, for only he and his gospel give us a standard or rule. What we are to *be*—disciples, imitators—comes before what we are to *do*. The RP calls for just such a reorientation, suggesting that penitents compare their lives with the example and commandments of Christ (RP 15) and the demands of the gospel (RP 22) in an atmosphere of faith, trust, and prayer. This is done in the light of God's mercy (RP 6b), and the goal is not static conformity to laws or abstract virtues but a continuing growth into likeness to Christ (RP 4, 6a, 7b, 15). The RP provides a model examination of conscience (Appendix III), where it is the Word of God, not rules and regulations, that calls to conversion. Beyond this, it contains no suggestions on how the Church is to fulfill this ministry, but it clearly seeks more than introspective analysis.

At its most effective, such a ministry is a formation that simultaneously develops a sensitivity to the presence of evil and a sense of responsibility motivating Christians to resist evil actively. Neither is possible without sharing the Spirit that animates the community of faith. Success thus depends on an evangelization and ecclesialization of conscience. This entails the task not only of revealing and clarifying authentic Christian values but also of assisting people in discerning and revising priorities in the community.

The liturgical goal should be to arouse a sense of culpability rather than simply an awareness of guilt. Guilt can leave people passive and powerless in the face of evil, waiting on God's grace to cleanse them, while culpability is also an experience of the Spirit that is powerful within the community of faith to assure victory and make resistance possible. Where guilt is too often a shallow and superficial emotional response, culpability has deep religious roots in a shared experience of faith. Penitential celebrations using parables or symbolic actions to clothe the challenge (and the basis for it) function prophetically to accuse individuals, stimulating a reflection process enabling them to see and name the form that the power of evil has taken in their lives. While it will have generic qualities in common with other people's sin, its unique coloring in their individual lives is what must be seen if conversion rather than cleansing is to take place.

The dialogue that takes place in the individual celebration, when that is part of a program of spiritual direction, serves the same prophetic function in an even more personal and pointed way when the confessor is skilled in this art (cf. RP 10). What is to be aimed at, both in this dialogue and in proclamation and preaching in communal celebrations, is a reflectiveness going deeper than a catalog of failings to recognizing weaknesses, that is, areas where the strengthening presence of the Spirit of Jesus is needed. This starts, maintains, or intensifies a continuing process of conversion. Psychological self-knowledge or the release of introspective guilt is left to the therapist. What is essential, then, particularly in the individual celebration, is the establishment of an atmosphere where prayer is shared and where what confessor and penitent are doing is ecclesial worship.

Focus on contrition has been more often psychological than religious. Conversion and its motives were psychologized in the late Middle Ages; this combined with an individualistic and ritualistic sacramental format and a legalistic discipline to encourage scrupulosity. Contrition was easily confused with humiliation and shame or regret and remorse as the penitent sought sacramental release from anxiety produced by guilt. Instead, the converting sinner should look to the Lord, not the self, recognizing sin as a threat to the covenanted relationship rather than a defect in the person; then the penitent can try to respond more adequately to a loving and merciful God.

Contrition too is progressive, part of the natural movement of conversion, with its completed form, perfect contrition, the expression of love and the result of spiritual maturation. The proper focus can be established only in a context of prayer and worship, of gratitude to God. (Thomas's insight into this is the basis of his conviction

275

that "ex attrito fit contritus.") The ecclesial dimension of contrition must be maintained, then, since contrition is perfected only in the Church, where the love that is received evokes love in return and where the liturgical experience of shared conversion and reconciliation is the foundation of a loving prayer of praise and thanksgiving.[14]

Penitential celebrations and communal celebrations of the sacrament promote this. To be contrite is to have become a penitent. To be a penitent is to have found God in a community that manifests that divine holy presence in its own penitence, that thus not only sharpens awareness of how far sin takes us from God but also holds out the promise of restoration and supports those returning. Since contrition's foundations are faith and love, only the love felt within a community of faith can engender it. Since contrition is an expression of love for the Lord, only a setting of prayer and worship can situate and focus it. An ecclesial emphasis, a process view, and an integration of the personal and communal dimensions established in the liturgical celebration make for an integral and balanced understanding and experience of contrition.

The RP balances the introspection of the Tridentine definition of contrition with the more dynamic, process-oriented and God-regarding view of *Paenitemini*.[15] Contrition is the interior of conversion, the scriptural *metanoia*. Using the scriptural term throws an entirely new light on the Tridentine definition and conversion itself.

"This is a profound change of the whole person by which one begins to consider, judge, and arrange his life according to the holiness and love of God, made manifest in his Son in the last days and given to us in abundance. The genuiness of penance depends on this heartfelt contrition: conversion should affect a person from within so that it may progressively enlighten him and render him continually more like Christ." (RP 6a)

276

Contrition's essential character in conversion and reconciliation is brought out again and again in the RP, particularly in treating of general absolution (RP 33, 35a, 60). The only use of the term perfect contrition is in the discussion of the value and importance of penitential celebrations (RP 37). (The RP nowhere uses the terms attrition or imperfect contrition.) More precisely, the RP speaks of a contrition perfected by love, a goal attained with the assistance of other worshipers and restoring the reality of ecclesial grace. Like Trent, whose doctrine is thus restated positively, the RP connects the restoration to grace outside the ritual celebration with a desire for the sacrament. The experience of reconciliation with the community is thus once again suggested as the symbolic reality and immediate effect of the sacrament. All that is lacking in the penitential celebration is the official proclamation and grant of reconciliation by the one authorized to do so.

Confession

If conversion begins interiorly with the realization that in God's holy presence one is revealed as a sinner called to loving communion, and even if it continues with the willingness to be transformed by that communion—what we have been speaking of as contrition—it does not stop there. Our human situation at the intersection of the spiritual and material planes requires expression. The ecclesial constitution of our Christian identity demands liturgical expression. A penitent Church is likewise a Church that sings the praises of the God that calls us out of darkness into divine light (1 Pt 2:9). This is, of course, the root source of the ancient Church's *exomologesis* and, in a weakened and reoriented form, the confession of tariff and modern penance. Penitents whose voices blend harmoniously with the grateful hymn of a reconciled community share its spirit of love and know themselves to be reconciled with God.

Ordained ministers preside at the Church's worship. In the ancient Church, the bishop's presence was ordinarily

required so that the laying on of his hands would officially sign restoration and solidarity. In emergencies
where death threatened, other Church officials—especially the presbyters, from whose number the bishop ordinarily selected his delegate for official functions, but
sometimes deacons as well—could be authorized to
preside at this act of worship. For a long time in the
early Middle Ages, even a lay person was considered
able to preside at confession—now an acknowledgment
of guilt and self-accusation—when no official was
available.

With emphasis on the power of the keys held by the
bishop (and delegated presbyters), lay confession disappeared, but Trent restated the tradition that the sincere
penitent—perfectly contrite—was really, though unoffi-
cially, reintegrated into the Church. The RP, by its statement that penitential celebrations are "very useful" when
no priest is available, resituates such unofficial reintegration within ecclesial worship, though without ruling out
other forms of unofficial ministry or even of unassisted
restoration to the Church in extreme cases. The Church is
willing to accept the sincere penitent who wishes to be
part of the community—which is what is meant by "the
desire for the sacrament"—the ultimate expression of the
early Church's decision not to leave any sinner isolated
and abandoned.

Ordinarily, however, the individual whose sin requires
the Church's ministry and assistance in conversion was
expected to share in the penitent community's praise of
the saving God. When these official supports are required
and what form the liturgy takes has, of course, varied
tremendously. Since the Middle Ages, such ministry and
liturgy have taken the form of a private confession at which
the duly authorized priest presides, and this form has
been required for any of a large number of sins regarded
as grave or mortal. The ministry gradually became the
opportunity for advising the penitent, and the penitent's

singing praise with the Church became the specific acknowledgment of all mortal sins.

Conversion, to be human, cannot remain interior—which is only contrition—but must find expression externally, particularly in relationships essential to the person's identity. For a person whose self-definition, in fact or by intent, includes membership in a Christian community as part of essential relatedness, conversion comes to external expression within that community. Both the incarnate character of the human being and the ecclesial nature of Christian conversion demand that contrition be evident to the Church. Self-realization and self-expression are correlative for people, and a Christian identity is not ordinarily achieved or maintained outside the Christian community. Converting sinners, then, have normally become penitents by showing themselves to the community and being officially recognized and accepted as penitents. Becoming a penitent has usually taken place in liturgy, and the Church has ministered by acknowledging itself as the same, proclaiming and confessing the mercy of God. The penitent's restricted participation cramped and eventually crippled the liturgy, making reform essential if the confession was to be recognizable as the Church's liturgy of conversion and reconciliation.

The problem of a sacrament of conversion and reconciliation in our times, then, is not only the problem of a consciousness of sin and a crisis of contrition but also a crisis of confession. This is the liturgy or service that the Church offers to God and its members, but the confession has largely ceased to be recognizable as a service of divine worship and has come to be regarded as an unproductive requirement of little benefit. Its liturgical poverty is glaringly evident when its recent form is compared with past liturgies. Its uselessness to penitents, however—or at least their perception of its unhelpful character, which comes to the same thing—emerges from analyzing their complaints. Such an analysis clarifies confession's function as a component of conversion and offers insight into how this dimension of the Church's ministry might be made more effective.

The basis for rethinking is that its function has varied tremendously in the Western history of penance. Accusation played a part in ancient penance when a person was denounced to the bishop's tribunal or when a person spontaneously sought counsel on whether to seek entry into the order of penitents, but it was minor in comparison to the central expression of conversion that was sought. That system looked for and supported the maturation of a contrition that was a reshaping of attitudes and priorities and expressed itself in a manner of life showing that the sinner had been rehabilitated. The inner reality of conversion resulted from external reform in the Church; liturgies where the Church lined up with the penitents in confessing God's mercy enabled them to be restored. Both interior conversion and external reform were the result of the Spirit's working through the Church; the penitents had an example as a model, loving encouragement supported their efforts, and prayers invoked the Spirit's transforming touch.

Confession, a basic element of conversion, is thus more than self-accusation. Confession as *exomologesis* was prominent in ancient penance, but confession as self-accusation was decidedly secondary. In tariff penance, self-accusation determined the satisfaction required; as self-humiliation, it was the sign that God rather than the self was put first. Once the penitent's efforts to change were officially observed and supervised only through repeated confession, the willingness to submit to such supervision and acknowledge failings became the touchstone of sincere conversion. In modern penance, confession often became a ritual end in itself. Here, as in other areas of liturgy, words displaced activity.

Unfortunately, ritual can substitute for reality. Penitents were once warned not to wait until their deathbeds, counting on reconciliation to compensate for the failure to do penance. Later they were warned to achieve a sorrow for sin that included a firm purpose of amendment and a complete or integral confession of all grave sins not yet confessed. The centrality of a ritual of self-accusation was thus complemented by the insistence that it express complete personal commitment and willingness to undergo conversion. Yet as the Tridentine insistence on a complete or fully personal confession came in the minds of many people to be primarily a matter of ritual enumeration, the danger of confusing ritual and reality increased.

Both the inner examination of the heart and the external expression of culpability and contrition are to be made in the light of God's mercy (RP 6b), a mercy that evokes praise. Establishing joyful confidence rather than law as the context counters the tendency of late medieval confession to foster anxiety and scrupulosity. Though this takes nothing away from complete confession nor denies the Church's ability to set standards for confession, it does further healthy growth and maintains the sacrament as worship. What is confessed or acknowledged is God's sovereign power to forgive. Loving mercy is no vague and vapid benevolence—it reaches into the life of *this* sinner and so some concreteness is required—but confession of sins is not giving information for its own sake.

Confession requires an openness on the part of the penitent and spiritual judgment on the part of the minister. When the confession is private and individual, an unstructured dialogue between priest and penitent and prayer together can do much to support maturation of motives and attitudes and help faith and hope to grow into love. Self-centered dispositions are purified as the penitent perceives God's love more clearly and is assured of pardon. A competent confessor is not only able to lead prayer but is also sensitive to what the person says, helping the individual identify the root difficulty, and to what the Spirit is doing, fostering awareness of how God is calling this sinner to conversion. As with contrition, so with confession: elements of the ritual bring to the surface a process taking place in the penitent's life and are sacramental to the extent that they do so.

How concrete and specific this confession must be in order to be sacramental has varied. In the early centuries, much of what is considered matter for confession today was not sufficient to allow entry into the order of penitents. However, as law replaced community in people's experience requirements were relaxed—or, from another perspective, the degree to which the official Church regulated its members' lives was extended—and formal or official penance became possible (or was required) in more and more cases. The historical trend has been to make confession more self-accusation than *exomologesis* and its completeness or integrity ever more specific and detailed, with an increase in the sins requiring official penance. This reached its apex in the middle of this century with Counter-Reformation spirituality and moral theology interacting to foster frequent, even devotional, confession.

By then, reversal of the trend had already begun both in theology and in law. Several factors contributed, particularly a retrieval of history,[16] a rediscovery of the social and ecclesial nature of the sacrament,[17] and the realization of current pastoral needs.[18] These led to legal recognition of circumstances excusing from the current requirements of integral confession, even while officials encouraged increasingly frequent confession.[19] Teaching and practice recognized the sacrament's ecclesial character and the inability of modern private confession alone to express that character.

The RP puts the Tridentine requirement of integral or complete confession in the context of divine mercy (RP 6b) and sees the requirement as part of the plan of a merciful God (RP 7a). It continues to state that such confession and absolution are the "only ordinary way" to reconciliation (RP 31),[20] but the atmosphere (the light of God's mercy) and purpose (the manifestation of conversion [RP 6b with 6d]) are clearly less legalistic. The same is true of the RP's understanding of grave sin, which differs significantly from the popular understanding. The omission of the traditional reference to number, species, and circumstances also shows that the RP is more concerned with sincere conversion than detailed confession, a significant shift in attitude and style of celebration. In any case, God forgives the sinner—what the confession signifies—not merely the sins confessed.

Current restrictions on the RP's communal celebrations have halted this development, though it is unclear whether this halt is a temporary plateau or permanent for the foreseeable future. The 1983 Code of Canon Law in many respects marked a reversion to legal formulations and attitudes characteristic of the period before the 1972 Pastoral Norms and the 1973 RP and is little different from the 1944 Instruction. Positions taken by the Congregation for the Doctrine of the Faith suggest that the congregation presumes no development in theology or practice has taken place since 1944. Yet, since the type and style of celebration mandated in the RP is far different from that assumed in the 1944 Instruction, current canonical legislation does not simply return us to the preconciliar situation.

Act of Penance (Satisfaction)
The phase of ecclesial conversion that received the most attention in the ancient period was the penance where individuals set about rebuilding their lives with the Church's assistance. It was still prominent in medieval penance, though it was reinterpreted as satisfaction for one's sins. Modern penance retained only a token of what theologians termed "satisfaction" and people called "the penance," though the tariff penance outlook endured in both. The Latin text of the RP uses *satisfactio* for this ritual element, while the English translation calls it the "act of penance," with "satisfaction" added in parentheses (RP 6d).

The long, severe penitential practices of the ancient period functioned, in context, as a means of liberation from underlying attitudes of sin. They showed the depth and sincerity of repentance by externalizing it and shaping a life centered on God rather than creatures. In a different sociocultural setting, such practices came to be interpreted more as the price to be paid for having sinned and, as the price was more than most people were willing to pay, the ranks of penitents dwindled.

Letting the debt be paid off with little fuss and without public knowledge seemed the solution in tariff penance, but the shift had been made from penance as a conversion of life to satisfaction expiating sins. Looking at items of behavior rather than manner of life required compensating for each detail that was out of line. The consequent accumulation of debts made the payoff impossible within an individual's lifetime. Refinancing (commutations and redemptions) was the only way to stave off bankruptcy. Reacting to the Celtic system that ultimately only compounded a hopeless situation, Church officials restored a link to the community by providing for a private ritual of reconciliation.

Once absolution began to precede satisfaction and sins were understood as forgiven by the priest's absolution, the postponed satisfaction was considered to deal with the punishment due to sin rather than the sins themselves. Since confession indicated willingness to pay and absolution was pardon, the debt was increasingly regarded as a token one. The Church then felt able to distribute dividends (indulgences) from its surplus (treasury of merits) so that penitent sinners could pay their debts, the temporal punishment owed for sin. Theologians still spoke of satisfaction, but post-Tridentine practice mitigated this even more, even though the 1614 ritual retained the notion that this was punishment for sin,[21] and it was increasingly symbolic. Almsgiving, fasting, mortification, or acts of service or devotion were recommended and were to be assigned in relation to the sins confessed, but generally the penance became a matter of prayers. A way of life became token prayers, individual and private as in the medieval system rather than communal and liturgical as in the ancient.

When writers interpret the historical development as simply a gradual evolution from severity to mildness—the result of not recognizing the changing sociocultural situation—they tend to regard the severity of the ancient system as provoking a crisis then (the usual interpretation today) or the mildness of the modern system as itself problematic (the interpretation of the Jansenist historians). A more nuanced interpretation differentiates the dissimilar sociocultural situations and the diversified functions. The ancient crisis was due less to severity than to the changing experience and understanding of sin and the Church. A parallel shift is probably at the base of the contemporary crisis as well.

Few modern authors give much place to notions of expiation or satisfaction. They usually recommend that the (act of) penance be a concrete expression of *metanoia*, a means of joining the Church in resisting evil in the world, an act of charity rather than a prayer.[22] Since conversion is always less behavior modification than the mystery of the Holy Spirit unfolding within that person's life, the assigned or chosen act of penance should serve as a focal point for experiencing and reflecting on that dynamic mystery. As a visible sign of invisible grace, still part of the sacrament, it becomes a way of facing the future as well as the past: not only undoing harm done and scandal given but preparing for future decisions by becoming alert to general values and building good habits. It links the sacrament with the penitent's life in an ecclesial way, symbolizing the penitential character of the Christian life as continual conversion and the penitent's share in the Church's struggle to overcome sin and achieve reconciliation in society.

Several factors lead contemporary authors to recommend a work of charity rather than a prayer: the new realization of the social and ecclesial effects of sin and sacrament, the reconciliatory nature of the sacrament, the need to express conversion in everyday life. The penance is then an act expressing (RP 6) and completing (RP 6d) the intent to be converted, an action mending one's life and repairing injury done, a remedy for sin by restoring order and an assist in renewal by seeking health (RP 6c, 18). This is the understanding in the RP, and so the English text's reference to the "act of penance" captures the sense, even though the Latin text retains "satisfaction." (The concept of temporal punishment due to sin—historically, the result of postponing satisfaction—is nowhere to be found in the RP.) The RP describes the work of satisfaction as having its force and power from Christ's satisfaction and as requiring not only penitential practices but especially the exercise of true love of God and neighbor (RP 25d).

Though the terminology of recent tradition is used and that understanding sometimes betrays itself (especially in RP 18c), the Tridentine view is balanced by a post-Vatican II nuance, particularly by the perspective of *Paenitemini*.[23] The act of penance expresses and completes conversion, showing that the penitent "again becomes part of the mystery of salvation and turns himself toward the future" (RP 6d). RP 5 links it with social action and the Church's ministry of reconciliation in society, since neither the penance assigned in sacramental confession nor penitential practices in general (particularly during Lent) can be adequately understood from the perspective of personal asceticism.

Absolution

The priest's absolution is differently regarded when penitents' acts in the sacrament are recognized as ritualizing the extension of baptismal conversion. Though authoritative as an act of one entrusted with pastoral care and authorized to preside at worship, it is no more official, ecclesial, and sacramental than the acts of the penitent. It cannot be regarded as the whole of the sacrament or as an automatic guarantee of divine forgiveness and ecclesial reconciliation, even if it does complete the sacrament.

The RP states explicitly that the absolution does complete the sacrament of penance (RP 6d). It does so by being a sign of God's mercy and pardon to the repentant sinner, a sign made in, by, and through the Church and a pardon received in, by, and through the Church. As Christ was visible sign of God reconciling and saving, so the Church, as Christ, extends that word and work to every time and place. The absolution, proclaimed by the presider as a ministerial act of the Church, consecrates the whole conversion process—intrinsically, not extrinsically—by revealing its term and goal, a reconciliation with the Church whereby "the Father receives the repentant son who comes back to him, Christ places the lost sheep on his shoulders and brings it back to the sheepfold, and the Holy Spirit sanctifies this temple of God again or lives more fully within it" (RP 6d).

Until the revival of communal celebrations, only the absolution gave explicit expression to the ecclesial character of the sacrament and showed that the whole conversion process takes place in the Church. Thus, theologians considered the *votum sacramenti* (the desire for the sacrament) necessary for forgiveness and reconciliation outside the ritual. More often, however, the absolution was seen as a judicial exercise of priestly power, just as the challenge to the sinner and the call to conversion were seen as stated through ecclesiastical legislation.

As in the case of integral confession, so with the judicial nature of absolution: the RP contains some limited but significant developments. The legalistic outlook on absolution is gone. The confessor's role as judge is given less attention than in the past, though it is by no means ignored; where it appears, it is decidedly more spiritual than juridical. RP 6b states that confession requires of the penitent an openness of heart and of the minister, "spiritual judgment by which, acting in the person of Christ, he pronounces his decision of forgiveness or retention of sins in accord with the power of the keys." Trent, in the same context, had used the image of the priest as presiding judge before whose tribunal all the facts of the case must be presented so that an appropriate sentence could be pronounced.[24] By qualifying the judgment as spiritual, the RP brings out its distinctive character in relation to the discernment of spirits (correlated with judgment in RP 10a) and thus sees the confessor providing the Church's support and encouragement in facilitating and authenticating penitents' conversion. Examination of conscience and confession, we have seen, are likewise less juridical. The RP attaches more importance to genuine ecclesial conversion and an effective reconciliation than it does to completeness of confession or the exercise of judicial power. In so doing, it partially reunites the private and public roles of the priest that were only loosely connected for centuries.[25]

Judgment, an authoritative response or decision, is a dimension of absolution but not the essence of the sacrament. It is, in fact, clearly seen as an element of absolution only when a grave sinner is absolved. In the case of the individual who by serious sin has ceased to live responsibly as a member of the community of salvation, the Church responds by recognizing the reality of (re-)conversion and restoring the person to a full part in the Church. In the case of those who have not sinned seriously, it accepts them as members of a penitent Church. In both cases, the absolution is the Church's official response to the penitent, not a judgment rendered on the confession, and has a clear relationship to the assembly that does eucharist because such an assembly is the visible expression of how we have been reconciled to God in Christ. Thus, the eucharist, previously noted as *the* sacrament of reconciliation because of Christ's sacrificial presence (RP 2), is the final expression of our reconciliation with God and Church (RP 6d) just as it is the final expression of initiation into the Church.

This relationship of the eucharist to penance—parallel to the eucharist's relationship to baptism-confirmation— raises questions regarding the Pastoral Norms' (Norm X)

288

prohibition of celebrating penance and reconciliation in connection with the eucharist. The draft rite of November 30, 1972, provided for celebration of the eucharist (beginning with the presentation of the gifts) after the ritual of conversion and reconciliation in a communal celebration. All the reformed rituals, except penance, provide for celebration in the context of the eucharist. While penance is a sacrament in its own right and not a means of preparation for the eucharist, the eucharist does complete it and there is no theological requirement that they be completely separate. The prohibition is probably intended to prevent an opportunity for general absolution.

Penance's relationship to the eucharist also suggests certain lines of thought regarding the need to celebrate penance prior to communion in the case of mortal sin. The sacrament is not a means of cleansing before communion but rather of official recognition as a member of the community celebrating the eucharist. Other values can take precedence over this and the Church can choose not to require it.

There has been development here, probably as the consequence of the liturgical renewal's emphasis on the importance of full eucharistic participation. Medieval confession was a means of purification before communion and Trent prohibited those conscious of mortal sins from communion (DS 1740, 1743). The RP does not mention this. *Eucharisticum mysterium* does, but its 1982 text states the common theological opinion that in necessity, with no confessor available, an act of perfect contrition (i.e., conversion) is sufficient. This was repeated in the Introduction to *Holy Communion and Worship of the Eucharist outside Mass*, with the added mention that the eucharist frees people from their daily faults.[26] Canon 916 of the 1983 Code amends this to speak of a "serious reason" rather than "necessity."

However, there is a theological problem in explaining how, in at least some cases, repentance without the sacrament of penance is sufficient for communion and if, in such cases, the eucharist itself readmits to the eucharist. The explanation is probably that the ordinary obligation of confessing grave sins before communion is an ecclesiastical law that the Church can suspend.[27] Franco Sottocornola, secretary of the group that produced the RP, states in his commentary that the objective necessity of participating in the eucharist is verified whenever a person is present; if no confessor is available, the sincere desire to receive communion and sincere contrition for sin suffices and the eucharist is itself the sacrament of effective reconciliation.[28]

THE VALUE OF PENANCE

The Introduction concludes its doctrinal considerations by restating penance's healing value. This value is as varied as is sin and its effects and consequences in the lives of individuals and community (RP 7).

The RP uses the traditional, two-category distinction of sin—grave (rather than mortal) and venial—but its descriptive definitions (RP 5, 7) bring out the relational character, just as its language throughout emphasizes social sin and the social dimension of all sin.[29] Grave sin means an individual has withdrawn from the communion of love with God; here the sacrament of penance restores penitents to the life they had lost. Venial sin means a person is weak and has failed to attain the full freedom of the children of God; here the repeated celebration of the sacrament offers strength. The language seems carefully chosen to avoid identifying sin with an external act and to direct attention to attitudes and power rather than mere acts. The vastly different effects of penance in these two cases almost implies two different sacraments!

Repeating the Council of Trent,[30] the RP states that each grave sin of which the person is aware must be confessed to a priest. However, the requirement is stated in terms of salvific relationships rather than legal and juridical re-

290

quirements; for example, "the plan of our merciful God" replaces *iure divino.*

How the RP states the value of frequent celebration for venial sins is likewise significant. "Frequent and careful celebration" is encouraged, but such a celebration is not a "mere ritualistic repetition or psychological exercise, but a serious striving to perfect the grace of baptism" (RP 7). The goal is closer conformity to Christ and a more attentive following of the Spirit. There seems to be a significant change in outlook from that under Pius XII,[31] particularly when the RP's remarks on frequent celebration are correlated with its affirmation of other means of expressing repentance and achieving reconciliation (RP 4, 37). The concept of "devotional confession" goes unmentioned.

An even clearer sign that the RP moves away from a view favoring frequent use of the sacramental ritual as a means of getting grace is the statement that the sacrament does not achieve its purpose unless it takes root in people's lives and moves them to "more fervent service of God and neighbor" (RP 7). The liturgy of penance is to be linked with the Christian life of love and service, and the celebration is then the Church's proclamation of faith, its thanksgiving for freedom in Christ, and its sacrificial self-offering in praise of God's glory while on pilgrimage. Grace as a matter of personal transformation is not an automatic consequence of ritual nor is it evident except in the penitent's life. It is not likely to happen on schedule. For that matter, it is unlikely to happen except to the extent that ecclesial conversion is furthered. (To claim otherwise is to deny the ecclesial nature and effect of the sacrament.) The penitential rite of the Mass and penitential celebrations are thus more likely to support such growth than is devotional confession.

The sacrament of conversion and reconciliation thus stands in close relationship to a life of conversion lived in a reconciling community. It cannot simply be reduced to a ritual. It is instead closely related to penitential practices, whether these are viewed as traditional ascetic means for achieving self-integration in order to surrender fully to God or as modern forms of accepting responsibility for serving others' needs. The sacrament and the virtue of penance are once more as closely linked as they were in ancient times, though both are understood in relation to the Church's contemporary mission.

NOTES

1. Christian Duquoc, "Real Reconciliation and Sacramental Reconciliation," *Concilium* 61 (1971) 26.

2. This was Cardinal Ottaviani's concern in the Congregation of the Doctrine of the Faith's letter *Cum Oecumenicum Concilium* of July 24, 1966. The letter complained that some explanations of penance as a means of reconciliation with the Church misinterpreted the conciliar teaching by saying too little about reconciliation with the God who is offended by sin and consequently deemphasizing personal confession by stressing only the social function of reconciliation with the Church. The portion on penance is in *Documents on the Liturgy*, p. 394 (DOL 178, no. 1227). An important essay of Karl Rahner's was occasioned by this letter: "Theology and the Church's Teaching Authority after the Council," *Theological Investigations* 9 (New York: Herder and Herder, 1972) 83–100. Pope John Paul II voices concerns similar to Ottaviani's in his postsynodal exhortation.

3. Appendix III, 3, iii, 1. The English translation asks: "Where is my life really leading me?" Contemporary theological literature on sin is extensive. Significant surveys in English include Eugene J. Cooper, "A Newer Look at the Theology of Sin," *Louvain Studies* 3 (1971) 259–307; B. Kiely, *Psychology and Moral Theology* (Rome: Gregorian University Press, 1980); Kevin F. O'Shea, "The Reality of Sin: A Theological and Pastoral Critique," *Theological Studies* 29 (1968) 241–259; Piet Schoonenberg, *Man and Sin: A Theological View* (Notre Dame, Indiana: University of Notre Dame Press, 1965).

4. For Trent's teaching, see Sessio XIII, October 11, 1551: *Decretum de SS. Eucharistia*, cap. 2 (DS 1638), and Sessio XXII, September 17, 1562: *Doctrina de SS. Missae Sacrificio*, cap. 1 (DS 1740),

cap. 2 (DS 1743); see also P. Gerardi, "Eucarestia e penitenza, sacramenti di riconciliazione, nella dottrina del Concilio di Trento," *Rivista di Teologia Morale* 5 (1973) 491–514.

For writings examining the relationship between eucharist and penance, see Edward J. Kilmartin, "Eucharist and Reconciliation" in "The Eucharist in Recent Literature," *Theological Studies* 32 (1971) 254–260, and for a report on discussions by liturgists, see my "Eucharist and Penance," *Worship* 50 (1976) 324–328. See especially Ligier's articles on Eastern penance; M. van den Nieuwenhuizen, "De Eucharistie als Sakrament van de Vergeving," *Tijdschrift voor Theologie* 9 (1969) 178–195; John J. Quinn, "The Lord's Supper and the Forgiveness of Sins"; J. M. R. Tillard, "The Bread and Cup of Reconciliation," *Concilium* 61 (1971) 38–54.

The penitential rite in the present Mass is the first such rite since the medieval general absolutions. It and the sign of peace may be significant influences on the number of people confessing, serving as expressions of reconciliation in community for ordinary sinners. For studies of the rite, see Joseph A. Jungmann, "De actu poenitentiali infra missam inserto conspectus historicus," *Ephemerides Liturgicae* 80 (1966) 257–264; Adrien Nocent, "L'acte pénitentielle du nouvel 'Ordo Missae': Sacrement ou sacramental?" *Nouvelle Revue Théologique* 91 (1969) 956–976; and Denis F. O'Callaghan, "The *Confiteor-Indulgentiam* and Forgiveness of Sin," *Irish Ecclesiastical Record* 160 (1966) 322–326; Mary Alice Piil, "The Penitential Rite of the Mass," *Hosanna* 1 (1982), No. 1, pp. 28–31. Penitential themes in the prayers over the gifts and postcommunion prayers of the ancient sacramentaries and the various forms of penitential rites in the Eastern liturgies are also worth investigating for understanding the relationship of penance to eucharist.

5. Instruction of the Sacred Congregation of Rites, May 25, 1967; AAS 59 (1967) 560–561, *Documents on the Liturgy*, p. 410 (DOL 179, no. 1264).

6. For an example of discussion at the Council, see Stefan László, "Sin in the Holy Church of God," in *Council Speeches of Vatican II* (Yves Congar et al., eds.; New York: Sheed and Ward, 1964), pp. 29–31, and for a synthesis, see Karl Rahner, "The Sinful Church in the Decrees of Vatican II," *Theological Investigations* 6 (1969) 270–294. In the same volume see "The Church of

Sinners" (pp. 253–269) and "Justified and Sinner at the Same Time" (pp. 218–230) and see also Patrick McGoldrick, "Sin and the Holy Church," *Irish Theological Quarterly* 32 (1965) 3–27.

7. Duquoc, "Real Reconciliation and Sacramental Reconciliation," p. 28.

8. Paul Greégoire, "The Use of Penance and the Sense of Sin," *Doctrine and Life* 22 (1972) 32–34.

9. The only recent negative assessments of the position appear to be those of Clarence McAuliffe ("Penance and Reconciliation with the Church," *Theological Studies* 26 [1965] 1–39) and Francis J. Connell ("Some Recent Statements on the Sacrament of Penance," *American Ecclesiastical Review* 155 [1966] 278–280).

10. See Karl Rahner, "Penance as an Additional Act of Reconciliation with the Church," *Theological Investigations* 10 (1973) 125–149.

11. The 1983 Code of Canon Law reverts to a preconciliar understanding, where the penitent is the passive individual recipient of the priest's ministration. Canon 960, for example, rewords RP 31 to make the Latin word for "faithful" singular rather than plural and uses the passive rather than active voice. In the RP as first promulgated, the faithful were regarded as actively involved in reconciling themselves with God and the Church. It has now been corrected. In general, changes in the wording of parallel passages heighten the importance of individual confession and the judicial character of priestly absolution, the major characteristics of late medieval penance emphasized by Trent as normative in reaction to the attacks of Protestant reformers.

12. The 1983 Code of Canon Law largely contradicts this. By failing to mention communal celebrations, regularly speaking of "confession," and being primarily concerned with restricting possible use of general absolution, the Code reverts to a preoccupation with integrity that fixes attention on past sin and leaves little room for praise and thanksgiving.

13. See especially Arnold Uleyn, *Is It I, Lord? Pastoral Psychology and the Recognition of Guilt* (New York: Holt, Rinehart and Winston, 1969).

14. Manual theology often had discouraging and unrealistic expectations, largely the residue of the attrition-contrition controversies, yet someone able to turn away from evil has already

overcome the only real difficulty impeding love of God. For this reason, Karl Rahner regards the distinction between perfect and imperfect contrition as irrelevant. See his *Allow Yourself to Be Forgiven: Penance Today* (Denville, N.J.: Dimension Books, 1978), pp. 37–38).

15. This is cited in RP 6a: "heartfelt sorrow and aversion for the sin committed along with the intention of sinning no more." See Council of Trent, Sessio XIV, *De sacramento paenitentiae*, c. IV (DS 1676).

16. As was noted in the introduction to Part One, the historical variation of the sacrament poses a crucial hermeneutical problem. It can be said, at the least, that for a millennium and more the Church's tradition maintained a materially different understanding of what constitutes integrity and which sins must be confessed than has been the case since. A less cautious, but still defensible, interpretation is that the ancient Church simply did not require integral confession except in the case of those sins whose gravity necessitated the formal process. In any case, the pre-Tridentine Western tradition, as well as the constant tradition of the East, must be part of the context for interpreting the statement of Trent that complete ("integral") confession is "iure divino." The basic problem here for the theologian is to distinguish the essential features of the sacramental encounter from those that are temporally or culturally conditioned, even when that conditioning takes the form of a conciliar dogmatic statement—which itself, of course, requires interpretation.

17. Primarily the result of historical studies, this has undoubtedly been the major contribution of twentieth-century theology to the ongoing development of the sacrament and received official acceptance at Vatican Council II. The full significance of this will probably not be fully evident for decades. The present transitional tension is largely due to the difficulty of integrating traditional spirituality and this contemporary (actually, ancient) conviction.

18. Such needs are not merely the consequence of a declining number of priests to serve as confessors. They go on to include, among others, institutional alienation (particularly from the penitential system) and the need to express and experience community support. Such needs would exist—and be perhaps even more intensely felt—were there a superabundance of clergy.

However, official recognition of such pastoral needs has been limited to situations where the proportion of clergy to laity has made it impossible to fulfill the Tridentine requirement.

19. It has been said that while Trent stated that integrity was required by God in some instances, it did not state when, where, of whom, or in what circumstances. Cf. Carl J. Peter, "Integrity Today," *Communio* 1 (1974) 71–72. However, the Church has indicated some instances when it is *not* required. Trent itself noted that physical impossibility excuses from confession, though not from the *votum* of the sacrament. Later theology extended this to moral or psychological impossibility and distinguished material and formal integrity.

20. The 1973 RP added: "unless physical or moral impossibility excuses from this kind of confession." The 1983 Code of Canon Law (canon 960) amends RP 31 to emphasize that "physical or moral impossibility alone excuses" and restricts the criteria for recognizing such situations. Another terminological difference: where Trent spoke of mortal sins (*peccata mortalia*) and the Pastoral Norms of lethal sins (*peccata lethalia*), the first committee drafting the reformed rite spoke of more grave sins (*peccata graviora*), sins that separate from Christ and his Mystical Body, and the RP uses grave sins (*peccata gravia*) to indicate those sins that must be submitted in individual confession.

21. "Let [the confessor] remember that satisfaction is not only a remedy for renewing one's life and a medicine for infirmity but also a punishment for past sins" (*Rituale Romanum*, III, I, 18). Cf. DS 1692.

22. For a reinterpretation of mortification, see Rosemary Haughton, "Penance and Asceticism in the Modern World," in *Sin and Repentance* (edited by Denis F. O'Callaghan; Staten Island: Alba House, 1967), pp. 73–92. I have utilized this understanding in my "Reflections on Penance," *Origins* 4 (1975) 525–528, and "Penance and the Life Situation of the Penitent," in *The New Rite of Penance: Background Catechesis* (Pevely, Missouri: Federation of Diocesan Liturgical Commissions, 1975), pp. 23–33.

23. See DS 1692 and *Rituale Romanum*, III, I, 18ff and cf. *Paenitemini*.

24. DS 1679–1683, especially the "praesides et iudices" of DS 1679, and cf. *Rituale Romanum*, III, I, 2, where the priest fills the

role "iudicis pariter et medici" but is finally spoken of as the "arbiter" between God and mortals. However, the ritual gives a great deal of emphasis to the confessor's medicinal role to balance this. The more heavily juridical model comes out of post-Tridentine manual theology. Though attentuated in the RP, it is restated in Canon 978, which again speaks of the priest as "iudicis pariter et medici."

25. Cf. above, p. 74, for the historical origin of this separation.

26. No. 23 (*Documents on the Liturgy*, p. 658 [DOL 267, no. 2101]).

27. The exclusion of the grave sinner from communion was not dogmatically defined at Trent as a matter of divine law. See Louis Braeckmans, *Confession et Communion au Moyen-Âge et au Concile de Trente.*

28. See "Les nouveaux rites de la pénitence. Commentaire," *Questions Liturgiques* 55 (1974) 102–104, and the General Instruction of the Sacramentary, 29, 30, 56a, b, g.

29. See especially RP 4, 5, 7, 18, 25c.

30. Sessio XIV, *De sacramento paenitentiae*, canons 7–8; DS 1707–1708.

31. Cf. *Mystici corporis*, 86, cited above, p. 188. See also Pastoral Norms, 3.

Chapter Nine

Liturgies of Conversion and Reconciliation

Providing for penance's liturgical celebration is a radical change from recent practice. Still, new structures and texts will not compensate for penance's past liturgical poverty unless we first regain the sense that it is worship, Christ's saving action present through the Spirit's work in the Church. The RP clearly states that penance is worship (e.g., RP 4, 7, 11), but the inability to see penance as the activity of the Spirit-filled community acting as the presence of Jesus' saving mystery is a major obstacle to full implementation of the RP and resolution of controversial questions, including that of general absolution.[1]

If penance is liturgy, the community engaged in ritual prayer, its focus must be God rather than forgiveness. The realization of sin and the experience of sorrow must grow together with a conviction of God's mercy in order to be more than regret or remorse. Confession must be a confident and humble proclamation of the Church's faith in a loyal God and gratitude and thankfulness for God's gift of forgiveness—in the spirit, if not the form, of the *berakah* and *exomologesis*—before it is admission of one's sins. The act of penance must show the intention to reorient one's life as worship, experiencing and proclaiming God's mercy there. A proper understanding of the priest's role as judge must flow from the recognition that penance is the Church's worship at which the priest presides. Priest and penitents together share and celebrate the liturgy by which the Church itself seeks and receives renewal in the Spirit of Jesus (cf. RP 11).

To separate the acknowledgment of sin and sorrow from the praise of God accomplished in the joy of the Spirit is to risk losing both. It is to fail to realize that penance as an act of worship is a means of participating in the Easter Mystery and thus a form of eucharist[2] to be completed in the eucharistic assembly. For this realization to take root in our communities, there must be a radical shift in mentality and style of celebration, or we will again find that disoriented piety and spirituality can do more to distort liturgical ritual than ritual can do to transform them.

Balancing and integrating the personal or individual dimension of penance and the ecclesial and social dimension has been a recurrent difficulty through the centuries. The RP makes penance's social and ecclesial effect central to redress the previous overemphasis on the personal, which led to an individualistic outlook. The individualistic view of sin and responsibility and a lack of social consciousness led to an excessively psychological and introspective vision of sin and confession, with minute schemata for examining conscience and a therapeutic use of confession. Sin was viewed moralistically and juridically; Christians were concerned with borderlines; morality and spirituality drifted apart. To counter this, penance must once more be conversion in the sense of the scriptural *metanoia;* the social dimension of sin and penance must be stressed; and the communal dimension must be normative for celebrating, so that the joy inherent in Christian penance and worship can surface once again.

The personal dimension finds expression in the penitential celebration and the communal celebrations of the sacrament as well as in the reconciliation of an individual penitent, so the normative character of the communal celebration need not obscure the personal aspect. Conversion and reconciliation may well, in fact, be more highly personal in the communal celebration than in the individual rite. Certainly the emphasis on conversion and reconciliation in the community must not be detrimental to the personal dimension; as individuals, we deserve a personal encounter with Christ and Christ himself requires it.[3] But we are also God's People redeemed and renewed in Christ, standing before God's throne. The RP shows in its summary that all God's actions in the history of salvation have been directed toward forming a community that is both reconciled and reconciling. This, until recent decades, had faded from the Church's consciousness and must now be restored. Good celebrations will foster and nourish this faith; poor celebrations will weaken and destroy it.[4]

MINISTRIES OF PENANCE AND RECONCILIATION
The RP's central emphasis on conversion and reconciliation in an ecclesial setting calls for penance to be set within the rhythms of personal and community life. For that to happen, both pastoral and sacramental ministry need the reorientation called for in RP 8–11: the community is minister and celebrant, and every role and office in the sacrament draws its power and motive force from that principle.

The Role of the Community
Christian conversion and each of its phases is always both personal and ecclesial, the personal encounter with a saving God in Christ, a Christ who is recognized only in the community of those identified with him as disciples. Since the emergence of medieval penance, the accent has been on the personal—more accurately, the individual—dimension, reducing conversion to the penitent's ritual acts made before the priest and reconciliation to the priest's absolution. The RP attempts to balance the personal and ecclesial dimensions by giving renewed expression to the Church's involvement in the whole process of conversion as well as in the reconciliation that completes it.

The RP's understanding of penance and reconciliation does not confine ecclesial ministry to the priest, even though his ministry is ordinarily required for the reconciliation of those who have been alienated from the Church by grave sin. RP 8 states that "the whole Church, as a priestly people, acts in different ways in the work of reconciliation." However, the examples it gives are largely vicarious, with the priest serving as proxy for the community. The call to repentance through preaching is mentioned, but present discipline ordinarily restricts that ministry to the ordained. Interceding for sinners and assisting them in confessing are part of the community ministry, but they need to be particularized. The final statement—that the Church becomes the instrument of conversion and absolution through the apostolic ministry—comes close to collapsing the process of conversion and the ministry of reconciliation into the ritual of priestly absolution. Though the title speaks of the role or function[5] of the community in celebrating penance, the framers of the RP, after a brief effort, revert to the standard outlook.

The community was actively involved in ancient penance. Its ministry was evident and effective, with nonordained members prominent in specific ministries to sinners and penitents. The community shared in praying for sinners and challenging them, in praying for penitents and reconciling them. Both the ordained and the unordained ministered as counselors and spiritual directors. Though in medieval penance—as in all medieval liturgy—the clergy assumed the community's role, the community continued to be involved in both solemn and Lenten penance. The nonordained continued to minister in lay confession. Only in the late medieval and early modern period, when individual auricular confession and priestly absolution became the sole symbol of conversion and reconciliation, was the community's responsibility and function forgotten.

As we recognize once more that initiation shapes ministers and that Christians become members of the ministering community of the faithful by baptism, we again begin to see how the whole of this priestly people is involved in the ministry of reconciliation. All the ways in which we support and encourage one another to be a communion of saints—the witness of our lives, public and private prayer, the informal and formal counseling and spiritual direction that we give, days and seasons and celebrations of penance—not only stand in continuity with the age-old forms of service to the kingdom, humanity, and sinners but are also much more fundamental forms of the ministry of reconciliation than is priestly absolution. They are likewise the only appropriate context for properly understanding and appreciating that specific ministry.

Penitential celebrations and intercessions in the prayer of the faithful are not ways of encouraging people to receive the sacrament more frequently or methods to prepare them for celebration or means of compensating for unavailable priests. They are as much a part of the sacramental process today as they were forms of the sacrament in previous ages. Indeed, all our gatherings (and particularly the ways through which we deepen our awareness of one another, attend to one another's needs, and interact with one another in our gatherings) express our character as a reconciling community, a community that makes welcome and warmly accepts. Consequently, all the rituals of hospitality in our worship are means and expressions of reconciliation when done with a consciousness of ministry: prayers for sinners and penitents in our general intercessions, less perfunctory (and, probably, less frequently used) forms of the penitential rite, a deeper understanding of the sign of peace, and all the ways in which our liturgies become community celebrations. Community prayer for sinners is of paramount importance, particularly in penitential celebrations and communal celebrations of the sacrament of penance. As in ancient penance, so today: the result of the penitent's striving for conversion and the community's prayer shows that God's forgiveness reaches mortals through the mediation of the ecclesial community, a sacrament of the risen Lord.

New ways of exercising this ministry of reconciliation need to be discerned. The starting point, the call to conversion, for example, is addressed personally to the penitent by God in Christ through the Church. For the last millennium authoritative binding has been almost exclusively legal and almost solely a hierarchical ministry. That the initiative is God's and the introduction into penance is a ministerial act of the whole Church and an exercise of its ministry of reconciliation as much as is its loosing needs to be more deeply appreciated and expressed ritually as well. That this binding is currently evident only in the Ash Wednesday liturgy, as the entire community enters penance, highlights the importance of Lenten celebrations.

In a complex society where we more readily recognize our interdependence and where the Church takes on a new role in society, the Church's service to the kingdom, humanity, and sinful individuals must take forms unimaginable or impossible in former ages. It must work for global peace and justice as well as respond to individuals' needs for healing. It must struggle to eradicate all forms of division and discrimination and transform sinful social structures—within itself first—as well as strengthen individuals to bear up under oppression and resist sinful influences. Community rituals must be a prophetic protest against social evils and a means of sensitizing participants to the part they play in causing, perpetuating, or tolerating such evils. They must also include, more than ever before, a consciousness of the Church's complicity.

Sacramental revitalization requires a sense of the Church as a reconciled and reconciling community, a community in which all members are coresponsible for mission and worship. The RP speaks, for example, of the laity as agents of reconciliation (RP 5, 8) and mentions their role in planning and preparing if celebrations are to be effective (RP 40b). A vision of Church and ministry far different from that of medieval and Counter-Reformation times

303

is evident here. Missing, however, and urgently needed is the realization that there are and can be specific ministries of penance and reconciliation other than that of the priest.

Such an experience of Church depends on well-prepared and well-celebrated community celebrations. The Christian community is unlikely to remain conscious of its identity or to be able to express it adequately except through consciously social activity. Ritual's function in focusing a world view and interpreting experience requires it. Unless a parish community gathers regularly for such celebrations, the revitalization of the sacrament of penance will be impossible; it will continue to be understood and used in a distorted and misleading fashion. Only through such celebrations will the Church community itself (rather than simply the priest as its minister) be realized as continuing the mission of Jesus as providing a place of reconciliation, the condition and the milieu of reconciliation with others and with God.

The Role of the Priest
Bishop and presbyter exercise their ministry of reconciliation by calling to conversion in preaching (especially in penitential celebrations and communal celebrations of penance), regulating the sacramental discipline, and declaring and granting forgiveness in the sacrament (RP 9). The priest's primary role, supervising the ecclesial process of conversion and presiding at the liturgical celebration of reconciliation, is an ecclesial role in worship, not sitting in judgment with a power that is purely and simply his. Affirming the community's role as primary, seeing the sacramental celebration as worship, and giving the proclamation of the Word first place in the priest's ministry are major steps in clarifying the priest's role in the sacrament and show that his ministry is much broader than hearing confession and giving absolution.

The RP situates the minister of the sacrament in an ecclesial context as representative of the Church community. He is minister of the Church (RP 6) and God (RP 6, 10d), acting in the person of Christ (RP 6, 9). God grants remission of sins through the Church, which exercises the ministry of this sacrament through bishop and priest (RP 6, 8, 9a).[6] This does not reduce the priest simply to a community spokesman, since his relationship to the community founds his relationship to penitents. He declares and grants forgiveness in speaking for the community of salvation as its shepherd and leader and, in the case of the presbyter, as one who participates in the bishop's ministry of oversight.

The bishop's traditional role as moderator of penitential discipline was restated at Vatican Council II[7] but has received little attention since. In the RP and canon law, the bishop is still envisioned as regulating the discipline legally rather than moderating it pastorally. There is little indication, for example, that he is as much expected to preside at community celebrations of penance as confirmation, though the latter role is likewise delegated to presbyters. Even his limited ability to regulate penance legally by approving confessors individually and authorizing communal celebrations with general absolution has been lessened in the new Code.

The competent minister, in the canonical sense, is a priest with the faculty to absolve, though neither ordination nor faculties ensure the ability to serve as confessor. (As is customary in the new rituals, the term priest [*sacerdos*] includes both bishops and presbyters.) Working in communion with the local bishop, presbyters share his responsibility for penitential discipline and thus, except when the penitent is in danger of death, must have the faculty to absolve (RP 9b). The 1983 Code simplifies this considerably: as a rule, a priest who has authorization anywhere has it everywhere, except where it is explicitly withdrawn.[8] There are evident pastoral advantages to this change but also unfortunate by-products: there is little indication that the priest is a minister of the local community and that the penitent is, first and foremost, reconciled in and to the local Church.

The emphasis on the ecclesial dimension of the sacrament and envisioning the priest's role as a ministry within the Church contrasts sharply with the late medieval and Counter-Reformation view of the priest as judge and an individual with powers received in virtue of ordination. Clericalization and juridicization were closely correlated in the changing medieval absolution formulas and in later theological developments, with the final indicative and juridical formula stating the priest's role in a fragmentary and polemical fashion. The absolution formulas in the RP give fuller expression to the whole Church's involvement in reconciling the sinner and situate the declaration of official judgment—the "I absolve you"—in the context of Church and of prayer.

The priest's proper role is presiding at the Church's worship. Therefore, what is reserved to him in penance is the official response to the penitents' manifestation of their repentance to the Church and the proclamation of the absolution that grants reconciliation, just as heading the table to proclaim the eucharistic prayer is his at the eucharist. Though for the first time in centuries penance is regarded as liturgical worship, the Introduction gives little attention to the priest as presider in describing his ministry (RP 9) and its pastoral exercise (RP 10). The only possible reference to communal celebrations is in the mention of preaching. Otherwise RP 9–10 has in view the reconciliation of individual penitents and devotes itself to expressions of ministry that are not exclusively the priest's. Still, whether in reconciling groups or individuals, the priest functions as the presiding celebrant at the Church's celebration.

Recognizing that the sacrament is ecclesial worship clarifies the priest's significance rather than diminishes it. Confession as a matter of personal catharsis can be made to anyone and anyone qualified may serve as spiritual counselor. However, to be ecclesial, conversion must be supervised, authenticated, or accepted by someone able to speak for the Church. Reconciliation must be granted by someone in such a position. Worship, to be the Church's worship, must be presided over by someone authorized to do so. But this official character is only a component of representing and embodying the community sacramentally, that is, in a human way. And so, even in the reconciliation of an individual, it is more appropriate to speak of the priest as presiding at worship than as presiding in court. His role is not authoritarian or patronizing—it is paternal only in the sense of revealing God's mercy—but neither is it therapeutic. Rather, it is sacramental (cf. RP 10c).

Recognizing penance as ecclesial worship puts heavier demands on the priest. Even the ultrarigid theological proponents of an *ex opere operato* efficacy of the sacrament required the penitent's personal involvement through faith and commitment and hoped for the priest's involvement in a similar manner. Now that is crucial for the proper and effective exercise of the ministry in this sacrament.

The ministry of confessor receives most attention, though of itself it is not exclusively a priestly ministry. Its historical development is a largely unexplored area in the history of penance.[9] In the ancient period, the bishop's position as community leader was the foundation for all the ways in which he ordered the community: admitting new members, readmitting penitents, ordaining presbyters and deacons, presiding at worship. The same held true when these functions were delegated to presbyters. However, supervising penitents, whether done by the bishop or delegated priest-penitentiaries, increasingly required the type of expertise expected of Eastern monastic confessors.

Tariff penance in its final form combined the two roles of spiritual counselor (supportive confessor) and community official (absolving judge) in the person of the priest. It thus reduced lay exercise of the ministry of confessor, since that role was increasingly regarded as official and authoritative. But not until the late medieval fixation on absolution as a ritual and rather mechanical means of forgiveness did the juridical dimension overshadow the spiritual, lead to the confessor being regarded as judge, and thus exclude laity from being regarded as confessors. Role changes in the course of the Reformation, Counter-Reformation, baroque period, and struggles with Jansenism gave the juridical dimension even greater priority.

Traditionally, then, the confessor has been more counselor and spiritual director—physician—than judge, even though restoration to the community was ordinarily reserved to the official who presided over its worship. Only as the shift is made from reconciliation in the community to direct forgiveness of the individual's sins (and thus repression of the ecclesial and communal dimension) did the situation change. At that point confession to the priest, who has the power to absolve, becomes crucial.

The question is whether the category of power is appropriate for understanding the priest's role in the sacrament of penance. Both sides in the sixteenth-century controversies presupposed it was, with Protestant reformers denying that priests possessed such power as unique mediators and Trent affirming it. The Counter-Reformation's reaction, emphasizing priestly power, served to diminish further what remained of the ecclesial view of the sacraments.[10] Now emphasis on the priestly character of the community of believers (as in RP 8) requires that the ordained minister's role be seen in the context of community and viewed as ministry rather than power. The clearly ministerial role of spiritual counselor is not reserved to the priest and the role that is uniquely his—accepting and reconciling penitents who have been excluded by grave sin—is not a personal power but an ecclesial ministry closely connected with ordering the community and presiding at its worship.

RP 10's description of this ministry—confined to individual confession—contrasts with the 1614 Ritual but is in line with earlier tradition. It has high expectations of the

confessor, requiring much more than ordination and juridical competence. It correlates the two roles of spiritual
counselor (supportive confessor or physician) and community official (absolving judge), giving primacy to the
confessor's pastoral role and linking the judicial role with
discernment of spirits (RP 10a), a charism traditionally
associated more with the role of spiritual guide. It ex-
pands the roles of physician and judge to include
leadership in prayer, discernment of spirits, and pastoral
dedication, as well as the human warmth of a friend,
making the ministry more akin to the ancient spiritual
counselor and modern spiritual director than the confessor of recent memory. (However, the 1983 Code of Canon
Law reverts to the Counter-Reformation view by using
the wording of the 1614 ritual, "judicis pariter et medici,"
in effect again giving priority to the role of judge [canon
978].)

The ministry requires a sensitivity to persons and the
Spirit that facilitates healing and offers encouragement
and guidance, a charism unfortunately not given by ordination. Though the RP by no means makes penance into
counseling or spiritual direction, it does recognize that
some spiritual counsel may be called for (RP 18; cf. RP 7c)
and bases it in human affection and the Spirit. A skill or
art more valuable in the exercise of this ministry than giving advice is that of attentiveness: listening in such a way as
to help the penitent clarify perceptions and feelings about
God, self, and behavior. Like laypeople who exercise this
ministry informally, the priest-confessor must be able to
listen sensitively and helpfully.

Discernment of spirits, linked in RP 10 with the office of
judge, requires a genuine concern and affection for people. It also requires a knowledge of God's workings based
on more than magisterial pronouncements and general
theological principles, though these are necessary for the
confessor's ministry. The evangelization of conscience—the
goal of penitential preaching—takes a more individual
and personal form in private confession, but even here it

must be a matter of assisting penitents to form conscience rather than making decisions for them or leaving them completely on their own.

To be able to reveal the Spirit—in other words, to be a sacrament oneself—requires the spirit of fervent, scripturally oriented prayer. Such prayer is not only a matter of the confessor's own spiritual life but also the presider's special ministry in the ritual event of penance, because preaching and leadership in ritual prayer are the two major forms that presiding takes in every form of penance liturgy. In the reconciliation of an individual, as well as in communal celebrations and every sacramental liturgy, breaking the bread of the Word and leading prayer are the basic expressions of priestly ministry.[11] By associating discernment of spirits with the judicial role, that of presiding, the RP seeks to ensure that spiritual counsel is always subordinate to worship and that instruction is not to the detriment of prayer but part of sharing the Word. The requirement of the seal—absolute confidentiality concerning anything that would be to the penitent's disadvantage—is seen in this same context (RP 10d).

The qualities required lead to the conclusion that not every priest is qualified to serve as confessor and that, so far as spiritual direction and counseling are concerned, others may be better able to provide this service. The priest's primary role is presiding, and no one incapable of this ministry should be ordained.

The Role of the Penitent

As full members of the community of the faithful, penitents are coresponsible with priests for the mission and worship of the Church. What the RP says of their role in the sacrament better applies to both communal and individual celebrations than does its description of the priest's ministry. The personal, ecclesial, and sacramental character of their actions (RP 6) makes them sharers in the sacrament and cocelebrants of the liturgy. They are not merely passive recipients of priestly absolution—that only com-

310

pletes the sacrament (RP 11). Calling them "faithful" (RP 2, 4), "member of the Church" (RP 3), and "disciple of Christ" (RP 6), as well as the usual "sinner" (e.g., RP 3, 5) and "penitent" (e.g., RP 6), brings out their ecclesial character. In their lives, penitents experience and proclaim God's mercy; in the sacrament, together with the priest who presides over the Church's worship, they are the community of believers celebrating "the liturgy by which the Church continually renews itself" (RP 11).

Authentic conversion, though always ecclesial, is ritually shown as such in penitential celebrations and the reconciliation of groups of penitents. In most cases, conversion has been completed before the penitent comes to the celebration and needs only to be accepted by the Church for reconciliation; the sacramental celebration must therefore be an experience that strengthens the penitent's relationship to God and neighbor. In those cases where repentance and conversion have only begun, the same experience will be the foundation for the growth in faith and love that is needed for reconciliation. In either situation, the responsibility of providing the human foundation for that experience in the sacramental ritual is the whole community's in communal celebrations and solely the priest's in the reconciliation of an individual. Whichever liturgical form is used, the penitent's understanding of the process of sanctification, individualistic or ecclesial, will largely determine his or her approach to the sacrament: whether it is regarded as spiritual hygiene or growth in love. However, the more evident the role of Church and the experience of community, the more likely it is that the penitent will enter fully into the Mystery of Christ.

CELEBRATING PENANCE AND RECONCILIATION
Conversion and reconciliation are ritualized in the liturgical celebration of penance. As a converting community, one that strives to surrender to the Spirit and be transformed, the assembly presents itself as model for peni-

tents and identifies with their struggle. As a converted community, one possessed by the Spirit and reconciled by Jesus to the Father, the assembly shares its Spirit with the penitents and identifies them with itself by accepting them. The activity by which it completes the sacrament is the memorializing or *anamnesis* of Jesus who welcomed sinners and ate with them (e.g., Lk 15: 2) because he recognized that God was loyal, present even in the midst of conflicts and transgressions. Its liturgy, then, is *eucharistia*, thankful praise and faith that God's love is found in such surprising places as sinners' lives.

Such celebration requires more than liturgical texts if the assembly's activity is to be the *anamnesis* of Jesus and if its liturgy is to be *eucharistia*. The fourth section of the Introduction, on celebration, indicates this broader character by beginning with brief statements on environment and time and then describing the activity of the celebrants. Its remarks on environment are, unfortunately, too brief to be helpful to church architects and its descriptions of the activity that takes place in the different sacramental forms make it difficult to get a sense of the overarching rhythmic structure of the celebrations.

The Environment of Celebration
The environment for liturgy has too often been given inadequate attention, yet space stifles and cramps or facilitates and enhances celebration. Until appropriate space is provided, the reformed liturgy is hampered, yet the RP gives little advice. RP 12 originally simply said that law determines the place and location for ministering the sacrament and made no distinction between the place for reconciling individuals and groups. The new Code provides some specifics.[12] Canon 964 states that confessions are ordinarily heard in a church or oratory (canon 964, 1), that the episcopal conference establishes norms for the location, but that there be must be locations, in an open place, with a fixed screen between confessor and penitent, available for those who wish them (canon 964,

2), and that confessions should not be heard outside the usual location except for a legitimate reason (canon 964, 3).[13]

As in all other cases, the communal celebration is normative: it best expresses the nature and effect of the sacrament and thus the ideal form of the sacramental liturgy. Sacrament is more action than thing, the action of a community, and this action generates and organizes space. Since liturgical space houses the activity of a community that welcomes and reconciles, the proper environment for the celebration is one where the local church can assemble, hear God's Word, respond in the prayer of faith and praise, and express itself as a reconciled and reconciling community.

Though receiving the Word and responding to it in faith and praise are central dynamics of the celebration, the assembly itself is the central sign and belonging to it the central experience. Unfortunately, the usual church building (particularly the two-room church that separates clergy and laity) impedes rather than enhances this experience. This is especially true when the assembly comes nowhere close to filling the space, but in almost every case the arrangement of the church and the furniture in it make it difficult for the assembly to be genuinely active. The activity of an inclusive, reconciling community might be represented graphically as an ever-expanding circle centered on God's reconciling Word. Therefore, the community should gather near the place of proclamation; if that is too far from the seating provided, the lectern should be brought closer. Since these celebrations will usually be scheduled in the evenings, proper use of lighting can enhance the sense of gathering together and minimize the empty feeling of the larger room.

When individual confessions take place as part of the communal celebration or after the penitential celebration, the places for confession should be carefully chosen to provide privacy without weakening the sense of being a gathered community. It is unlikely that either reconciliation rooms or conventional confessionals—still less the sacristy!—will be appropriate, since these draw priests and penitents away from the assembly. An ideal spot—indeed, the classical place for reconciliation—is the presidential chair. Others are the baptistery, the place for sacramentalizing the Christian's first and lasting conversion; near the Table, where common union in Christ is celebrated and actualized; and the place for reserving the eucharist, the enduring pledge of the covenant of reconciliation—presuming that all are part of the assembly space. Since individual confessions are usually part of a communal celebration only when the assembly is relatively small, other parts of the church might be usable.

For reconciling individuals, the bishops of the United States have approved and encouraged the use of rooms properly laid out and decorated that are designed for the celebration of the sacrament.[14] Whether called reconciliation rooms or confessionals, they are necessary for the proper celebration of the reformed liturgy of penance. Its celebration is almost impossible in the dark box in which, since the seventeenth century, priest and penitent have been closeted with a barrier between them. As the bishop's chair was the place of reconciliation in ancient penance, so the priest's home was the original place for individual confession. This suggests that a homelike atmosphere is more appropriate than an institutional one. The sacrament's social nature and effect suggests that the ideal location is a small chapel or room, a warm, open setting where both confessor and penitent may be comfortable and relaxed and engage in a prayerful exchange. Both can focus on the Word and share the prayer of faith in response to it. The prayerful, conversational dialogue that the confession of sins should be and the spiritual counsel that may be appropriate can flow more easily there. Certainly, the extension (or imposition) of hands called for in the rite as symbol of reconciliation is not possible in the confession box.

314

The 1983 Code requires that a screen be available for penitents who wish to use it, but the option of anonymity is the penitent's, not the priest's. Since it hinders the expression of the sacrament's social nature and effect, its use is no longer required. In time, as adequate catechesis is provided, as the reformed liturgy is implemented, and as trust deepens between priest and penitents, it probably will rarely be used. The room should be designed so that the penitent, on entering, is not visible to the priest and sees both a simple grill or screen with kneeler and chair and a conference area for being seated to speak directly with the priest. Penitents can then choose to celebrate the sacrament with the priest either anonymously or face-to-face. The screen should be made so that it is not simply a blank wall to which the penitent speaks; loosely woven cloth, with lighting carefully arranged, can provide for the penitent's anonymity while allowing the priest's features to be seen. Those unable to kneel comfortably should have the option of a chair.

The conference area, warmly lighted and inviting, should contain several chairs (perhaps arranged around a low table), both to allow couples and small groups to celebrate the sacrament together and to permit a penitent to choose a place to be comfortably seated. The room should not be so small as to give the impression that God's mercy is cramped and restricted. Color, carpeting, windows, and art work should make it uncluttered, warm, and welcoming. In other words, it should be a simply and tastefully decorated living room. The Book of the Word, recording God's call seeking our response, is, apart from the assembly, the most important symbol in every celebration; the scriptures should therefore be prominently displayed and accessible for use. A large candle and a well-designed cross may also appropriately be used.

Deciding where to locate the reconciliation room will be difficult in most older churches and poor choices have frequently been made. Likely possibilities include a former baptistery, a sacristy or storeroom, an usher's room or crying room or shrine area. However, it is important that it be easily accessible, large enough to be comfortable— existing confessionals are, in almost every case, too small to be renovated—and clearly permanent. Ideally, it should not be used for any other purpose.

Planning groups should also give careful attention to other appropriate symbols in celebrating penance, both environmental symbols—such as lighting, visuals, candles, cross, book, water, and plants—and assembly symbols—posture, gesture, movement, silence, interaction, sign of peace, and the like. The presider's liturgical vestments, another aspect of symbolism, are left to the regulation of local ordinaries (RP 14). The alb and purple stole are generally appropriate. The flimsy purple ribbon that in the past substituted for the stole in the confessional should be disposed of.

The Time of Celebration
Since the celebration of penance must be carefully integrated into the rhythms of community and personal life, Lent is the most appropriate time for celebrating it (RP 13) and the best time to impress on people that immersion in penance is part of a lifelong process. This is the season when the Christian community leads catechumens to the font of life and itself seeks renewal in the Easter Mystery. Though the Introduction fails to mention Lent's baptismal base, baptism gives the season its conversionary character (cf. Appendix II, 7–13). As a time of conversion and of being reconciled with God and neighbor, it is a period that every community should mark by carefully prepared penitential celebrations (RP 13, 40b; Appendix II, 5).[15]

When developed in tandem with the ceremonies that mark the catechumens' journey to Easter, such celebrations are a superb means of supporting the Christian's lifelong conversion, reinvigorating the sacrament of penance, and preparing the community to celebrate Easter.[16] On Ash Wednesday, the community hears the call to conversion and commits itself to penance. Weekly celebra-

316

tions, either in place of familiar Lenten devotions or combined with them (cf. Appendix II, 19), extend that call and commitment throughout the season. They might do so by challenging the community with the reality of sin (first week) and the Christian call to holiness (second week) and by supporting the community and individuals in expressing guilt (third week) and changing their lives (fourth and fifth weeks). They should lead to communal celebrations completing the sacrament during Holy Week, before the triduum, so that the community, reconciled and renewed, is ready to celebrate the Easter Sacrament.[17] If linked with carefully chosen individual and communal practices of penance in the spirit of *Paenitemini*, penitential celebrations also promote the integration of Lenten liturgy and Lenten life. Such community celebrations should prove valuable means for reintegrating once-alienated members into the community.

Though not a penitential season, Advent, as a time of joyful expectation, is also a likely time for a community to celebrate the sacrament. Other days of prayer and penance for a parish, diocese, or nation—the transferred ember days (*Sacrosanctum concilium*, 105; *Paenitemini*)—can also be appropriate times. They should be carefully chosen to fit the season or the rhythm of the liturgical or civil calendar and well planned in order to make them red-letter days in the life of the community. Pastors and others responsible for the worship-life of a community need to be alert to these times and to special occasions in its life or the life of groups within it that call for such celebrations. Various renewal events (such as retreats, marriage encounters, cursillos, and missions) or sacramental preparation programs can, for example, be appropriate times for parish or group celebration.

The sacrament of penance may, when necessary, be celebrated at any time on any day. Though a priest is expected to respond when requested (RP 10b), every parish will have regularly scheduled times when the priest is available for individual celebrations. (RP 13 notes that this is to be outside the time of mass.) Each parish needs to determine an appropriate schedule. During Lent and on days of penance, as well as on a weekly basis, parishes should see to the availability of priests for individual as well as communal celebration. Friday, as a weekly day of penance (canon 1250), might be a good time in some communities. Though the pattern of Saturday afternoons and evenings has been customary, it is often no longer practical because of weddings and vigil masses. It is also likely to reinforce what remains of the confession-before-communion syndrome or encourage the view that the sacrament is needed only by those who have sinned gravely, so that they can receive communion at Sunday mass.

Annual, seasonal, and weekly rhythms of celebration can be established for communities, but it is not as easy to determine a recommended frequency of celebration for individuals. Only those conscious of grave sin are required to celebrate the sacrament; they are expected to do so once a year (canon 989) and should be able to do so before the Easter communion (canon 920). Mortal sin will be rare in the life of a Christian, but the practice of confessing venial sins is certainly recommended in RP 7 and canon 988. However, RP 7 calls for "frequent and careful celebration" in terms far different from those current in past decades. Other means of forgiveness of daily faults are recognized, and the idea of getting grace or using devotional confession as an ascetic discipline to root out faults is absent.

The criterion of frequency is intensifying the spirit of ecclesial conversion that flows from baptism (RP 7). Conforming oneself more closely to Christ and being more attentive to the Spirit is possible in many ways, but celebrating the ecclesial dimension of conversion is hardly possible apart from the Church and its celebrations. All should participate in the Church's Lenten celebration of conversion. Beyond this, an individual's ecclesial sense will affect the extent to which he or she shares the rhythms of the community's celebration of conversion and reconciliation and the community's sensitivity to its sinfulness will affect how often it gathers. Strengthening this ecclesial sense will be more productive in increasing frequency of individuals' participation than harping on frequent confession. A lesser frequency than was customary earlier in this century should not be taken as indication of a penitential void in the lives of Catholics.[18]

The Structure of Celebration
All the celebrations of penance and reconciliation have a common structural rhythm, dynamics in which participants engage in ritualizing penance: the familiar liturgical pattern of gathering (an introductory rite), listening (celebrating the Word), sharing God's action (conversion and reconciliation), and departing (concluding rite). The rhythm is most complete and clearest in the third rite, where penitents express their conversion to the Church as a group and are reconciled as a group. It is also strong in the second rite, though there can be a break or hiatus while penitents make their individual confessions. The rhythms are weakest and least apparent in the first rite. They are strong but incomplete in penitential celebrations, which lack reconciliation.

Gathering: The Introductory Rites
Gathering or assembly is the sacrament of Church and the prerequisite for all worship. It is basic to initiation and penance, since both present the central reality of the Christian Mystery: initiation in order to form community, penance in order to reform it. The baptismal process, particularly through the catechumenate, introduces people into the Christian community and the reconciliatory process, particularly through penance, returns them to it.

Since the transformation or reformation of individuals in the sacramental process depends upon the Spirit that enlivens the community, the extent and intensity of the community's presence impedes or enhances the work of the Spirit. This realization underlies the insistence of the council that communal forms of celebration are always to be preferred to individual and quasi-private forms (*Sacrosanctum concilium*, 26–27). Rediscovering the communal nature of the sacraments has been a major factor in revitalizing theology and celebration. Its expression in celebrating penance is the primary principle of reform and means that the communal celebration is normative, since reforming the community or returning to it is the basic human experience.

The introductory rite in such celebrations is primarily concerned with ensuring that the penitents form an assembly. Since music helps express and strengthen the necessary bonds, RP 23 calls for a suitable hymn to be part of the gathering rite. The presider's greeting, a brief introduction to the service, and prayer are the other elements indicated (cf. RP 48–50, 94–100). A somewhat different order of service than that given in the RP's models might better achieve the purpose. To prevent the assembly from responding passively to the presider, it would be well for people to take time to greet one another as well as responding to the presider's greeting. A call to worship, not simply an introduction or explanation of the service, should direct their attention. Singing the hymn then symbolizes unity, and time spent in prayer shapes the assembly as a worshiping community.

The RP is clearer than other rituals and the Sacramentary in stressing that this prayer is the prayer of the assembly, not of the presider; it calls for silent prayer that the presider completes with a brief summary prayer (RP 23, 50). The period of silence should therefore be long enough for prayer to take place and probably longer than would be appropriate at mass. The six opening prayers offered as models are called "prayers over the assembled people" in the Latin of RP 97, a title reminiscent of the ancient prayers for penitents and appropriate enough since the first four are from ancient sources.[19]

In all celebrations, the experience of community is the means whereby God's converting and reconciling presence enters into penitents' experience. Though the expression of community is minimal in the reconciliation of an individual penitent, the atmosphere and formulas of the rite are calculated to impress on both penitent and priest that together they represent the Church seeking renewal. The emphasis given the priest's friendly welcome to the penitent and the penitent's disclosing something of his or her life as a basis for the relationship and conversation shows the RP's intent to establish a sense of community between the two at the beginning of the celebration. The priest's attentive listening and warm acceptance and the gesture of imposing hands all symbolize community with the Church.

Listening: Celebrating the Word

Celebrating the Word shows that the gathering community of faith has as its inner dynamic God's creative presence. In the gathering of a converting and reconciling Church it shows that conversion—even the very recognition of the need for it—comes from God's Word. The members of the assembly again hear their call to be the People of God, know the deep source of their identity, examine their lives in the light of the Word, and are able to respond in the trusting commitment of conversion and faith. For that reason, the Constitution on the Liturgy restored the primary place of scripture in liturgical celebration (*Sacrosanctum concilium*, 24, 35) and the RP gave it primacy in every celebration of penance in order to underline that penance is a matter of ecclesial prayer, joyful praise, and confident worship (RP 17, 24–26; cf. RP 51–53, 101–201, and Appendix II) centered on the present action of a merciful God rather than on the penitent's past sins.

The general principles for the celebration of the Word apply.[20] One or more readings may be used. When there is only one, it should be from a gospel. When there are several, a psalm, hymn, or time for silence may separate them to provide opportunity for reflection and commitment (RP

24). Since the purpose of penance is to recall the assembly to its first commitment, the readings should not only challenge by developing or deepening a consciousness of sin but also support a confidence in God's mercy. They do so by proclaiming God's readiness to forgive the repentant as this is shown in Christ's Easter Mystery (RP 24). Nonscriptural readings meeting these criteria may also be used (RP 36).

The RP provides the largest lectionary of all the reformed rituals (RP 51, 101–201; Appendix II).[21] Text alone is not enough for this to be the Word of God, however, nor does reading ensure celebration. That is why the RP distinguishes between "The Reading of the Word of God" in the private celebration (RP 43) and "Celebration of the Word of God" in the communal celebrations (RP 51). Readers should proclaim the Word so as to help the assembly listen and receive the Word. Homilists should remember that their purpose is to reveal and strengthen the links between the Word and the community's life, leading people to a deeper consciousness of sin's power in their lives and to a commitment to conversion (RP 25; cf. RP 9, 24, 52). For this reason, the homilist (and confessor) must be careful not simply to moralize or examine consciences for people. The Word, reverently proclaimed and carefully explained, itself examines hearts. Therefore, ample opportunity for silent reflection is particularly important.

Silent reflection after the homily and before the liturgy of penance is primarily for examination of conscience (RP 26). The priest, a deacon, or another minister may offer considerations for reflection. A litany format may also be used. In either case, this can serve as a homily if it is based on the scripture just proclaimed, but then in particular it should be carefully planned to fit the assembly. Silence for examination of conscience and commitment to conversion is the essential element, but leading the assembly in such an examination can be an important means of formation.

This examination of conscience in light of the Word ordinarily takes place before the liturgy when a penitent is reconciled privately. How it is done in penitential celebrations and communal celebrations of penance will be the major way for individuals to learn how to deepen their consciousness of sin and broaden their horizons for recognizing it. In every case, the person of Christ, whose Word resounds in human life and the Church, is the standard, not an abstract list of rules or of virtues and vices. The example given in Appendix III is a partially updated format. Though it should not be read aloud in a service, it does show how the Word of scripture and the person of Jesus are primary. Its questions are posed in the first person, but it avoids introspection and scrupulosity by fostering a lively social and ecclesial sense. It would be helpful if penitents preparing for individual reconciliation used a passage of scripture to set the proper tone before examining their consciences and then used the same scripture in the ritual celebration.

Sharing: Ritualizing Conversion (and Reconciliation)
Conversion is ritualized in every liturgy of penance either to deepen penitents' consciousness of what they are involved in or to relive and cap off the phases of the process they have in some way completed. These rituals are the acts of the penitent and form part of the sacrament. Penitents glory in God's mercy as they admit their sinfulness and commit themselves to changing their lives. The Church, in the person of its minister supervising and presiding at the celebration, can then respond to what the penitents express by supporting them with its prayer in penitential celebrations or by granting reconciliation in the completed sacrament.

Though the three sacramental rites and the penitential celebration are quite similar in overall structure, they differ most in this area. The most radical difference is in how the Church responds to the ritualization of conversion, whether by a prayer of forgiveness or by not only praying for forgiveness but also granting reconciliation.

In the penitential celebration, conversion is in process. It is not considered mature or definitively manifested but is expressed in order to seek the Church's support. Penitents pray together, acknowledging their sinfulness and repentance and seeking forgiveness. They either engage in a ritual action symbolizing life-change or commit themselves to an actual indication of such conversion. The presider—who need not be a priest—responds to their desire for conversion by voicing the Church's prayer, seeking God's assistance for them and offering its support.

In celebrations of the sacrament, the conversion of the penitents is regarded as sufficiently matured and definitive to be officially accepted by the priest in the name of the Church. Penitents ritualize their conversion by praising God's mercy as they repentantly admit their sinfulness and accept the assignment of an act of penance. The Church responds by praying for their forgiveness and granting them reconciliation.

The manner in which penitents show their repentance to the Church—and, to an extent, the purpose for which they do so—and the manner in which the Church responds also differ in the three forms of the sacrament. In the fully communal celebration (with communal confession and communal absolution), mature, ongoing conversion and reconciliation to the community and God—the central orientations of the RP—are paramount. More than in the other celebrations, stress is placed on penitents' personal responsibility to continue conversion and seek whatever support might be needed. In the individual celebration, the penitent manifests conversion more specifically by a complete disclosure of sins; this is done to seek the confessor's counsel and prayer as well as a personal assurance of forgiveness and reconciliation. In the rite where individual confession and absolution are situated in a communal context, penitents show the Church as a whole their repentance and express it to the priest in private confession. Though the setting restricts counsel and prayer, both are possible.

In the sacramental rites, where the Church responds to the manifestation of repentance by praying for forgiveness and then granting reconciliation—theologically, reconciling them to the Church as a sign and cause of reconciliation with God—the true meaning of confession is shown in the penitents' praise and thanksgiving to God for the mercy they have received. This is again clearest in the third rite where the assembly replies to the public proclamation of reconciliation with a song of praise. In the second rite, where the sense of being a gathered community may have dissipated somewhat during the time for individual confession and absolution, this extends into a prayer of thanksgiving by the priest, further expressing the spirit of gratitude and concluding the community's proclamation of praise for God's mercy. Several model texts are provided (RP 57, 207–211).[22] In the individual rite, priest and penitent use a short passage from the Psalms (118:1, 136:1) to verbalize their *berakah* response to God's word and deed.

Departing: The Concluding Rite
There is always something incomplete about liturgical celebration, something that remains incomplete until God's kingdom comes. The unfinished business here is that a reconciled community must be a reconciling community. Thus, what the assembly has experienced of God must now be extended and shared in the lives of its members. Conversion and reconciliation are always incomplete until they take root in penitents' lives and move them to a stronger and more loving service of God and neighbor (RP 7). In concluding the celebration, the priest asks God's blessing on the penitents' efforts and sends them forth in peace.

Music in Celebration

As an especially strong and vibrant form of ritual prayer, music is vital to expressing and supporting the major rhythms of the community celebrations.[23] At times, music is a constituent element of the rite (e.g., the proclamation of praise)[24] at others it accompanies ritual actions (e.g., the individual confessions or the individual laying on of hands)[25] or is the means whereby the mystery is proclaimed and presented (e.g., the absolution).[26] It must always be an important part of planning and preparation.

The gathering or opening song is always important for uniting the assembly and expressing its God-center. Since it helps set the tone for the celebration, the song or hymn should express grateful confidence in God's mercy. Both the words of the text and the mood of the melody should help form the converting assembly in a spirit of communal reflectiveness and celebration. Hymns that are too slow moving, individualistic, or sentimental should be avoided. While music here supports the act of gathering, it also embodies ritual prayer and care must be taken to respect the integrity of the prayer of converting penitents in both form and style.[27] The images of God in the songs, for example, must be both strong and specific to support the experience of reconciliation.

Sung prayer is always recommended for the psalm and gospel acclamation during the celebration of the Word and it may also be appropriately used following the homily. Prayer here is a response to the Word and should have an obvious relationship to the Word that has been or will be proclaimed. The freedom and flexibility permitted in these celebrations mean that it need not be a psalm. However, it should be scripturally based, since the scriptural expression of the range of human emotions is usually both deeper and more sound than that of more recent writers. Here, music both extends the proclamation of the Word and confirms our reception of it. Since prayers are heard as well as prayed, a responsorial mode (cantor and congregation) is advisable, though simple meditative listening is possible if the assembly is heavily engaged in singing at other times in the celebration. Some instrumental music before and after the song may also assist reflection. If there are only two readings, the gospel reading should be the focus. Soft instrumental music is best during the time for reflection and examining conscience.

In the rituals of penance and reconciliation, two elements particularly call for community song: the general confession and the thanksgiving. While a hymn is possible for the general confession, a litany alternating between deacon (or cantor) and assembly—in the style of the general intercessions—is probably better, since it can be written with the particular celebration and congregation in mind. If a hymn is used, it should be carefully chosen; the mood of the confession is more joy and relief than wallowing in guilt. The Lord's Prayer, which is always part of the general confession, may be the sung prayer here. When individual confessions are part of the celebration, some congregational songs—carefully selected!—may be used to accompany them if this will take a long time. Otherwise, soft instrumental music to encourage reflection and meditation is advisable, but it must be performed well since it needs to hold the assembly's attention. Silence will almost always be a more effective symbol than recorded music. Song may also accompany the individual laying on of hands if this is used in the third rite and it may also very effectively be used in proclaiming the absolution. A focal point in the sacramental celebration that is not in the liturgy of the penitential celebration is the hymn of praise and thanksgiving. It must be carefully chosen, since it is a high point and the song stands on its own as a constitutent part of the rite.

The concluding rite should be done simply. A closing hymn almost immediately after the hymn of thanksgiving is pointless. A lively instrumental will be more effective as an accompaniment to people's departure, particularly if they are to socialize.

Differences among the rites call for varied application of principles to achieve the particular purpose of each celebration. We will discuss the rites in the order they are given in the RP, proceeding from the most familiar (the rite for reconciling an individual penitent) to the least familiar (the fully communal rite for reconciling a group of penitents) and concluding with the penitential celebrations.

Reconciling an Individual Penitent

In the Tridentine Ritual:	*In the Vatican II Ritual:*
Gathering: The Introductory Rite	
Preparation	Preparation
	Priest's welcome
Sign of Cross	Sign of cross
	Invitation/Call to worship
[Priest's questioning]	[Penitent's introduction]
Listening: Celebrating the Word	
	Reading from scripture (optional)
[Catechesis]	[Silent reflection/prayer]
Sharing: The Rite of Penance and Reconciliation	
Confession (general and specific) and counsel	Confession ([general] and specific) and counsel
Assignment of satisfaction	Acceptance of act of penance
	Prayer of the penitent
Absolution (act of contrition during)	Absolution
(Prayer for penitent)	Proclamation of praise
Departing: the Concluding Rite	
(Dismissal)	Dismissal

Unlike the Tridentine format, this rite in the RP is clearly liturgy. Its dynamic rhythm is that of communal worship, even though the rhythm is restricted and its peaks somewhat lowered by the limited community active in the celebration. Since the assembly, here composed of priest and penitent, celebrates the liturgy, the RP indicates the parts of both. (The Tridentine ritual was concerned with only the priest's functions.) The priest, appropriately vested, presides, but he and the penitent together are the sign of the Church's gathering and the symbol of how the Church, in realizing itself as a reconciling community, is renewed (RP 11). They gather, share the Word, experience their gathering as the sacramental locus of God's converting and reconciling presence, and then depart.

As in other liturgies, the introductory rite is concerned with the Church assembling for worship. In the context of the restricted community of penitent and priest, this means relating personally to one another in sharing faith and prayer—a vivid contrast with the courtroom protocol on which the Tridentine ritual was based, a secular model where rituals are designed to depersonalize and prevent reconciliation. In the Tridentine ritual, the priest called upon to hear a confession was advised first to pray for divine assistance in performing his ministry. The penitent was expected to examine his or her conscience and to approach the tribunal with due deference. In the RP, priest and penitent are both advised to prepare for sacramental celebration: the priest, by invoking the Spirit for enlightenment and charity; the penitent, by comparing his life with Christ's example and teaching and by praying for forgiveness (RP 15).

A religious atmosphere of prayer and worship is thus present from the beginning, as is a concern for human community lacking in the Tridentine ritual. Since presiding at liturgy is not a matter of mechanically and impersonally going through ceremonies but rather of bringing together and leading a worshiping community, the priest extends a warm, informal welcome (RP 16, 41). If priest and penitent are not acquainted, the penitent says enough about his or her state in life, last confession, particular difficulties, and the like to establish the minimal relationship needed for celebration and the confessor's ministry (RP 16). All of this may be done through informal conversation. Such preliminaries, more than pleasantries, are the beginning of celebration. The Tridentine ritual advised the priest, if necessary, to question the penitent regarding state in life and performance of obligations connected with the sacrament, but interrogation is a poor way to begin. The confessor's first ministry is that of a host, making the penitent welcome and comfortable.

If the confessor is to support the penitent in ritualizing and sacramentalizing conversion, he needs some sense of what the penitent intends. If he must wait until the confession of sins to learn what motivates the penitent's presence (and even then he can often only speculate), valuable opportunities will have been lost and both the introductory rite and Word-liturgy will have been little more than formalities. Penitents should briefly indicate (or be asked) why they have come. Is it because they are conscious of serious sin or have been away from the Church? Because they are at an important turning point in life or want to begin taking their faith-commitment more seriously? Because they need some help in living the Christian life or want to reaffirm their commitment? Because they are conscious of failings in following Christ, faults that need correction? Any of these may motivate the penitent and be reason to celebrate the sacrament.

Or it may be something else—fear of God or of one's past, habit or a sense of duty, neurotic guilt, or devotional needs. In such cases, counseling or instruction is called for, but not the sacrament. If no conversion is taking place, there is nothing to ritualize, no reason for reconciliation, and no sacrament to celebrate. In older terms, there is no matter for the sacrament—and again confessing past sins, reopening old wounds, is artificial, inappropriate, and an attempted misuse of the sacrament. Such needs are better met in other ways.

The priest must remember that his primary role is to preside over Church worship and maintain it in proper order. The purpose for penitent and priest coming together is God, Father, Son, and Holy Spirit. If necessary, after visiting informally, the priest leads into the ritual sign of the cross, which he should make, slowly and reverently, with the penitent. Then the priest, as presider, calls the penitent to worship by an invitation to trust and confidence in God (RP 16), using texts provided (RP 42, 67–71) or another, scripturally based invitation of his own. This too is a new element, important for establishing the proper tone. It puts God, not human sinfulness, first; it serves to introduce the Word; it may be appropriately nuanced to reflect the kind of conversion that is being celebrated. It should have the ring of one human being sharing faith with another and not be simply a formality.

The major structural innovation in this rite is the provision for sharing the Word, a lack in the Tridentine ritual that the final first draft of the reformed rite did not remedy. In the RP, this sharing of the Word is labeled optional—unfortunately and inconsistently, considering the importance of the Word in recognizing sin, receiving the call to conversion, and establishing the sacrament as confident praise of a merciful God (RP 17, 43). It should not be omitted without a reason proportionate to the importance of the Word in relation to the sacrament (cf. RP 17, 22, 24). The Word may be used in preparation, so that the examination of conscience may be made in response to the evangelical demands, but even then it is advisable to include it; the Word helps prevent confession from degenerating into self-criticism or the priest's counsel from becoming amateur psychotherapy.

Even if the scripture passage does no more than put priest and penitent into a calm, meditative state of mind, it has served a purpose. It may be chosen and read by priest or penitent and should, if possible, be appropriate to the penitent's motive for celebrating the sacrament. Several short texts are given in RP 43 and RP 72–83 and a large number of longer readings are given in RP 101–201; other texts may be chosen and used (RP 43, 84). If the penitent has no special reason for the celebration, part of one of the Sunday readings might be used, if it calls to conversion or confidence in God's mercy. Whatever the text, the scripture should be read aloud, slowly and thoughtfully, with a pause afterward for reflection and prayer. (Notice the suggested introductions to some of the readings.)

Unmentioned in the RP—but important if this is to be a genuine celebration of the Word to the extent possible rather than the reading of a snippet of scripture—is a sharing of thoughts and prayer in response to the Word. The priest may make a comment, invite a response from the penitent, or suggest that both spend a few moments in silent prayer before continuing.

They both respond to the Word primarily through the shared liturgy of penance and reconciliation. As in the introductory rite, the atmosphere is primarily that of a worshiping community—here, of a personal encounter in faith and prayer. Though the structure closely parallels the Tridentine rite, there is a radical difference in atmosphere and understanding because of the climate of shared ritual prayer and the power of the Word that has been celebrated.

The penitent first ritualizes penance or conversion, confessing sins and accepting an act of penance (RP 18, 44) and then, in prayer, asking forgiveness (RP 19, 45). This is clearly a liturgy, part of God's dialogue with sinful humanity, and is celebrated by the penitent. The priest assists as needed. The penitent may begin with a formula of general confession. This is a matter of individual preference, but probably advisable since it is more akin to the ancient *exomologesis* than the specific and integral confession that follows. Though the complete confession acknowledges areas of sin where God's mercy is experienced or needed, the basic statement is simply that one is a sinner. The priest responds, supporting the penitent's conversion by encouraging contrition—culpability combined with faith and love—and offering advice on renewal, including an appropriate act of penance. It is important that this conversation show the confessor as a supportive counselor rather than a distant authority figure.

The responsibility for the completeness of confession is primarily the penitent's; honesty and sincerity are to be presumed. Since this is more a matter of self-presentation than detailed information on the past, the confessor should rarely interrupt with questions or commentary. Unlike the Tridentine ritual, the RP is more concerned with the penitent's self-disclosure (cf. RP 7b) than with details of number, species, and circumstances. The confessor should minister in the same spirit. Except when the penitent needs or asks for assistance or is obviously in need of instruction, the confession should simply be accepted without probing or second-guessing.

The dialogue that takes place between priest and penitent in the confession has two purposes. The first is uncovering sinfulness so that conversion can be supported; this requires the gift of discernment. Discussion in depth—to uncover a root sin—will not ordinarily be required, but, in any case, it is not psychotherapy for cathartic relief but religious counseling for spiritual growth (cf. RP 44). Remembering the second purpose of the dialogue should keep conversation on the proper track: it is intended to evoke prayer. Both the penitent's confession and the priest's counsel are aimed at acknowledging God's sovereign power shown in a readiness to forgive and reconcile. Scolding and browbeating are altogether alien to the sacramental celebration.

In the course of this conversation, it should be possible to identify particular areas where renewal needs to continue. The priest may invite the penitent to propose specific steps toward renewal or make suggestions himself, and the penitent should commit to one of these as an act of penance, whether prayer, self-denial, or service. While the penance is partly a way of undoing past harm done, it is more a way of being healed and moving forward. Therefore, it should relate to the penitent's confession and be more than a token prayer.

The penitent's prayer is a prayer for pardon, preferably scripturally based, showing contrition and resolve to pursue renewal (RP 19). Penitents may prefer to kneel for this, the high point of their liturgy of conversion, which sums up what has preceded and ensures that it is put into prayer. Several formulas are provided as models (RP 45, 85–92). Though some are more petition than praise, all are better than the traditional act of contrition. It too, though hardly scriptural, is included but with a deeper expression of consciousness of God's mercy and trust in the Lord: Jesus, not the penitent's action, is the source of forgiveness. Penitents may recite or read one of these prayers or use their own words. It may sometimes be better for priest and penitent to pray the Lord's Prayer together, as the preliminary draft of the RP had proposed and as is done in the communal celebrations.

It is important to notice that the liturgy provides for two distinct moments of prayer here: the penitent's prayer of conversion and the priest's prayer of reconciliation. The old practice of the penitent rattling through the act of contrition while the priest did the same with the absolution was inappropriate, as was the more recent practice of having the penitent say the prayer before entering the confessional in order to listen to the absolution. The nature and importance of both prayers in the liturgy should be respected.

While the RP does not mention it, the priest may appropriately pray into the absolution—expressing his prayer for the penitent, seeking healing, forgiveness, and strength for renewal. If the two have been seated, the presider may wish to stand for this prayer, but it is better not to impose hands until it is finished in order not to confuse the distinct gestures of exorcism and reconciliation. The same is ordinarily true of the anointing used by some confessors. While this is an excellent ritual expression of the prayer for healing, if done regularly in such close proximity to the reconciliation, it can be confused with the laying on of hands or even substitute for it, as has happened in the past. Since it is more an expression of healing than reconciliation, it centers attention on the individual rather than on the individual's reconciliation to the community. In the private celebration, it also gives too much prominence to the priest.

The priest's primary role is officiating at the liturgy of reconciliation, the Church's response to the penitent's assurance of conversion. If penitent and priest have sat face to face in the conference area, the priest should stand and move closer to the penitent. The RP directs that he extend his hands, or at least his right hand, over the penitent for the formula of absolution and make the sign of the cross over the penitent during the final words, to which the penitent responds "Amen" (RP 19, 46). Physical contact is more expressive than words. Hands should be imposed in silence for a few moments before beginning the absolution and after completing it. Both priest and penitent should be comfortable with this gesture, a ritual symbol that divine forgiveness comes through the Church and human acceptance. The penitent knows the mercy of God through solidarity with the community in which the Spirit is given and through restoration to its eucharistic assembly.[28]

The absolution formula says what the gesture does and is a rich summary of the Church's theology of the sacrament (RP 19). Though Christ's mediation is weakly expressed and reconciliation to the Church is unmentioned, the formula, a new composition, combines the major scriptural themes in a compact fashion: humanity's reconciliation comes from God's merciful initiative in Christ; it is a participation in Christ's Easter Mystery by the power of the Spirit, sought and given through the Church.[29] The formula is not as clearly prayer as it might be. "Blessed be God, the Father of mercies!" would be a better beginning, or it could be addressed directly to God. Similarly, the shift from prayer to judicial declaration is awkward, made only with the conjunction "and." However, the element of proclamation is strong. If it is used in its present form, it will be up to the priest to proclaim it as prayer—clearly, slowly, and reverently, like the eucharistic prayer.

The absolution is considerably longer in the RP than it was formerly. How much prayer and worship are appreciated will determine whether the full formula is kept or whether the skeletal celebration of the past will be resurrected. Those satisfied with the minimum required for validity will ignore the rubric that only in imminent danger of death may the confessor shorten the formula to the "essential words" (RP 21). Convenience alone, however, does not justify abuse. As mentioned before, adaptation must respect an element's significance.

The liturgy of reconciliation then concludes with praising and thanking God for the mercy shown and pardon received (RP 20, 47). A short scriptural text from the Psalms (118: 1; 136: 1) expresses the priest's and penitent's response to God's reconciling action. It sums up the climate of human acceptance, affirmation, support, and faith-sharing and the climate of praise and prayer. Though frequently omitted or done only by the confessor, it is an important expression of the ancient *berakah* prayer form.

The concluding rite is a simple dismissal. The priest sends the penitent in peace to be a sign of God's reconciling love by continuing conversion (RP 21, 47). Additional texts in RP 93 are less appropriate, since they do not involve the penitent.

Reconciling Groups of Penitents

Rites for Groups of Penitents
Gathering: The Introductory Rites
Song
Greeting
Introduction/Call to Worship
Opening Prayer

Listening: Celebrating The Word
Reading(s)
Homily
Examination of Conscience

Sharing: The Rite of Penance (and Reconciliation)
Penitential

Celebrations:	*Rite 2:*	*Rite 3:*
Confession	General Confession	General Confession
	Confession Prayer	Confession Prayer
	Litany or Song	Litany or Song
	Lord's Prayer	Lord's Prayer
[Action]	Individual Confession	
Prayer	Individual Absolution	General Absolution
	Proclamation of Praise	Proclamation of Praise
	Concluding Thanks-giving	

Departing: The Concluding Rite
Blessing
Dismissal

A communal rite is appropriately used whenever a number of penitents gather at the same time to celebrate the sacrament (RP 22). Though these rites differ in the central liturgy, they all clearly express the rhythmic structure discussed earlier and give primacy to the action of the assembly. Paradoxically—because the celebrating assembly is a symbol not only of itself but also of the Church and thus of Christ—the gathered group of penitents supports the conversion of each of its members and, in reconciliation, reconciles each penitent to itself as sign of reconciliation with God. The support offered conversion is clearer and stronger in the penitential celebration, but it is ritualized briefly in the sacramental celebrations just prior to reconciliation. However, the reconciling community is the primary symbol in this sacrament, as is most clearly and intensely experienced in the celebration with communal confession and absolution.

Communal Celebrations with Individual Confession and Absolution
The introductory rites (RP 23; cf. RP 48–50 and 94–100) and the celebration of the Word (RP 24–26; cf. RP 51–53,

337

101–201, Appendix II) follow the model common to all the communal celebrations. However, after the assembled community receives the Word, each of the two sacramental celebrations and the penitential celebration follow different paths. In the celebration with individual confession and absolution, this part of the liturgy is titled "Rite of Reconciliation" (RP 27, 54). As in the other sacramental formats in the RP, the ritual of reconciliation overshadows the ritual of conversion or penance, which is emphasized only in the penitential celebration. Here, because of the time needed for individual confessions, it is fused with reconciliation.

The deacon (or other minister) invites the assembly to kneel or bow for a general confession, such as the "I confess" (RP 27; cf. RP 54, 202–203). Then, they stand for a litany or song seeking mercy and forgiveness (RP 27; cf. RP 54, 204–205). The model litanies provided are drawn from various scriptural, patristic, liturgical, and conciliar sources. Like the invocations of the litany, songs chosen should reflect confident trust in God's mercy while confessing sin and expressing sorrow or asking forgiveness. The Lord's Prayer always completes this communal ritualizing of conversion.

Not suggested in the RP, but an effective symbol and witness, is the giving of stoles to the confessors by the presiding priest and their confessing to one another and receiving absolution before going to their places. (This presumes, of course, that those who are to serve as confessors have been members of the assembly and shared in the celebration to this point.) Other members of the assembly who wish to do so then confess their sins, receive necessary counsel, and are assigned a penance, thus completing for each the rite of conversion. The rite of reconciliation begins immediately and individually, as the confessor absolves with the same formula and gesture as in the first rite (RP 28; cf. RP 55).

As the rite of conversion begins publicly and becomes private, so the rite of reconciliation begins privately and becomes public. The priests return to the sanctuary and the presider invites all to join in thanksgiving and praise to God for the mercy received. A psalm, hymn, or litany may be used (RP 29; cf. RP 56, 206). This proclamation of praise is concluded by the presider's prayer of thanksgiving (RP 29; cf. RP 57, 207–211). In the concluding rite, the presider blesses the people and then he or the deacon dismisses the assembly (RP 30; cf. RP 58–59, 212–214).

Communal Celebrations with Communal Confession and Absolution

The structure of this celebration differs only slightly from that used for communal reconciliation with individual confession and absolution (RP 35, 60). The members of the assembly who wish to be reconciled together ritualize their penance (conversion) and are then solemnly reconciled. All the differences—and even the disciplinary restrictions on this rite—serve to indicate that the second rite is something of a compromise.

Sincerity of conversion receives greater emphasis in this rite than in any other. During or after the homily, penitents are instructed on the essentials of conversion required for reconciliation: contrition for sins, the resolution not to commit them again, and the intention to try to undo harm done or scandal given (RP 33, 35a, 60). They must also intend to confess later any grave sins of which they are conscious (RP 34, 35a, 60). Those who judge themselves maturely penitent in this sense are assigned an act of penance and invited by the deacon, another minister, or priest to join, by a symbolic action, the ranks of those ready for reconciliation. They then make a general confession, followed by a litany of confession (like the general intercessions) or penitential song and the Lord's Prayer. The ritual of penance is thus virtually identical to that in the second rite, with the exception of the instruction on the essential conversion required—added, it seems, as a precaution against misunderstanding and abuse.

The RP mentions kneeling or bowing as appropriate ways for penitents to show that they consider their conversion complete (RP 35b, 61). However, episcopal conferences may determine another appropriate sign (RP 35b, 38b, 61). In the United States, the presiding priest may decide this. A verbal proclamation fashioned after the model of the renewal of baptismal promises or joining hands are possibilities in exceptionally large assemblies, but ordinarily something more is needed. A better symbolic expression of such a conversion is stepping forward to receive the imposition of hands. Since this is not the rite of reconciliation, other ministers can assist or members of the assembly can impose hands on one another in prayer and then exchange the sign of peace. In any case, the rite must be well and carefully done to be an effective expression of sincere conversion and desire for reconciliation.

Reconciliation, like conversion, is more prominent in this rite than in any other. As community leader, the priest accepts the signs of conversion and readmits the converted. As leader of the community's worship, he proclaims the prayer of reconciliation in penance as he proclaims the eucharistic prayer at eucharist. The priest calls upon the grace of the Spirit in proclaiming Christ's victory, extending his hands over the penitents to absolve them (RP 35c, 62).

Though the absolution formula used in the other rites may also be used here, RP 62 provides a proclamatory formula in the form of a solemn blessing that is more clearly prayer. It too echoes several passages of scripture.[30] At first, it seems trinitarian in a somewhat artificial way, with the first section speaking of the Father, the second of the Son, and the third of the Spirit, but the first two each dovetail into the section that follows and the third points to the life of the Church. Again, however, the juridical formula—"And I absolve you . . . "—seems simply tacked on. The absolution could be even richer and more effective if preceded by a sung prayer of praise in the preface or *berakah* form with congregational acclamations, not provided in the RP. However, adding it is a legitimate expansion of the rite (cf. RP 40a). At the least, the absolution itself should be set to music, sung by a capable presider, and responded to enthusiastically with a series of solemn "Amens" or another congregational acclamation.

As in the other rite for reconciling a group of penitents, the ritual of reconciliation concludes with the assembly's praise and thanksgiving to God in song (RP 35d, 63; cf. RP 29). Since the communal confession of God's goodness is already prominent, the concluding prayer of thanksgiving found in that rite is omitted as unnecessary (RP 35d, 63; cf. RP 29, 57). The service concludes immediately with a blessing and dismissal. As in the days when reconciled penitents were invited to dine with the bishop, the assembly should have the opportunity to socialize together after the liturgy, expressing informally the reconciliation they have celebrated liturgically.

Penitential Celebrations
The penitential celebration follows the structure of celebrations of the Word. The assembly gathers, celebrates the Word, expresses repentance and conversion and offers support and encouragement through prayer, example, and caring, and then departs. Though this is a genuine assembly of the Church, the presider need not be a priest.

This service calls for more silent personal reflection and interaction among the participants. They should, to the extent possible in a particular group, reveal their needs and minister to one another by sharing what they hear of the Word, not only in the service but also in their lives and experience. This will probably be easier if the assembly, at certain points, can divide into smaller, more homogeneous groups and if a leader in each group facilitates the mutual ministry.

At the heart of the penitential celebration is the liturgy of penance or conversion. Having heard God's Word calling to conversion, the members of the assembly acknowledge their distance from God and others because of their sins. They make a gesture to show their desire to turn again to God and hear the prayer of the Church supporting their desire and interceding with God for them.

The examination of conscience is especially important here for developing the understanding of sin and forming conscience, both crucial to authentic conversion. It both forms and informs and also counters individualistic and legalistic tendencies. It need not be as specific as some litanies of confession in ancient communal celebrations or the confessor's interrogations in medieval confession, but it should assist penitents in probing their lives to uncover basic attitudes that obstruct their experience of the Spirit and hinder their growth. It may take the form of brief reflections or series of questions by a leader, with intervening periods of silence, or a litany of confession to which all respond and, if the space permits, may be reinforced with accompanying slides.

Penitents have sinfulness in common, whatever the specific forms it takes in their individual lives. The general confession acknowledges this to the Church by admitting that the penitents, by sinning against God and neighbor, have failed to live in the Spirit of their baptism and have thus offended against their Christian community. While confession is oriented toward praise and the proclamation of God's holiness, in the penitential celebration—as in the ancient entry into penance and the ancient prayers during penance—the accent is on deepening an awareness of sin's damaging effects in people's lives and in the Church.

The same is true of the act of penance. As a response to God's redeeming Word, it has a dimension of praise and thanksgiving, but in the context of the penitential celebration, it is primarily a concrete way of beginning to cause change by a symbolic reform of attitudes. While it extends beyond the celebration into penitents' everyday lives, there should be a symbolic gesture to mark its beginning. If, for example, the penitential celebration centers on home life, at this point in the celebration family members might spend a few minutes in conversation to decide in what specific way they, as a family, will begin to experience the Spirit's transforming presence—perhaps by beginning their evening meal with prayer or a scripture reading or by each week meeting to discuss and assign chores. They could then commit themselves to this by holding hands as one member voices their prayer within the group.

The assembly of penitents concludes its confession of sin and expression of conversion, praying the Lord's Prayer, asking to be reconciled as they reconcile. The Church, through its presider, acknowledges the assembly of penitents as its assembly—as the Church—by making their prayer its own and asking God's forgiveness. This, like the rest of the liturgy of conversion, finds a place in the three sacramental rites, though there it is shorter and overshadowed by the grant of reconciliation. Here it is given the place of prominence. Some of the models in Appendix II, in fact, utilize prayers that, in ancient liturgies, so closely identified the Church's prayer with that of the penitents as to bring about their reconciliation.[31]

After this prayer for the penitents, the service concludes with a simple dismissal. The simplicity of the prayer for the penitents and the concluding rite, after the more elaborate ritual of penance or conversion, gives a sense of incompleteness, even abruptness—as it should. The penitents' conversion is still developing, still growing, not yet mature enough for them to be sacramentally reconciled.

NOTES

1. For centuries Western theology has largely ignored the role of the Spirit in reconciliation except as individual healing. Re-

covering in theology the pneumatological role of the community and giving corporate expression to the Spirit's function in celebration is crucial to dispelling the confusion that surrounds the discussion of general absolution and to making full use of the RP. See J. C. Nuttall, "The Holy Spirit and Reconciliation," *Clergy Review* 68 (1983) 408–410.

2. Jean Leclercq, "Confession and Praise of God," pp. 169, 176.

3. John Paul II, *Redemptor hominis*, 20 [*Documents on the Liturgy*, p. 440 (DOL 191, no. 1331)]. The same emphasis on personal conversion, making of the individual a "reconciled world," dominates *Reconciliatio et Paenitentia*.

4. Cf. *Music in Catholic Worship* (Washington, D.C.: United States Catholic Conference, 1972), p. 6.

5. In the Latin. The English title is simply "The Community in the Celebration of Penance."

6. This formulation is somewhat misleading, as the RP speaks in general of the community's role and fails to indicate specific ministries other than the priest's. The Church exercises several ministries in the sacrament, including, through bishop and priest, that ordinarily required for the reconciliation of someone who has sinned gravely, but the sacrament is not confined to such limit-situations. RP 11 envisions the setting where an individual is privately reconciled by a priest and does not exclude other ministries outside this setting.

7. *Lumen gentium*, 26; *Presbyterorum ordinis*, 5; *Christus dominus*, 15.

8. See canons 967–975, especially 967, 2 and 974, 2. Except for canon 966, the Code speaks of the faculty with regard to confessions rather than absolution. The customary terminology is inaccurate: granting absolution, not hearing confession, is the official restoration of the penitent to the Church and the prerogative of the priest in the case of grave sin.

9. For a survey, see J. van Laarhoven, "Een geschiedenis van de biechtvader," *Tijdschrift voor Theologie* 7 (1967) 375–422. For an analysis of three historical examples of the confessor (desert, monastic, and Counter-Reformation), see Raymond Studzinski, "The Minister of Reconciliation: Some Historical Models," in *Background and Directions* (Nathan Mitchell, ed.; *The Rite of Pen-*

ance: Commentaries, v. 3; Washington, D.C.: The Liturgical Conference, 1978), pp. 50–61.

For the confessor's role in the RP, see Gerard T. Broccolo, "The Minister of Penance" in *The New Rite of Penance: Background Catechesis* (Pevely, Missouri: Federation of Diocesan Liturgical Commissions, 1974), pp. 50–64; Francis J. Buckley, "The Paschal Mystery and the Priest in the Sacrament of Penance," *Lumen Vitae* 31 (1976) 223–233; Joseph M. Champlin, "The Role and Qualities of a Good Confessor," *Homiletic and Pastoral Review* 75, No. 6 (March 1975), pp. 6–21; D. Joseph Finnerty, "What Does the New Ritual of Penance Expect of the Priest?" *Review for Religious* 35 (1976) 3–13. Regis Duffy suggests a helpful model that respects the individual rite's sacramental character: "Concelebration of Penance and a Therapeutic Model," *Worship* 48 (1974) 258–269. For seminary education and training, see A. Chapungco, "Teaching and Celebrating the Sacrament of Reconciliation in Seminaries," *Seminarium* 31 (1979) 706–720.

10. As indicated above, page 195, note 10, the Tridentine ritual seemed almost purposely to remove the few ecclesial references and elements of lay participation that remained in its sources. The new Code does much the same; for example, contrast canon 960 with RP 31.

11. See, for example, Michael Scanlan, "Penance as Prayer," in *The New Rite of Penance: Background Catechesis,* pp. 36–39.

12. The revised text of RP 12 reads, in the ICEL translation:

"The sacrament of penance is ordinarily celebrated in a church or oratory, unless a legitimate reason stands in the way.

"The conferences of bishops are to establish the norms pertaining to the confessional, which will include provision for clearly visible confessionals that the faithful who wish may readily use and that are equipped with a fixed screen between the penitent and the confessor.

"Except for a legitimate reason, confessions are not to be heard outside a confessional."

13. The new Code makes no change regarding the reconciliation rooms that have become common, though the "sedes confessionalis" referred to in canon 964 has caused confusion. Literally it is the confessional location, so named because of the confessor's chair; as in the Sacramentary, "sedes" designates the pre-

sider's place. Because of the Tridentine ritual's requirement that the location include a fixed screen between confessor and penitent (*Rituale Romanum*, III, I, 8), the confession box became customary. Since canon 964, 2 (cf. RP 38b) states that the episcopal conference is to establish the necessary norms for the "sedes confessionalis" and that "sedes confessionales" equipped with a fixed screen between penitent and confessor are to be available for penitents who wish to use them, it is not the confession box but the possibility of confessing through a screen that is mandated. "Sedes confessionalis" is thus confessional in the sense of location for confessions, not confession box.

14. See Bishops' Committee on the Liturgy *Newsletter* 10, No. 12 (December 1974); *Commentary on The Rite of Penance* (Study Text IV; Washington, D.C.: United States Catholic Conference, 1975), pp. 23–24. I have used guidelines prepared by various diocesan liturgy offices for the following comments on confessionals or reconciliation rooms.

15. *Sacrosanctum concilium*, 109; *Paenitemini*, 9; canons 1249–1253.

16. The Congregation for Divine Worship noted the link between penitential celebrations and catechumenal scrutinies and proposed their use in preparing uncatechized Catholics for full participation in Church life. See "Reflections on the *Rite of Christian Initiation of Adults*," Chapter 4 [*Documents on the Liturgy*, p. 763 (DOL 302, nos. 2496–2497)]. As will be discussed in the next chapter, such a format suggests an order of penitents. Sample celebrations given in Appendix II are based on the theme of strengthening or restoring baptismal grace (7–13), the base of all postbaptismal conversion (RP 2), and the theme of preparing for a fuller sharing in the Easter Mystery (14–19).

17. A set of penitential celebrations for Lent that I developed using this pattern may be found in *Renewal and Reconciliation*, pp. 39–60. It is important that ample opportunity for completing the sacrament be provided *before* the triduum so that the whole community can join in that Easter celebration without the distraction of other liturgies. The ancient Roman pattern was to reconcile penitents on Holy Thursday morning so that the community, made whole by the restoration of its penitents, could enter into the Mystery. As noted in the present Sacramentary, the sacraments are celebrated on Holy Saturday only for those in danger of death.

346

The November 30, 1972, draft of the new rite produced by the second committee (Schema 387 [De Paenitentia, 14, Addendum]) suggested in its set of penitential celebrations the possibility of a celebration of penance beginning on Ash Wednesday, continuing with penitential celebrations during the season, and concluding during Holy Week with a service of confession and absolution.

18. For applications of this principle (assessing devotional confession more positively than I have), see David N. Power, "The Sacramentalization of Penance," *Heythrop Journal* 18 (1977) 5–22, and "Confession as Ongoing Conversion," *Heythrop Journal* 18 (1977) 180–190.

19. The themes of the prayers and their sources are noted by Franco Brovelli, "Il nuovo 'Ordo Paenitentiae' alla luce della storia della liturgia" in *La Penitenza* (Quaderni di Rivista Liturgica, N.S. 3; Turin Elle di Ci, 1976), p. 161. The first and third are from the *Sacramentarium Gregorianum*, the second from the *Oracional Visigotico*, and the fourth from the *Gelasianum*.

20. *Inter oecumenici*, 37–39 (*Documents on the Liturgy*, p. 95 [DOL 23, nos. 329–331]) is cited in RP 36. See also *Musicam sacram*, 46 (*Documents on the Liturgy*, p. 1302 [DOL 508, no. 4167]) and the sections of the Sacramentary's "General Instruction" on the Liturgy of the Word. Most liturgy planning handbooks contain helpful advice.

21. For commentaries and applications, see Robert Crotty and John Barry Ryan, *Commentaries on the Ritual Readings* (New York: Pueblo, 1982) pp. 77–151.

22. Brovelli, "Il nuovo 'Ordo Paenitentiae,' " p. 162, notes the themes and sources of the seven models. The first three and the last are new compositions; the fourth and fifth are from the *Missale Gothicum* and the sixth from the *Missale Gallicanum Vetus*.

23. *Liturgical Music Today* (Washington, D.C.: National Conference of Catholic Bishops, 1982), no. 27. I have also utilized guidelines offered by various diocesan liturgical commissions.

24. RP 56; *Liturgical Music Today*, no. 10.

25. *Liturgical Music Today*, no. 9.

26. Cf. *Liturgical Music Today*, no. 10.

27. For insightful reflections, see Don Saliers, "The Integrity of Sung Prayer," *Worship* 55 (1981) 290–303.

28. See my "The Imposition of Hands in Penance: A Study in Liturgical History," *Worship* 51 (1977) 224–247. The story of its gradual mutation and eventual loss is an apt summary of the history of penance. As stated at the council, its restoration is a key element in expressing the new orientation of the sacrament.

29. The formula weaves together several scripture texts (see especially 2 Cor 1: 3, 5: 18–19; Rom 5: 10; Jn 20: 22–23). The weaknesses in the formula are largely due to theological and polemical preoccupations; see above, Chapter Seven, for the controversies surrounding absolution formulas during the drafting of the rite.

30. See especially Eze 18: 23 and 1 Jn 4: 9–10 for the first section, Rom 4: 25 and Jn 20: 22–23 for the second, and Jn 20: 23, Eph 2: 18, and 1 Pt 2: 9 for the third.

31. The prayer for forgiveness in the first Lenten service (Appendix II, 13), for example, is from the *Liber Sacramentorum*, I, XXXVIII (Mohlberg, ed., nos. 358–359, p. 57) and follows an address to the assembly based on the deacon's address to the bishop requesting reconciliation of the penitents.

Chapter Ten

Shaping the Future

In the mid-twentieth century, penance reached the peak of its centuries-long growth in prominence and apparently began a sharp decline. The widespread disaffection from the form of the sacrament identified with Counter-Reformation Catholicism has been a quiet rejection, more like the postfifth-century decline in vocations to the order of penitents than the vociferous condemnation of the sixteenth-century Protestant reformers. Still, such a radical change raises critical questions regarding the current situation, its relation to the tradition, and future directions.

A CONTEMPORARY CRISIS?
Significant changes in penitential practice since the 1950's have led many authors and Church officials to speak of a crisis of penance, even though they find it difficult to agree on its signs, nature, and causes. Fewer confessions are certainly a fact. A study made by the National Opinion Research Center shows that in the 1964–1974 period the number of American Catholics confessing monthly declined from 38 percent to 17 percent, while in the same period churchgoers receiving communion weekly increased from less than one-fifth to more than one-half[1]—a reversal of the post-Tridentine correlation of increased frequency of communion with more frequent confession. A 1978 Gallup poll indicated that a similar number (18 percent) had confessed in the previous month. Responses to a 1982 survey by the Southwest Liturgical Conference (Region 10 of the Federation of Diocesan Liturgical Commissions) showed that 8 percent normally confessed every

few weeks or more often, 30 percent every few months or more often, 23 percent about twice a year, 15 percent about once a year, and 11 percent every few years. The Notre Dame Study of Catholic Parish Life, looking only at active Catholics, found that 27 percent never confess, 35 percent confess once a year, and only 6 percent confess monthly or more often. Less frequent confession appears to be the practice not only of those who might be called marginal Catholics but even of those usually considered devout—including priests, religious, and seminarians.

Some observers see these statistics as a sign of spiritual carelessness or as the result of inadequate teaching and even disobedience to magisterial directives on the part of priests and theologians. The sense of sin has been lost, they say, or people have an inadequate understanding of the sacrament. Individualism and secularization have blunted our sensitivity to sin, the social sciences have promoted an ethical relativism and diminished people's realization of individual responsibility.[2] Other commentators point to persistent defects in our manner of celebration—an anonymous, impersonal, legalistic, mechanical form encouraging childish dependence, a ritual routine with little expression of prayer or worship, defects unremedied by the RP because it is rarely fully implemented. (Interestingly, Church officials tend to speak of the loss of the sense of sin, religious educators of a lack of understanding, and liturgists of inadequate forms of celebration.)

Others are relatively unconcerned over the statistics. They look at the former frequency rather than the decline and see a practice centered more on security and forgiveness than on reform and reconciliation, an understanding of sin fixated on actions rather than on attitudes giving rise to them, an individualistic view of morality often preoccupied with sex, an unhealthy link between assuaging guilt and preparing for eucharistic communion, an understanding of sacrament and grace isolated from life and confined to ritual. The current decline corrects a previous imbalance, they say, and shows that conversion and reconciliation, the real grace of the sacrament, can be symbolized in other ways. They admit that dissent in the area of moral values is a factor—contraception in particular—but point to studies where people clearly aware of sinful alienation and the healing touch of divine reconciliation rarely recall confession as such an experience.[3] They suggest a correlation between more communions and fewer confessions: the realization that the eucharist is *the* sacrament of reconciliation, with the penitential rite and sign of peace serving the function previously filled by devotional confession. They ask if people are perhaps looking elsewhere for support in the life of Christian conversion and an experience of reconciliation.

While a statistical decline in confessions may not be evidence of crisis, the virtual disappearance of such penitential practices as fasting and abstinence after the revision of the disciplinary regulations does raise a question. Is anything like Augustine's idea of everyday penance any stronger today than in the days when Saturday confession was almost as much a mark of the Catholic as Friday abstinence and Sunday Mass? There are ambiguous signs, to be sure, with prayer groups and sharing groups and social action groups perhaps the strongest, but there is the nagging fear that the average Catholic may be relying too much on the Mass to fill devotional needs and express all dimensions of prayer and worship.

Whether celebrated frequently or rarely, communally or privately, penance has always been particularly sensitive and vulnerable, a critical and controversial point in Christian life and worship. It is the point in real life where a number of basic elements of Christian experience intersect: our awareness of sin, God's call to conversion, our interior response to God and others and the external expression of that response, God's reconciling act made tangible in Jesus and reaching us through the community of his disciples. For over a millennium, it has been the one place where those baptized as infants could ritually experience something of the catechumenal struggle to be converted and transformed into Christ. Admittedly, the contracted rite that we have celebrated is little more than a skeleton of this Easter Mystery, much like the mass reduced to consecration and communion: no gathering of a reconciling community, no divine Word calling to conversion, no human word of dialogue and prayer responding in praise and thanksgiving, no sense of being sent to reconcile. What remains of a process of conversion and reconciliation has been isolated from the life of the community, reduced to a ritual, and almost totally individualized.

At the same time that the focus of penance narrowed, its field of application broadened. No longer confined, as in the ancient period, to a time of radical conversion—the reconciliation of a serious sinner to the Church—it has been used in many ways: to ritualize a radical deepening of conversion at critical stages of growth, as a means of purification from lesser sins, as a devotional aid, as a source of counseling or spiritual direction, and even, in first confession, as an ersatz confirmation, a step in initiation, a rite of passage with little connection to a sense of sinfulness or an experience of the need for conversion and reconciliation. Despite its historical flexibility, the sacrament has been strained to the extreme in recent centuries because of a limitation of symbolic language to the single symbol of individual confession and absolution and, at the same time, its extension into a number of situations of varying meaning.

If there is a crisis of penance, it is that an impoverished and limited ritual language, spread so thinly, is still expected to express our experience of the mysterious character of a forgiving God. The question of God is indeed central.[4] God has always been a cause of crisis, stretching and shattering the symbols through which we struggle to express faith, forcing us to find new ones. Trent met the Reformation controversy over the procedures of post-baptismal conversion by reaffirming and rigidly maintaining the symbolic language then in use. The crisis today, still revolving around that format, takes a somewhat different direction, raising the question of whether that language alone is adequate to meet current pastoral needs.

How the crisis is viewed determines the solutions proposed. If the crisis is statistical infrequency or a deficient sense of sin or sacrament, then preaching, catechesis, and education will reform individuals' behavior, attitudes, or knowledge. If it is an inadequate rite, then research and new rituals are the solution. But if the problem is our experience of a transcendent God and our self-understanding in faith, then more is involved: the reform of penance is only one aspect of a general pastoral renewal and reform of the Church in all its aspects.

Community celebrations of conversion and reconciliation have been a significant part of penance reform since the middle of our century and have a prominent place in the RP. Such celebrations do not, of course, make the mystery more transparent or the response of faith more facile. To believe in a God who loves and forgives is no less total a commitment in a community celebration than in an individual one. But there it is perhaps easier for us to stand before God and let ourselves be touched and transformed. We need the strength, warmth, and reassurance that comes through the experience of a faith that is shared. Faith may be no easier, but God's healing touch is more easily felt through the healing touch of others. That, at any rate, seems to be what the Christian sacraments have always had as their inspiration.

Manual theology identified the sacramental *opus* with the mechanics of ritual. If the ritual was done properly and the penitent put no obstacles in the way of grace, the effect was infallible and guaranteed. However, forgiveness and grace were not open to experience. For many people today an effect not experienced hardly matters, a factor influencing the decline in confessions. Starting from the premise that the ritual is the sacramental *opus* leads some observers to conclude that less frequent participation in the ritual implies a penitential void, yet affirming an abstract inner transformation—that cannot be experienced but happens when the priest absolves—no longer suffices when there is a new sense of lay independence and a new sense of being the Church. The outlook cautiously and ambiguously presented in the RP suggests a new starting point for understanding the meaning of *ex opere operato*, the Spirit of Christ at work in the life of the Church. For those who celebrate the sacrament of penance the sign effects what it signifies only to the extent the Church is, and is perceived as, a reconciling community. The call, then, is not to individuals to confess more often but to the Church to be converted. (It would be curious if the problem of penance reform had to be stated in terms of reforming individuals' behavior when that is the concern of the sacrament!)

The root difficulty lies in achieving a credible experience of a penitent Church, a reconciled and reconciling community that mediates the experience of a merciful, compassionate, and loving God. It is safe to say that the majority of Catholics do not perceive their Church as a reconciling community, even though they may themselves celebrate the sacrament of penance with some regularity for various reasons. The 1982 survey of the Southwest by the Federation of Diocesan Liturgical Commissions (FDLC) showed that 76 percent of the respondents confessed once a year or more frequently. The survey listed several groups of Catholics who could be regarded as somehow alienated from the Church: those who have fallen away, the divorced and remarried, former religious and resigned priests, those involved in abortion, and homosexuals. In every case, the majority of respondents did not perceive the Church to be reaching out to reconcile, ranging from 75 percent who felt that the Church was not reaching out enough to those who have fallen away to 51 percent who felt it was not reaching out enough to homosexuals. Fourteen percent said that the Church should not reach out to homosexuals and 6 percent said it should not reach out to those involved in abortion, a sign that blame does not belong only to those who set policy.

The point is not so much that the Church does not attempt to reconcile the alienated as that its members do not expect or perceive it to do so. Bishops voiced similiar convictions at the 1983 Synod: the Church cannot be a reconciling force in society if it cannot reach out to its own marginal and alienated members. (Pope John Paul II countered this in *Reconciliatio et Paenitentia,* 34 by insisting that such people as the divorced and remarried and resigned priests lack the required dispositions or objective conditions for the sacraments.) A fortiori, the sacrament whose nature and purpose is reconciliation cannot be convincingly and effectively celebrated in a Church regarded as neglecting to reach out to challenge, support, and reconcile those who are alienated from it. That, it seems, is the real crisis of penance, for those are the essential dimensions of Church ministry in this sacrament.

TRADITION AND CELEBRATION

How the community of faith has ritualized conversion and reconciled penitents through the centuries occupied our attention earlier. Such a study is a crucial, though preliminary, part of the ongoing reform called for at the council. Variety, complexity, and even confusion are probably the first impressions given by an overview of the history of penance. Since almost anything imaginable seems to have a precedent, is there anything helpful in that history? Or is its study only of interest to the antiquarian?

Obviously, we of the twentieth century would have even less success than those in the ninth in attempting to revive fifth-century liturgical and disciplinary forms. And while instances of readmission to communion without institutional penance or of changing norms on prohibited life styles might attract a more than casual interest from those dealing with the problems of the divorced and remarried or the active homosexual, the parallels are not necessarily complete. Changing patterns of recognizing

355

and naming sin or precedents in reconciling or absolving penitents after a confession that differed vastly from our own customary form might seem instructive in dealing with current pastoral problems in the area of penance, but cultural artifacts must be interpreted within their own context and may not function satisfactorily outside it.

Variety itself should catch and hold our attention. Were the fact not so evident, we would surely deny that such varied forms could all be the same sacrament. That is perhaps why some historians have tried so desperately to find modern private confession in the ancient period. Variety, of course, establishes a problem for theologians; is there a constant, a *substantia* of the sacrament in the Tridentine sense, beyond the Church's control and power to change? If so, what is it and when are Christians called to celebrate it? A similar question is posed to liturgists; where is the "organic continuity" proposed by Vatican Council II (*Sacrosanctum concilium*, 23) as a guiding principle for liturgical reform and innovation? Even canonists and Church officials must deal with the question of how much they are bound by past precedent. Historical data alone cannot answer such questions, of course, but the historical variations do seem to indicate that the dominant concern at each stage of development—even when other factors interfered—was to respond pastorally to members' current needs without necessarily elaborating a theory on the limits of possible adaptation.

A major difficulty is that few historians of penance have attempted to discern a pattern of significant relationships between developing forms of penance and other factors. Penance has generally been studied in isolation and what has usually been studied is how people thought about and theologized it. Few scholars have tried to relate the development of its liturgy and discipline to sociocultural factors in the Church and society or to concurrent developments in the experience and understanding of the Church community, redemption, baptism, eucharist, sin, grace, and so on.

356

For example, it seems quite likely that the development and spread of the monastic form of tariff penance was closely related to other developments at the same time: rapid growth through mass conversions, the breakdown of the catechumenate system, the disintegration of the initiation process, the loss of the sense of community in the Church, changing models of redemption, a regression to a pre-Christian understanding of sin, a changing experience of the eucharist resulting in increasing clericalization and congregational passivity. Is it only a coincidence that the private mass, private penance, and absolute ordination developed at the same time as well? All seem to be indications of a divorce between community and worship. The wider society was also undergoing change. The loss of classical culture, the breakup of the empire, large-scale migrations, and barbarian invasions must also be taken into account.

Without this kind of preliminary historical analysis, it is difficult to see how the theologian's conclusions can go far beyond either guesswork or the unfolding of presuppositions, neither of which is adequate foundation for the decisions of Church officials. Historians of dogma and systematic theologians, even those of the caliber of Rahner, Poschmann, and Vorgrimler, frequently fail to make adequate use of liturgical sources or to relate their analysis of past theologies to other factors. Yet how are we to theologize about penance without studying how believers have experienced and celebrated it?

On the basis of our own study, it seems possible to sketch at least the outline of a theory of the development of penance: first in the form of the main features of the changing experience of the sacrament, then in terms of the pastoral concern at each critical transition, and finally by an indication of the dynamics that seem to be the major constants in the history.

Ancient penance provided community context and structures for conversion. Called from sin by the witness of the community's life, penitents felt the community's support, encouragement, assistance, and prayer during the process of detachment from sin and reintegration into the community's way of life. This process and the community structures provided paralleled those of initiation and the catechumenate. In the liturgical entry into penance, repentant sinners were reconsecrated to a life of conversion. During their time as penitents, they continued to receive attention in the liturgy and, presumably, other forms of ministry. The imposition of the bishop's hand completed the communal penitential process. Done at the assembled community's intercession and in its presence, it was the Church's prayer invoking the Spirit and reconciling the penitent to the Church. It restored the *pax ecclesiae*, the peace of the Church, and the *ius communicationis*, the communion of the Holy Spirit in the Church, which, like initiation, reaches its completion in the community eucharist. The ritual gesture of the laying on of hands is a rich symbol of the ancient experience of penance, even though, in some cases, the gesture was becoming an anointing after the model of the postbaptismal anointing.

During the medieval period, the imposition of hands, where it still took place, was beginning to mutate into other less obvious and less personal gestures: the imposition of ashes, anointing, touch, extended hands, the placing of the stole into the penitent's hands. There was little appreciation of the relationship of penance to initiation as infant baptism was the norm and the initiation process had disintegrated. Both the Spirit and the eucharist consequently received less attention. With the rise of private penance, the community's role was less important than in the ancient period. The rite completing penance was generally still a prayer (supplicatory absolution) and the ecclesial context was not totally forgotten. The primary emphasis, though, was no longer reconciliation with the Church, the communion of the Holy Spirit, and readmission to the community eucharist but forgiveness and restoration to grace at the judgment of the bishop or, usually, the priest. The penitential process first collapsed into two rites separated by a period of penance and then, with the joining of confession and reconciliation, into a single rite.

The change in the ritual gesture in the modern period is again an apt symbol of the change in the penitent's experience. The imposition of hands became the raising of the hand toward the penitent and the sign of the cross over him or her—all invisible because of the confessional. The process of penance had been reduced to a rite understood in its totality almost exclusively in juridical and impersonal terms. There was little or no advertence to the Spirit, the eucharist, or the Church community. Forgiveness and restoration to grace became the impersonal focus of an individualistic rite where the grant of faculties to the confessor was almost the only link with bishop and Church.

In the early Church, the laying on of hands in penance and reconciliation was closely connected with the Holy Spirit active in the community and associated with the Church's prayer for its healing and wholeness through the reincorporation of the repentant sinner. The gesture during penance was a sign of consecration and exorcism. At reconciliation, it signified the Church's acceptance and the penitents' return to the communion of the Holy Spirit. Its gradual mutation and disappearance accompanied the progressive individualization and subjectivizing of the penitential system—and clericalization—and thus appear to correlate with the degree of social cohesiveness in the Christian community and the extent to which individual Christians defined themselves as Christians in terms of that community. These changes also seem linked with the displacement of the tactile and active dimensions of liturgy by the ocular and auricular. A life process reflected and defined by communal worship became mechanical ritual. Liturgy and liturgical gestures ceased to be personal activity in a communal setting and became things.

Numerous other correlations could probably be made as well, particularly with a changing understanding of sin (more external, legalistic, and individualistic) and a varying evaluation of the body and its relationship to salvation (including the bodiliness of the Spirit community). Certainly, the correlation with the emphasis given the ecclesial dimension of the sacrament and the Christian's sense of relation to the Church community should be apparent. At any rate, it is interesting that the restoration of the gesture in the 1973 Rite of Penance was preceded by a rediscovery of the communal dimensions of the sacrament of penance, an emphasis on active participation in the liturgy, and a new attention to touching and personalism in our culture.

The dominant concern at each critical point of transition in penance's history was a pastoral one, even though that was at times obscured by such factors as a tenacious holding on to outmoded forms or to a jealous maintenance of official prerogatives. The gradual broadening of the horizon of the Church's penitential experience seems to center around a specific question: can the Christian community be unconcerned about those who have abandoned its way of life and can it leave them, if repentant, isolated from the community and without reconciliation? At every stage of institutional development, the answer was based on foundational postulates derived from the experience of redemption and already recorded in the scriptures: the relationship between Christ and Christian is the basis of the Church as a community of disciples; sin is a wandering away from discipleship and separates the sinner from the community; sin affects the very being of the Christian and the community; the community must deal with this threat and seek to restore its wholeness by regaining its lost member.

The changing understanding of sin and manner of ministering to sinners are of less significance than the foundational postulates upon which the apostolic ministry of reconciliation is based. Actions (e.g., parents marrying their daughter to a Jew) and life styles (e.g., serving in the military or working as an actor) once prohibited to Christians came to be accepted. The ministry has been more or less public at different times, it has sometimes been required for a particular sin and sometimes not, it has in some ages been exercised in a variety of ways and in others in only one. However, the rule is that the Church has eventually, however reluctantly, attempted to minister to those then regarded as alienated, trying to reconcile them.

That this double pastoral thrust is central can be seen by an examination of the developmental crises in the history of the sacrament. The possibility of forgiveness by the Church for certain sins committed after baptism was the first of these and already apparent in the scriptures. It was resolved by the gradual development of institutional structures for dealing with certain sins that were regarded as particularly threatening to a community whose way of life was discipleship. The second crisis was the question of the conditions for such ecclesial forgiveness in a changing milieu. Third-century Christians quarreled over reconciling certain classes of sinners. This was resolved through establishing the canonical system of penance during the fourth and fifth centuries. This system concerned itself only with certain specific sins, dealt with them and ministered to the sinner through public procedures, and restricted forgiveness of these sins through these procedures to once only.

The rigid and unyielding character of this canonical structure, and particularly its refusal to grant a second such concession of forgiveness, was the starting point of another crisis in the early Middle Ages, when this official form of Church forgiveness seemed out of the question for most people, not only because of its severity but also because it no longer corresponded to their experience. As ancient penance in its final form collapsed, the Celtic monks, through their pastoral initiative, attempted to fill the vacuum left by the pastoral ineffectiveness of the canonical system, but their effort failed to gain official approval. A third crisis arose over the possibility of repeated forgiveness. It was eventually resolved by affirming this possibility, providing for it through a private ministry, and extending these private procedures to all sins. The compromise between monastic penance and public penance that came into being during and after the Carolingian Reformation resolved the crisis by providing a private penance that made repeated forgiveness possible.

However, this too contained within itself the seeds of another and even more bitter controversy that grew through the Middle Ages and ended in the Protestant Reformers' rejection of individual auricular confession and priestly absolution. The fourth crisis—that of the required procedures and ministers of forgiveness—has not, it seems, been resolved as yet. To the fathers of the Council of Trent, the problem and solution were as simple as these had seemed to the bishops of the Carolingian reform councils. The problem was contempt for ancient tradition and rejection of the Church's official structures. The solution was reaffirming their value and encouraging their use. Trent responded to the Protestant attempt to carry individualization to its extreme by insisting on integral confession to the Church's minister in order to meet its responsibility to penitents and reconcile them. Though this solution worked for a time, the contemporary questioning of the Tridentine insistence suggests that it may not have been a final solution and that the crisis is not yet fully resolved.

At each stage the Church's concern was to help repentant sinners return, yet each resolution contained an inherent tension, making further development necessary. Affirming the possibility of forgiveness led to the question of conditions. The eventual inadequacy of the conditions set, as pastoral situations changed, led to granting unlimited forgiveness on an individual basis through official structures and procedures. In reaction to the Protestant rejection of these structures and procedures, Trent insisted on them even more rigidly, without considering whether a changing pastoral situation might call for something more.

Careful study of such prior crises and developments, particularly the points of transition, should offer valuable insights for us. In all such cases, the evolution of the penitential discipline was only one aspect of the Church's coming to terms pastorally with a situation where earlier solutions appeared unresponsive to current needs. At each stage the Church's answer to the question of abandoning sinners and leaving them unreconciled was an emphatic "no."

Taking into account the foundational postulates upon which the answer depends, can we make any generalizations about constants amid the historical variation? Simply put, two social dynamics appear to have been at work in every historical form of the sacrament: challenge and support—or, in scriptural terminology, binding and loosing. The community faces the fact of sin in its members and confronts them with their guilt, challenging them to return to their commitment. If they repent, it then assists them in their conversion and progressive reintegration into the community and finally, when ongoing conversion is sufficiently underway again, reconciles them. Yet the ministerial means through which these social dynamics have operated have varied extensively.

The ways of challenging sinners (binding) have been affected by many factors, not least of all by how sin was understood and by the Church's sociocultural situation. The stronger the sense of being community and Church, the more social was the concept of sin, the more limited was the number of sins dealt with formally and institutionally, and the more communal or public were the procedures and ministries. With a decline in the sense of community (largely due to too rapid growth and inadequate provisions for socializing and forming new members), the concept of sin became more individual, the number of sins to be submitted became more extensive, and the ministry and procedures became more limited, individual, and private. At the end, individuals confronted themselves with the fact of sin by a personal examination of conscience and excluded themselves from the community eucharist for any one of a large number of mortal sins. A social dynamic was still at work, though it was not so clear as in earlier centuries. The presence of the community was mediated through its understanding of sin (either internalized by the individual or read off a formal examination of conscience) and through its regulations on eucharistic participation. In these more impersonal ways, it was still the community that confronted and challenged the individual, but it was law rather than community that was uppermost in the individual's experience of being confronted with the fact of sin and guilt.

There appear to be two means through which the community has offered support to the converting individual. The first is that after individuals have responded to the challenge, they are assisted in admitting and expressing guilt and repentance. In ancient penance, this took place through the (probable) private counsel with the bishop or his delegate and through public admission into the order of penitents, with private auricular confession fulfilling this function in tariff and modern penance. In ancient penance, this expression of guilt and repentance was regarded as a progressive thing and so the community's support and prayer and formative example (and, probably, more specific forms of ministry) continued to be given to the repentant throughout their time in the order of penitents. In tariff and modern penance, it came to be regarded as a preliminary to the sacramental ritual wherein it was verbally expressed.

The second means of ministry involves the community's support in undoing the remnants of past sins, obstacles to being completely aligned with the community of disciples, and support in beginning anew, whether interpreted as reformation or satisfaction (the latter as either rehabilitation or punishment). Where reformation or rehabilitation was sought, as in ancient penance, a process similar to the catechumenate tried to rebuild bonds of relationship to the community and reorient personal attitudes and priorities. Where punishment was sought, as in medieval penance, self-denial and prayer were imposed and the community provided external means (e.g., indulgences) to help pay debts owed for past sins. In either case, the process was completed by ritually reintegrating the penitent into the community and its assemblies.

The historical development of the sacrament seems to have affected the means of support in much the same way as it did the dynamic and ministry of challenge: in the direction of progressive individualization and privatization and the weakening of obvious social and ecclesial bonds. Thus, the support community for expressing guilt and repentance was reduced to the priest. The link to the Church in reducing or removing the remnants of past sin (initially regarded as behavior or attitudes, later as guilt and punishment)—beyond the priest's assignment of satisfaction—was, in the private system, initially limited to commutations and indulgences and then extended to include the priestly absolution that also reintegrated the person into the community. At least in theory, the priest functioned as the Church's official representative and minister rather than as a private individual, but even this social link was rarely perceived as such. In practice, the priest rather than the community came to be foremost in the individual penitent's experienced of being loosed from sins.

The structures through which the Church community and its pastors have aided the conversion of sinful members and reintegrated them into the community have varied considerably through the centuries and have likewise undergone considerable reinterpretation. For example, the modern ritual of confession has had to carry the full weight of what an earlier age distributed over time and throughout the community. As a consequence, an individualistic ritual forgiveness of sins (basically regarded as purification or liberation) has been sought rather than the experience of reconciliation with God and Church. The social structures are hardly seen as such and are accordingly maintained by law and the appeal to a special pastoral power.

Historically, the telescoping of the conversion process, the reduction of a life process to a ritual, and the privatizing of the ritual appear to be at the heart of the contemporary crisis regarding the ministry and procedures of ecclesial forgiveness and reconciliation. The renewed emphasis in the Vatican II reforms on conversion as a lifelong affair, the interrelation of liturgy and life, and the role of community—a reconciling community—in celebration seem designed to respond to precisely these points.

The call to conversion through confrontation and challenge—binding—and reconciliation through support in conversion and through reintegration—loosing—have been constants in the dynamics of penance. The penitent's manifestation to the Church of conversion and the Church's expression to the penitent of forgiveness and its inclusion of the penitent in its prayer and worship have been constants in the liturgical celebration of conversion and reconciliation. In most respects, the ecclesial dimension was steadily weakened in the course of centuries; the liturgical and sacramental aspects of conversion and reconciliation were likewise lost. Here again, the Vatican II reforms seem designed to respond to these needs by enabling penitents to show their conversion to the Church as a community and by enabling the Church as a whole to show the penitent forgiveness and acceptance. The third liturgical rite for the sacrament in the RP is clearest in this regard, because it places the greatest emphasis on the penitent's sincere conversion and the Church's reconciling character bringing penitents into its assembly for worship.

The restrictions placed on this new form, even though it fulfills doctrinal mandates, suggest that once more, as in the third-and fourth-century clash with Novatianism, doctrine has outstripped discipline. Perhaps the old discipline will again be officially maintained and popularly ignored until intrinsic contradictions fully unfold. Official insistence on the past official form also makes it tempting to draw parallels with such periods as the Carolingian Reformation. However, in neither case is the parallel complete. Perhaps the major conclusion to be drawn is simply this: in the Church, as in other institutions, policy is frequently contrary to self-interest and members' advantage, even when there are viable alternatives.

CONTINUING REFORM AND RENEWAL

Though the guiding principles of penance reform laid out by Vatican II and postconciliar commissions are clear enough, their expression in the RP and subsequent developments has not always been equally evident. Generally, this is because of the restricted recent tradition requiring individual confession and absolution for every type of conversion. In addition, in many parishes and dioceses, implementation of the RP has been halfhearted and inadequate due to misunderstanding, timidity, or outright opposition.[5] And in some cases, local Churches attempting to follow those principles have been reined in by higher authorities.

Apart from inconsistencies and defects, there is the more important fact that the various rites provided in the RP are not interchangeable but rather are directed toward different situations in the lives of individuals and communities. The unique values of each rite, together with their strengths and weaknesses, provide the basis for continuing reform.

Reconciling Individuals

The RP's rite for reconciling individuals has a richness of context and expression lacking for centuries, yet unless popular understanding and spirituality are reoriented it is probably doomed to disuse or distortion. The depth and extent of prayer and dialogue for which it calls are alien to most people's past experience and frequently upsetting. Its attempt to establish and maintain an ecclesial sense is almost totally dependent on the celebrants' maturity of understanding. An outlook centered on ritual forgiveness parries its thrust toward reconciliation and finds its celebration of the Word pointless or no more than ceremonial enhancement. The intense experience of conversion and reconciliation that this rite expects is neither called for nor possible in every expression of Christian conversion; even in the case of the person who has sinned gravely, deep personal self-expression has not always been within the ritual. Since it can hardly be expected in a regular or even ordinary celebration, the rite, as it is structured and intended to be celebrated, may be more suitable for extraordinary situations. It is, for example, the best form when an individual has serious difficulties and wishes assistance in the context of the sacramental celebration. It is also the appropriate form at some important juncture when the individual needs help in discernment or wishes a means of intimate and personal self-expression. Either practice will reserve this rite for such occasions or it will be twisted to fit the presuppositions of priests and those penitents who will use it—unless its real value can be made clear and the spirituality of both priest and penitent can expand to include its riches.

There are other problems. Can two people celebrate, particularly through a screen? Can the distinct elements of conversion—counseling and direction, celebration, and reconciliation—take place without confusion in a relatively short time? Is there, in fact, a clear, consistent model for what should happen or is the RP trying to blend elements that are too diverse?[6] Even the shared-prayer model proposed earlier can be difficult to follow in practice. Confusion about the nature of sin compounds this. Sin was previously clear—external, objective criteria made it clear—and the straightforward confession ritual matched it. The new rite, approached with this understanding, raises other questions: Why dialogue if sins are clear?

How can we focus on the future by concentrating on past sins?[7]

Though the rite's historical origins and recent use suggest a close relationship to pastoral counseling and spiritual direction, sacramental celebration is neither. Private confession may have originated in Eastern monasticism, but Eastern Churches, unlike the Western, have generally separated sacramental confession and spiritual direction, since spiritual direction is a charism unrelated to ordination.[8] Direction was probably provided in the ancient order of penitents but not in liturgical celebration. The close link between the sacrament and spiritual direction in recent centuries occurred primarily because the individual format was the only sacramental form available and because private confession provided a ready access to pastoral counseling. However, this link has come into question. Seeing the sacrament's relation to a life of continuing conversion seems to maintain the link, but recognizing the sacrament as worship weakens it. Is it fair to the presider to expect competence as spiritual director and pastoral counselor? Is this a proper use of the sacramental setting or detrimental to both the sacrament and spiritual direction or counseling? Too often the link can lead to regarding the sacrament as simply therapeutic or purificatory and as a somewhat mechanical means of receiving grace.

While some counseling will frequently enter into the celebration (cf. RP 7c, 10, 16, 18, 44), it is unlikely, in context, to be sufficiently deep and broad to serve as spiritual direction. Nor is every confessor competent to serve as spiritual director. Both sacrament and spiritual direction would likely benefit from a clear distinction between the two. When regular celebrations are part of programs of spiritual direction—rather than making direction part of celebrations—the differing purposes will more likely be kept in mind. Then the sacrament's place in the penitent's spiritual life and its role in spiritual growth will be evident: the sacrament is an aid in attaining the fuller liberty that is a progressive transformation in likeness to Christ and a support in continuing the life orientation begun in baptism (RP 7b; cf. 2, 4, 6a). Then, however, it is important not to make the sacramental liturgy into a routine ritual wrap-up to a spiritual conference.

So far as pastoral counseling is concerned, the worship setting of the sacrament is not ideal. If an individual truly needs help in dealing with serious personal difficulties, giving it where reconciliation follows so closely on the ritual expression of conversion restricts what can be offered and risks making it perfunctory. Realistically, however, it is, for many people, the easiest way to find help in confronting personal problems and the dialogue between confessor and penitent and penitents' needs may lead to some measure of counseling. The confessor can suggest making a counseling appointment at another time in a nonsacramental context, but he cannot, like the priest and levite, pass by someone in need in order to go up to the Temple. The best that he can do is try to maintain a spirit and atmosphere of shared prayer and bring himself and the penitent to the point of liturgical celebration.

The same is true when informational or formational questions are directed to the confessor. The setting is not conducive to a searching analysis of the historical development of Church teaching on a moral issue or to an examination of current theological interpretations or to assisting an individual toward an informed conscience, any more than the pulpit is the place for detailed exegesis or a theological lecture. Still, some of this catechesis and counseling—and even evangelization—may have to be done in liturgy or it will not be done at all. In every case, the present need of the penitent takes precedence over anything that does not of itself distort the presentation of Christ's Easter Mystery.

Communal Reconciliation with Individual Confession
The communal rite for reconciling a group of penitents with individual confession and absolution is much more suitable for ordinary and regular confession where the

individual needs no special support but wishes more intimate self-expression. It efficiently blends the values of personal expression (from the first rite) and communal setting (from the third). It makes possible a more frequent private confession by members of a community when time is not available for celebrating the individual rite properly with each or when such celebration is not necessarily called for and does so without totally sacrificing the values of a community celebration.

Nevertheless, its weaknesses suggest that it is usable and valuable only in relatively small and homogeneous groups such as religious communities or special groups within a parish, unless private confession is the paramount value and efficiency a close second. The very reason for appreciating this rite—its communal character—was also the base for criticism only a few years after its introduction, even before the RP appeared, and those criticisms still seem to hold. Though it restores an experience of community to the celebration of the sacrament, the withdrawal into private dialogue with the priest at its high point gives the impression that the community's presence is little more than physical—a matter of ceremonial enhancement—and that the liturgical celebration is but preparation for the sacrament, impressions at some points reinforced by the RP (e.g., RP 22) and by Pope John Paul II (e.g., *Reconciliatio et Paenitentia*, 32).

In a sense, this rite is more individualistic than the first rite since it seems almost totally oriented toward individual confession and absolution. Even when the liturgy is well prepared and celebrated, there is little interaction except with the priest. Where penitents' ecclesial sense is weak, they are likely to leave after making their confession and receiving absolution; those last in line return to find that the community to which they were reconciled has gone.

Depending on numbers, the service ranges from awkward to unmanageable. It is awkward because of repetitiveness (general confession and then individual confessions) and an incomplete parallelism (individual absolution but no communal absolution). When penitents are many and confessors few, the service becomes unmanageable. A quick impersonal routine results. The interaction between priest and penitent, which is the real value of the individual rite, is minimal and the established experience of community diminishes during the confessions.

Perhaps the most telling criticism is that this rite is a compromise and a hybrid, inadequately communal and insufficiently personal—and thus in reality more individualistic than the private format it is intended to reform.[9] Still, defects can be remedied to some extent and certainly do not mean that this form is without value. Nor are the individual and communal forms in competition; the criticisms can also be applied to celebrations with general absolution. If there is a correlation between what is expressed in the celebration and what penitents experience in their lives, the presence of others will offer more than ceremonial solemnity. Where there is a reasonably strong sense of community, people will be willing to wait until all have confessed, recognizing that they can minister in the meantime by their presence and prayer.

The major difficulty is that the effectiveness of this rite does not depend only on proper preparation and planning. It also requires a sufficient number of confessors— perhaps one for every ten penitents expected[10]—to allow individual confessions to take place in an appropriate manner without a delay that will destroy the rhythm of the celebration or the sense of community achieved. It is increasingly difficult to provide enough confessors, an indication that this service is not fully responsive to pastoral needs in most parishes. Unless the assembly is relatively small and homogeneous or—not recommended!—confessions are done in assembly-line fashion (e.g., with penitents advised to confess only one or two sins), it would be better to have a penitential celebration with later opportunities for individual reconciliation or use the fully communal form of the sacrament. This does not mean that this form is merely transitional, a way of leading people from the customary to the fully communal form,[11] but experience both before and after the RP suggests that its effective use is restricted to a diminishing number of situations as the number of priests declines.

Even granting the need or value of including individual confession in a communal celebration, reconciliation of its nature bespeaks a return to community. Individual and private absolution is inconsistent with the overall orientation of the rite. Whatever place specific confession and specific counseling had in ancient penance, reconciliation was given to all the penitents at once; the plural form of the prayers of reconciliation was even retained for the solemn Holy Thursday rite in the modern Roman Pontifical. In the formative years of communal celebrations, public absolution of the group by the presiding priest often followed individual confessions. The first commission charged with drafting a reformed rite had intended to incorporate this practice, but the tenth of the Pastoral Norms prohibited it, requiring each penitent to be absolved by the priest to whom confession had been made.

Though no reason was given, it seems due to the Pastoral Norms' distinction between the sacrament and liturgical celebration (with the sacrament identified with individual confession and absolution and the liturgy regarded as extrinsic ceremonial) and the conviction that only the priest who has heard the penitent's confession can absolve.[12] The distinction between sacrament and liturgical celebration is based on false assumptions; the RP sees every form of the sacrament as liturgical worship. The concern regarding the absolving priest—including the proposal that all priests absolve simultaneously—is the consequence of a clericalism that fails to recognize the presbyters' relationship to bishop and Church and instead sees them having a personal power received in ordination. The presiding presbyter absolving the penitents, even if he has not heard each one's confession, acts as the bishop's delegate, just as do the other presbyters. If there was a specific confession in ancient penance, the one who reconciled the penitents was not necessarily the one who had heard their confessions and counseled them to enter penance.

The discipline prohibiting communal absolution after individual confessions lacks theological rationale and is little more than a concession to canonical custom, since everything in the rite seems to lead to such a grant of reconciliation. The discipline should be revised to conform more closely to the reform's guiding principles. Where this sacramental format is used, it would be better if penitents confessed individually to the priests while standing in full view of the assembly but at a sufficient distance to maintain privacy—screens could still be provided—had hands imposed on them in silence, and then were absolved all together by the presiding priest, with the other priests extending their hands over the assembly. A concelebrated or simultaneous absolution is unnecessary, theologically misleading, and liturgically confusing. Even a strict interpretation of the Tridentine requirement of individual confession should not preclude this change.

Communal Reconciliation

The fully communal form of celebration found in the third rite of the RP likewise has clear values for certain situations, though *Reconciliatio et Paenitentia*, 33, mentions only the values of the first two forms. Even more than the second rite, it makes frequent celebration of the sacrament possible without sacrificing the expression of community. It gives clearer expression to the guiding principles of the reform than do either of the other rites. The need for both conversion and reconciliation to be sincere and authentic dynamics in the life of both individuals and community is more prominent here than in the first two rites. The form is particularly valuable when a community confronts a common state of sinfulness or divisions within itself and seeks reconciliation or when members of the community wish

374

to renew their commitment but do not need special guidance. Though not canonically recognized as such, it is an ideal form of the sacrament for ordinary sinners in ordinary situations, even if the dialogue of conversion and reconciliation cannot become as specific and personal in it as in other forms.

Despite its potential, the third rite is canonically restricted. In both the RP and the 1983 Code of Canon Law, complete individual confession and absolution are the ordinary means of reconciliation after grave sin, with only physical and moral impossibility excusing from them (RP 31; canon 960).[13] The question of how often such situations may exist is not addressed, nor is the possibility that the varied forms of the sacrament may be complementary and intended for penitents in different situations. The regulation seems something like a prescription from a doctor who is unable to distinguish headache from heart attack and gives a shot of adrenalin for both: preoccupation with individual confession betrays a fear that someone somewhere might abuse the sacramental sign of divine mercy and compassion.

Though the Code is more negative on communal absolution, canon 961's two examples are essentially the same as those in the 1973 text of the RP: (1) imminent danger of death, with no time to hear the confessions individually; (2) the proportion of penitents to priests is such that confessions cannot be heard properly within a suitable time,[14] with the consequence that the faithful, through no fault of their own, would be forced to go for a long time without the grace of the sacrament or without holy communion,[15] but a large crowd at a festival or pilgrimage is not sufficient reason for communal absolution.[16] The first example is not altogether appropriate: it is clearly an emergency situation, in which this third rite would be as physically impossible to celebrate properly as would be the first or second rites; a short form for such emergencies is provided in RP 64–65. The second example is not an emergency but is proposed as an exceptional or extraordinary situation when it would be physically impossible to celebrate according to the first or second rites, with long deprivation of sacramental grace or communion apparently considered as serious as the danger of death. (Pope John Paul II, unlike many commentators, speaks of "grave necessity" rather than "emergency" in *Reconciliatio et Paenitentia, 33.*)

The question of extending this rite beyond the extraordinary situations envisioned is, admittedly, difficult to resolve. However, development in official discipline over recent decades is significant and suggests a profitable line of thought. Though the development in official discipline has been primarily canonical, it does show a gradually deepening understanding of excusing causes, a gradually broadening field of application, and a growing willingness to respond to specific pastoral needs. This development has been halted—but only to some extent reversed—by the 1983 Code of Canon Law.

1. The understanding of causes excusing from complete confession developed rapidly in the context of the World Wars and was officially acknowledged by several Roman indults.[17] These indults reconciled Trent with a new situation by permitting general absolution in situations where death was an imminent threat and individual auricular confession was impossible.

2. The clearest official recognition of a developing understanding was the 1944 Instruction of the Sacred Penitentiary.[18] This too was primarily concerned with the emergency situation of those in imminent danger of death but extended previous law by acknowledging the possibility of "another altogether grave and urgent necessity proportioned to the gravity of the divine precept of integrity of confession." Long deprivation of sacramental grace *and* holy communion when the penitents' were not at fault was noted as such a necessity and the bishop's permission was required for legality. Frequent mortal sin was presumed; deprivation of absolution meant deprivation of communion.

3. The willingness to confess subsequently any mortal sins thus absolved was stated as a condition of validity in these documents. However, in the 1960s several papal indults granted a *specialissima facultas* for general absolution without mentioning this obligation. These indults were generally for situations of persecution or other difficult pastoral situations.[19] Pope John XXIII's 1962 permission for the Sudan explicitly stated that the concession was complete, absolute, and without condition and that there was no requirement of subsequent confession.[20] These indults were not publicized and have generally not been taken into account by theologians or canonists.

4. The 1972 Pastoral Norms, universal laws rather than particular indults, substantially repeated the 1944 provisions but extended their field of application by requiring only a "grave necessity" rather than an "urgent" one. The cautious approval given communal celebration introduced a totally new factor: general absolution not only as a grant of forgiveness after a private act of contrition but also as communal reconciliation in liturgical worship. As a consequence of liturgical reform, there were heightened expectations regarding communal participation in sacramental worship, particularly by receiving communion. The medieval and Counter-Reformation preoccupation with sin had also been tempered somewhat by the council. The third Norm, unlike the 1944 Instruction, refers to deprivation of sacramental grace *or* holy communion. Likewise, because of conciliar developments, the priest was allowed to decide to give general absolution in situations not foreseen by the bishop if the bishop could not be contacted beforehand.

5. The RP repeated the 1972 Norms but established significantly higher standards for all celebrations than existed in 1944 or even in 1972. A communal rite (with individual confession and absolution) is regarded as an ordinary and normal form of celebration, a significant shift from the attitude evident in the Pastoral Norms. The emphasis given the Word, prayer, and personal dialogue means that individual confession is now much more than

merely the confession of sins, assignment of penance, and giving of absolution. Quick, almost mechanical confessions are no longer satisfactory. Hearing individual confessions "properly within a suitable period of time" thus has an altogether different meaning in the RP than it did in the Pastoral Norms. Even though the Pastoral Norms are substantially repeated in the RP, the manner in which the regulations are to be applied is altogether different.
6. Despite the proposed purpose of revising church law in the light of Vatican II, liturgical legislation in the new Code, particularly in the canons on penance, often ignores the conciliar mandate and the principles of the liturgical reform. The Code's restrictions on general absolution attempt to return to the letter of the 1944 Instruction, even to the point of not allowing priests to decide in cases of necessity unforeseen by the bishop, but with an outlook actually more restrictive, considering the theological and liturgical development that has taken place since 1944. The postsynodal exhortation, *Reconciliatio et Paenitentia*, though not carrying the force of law, strengthens this attempt (33).[21]

The presumption (except in the papal indults of the 1960s) is that a complete individual confession is required by divine positive law, which does not bind so long as it is impossible to observe. When circumstances make it physically or morally impossible, the obligation ceases until such confession is possible. Confession is not dispensed with but postponed until after the absolution, just as an earlier age postponed satisfaction until after the absolution. Long-standing practice to the contrary can be found in the past and was permitted in certain situations in the 1960s. Ancient tradition did not require specific confession or, at least, had a vastly different understanding of which sins needed to be confessed.

In any case, the examples given in the RP and the Code can still be faulted for being examples only of situations where confession is *physically* impossible. No examples are given of situations where confession is *morally* impossible, yet they exist and, according to present understanding and discipline, permit the postponement of confession as long as they last. Many people alienated from the Church are unable to bare their souls before they experience acceptance, welcome, and love. The aversion of large numbers of people to individual confession makes such a celebration of sacramental grace impossible for them except on rare occasions. The inability of available priests to serve satisfactorily as confessors or of penitents to relate to the priests available makes individual confession morally impossible. The presence of a large number of people wishing to celebrate the sacrament together but unable to do so with individual confession because of a lack of confessors deprives them of the experience and celebration of sacramental grace in a clearly communal and ecclesial fashion. People may wish to continue their conversion and experience sacramental reconciliation with God in the Church but simply be psychologically unable to do so in individual confession—as RP 34 seems to acknowledge.[22]

The documents are not clear on the values that can be realized in individual integral confession, perhaps because they are too rarely experienced. The most important of these values, from the historical perspective, is the guidance and direction the Church is duty bound to offer converting sinners as part of its service to God's kingdom and to society as well as the penitents themselves.[23] Individual auricular confession undoubtedly realizes values that cannot be realized in other sacramental forms, values intimately linked with self-disclosure for healing, personal encounter with Christ, transparency to the Lord, and receiving assistance in conversion. But other forms realize values that the individual rite cannot, particularly that of communal worship. The history of penance shows that individual integral confession is a historically conditioned form of the sacrament. Church law and theology acknowledge that the requirement of integral confession is a conditioned necessity and that physical and moral impossibility can excuse from it. Church law and theology further acknowledge that integral confession's value is likewise conditioned and that proportionate values can take precedence. As moderators of the penitential discipline weighing the pastoral situation and needs of their people, bishops should—as some have done in practice and as others in the 1983 Synod begged for—establish realistic and pastorally sensitive guidelines for recognizing the situations that call for this rite,[24] for they are not as extraordinary as the regulations imply.

However, the Church cannot dispense with the requirement of conversion. Ordinarily, the Church prepares sinners to be reconciled by offering guidance and direction and by cooperating with their conversion through prayer, example, and love. As in every past and present form of penance, the grant of reconciliation is meaningless and ineffective without sincere conversion. The Church must authenticate the conversion and ensure that penitents are properly disposed (cf. RP 33, 35). In the sixteenth century, private confession seemed to be the only way to do this. That is no longer the case in a Church that does not confine its ministry to priests, provides many ways for people to share faith and prayer and challenge and support one another, and calls all to take responsibility for the Church's mission and worship and for their own spiritual growth. Intelligible liturgy, scripture study, prayer and sharing groups, spiritual direction, retreats, social action groups, and a multitude of other means provide a formation undreamed of at Trent and vastly more effective than private confession. In such a pastoral situation, the Church need no longer insist inflexibly that confession always precede absolution.

People formed into a converting and reconciling community need to celebrate their identity together. It is because of the third rite's central emphasis on sincere conversion and genuine reconciliation that the most care must be taken in its planning and celebration. Here, even more than in the second rite, the ritual of conversion is overshadowed by the ritual of reconciliation and risks being as perfunctory as a routine individual confession. It is not enough to refine the ceremonial, whereby penitents declare their intention to receive general absolution. What needs strengthening is the prayerful dialogue that is at the heart of conversion, a dialogue that is not exhaustively expressed even in complete confession. Where a community has followed the path of conversion together, particularly during Lent, and at stopping points along the way gathered its members to express their penitence and minister to one another, that community is ready to celebrate reconciliation together and be renewed in the Easter Mystery.

Two further points need to be addressed in connection with the fully communal rite: the assignment of an act of penance and the subsequent confession of grave sins. Both of these are required in the RP, both have been criticized, and, like the requirement of individual absolution in the second rite, both seem inconsistent with the rite's central orientations.

The act of penance was once a long period of conversion preceding reconciliation. As absolution came to be given immediately after confession, an act of penance or satisfaction was seen to have only relative value. It could be postponed in order to realize the higher value of restoring communion immediately. Confession absorbed its importance and the act of penance atrophied, becoming little more than a token of sincerity. When complete confession is similarly relativized by postponement, the act of penance becomes even more clearly secondary, an appendage with little apparent meaning or significance. As a consequence, even in the second rite where an act of penance appropriate to the sins confessed can be determined, it has increasingly come to be identified with the prayer or hymn of praise and thanksgiving that concludes the ritual of reconciliation. Frequently, confessors assign no penance other than this prayer or hymn. Perhaps they reason that God's only condition for forgiveness is the sincere repentance that is able to receive it and that requiring anything more implies an exchange and limits grace.

Yet RP 35a and 60 indicate that some "form of satisfaction" or "act of penance" should be proposed for all the penitents, to which each can add something personally chosen. Does this further conversion, or is it, like the instruction on the essentials of conversion, no more than the retention of a custom, a token attempt to express all the elements once fully present in canonical penance? What does it add to the assembly's expression of penitence or to its efforts to live the Christian life? Does the Church meet its responsibilities if the homily or instruction points to the need to live out conversion, to repair harm done and serve God and neighbor with greater commitment? After individual confession, especially in the first rite, the assigned act of penance can be a helpful and specific suggestion on how to express conversion in everyday life. This necessary change in a person's life is even more emphasized in the penitential celebration. Its ceremonial inclusion in this rite through the perfunctory assignment of a vague act of service or charity seems more to trivialize than further sincere conversion, unless all have come to seek God's pardon for a collective sin.

The question of the required subsequent confession of grave sins is more complex and no more easily resolved than that of general absolution itself. The requirement is clear in the RP: penitents are to resolve to make it, they are to be instructed to do so, and this resolution, simultaneous with the other dispositions required (but not the act of penance), is an apparent condition of validity (RP 33).[25] Unless they are somehow prevented, penitents are to fulfill this obligation as soon as possible before again receiving general absolution and, unless it is morally impossible, at least within one year (RP 34).[26] (The mention of moral impossibility is significant, since it must add something to the previous statement that a good reason can prevent fulfilling this obligation. Is it a recognition that for some penitents individual confession is morally impossible?)

A major question hinges on the nature of sin, particularly of grave sin and its frequency in the life of a Christian. It is doubtful that grave sin, as it is understood in the RP and contemporary theology, occurs often, although the popular understanding of mortal sin has regarded it as relatively common. If it does not, then the Tridentine requirement of individual confession obliges very few individuals.

In any event, requiring a subsequent confession of these sins, at which absolution will again be given, implies more a stay of execution than a judgment of pardon.[27] The existence in the sixteenth century of only a single symbol of postbaptismal conversion explains the significance of the Tridentine requirement, as does the continuation of the same state of affairs in the Post-Tridentine Church, but the RP's provision of other forms raises new questions. How is the requirement of subsequent confession to be explained? Is confession now a dispensable requirement? Must it be retained in at least a token form—that is, mentioning in one's next confession grave sins already forgiven by general absolution—as the act of penance has been in recent centuries? If it is retained, what is its purpose and meaning?

A frequent explanation is that the confession that the reconciled penitent owes the Church, like the long period of penance in the ancient Church and like the medieval satisfaction that had to be paid off, prevents the grace of reconciliation from being cheapened and ritual forgiveness from becoming too easy and thereby trivial. However, this seems contrary to the lessons the Church has learned historically. In the course of the second- and third-century controversies, it realized that it could sign its holiness better by reconciling sinners than by excluding them. In the passage from public to private penance, it admitted that its requirements might be keeping people from God rather than bringing them closer. In the ninth and tenth centuries, it recognized that more was to be gained by postponing satisfaction than absolution. In this century, it is learning that delaying another part of the sacrament, confession, can be beneficial. Immature penitents can substitute the communal service with general absolution for real conversion, but that is the risk run by every ritual. It is hard to see how paying a price guarantees conversion or appreciates grace.

Another possibility is that confession, whether before or after absolution, is primarily conditioned by the penitent's need.[28] While this is a major factor, the history of penance indicates that the sacrament has a wider purpose than penitents' needs. That purpose involves the character of the Church and the furtherance of its mission. Complete confession, like the act of penance, has enabled the Church to fulfill its responsibilities to God, human society, and penitents by guiding and directing its members' conversion. The need for the Church's involvement does not cease, even if circumstances prevent penitents from making a complete confession for a time.

But since the postponement may be indefinite—as long as confession is impossible—one wonders if the *penitent's* obligation continues beyond the need upon which it was based. The penitent when reconciled may still need help to make conversion authentic, but that help will probably be found in time, even if confession to the priest remains impossible. Individual confession is, after all, not the only way for the Church to support its members' conversion. It may indeed have been the only way envisioned at Trent, and it may still be the best way (even if unavailable) for some penitents who need special help, but most pastoral situations contain other means. Continued preoccupation with individual confession may, in fact, distract us from other means or seem to excuse us from developing them. Individual confession alone would unlikely be of much help in a pastoral vacuum; if there are no formal means, there is always the ministry of a friend and fellow

Christian. Should the penitent's conversion mature to the point of no longer needing special support in individual confession, the penitent's obligation to seek it would seem to cease, though the Church's responsibility to provide it and other means does not.

If the obligation can cease—since it is not absolutely essential to every form of the sacrament—is it a disciplinary requirement that can be dispensed with? The first commission involved with drawing up a new rite concluded that subsequent confession of sins after general absolution could not be shown to be absolutely necessary and was an interpretation of divine law that the Church does not have to insist on and has sometimes not required. That is an accurate presentation of one strand of our tradition. Certainly, the Church cannot dispense with the requirement of sincere conversion or with the responsibility to assist it. However, it can as readily not insist on subsequent confession as not insist on prior confession. It can equally declare that there is no obligation—as it has in a number of twentieth-century indults. *Qui potest plus, potest minus*: if it can leave to the penitents' judgment whether conversion is sufficiently mature to receive general absolution, it can likewise leave to their judgment whether they need the special assistance of individual confession.

Abuse is undoubtedly possible. Popular attitudes regarding sin and forgiveness may identify sin with the infraction of a law and forgiveness with the performance of a ritual; using the fully communal celebration without careful preparation may actually reinforce such attitudes. Nevertheless, to cite another old Latin adage, *abusus non tollit usum*. Many communities are prepared to benefit from these celebrations and the decline in available clergy will make them increasingly common. Unless ritual efficiency and canonical compliance are our major goals, it is imperative that discussion shift from canonical debate to community renewal.

Penitential Celebrations

Crucial to developing coherent forms of penance for our times is a sound comprehension of the dynamics of conversion. Only with a grasp of these dynamics will we be able to develop community structures for supporting it and rituals for celebrating the reconciliation of the converted. Penitential celebrations, though rarely used in English-speaking countries (probably because of their nonsacramental character), are the likeliest laboratory for these developments. They are potentially the most valuable rite in the RP for fostering ongoing conversion, revitalizing the various structures in community life for supporting such conversion, and broadening the understanding of ministry.[29] Though the models provided in the RP are unimaginative and still heavily clerical and verbal, the freedom and flexibility for adaptation offer rich possibilities.

These celebrations are also a focus for basic theological questions that may not only indicate the Church's responsibility to support its members' conversion but also suggest some ways to meet it. As an example, the Church's prayer for penitents—the ritual highpoint of the liturgy of penance in these celebrations that lack a liturgy of reconciliation—raises important questions. Precisely what does it mean to the penitents that the Church identifies their prayer as its own and identifies itself with them? Are they no different at this point than when they were isolated individuals following the path of conversion and repentance?

As the modern penance celebrations came into use, the sacramental character of the penitential celebration was a matter of controversy. Though most parties to the discussion were willing to admit the celebration's value in promoting repentance and obtaining forgiveness of venial sins, they were not equally willing to acknowledge its sacramentality. Even excluding the matter of integral confession, questions arose because the penitential celebration lacked an absolution formula and instead had an authoritative, presidential prayer for the penitents' forgiveness.

The questions still remain—though controversy has cooled—and concern the criteria of sacramentality. Is the basic determinant of sacramentality "the *manifestation* of personal sinfulness before the community of the faithful or possibly before the qualified representative of that community"?[30] Or must the Church's official minister, the priest, explicitly declare the penitents' forgiveness either by an indicative absolution or a prayer intended for their reconciliation or otherwise accept their conversion as authentic and restoring them to communion? To what extent is an official declaration by the Church needed to answer these questions?

Several historical points enter in here and perhaps the most crucial is the evaluation of Celtic penance. Indicative absolution formulas were admittedly a late development in the West and are still rare in the East, but Celtic penance apparently lacked any absolution. Like the penitential celebrations, it was not always presided over by a priest and it moreover went counter to official Church policy on what was required for serious sinners to return to communion. In it and in lay confession the penitent could, if necessary, manifest repentance to an unordained Christian. As the sense of ecclesial worship was lost, such confession came to be made directly to God without Church mediation, sometimes as a concession (by John Chrysostom and, later, in the Carolingian Reformation) and sometimes on principle (in the Protestant Reformation).

If repentance must be manifested, is its private manifestation in prayer sufficient? If so, what place does the Church have in our relationship with God? Most basically, is penance's nature and effect truly social? To raise Celtic penance as precedent for contemporary questions is not anachronistic or a matter of historical pedantry. What is at issue in both cases is the basic substance of the sacrament, something that Trent declared beyond the Church's power to change. The question is particularly acute when preoccupation with the Tridentine requirement of individual confession threatens to paralyze the ecclesial imagination and prevent the development of penance. For example, in its document prepared for the Synod, the International Theological Commission recommended in place of the fully communal celebration that individuals be encouraged to perfect contrition and that the ecclesial dimension of conversion be provided for through penitential celebrations, since this would make it easier to explain the obligation of subsequent confession. Though good advice, it is given for the wrong reason and perhaps suggests a solution to a different problem.

The nature of the prayer blessing God and seeking forgiveness and grace for the repentant is, it would seem, key to the puzzle of penance's past and future. The basic question is whether such a prayer today, sincerely meant, can lack sacramental and ecclesial effect if the penitents who form the assembly at the penitential celebration, whatever their past sins, are sincerely repentant, even if the priest (or other presider) lacks the intention to minister sacramentally or expressly excludes that intention and even if the celebration is not canonically recognized as sacramentally valid.[31] If not, then the ecclesial and sacramental effect is the act of the assembly, with its presider voicing its prayer (even if it is contrary to his will).

The assembly is primary in the celebration and penance's nature and effect is social and ecclesial. Does that mean that, if necessary because of the unavailability of a priest, any of its members may represent it (because the Church's gathering needs a presider) and any repentant sinner present is returned to its community (because grace needs a sacrament and the Church's repentant gathering is a reconciling force)? The practice of lay confession implied it, as do the principles of contemporary sacramental theology. Scholastic theology, based as it was on penance as interior repentance rather than reconciliation with the Church, came to other conclusions. Since the mediatorial role of the Church had been lost sight of, scholastic theology generally spoke only of the individual's perfect contrition and then had difficulty explaining the priest's role except in terms of exercising a juridical power.

Though the RP insists on the nonsacramental character of these celebrations, the distinction, more canonical than theological, is based on the premise that only the Tridentine form can be sacramental. Yet every celebration of the Word has a sacramental character and this is the case in penitential celebrations even if absolution is postponed. There is an incompleteness, but it is difficult to deny any sacramental character to a celebration where sinners present themselves as repentant to the Church and where the Church welcomes them, identifies with them, and responds with its prayer for their forgiveness. Here there is certainly forgiveness for individuals' venial sins (RP 4), since the renewal of grace that results from reconciliation with the Church is not required. God's reconciling presence in the Church is experienced even by the repentant person conscious of grave sins (RP 37), not so much apart from absolution as prior to it. The Latin text of the RP suggests grammatically, by its use of the intensive, that such celebrations share in sacramentality. It would be better to say that the penitential celebration is not the full celebration of the sacrament—it lacks the recognition of the authenticity of the penitents' conversion and the grant of reconciliation that completes the sacrament—than to say that it is not sacramental. Clear distinctions can always be made in law, but in the actual life of a community such realities as belonging (communion) are more a matter of degree.

Renewing the Spirit of Conversion
Vastly more important than how to offer reconciliation is how to call to repentance people whose lives seem hopelessly entangled in situations of evil beyond their control or even notice. More crucial to the Church's identity and mission than debates over general absolution and criteria of sacramentality is how to call to conversion Christians who use religion as a defense against God's demands.

These other questions and debates are important. But before there can be reconciliation—if it is not to be cheap grace—there must be awareness of the conflicts and differences that are not obliterated by confession and absolution and that make even the sacrament of reconciliation a proclamation of hope and promise. Before appropriate celebration structures can be planned and implemented, there must be a realization (in Newman's sense) of the Church's mission and its members' call to ministry, but new forms of the sacrament are more likely to grow out of penitential celebrations than out of the three officially sacramental forms.

The commitment to declericalizing ministry that the Rite for Christian Initiation of Adults makes is not matched by the Rite of Penance, despite the historical parallels between initiation and penance. In every age, the liturgical celebration of penance has closely paralleled the liturgical celebration of initiation. When new Christians were formed as members of the faithful by being initiated into community life and then, after baptism, admitted to the eucharistic assembly, penitents were reformed through a similar process before rejoining the assembly of the faithful. When Christians were made simply by being baptized, penitents were readmitted by a similar ritual. Now that the Church again baptizes infants and initiates adults into a ministering community, it is strange that its Rite of Penance presumes adult celebrants but recognizes only one minister and provides rituals of reconciliation but no process of supporting reformation.

Maintaining the traditional parallel between initiation and penance—a parallel that, theologically, sees penance as postbaptismal conversion—seems to require a form of penance akin to the catechumenal formation of the Rite for Christian Initiation of Adults. Such a reformation in the spirit of ongoing conversion and renewal inspired the ancient order of penitents. A similar structured process of reformation, supporting conversion in order to achieve a genuine reconciliation, is needed today.[32] Experience with the catechumenate is giving us greater facility in providing support for people undergoing conversion, and scattered attempts have been made in recent years to provide such a ministry to those undergoing reconversion— often through the catechumenate. Many catechumens are in practice actually penitents: individuals baptized in other Christian communities and now entering the Catholic communion or individuals for a time alienated from the Church and now returning to its communion. To treat them as though they had not already been admitted to the ranks of the faithful by baptism is insulting both to them and the Spirit that has set a seal on them. Penitents may in fact have many things in common with catechumens and even share with them in aspects of the formation process—it is more process than program—but the reality of their baptism cannot be overlooked.

Speaking in the 1983 Synod of Bishops and basing himself on the discussion by the penance work group of the North American Academy of Liturgy, Cardinal Bernardin proposed a new, fourth form of sacramental celebration that would respond to the need to form people in a spirit of ongoing conversion.[33] This would be a four-stage process, paralleling the catechumenate and offering community support in reconversion: (1) a confession of sins; (2) a program of conversion emphasizing spiritual direction and community prayer; (3) celebration of the ritual of reconciliation; and (4) prolongation as a mystagogia. Cardinal Bernardin noted the relationship of his proposal to the ancient order of penitents and the Church's recent experience with the revived catechumenate.

Like those proposing to enter the catechumenate, prospective penitents would be interviewed to discern whether such therapy and reformation is called for or would be beneficial. The specific confession of sin and initial counseling would thus take place privately, but there would also be a public reception of penitents to mark the liturgical beginning of their being formed again as members of the faithful. Such a liturgy, like the ancient *exomo-*

391

logesis, would be the Church's challenging them to allow themselves to be converted and the public acknowledgment that they have, in fact, been estranged from their covenant community. It would also express gratitude to a compassionate God who calls them back and enables the return and it would be the opportunity to ask the community's commitment to prayer, witness, and loving support.

During their time as penitents, like the catechumens, they would share in the Sunday Liturgy of the Word—their presence acknowledged through special prayer—and then leave to meet together for prayer, instruction, and discussion. Reeducation in the Christian fundamentals that are the content of catechumenal catechesis and formation in prayer would be the focus of these ascetical meetings. Penitents would also meet regularly with spiritual directors and sponsors. A significant part of the process, as in the catechumenate, would be involvement in some form of Christian service. For the most part, much of what the community needs to provide for them is quite similar to what catechumens require and the two groups, if small enough, could often work together.

When those selected as ready for baptism enter into the final period of preparation, Lent, penitents ready for reconciliation would do likewise. On Ash Wednesday, as the community commits itself to Lenten penance the penitents would be publicly received with the laying on of hands and communal prayer. They would commit themselves to a special process of spiritual renewal and reconversion during Lent and the community would promise to walk with them. During Holy Week, probably on Wednesday or Thursday, they would be solemnly reconciled in a communal celebration and return to the eucharist. Then, during the Easter season, the formation process would continue with special attention to the sacramental experience and personal prayer, with the goal of helping the reconciled penitents develop a sensitivity to the God who speaks in the whirlwinds and whispers of life as well as in the privileged moments of sacramental celebration.[34]

Calling for such a structured ministry and celebration does not deny that means of renewal already exist. Adult education programs, prayer groups, pastoral counseling, spiritual direction, retreats, recollection days, renewal programs, the Cursillo, and similar ways of promoting ongoing conversion are obvious examples. However, it does recognize the special needs of those penitents who have, for example, been away from the Church for some time or who have never had an adequate Christian formation. It also recognizes that some individuals need special support and encouragement to mature in the spirit of ongoing conversion. Such needs for special ministry are, in a sacramental Church, closely related to worship. They therefore need to be responded to liturgically and sacramentally as well as through other pastoral means.

Nothing in present discipline prohibits the development of a modern order of penitents, though the name does need to be changed. The Rite for Christian Initiation of Adults grew out of the recognition of similar pastoral needs and was based on attempts to minister to those needs. Communal celebrations of the Rite of Penance are likewise the consequence of local communities seeking to minister to members' needs. Academic research and pastoral practice in some communities at present are valuable guides to a Church that recognizes the need for conversion and reconciliation as it finds its way into the future.

The shape and structure of such a process are less important than the fact that it, like the catechumenate, calls members of the local community to be ministers to one another in furthering conversion as well as celebrants in the sacrament of reconciliation. This no more denies the role of the priest-presider than the role of the assembly relegated the bishop to insignificance in the liturgy of canonical penance. However, it does imply that, as in initiation, there can be a variety of ministries. In both cases, such a process calls forth, for example, catechists (there can be no formation without accurate information), counselors, confessors, and spiritual directors (guides help prevent taking wrong turns on the journey of conversion), sponsors (a journey is easier and seems quicker with a companion), and the Church's assembly (we all travel the pilgrim path).

Ministers like these are lay confessors, extensions back into the community of a ministry of mutual correction, shared counsel and prayer, and mutual acceptance that came historically to be confined to clerics. The pastoral care of catechumens is no longer confined to priests, and similar ministry to penitents need not be. Such ministries exist now, of course, though they are too rarely acknowledged as ministry, let alone sacramental ministry. Establishing them in penance, as we have, to an extent, in the catechumenate and eucharist, may help as significantly in reforming a penitent Church as in forming a community of disciples.[35] Few may enter it—just as only a minority go through the catechumenate at any one time—but all will be challenged by their witness.

The exercise of such a religious role by lay people who serve as spiritual directors or simply as friends and confidants to others, whether in a private or group setting, is an important, though often unnoticed, ministry of peers. It is also the type of situation where people who often do not experience forgiveness and reconciliation in the sacramental ritual do encounter God and are graced. This suggests that in discussing liturgical rituals we need to look more closely at the actual times and ways transformation takes place so that we will be in a better position to celebrate it. Keeping close to Christian reality may make it easier to frame both liturgies and laws that are not out of touch with the workings of the Spirit.

In the case of sinners not subject to the official discipline, such situations are sacramental, like medieval lay confession, even if not the complete sacrament. They are also a less formal and juridical expression of the ecclesial dimension of the sacrament, expressing and structuring lay participation and ministry beyond the mutual prayer that is a primary element of communal celebrations. Such situations are, quite obviously, expressions of ministries that have been constant in penance: mutual correction and conversion; the promise of grace; support, encouragement and advice; and prayerful intercession.[36]

However, there is a wide gulf between our times and those when lay confession was a more common practice. In the intervening centuries, ecclesial worship became an extraordinary liturgy, confession and absolution became the official means of reconciliation for all grave sins, and sins excluding from eucharist expanded in number. Those officially excluded from the eucharistic community must still be officially reconciled to it. In the ancient period, only the bishop could reconcile; in the medieval and modern periods, only the priest. Lay ministry began to shrink as clerical ministry expanded and law limited the number of sinners who could share the eucharist. In a situation where exclusion from the eucharist is the consequence of grave sin or the result of long alienation, only those authorized to do so may claim to reconcile in the name of the Church. From our perspective, then, we need to note that confession as such is not the sacrament, nor is counseling as such an act of worship; consequently, the one who reconciles the person excluded from the eucharist should be able to preside at the eucharist. Nevertheless, it is not the presence of the priest that makes the gathering into Church nor does he simply administer the sacrament to a suitably disposed penitent. It is imperative that all members recognize their responsibilities and roles if the Church is to be a reconciling community.

THE NEED FOR RECONCILIATION
Christians today need to follow the path of conversion and reconciliation no less than those who went before, and doing so is not any easier now than it was then.

However, the council, its liturgical reforms, and particularly the RP, are clearly a commitment on the part of the Church to follow that path.

The problem of penance reform cannot be looked at in isolation, no more than any of the elements of the contemporary theology of penance can be looked at apart from their context in the whole of that theology. Penance reform is one dimension of the total reform of a penitent Church. Ultimately, only the experience of the Church as a reconciling community can serve to support its members' conversion and point them toward the experience of reconciliation with the transcendent God who always stretches out a helping hand. To be credible and effective, rites must be rooted in the life of the community and shown in the community's dedicated service of God and neighbor. Ecclesial credibility is a prerequisite for sacramental credibility, since sacraments are celebrated in an ecclesial context and the reality to which they point is lived there. No rite can guarantee either conversion or reconciliation, but if either involves the Church, the Church must be experienced as a reconciling community.

Urgent though the need is for reconciliation in society, the present state of penance is a clear sign of the need for reconciliation within the Church. The need is not simply for more frequent confession and absolution. That has itself been a source of the so-called crisis of penance, as conversion, a process of life in Christian community, was compressed, individualized, and identified with a ritual. The fixation on the single form of the sacrament is evidence of the medieval Western alienation from the Catholic tradition of worship and the preoccupation with frequency is evidence of the Counter-Reformation Church's alienation from the lived experience of faith. The return to the sources of faith and the commitment to incarnation in the contemporary world called for at Vatican II was an effort to overcome that alienation. The question is whether the conversion that was begun there will continue over the long haul.

The Counter-Reformation Church was characterized by its reliance on authority as source of meaning and value. This showed itself in theology's frequently literalistic interpretation of conciliar teachings, particularly those of Trent, in isolation from the wider tradition of faith. It showed itself in the canonization of inherited liturgical forms and styles. It was also seen in pastors (both bishops and presbyters) feeling compelled to keep looking over their shoulders to see what the central administration wished. Here too Vatican II proposed a new beginning. Now the gap between ecclesiology in theory (e.g., collegiality and the real ecclesial character of local Churches) and ecclesiology in practice must be overcome if reconciliation is to take root in ecclesial life as a whole.

An ecumenical effort is needed to reconcile the Tridentine tradition with its scriptural and patristic roots and the Western tradition with the Eastern. Both history and current practice outside the relatively narrow Counter-Reformation tradition suggest, for example, that personal repentance can be ecclesially manifested and an authorized ministry can grant reconciliation other than through individual confession and absolution, even in the case of sins that the later tradition has considered grave. Trent's limited historical knowledge and inheritance of medieval defensive isolation kept this from being recognized at the time. It has been rediscovered since. It should be publicly acknowledged and officially acted on. A theological methodology preoccupied with the state of the tradition at a single historical moment and proceeding with a literalistic interpretation of limited and historically conditioned teaching is not pastorally helpful.

The limited liturgical experience and restricted liturgical forms of the Middle Ages were canonized at Trent and remained a model for nearly four centuries. The separation between liturgy and spirituality continued to grow throughout that period. Concentration on sacramental confession and absolution led, in practice, to a neglect of other forms of conversion and reconciliation. Vatican II called for a new integration of liturgy, spirituality, and Church mission. The new social and ecclesial consciousness and the old personal and individual piety are not yet adequately synthesized, as is evident in many curial and papal texts as well as in the RP. An emphasis on the Church's mission of reconciliation and the insistence on ritual individual confession as *the* means of forgiveness do not harmonize well. Nor is the rediscovered sense of liturgy as the activity of the Church gathered for worship well expressed when the passive reception of absolution is the normal means of experiencing reconciliation with the Church.

The gap between sacramental liturgy and classical sacramental theology thus needs to be overcome. Post-Tridentine theologians have often theologized on the basis of past sacramental theologies and have too rarely understood or even noticed the expression of faith in celebration that is supposed to be their base of reflection. Contemporary sacramental theology works with lived meaning and the classical scholastic categories are unable to deal with this, as is evident when they are used to analyze the validity of general absolution or distinguish between sacramental and nonsacramental forgiveness. Is the narration or enumeration of mortal sins in individual confession necessarily more personal than a wholehearted participation in a communal celebration? Can a sacramental church be satisfied simply with encouraging perfect contrition when sufficient confessors are not available, even if (nonsacramental) penitential celebrations are used to express the ecclesial dimension of this contrition and even if the necessity of later confession is thus more easily explained? Systematic theologians, still generally operating as dogmatic theologians, need to give sustained attention to the nature and concept of sacrament and the criteria and determinants of sacramentality and not measure reality by categories derived from an altogether different experience of sacramental worship.

In many respects, both in the late Middle Ages and throughout the age of the Counter-Reformation, private confession to the priest functioned as a clear sign of the acceptance of Church discipline and authority. The understanding of sin made sin easy to commit and the understanding of confession made forgiveness easy to obtain. Change here does not necessarily mean that the sense of sin and conversion is lost. Neither does it mean that discipline disappears or that authority abdicates, whether the authority be that of the presbyter presiding at the celebration of reconciliation or the bishops and the chief bishop presiding in the agape that is the Church. Vatican II sought a new balance between primacy and episcopacy in recognizing the work of the Spirit throughout the Church. The Synod of Bishops was intended as a structural means of implementing that end. How much of a role the Church's pastors will actually have in establishing policy and making decisions still remains to be seen. Will administrators react to emergency situations by providing exceptions to normal rules or will the riches of our tradition of faith be used to nourish people pastorally? Much of the ambiguity and ambivalence in the area of penance on the theological level is because of a preoccupation with Trent at the expense of the Catholic tradition and even more, on the level of Church authorities, it is frequently a regression from both the spirit and the letter of Vatican Council II. This is true as well in the understanding and expression of the Church's nature and relation to salvation, but it is most evident when it fixes on the reconciliation of an isolated individual penitent and the ritual expression of clerical authority in that context.

Perhaps most of all, on the pragmatic level, the decision must be made on whether the commitment and resolutions made after the review of the Church's life at Vatican II will be stuck to. History suggests that neither theologians nor Church officials are immune to the human tendency to equate change with loss. The first flush of enthusiasm has waned after 20 years and it is tempting to return to the old securities of the Counter-Reformation Church. Many theologians and administrators stand in a position similar to that of those who, in patristic times, opposed extending reconciliation to certain sinners or of those who, in later centuries, opposed new pastoral initiatives when canonical penance had ceased to meet the Church's needs. Now, as then, fear is useless and what is needed is trust in a loving God who seeks to make that love evident in a reconciling community.

The Church of the late Counter-Reformation period found the clicks of the confession counters reassuring, but they are unlikely to be heard again. In times of transition such as our own, confusion and ambivalence seem to rule. The temptation is to hold on to old forms as certainty and security rather than to continue forward in faith. Yet the crisis of penance—if there is one—may be more the beginning of the new than the ending of the old.

The tradition that past communities of faith have shaped can, in our hands, continue to grow. For the time, there is tension: sometimes between old sacramental habits and new sacramental attitudes, sometimes between the pastoral implications of sacramental theology and canonical requirements, always between human inertia and the call of Christ's Spirit. The need for reconciliation—on many levels—is, for the believer, Christ's challenge to his Church to be converted, and the support that is needed to meet that challenge is present in his Spirit. In every case, the power of that Spirit, reconciling us to God in Christ, offers both challenge and support. A sense of how that Spirit has worked in the community of faith to shape our tradition gives us confidence to continue the work of sacramental reform and renewal as well as that of conversion and reconciliation. The future of a reconciling community is ours to shape.

1. Data from the first survey are in Andrew M. Greeley and Peter H. Rossi, *The Education of American Catholics* (NORC Monographs in Social Research, No. 6: Chicago: Aldine, 1966), pp. 57 (Table 3.1), 238 (Table A-2.2). The results of the 1974 survey are in Andrew M. Greeley, William C. McCready, and Kathleen McCourt, *Catholic Schools in a Declining Church* (Kansas City: Sheed and Ward, 1976), p. 125.

2. At the Synod, Cardinal Joseph Ratzinger, head of the Congregation for the Doctrine of the Faith, beginning his historical sketch with Trent, insisted that personal confession is normative for the sacrament and that more extensive use of communal celebrations would be giving in to contemporary trends of depersonalization and collectivism. See *Origins* 13 (1983) 331–332. Bishop Austin Vaughan's remarks on sin (*Origins* 13 [1983] 332–334) and devotional confession (*Origins* 13 [1983] 351–352) were in a similar vein, claiming that the sensed need for redemption has diminished and that routine devotional confession has to be encouraged. Cardinal Silvio Oddi, head of the Congregation of the Clergy, went even further. He charged that perverse theological opinions, defective catechesis on sin (particularly with children and linked with the question of first confession), and defective seminary training were causing crises of clerical identity, attitudes adverse to authority, and neglect of this ministry. See *Origins* 13 (1983) 373–376. At St. Charles Borromeo Seminary in Philadelphia on April 21, 1982, Cardinal Oddi linked clerical identity with several matters: "It is not by chance that, as confession lines grow shorter, communion lines grow longer, or that, as the number of extraordinary ministers of the eucharist increases, confessionals are disappearing from churches."

In general, the remarks of Ratzinger, Vaughan, Oddi, and others like them sound curiously akin to the remnants of Jansenism against which Pius X struggled in encouraging more frequent communion. (See above, p. 186f.) When individuals who regard confession as a purificatory preparation for communion begin to experience the reconciliatory power of the eucharist and their role as celebrants, the understanding (and frequency) of celebrating penance necessarily changes. The fathers of Trent encouraged frequent communion and Pius X renewed their efforts, but neither Trent nor he imagined the full impact it would have.

3. See Kathleen Hughes, "Liturgical Reconciliation and Spiritual Growth," *Spirituality Today* 30 (1978) 211–224, especially p. 217. In the 1982 Southwest Liturgical Conference survey, only 37 percent of those interviewed had their most intense experience of forgiveness in the sacrament. See also L.-M. Chauvet, "Pratiques pénitentielles et conceptions du péché," *Le Supplement* 120–121 (March 1977) 41–64, for a French study analyzing how the concept of sin is affected by the experience of communal celebrations; Sister Laurence Murray, *Confession: Outmoded Sacrament? An Inquiry into Teenage Opinion* (London: Chapman, 1972); and Piers Linley, "The Falling Number of Confessions—Development or Deviation?" *New Blackfriars* 51 (1970) 388–395, 433–442.

4. Carl J. Peter, "Renewal of Penance and the Problem of God," *Theological Studies* 30 (1969) 489–497.

5. The 1982 FDLC survey in the Southwest indicated that approximately equal numbers of those responding had received no instruction, adequate instruction, and some instruction but not enough. In some dioceses, over half had received no instruction whatsoever. Nearly one-third of the respondents had not attended a communal service with opportunity for individual confession and a quarter did not even know what it was. The Notre Dame Study of Catholic Parish Life shows some confusion in this regard; many people were either unaware that their parishes offered communal celebrations or thought that such celebrations were illegal.

6. John E. Price and R. George Sarauskas, "Second Thoughts on the Rite of Reconciliation," *Chicago Studies* 18 (1979) 223–232, summarize the contrasting approaches of the old and new rites and point out the need for a consistent model. The therapeutic or interpersonal model expects too much of most confessors. The celebration model requires presidential style rather than counseling skills but is more appropriate with a group. The symbolic encounter with God model was possible for many penitents in the confession box but is difficult now in the structure, setting, and orientation of the RP.

7. For the understanding of sin in the RP and the problems that arise, see J. McSweeney, "Reconciliation and Changing Attitudes to Sin," *The Furrow* 29 (1978) 636–640; Thomas J. Murphy, "Sin and Reconciliation in a Time of Confusion," *Chicago Studies* 17 (1978) 371–383.

8. P. de Regis, "Confession and Spiritual Direction in the Oriental Church," in *The Sacrament of Penance* (Marie-Bruno Carra de Vaux Saint-Cyr, ed.; Glen Rock: N.J.: Paulist Press, 1966), pp. 92–94.

9. Gérard Fourez, "Towards a Truly Communal Christian Penance," *Lumen Vitae* 25 (1970) 664.

10. Few diocesan guidelines do more than cite the law: insufficiency of confessors in relation to the number of penitents. One, from Little Rock, Arkansas, mentions that for the second rite there should be one confessor for every 15 to 20 penitents. This seems too few: the confessions, unless rushed, would easily take 40 minutes and would completely disrupt the communal character of the service. The liturgy of penance and reconciliation within the communal celebration should probably last no longer than the liturgy of the eucharist at mass and the confessions themselves should therefore take no longer than 15 minutes at the very most. Even the rule suggested here (one confessor for each ten penitents) cannot be applied rigidly, since the average length of such confessions varies from parish to parish. The number of confessors required and their availability must be determined in view of past experience and particular circumstances.

11. James McCue, "Penance as a Separate Sacramental Sign," *Concilium* 61 (1971) 62–63, among others, sees it based on the conviction that people should go to confession regularly and that this makes the duty more palatable. He thinks that the semi-public rite will prove less viable than the private and public forms as the sense of obligation dies.

12. See Francis J. Connell, "Common Confession Rite," *American Ecclesiastical Review* 156 (1967) 409.

13. The Code changes RP 31 slightly to emphasize that such confession and absolution are the "sole" ordinary way, with physical or moral impossibility "alone" excusing from this requirement. (The obligation applies only to those conscious of grave sin.) The original text went on to state that "Special, occasional circumstances may render it lawful and even necessary to give general absolution to a number of penitents without their previous individual confession" and then gave the examples and conditions. It now reads that "Absolution without prior, indi-

vidual confession cannot be given collectively to a number of penitents unless . . . " and the conditions are given.

14. The Latin of the RP and the Code, translated literally in the original ICEL text, is *intra congruum tempus*. The amended ICEL text has "reasonable time," which is misleading: what is otherwise "reasonable" may not be "suitable" in a liturgical celebration. The celebration should not be so long as to inconvenience seriously the participants or cause some to leave after their confession and absolution or break the rhythm of the celebration.

15. Moralists have generally considered three days to be a long time without access to sacramental grace or communion, but the general interpretation of canon 2254, 1, of the 1917 Code regarded one day as a long time. See H. Wagnon, "Les 'Normae pastorales' pour l'administration de l'absolution sacramentelle générale," *Revue Théologique de Louvain* 4 (1973) 53, 55.

16. The confusion introduced by the last clause is due to canon 961, 2, which seemingly ends by forbidding what it had first permitted. The third Pastoral Norm and the RP stated that a large number of penitents on such occasions would not be sufficient reason for general absolution if confessors could be made available. Canon 961, 2 states: "The need is not regarded as sufficient when confessors are not available solely because of a large number of penitents, such as can happen at some festival or pilgrimage." Curiously, all the texts here have in mind the 1944 Instruction that cites a laxist proposition condemned by Innocent XI (DS 2159)—condemned as "at least scandalous and dangerous"—but neither the original proposition nor the 1944 Instruction adverted to the *proportional* relationship of confessors and penitents. Canonists will have to strain to make sense of this text. It perhaps means that in such a situation penitents could receive the sacrament at some other time, before or after the festival or pilgrimage, but that is not really to the point.

17. See, for example, AAS 7 (1915): 72, 282; 31 (1939): 710–713; 32 (1940): 571. Canonists analyzing the twentieth-century developments can come to different conclusions. See, for example, Peter D. G. Smith, "General Sacramental Absolution," *Studia Canonica* 12 (1978) 225–263. See also Brian Newns, "General Absolution: Tradition and Recent Trends," *Clergy Review* 62 (1977) 62–68. For a useful collection of articles, see *General Absolution:*

Toward a Deeper Understanding (Chicago: Federation of Diocesan Liturgical Commissions, 1978). For discussion in light of the 1983 Code, see Ladislas Orsy, "General Absolution: New Law, Old Traditions, Some Questions," *Theological Studies* 45 (1984) 676–689.

18. AAS 36 (1944) 155–156.

19. These include, from the Congregation for the Propagation of the Faith, Prot. Nr. 2995/62, dated June 18, 1962; and Prot. Nr. 856/63, dated March 1, 1963; Prot. Nr. 2073/66; Prot. Nr. 3076/66.

20. See the 1983 Synod intervention of Gabriel Wako, "When General Absolution Is Needed," *Origins* 13 (1983) 368; Desmond Morrison, "Confession and the New Code," *The Furrow* 20 (1969) 526.

21. As the title suggests, such documents have an exhortative, not a legislative or doctrinal intent. Cf. Francis G. Morrisey, "The Canonical Significance of Papal and Curial Pronouncements" (Canon Law Society of America, n.d.), p. 3.

22. Authors have called attention to such cases for years, but officials have failed to take note of their suggestions or have been reprimanded for acting on them. For similar examples, see M. Huftier, "Integrité de la confession ou démarche progressive vers la vie spirituelle," *L'Ami du Clerge* 76 (1966) 683–687; Carl J. Peter, "Integrity Today?" *Communio* 1 (1974) 75, 78; Hurley, "Communal Absolution—Anatomy of a Decision," pp. 203–206; Michael R. Prieur, *The Sacrament of Reconciliation Today* (Bethlehem, Penn.: Catechetical Communications, 1973), p. 33; L. Rossi, "Quando la mancanza di confessori genera il caso di necessità," *Settimana del Clero*, July 30, 1972, p. 1; Cuthbert M. Whitley, "Understanding and Attitudes: Some Suggestions for Appreciating Communal Penance," *Review for Religious* 30 (1971) 225.

23. Cf. Carl J. Peter, "Integrity Today," p. 63.

24. See RP 32, 39 and canon 961. Where the original text had the bishop decide, after consultation with the national conference, whether the conditions for general absolution existed in his diocese, the new text, amended by canon 961, states: "To make the judgment on whether the requisite conditions already stated in no. 31b are verified belongs to the diocesan bishop. After con-

sidering the criteria agreed on with the other members of the conference of bishops, he can decide which cases involve the need in question." The national conference of bishops is thus to decide the meaning of "grave necessity." RP 39b now reads: "to make the decision, after considering the conditions required by the law (see no. 31b) and the criteria agreed on with the other members of the conference of bishops, regarding the cases of need in which general absolution may be permitted." Paragraphs 32b and 40c, which allowed priests to use their prudential judgment if a grave necessity not foreseen by the bishop should arise, have been deleted. Canonists or higher authorities will have to decide whether the situations are *examples* of grave necessity or the *only* situations where communal reconciliation is permitted. Usual principles of canonical interpretation would suggest that the list is not taxative: laws permitting access to the sacraments are to be interpreted as broadly as possible.

25. The ICEL text says it is required for validity. The Latin text of the Pastoral Norms (VI) and RP 33 speak of them as *ad valorem sacramenti requisitis,* a term that is not as legally precise as *validitas.* Despite canon 962, 1, it is doubtful that validity could hinge on such an intention.

26. Canon 963 inserts "as soon as they have the opportunity" in RP 34. Canon 989 requires annual confession, but it clearly states that only those conscious of grave sins are so obliged.

27. This was the opinion of the Ghana bishops at the Synod. See their intervention, "Reconciliation and African Realities," *Origins* 13 (1983) 350. Zoltan Alszeghy does regard general absolution as provisional; see "La confessione dei peccati sacramentalmente perdonati," *Civiltà Cattolica* 130 (1979) III, 13–24.

28. John Gallen, "General Sacramental Absolution: Pastoral remarks on Pastoral Norms," p. 115.

29. RP 37; Appendix II, 1; cf. Pastoral Norms, 10. For model celebrations, see *Penance Celebrations* (National Liturgical Office, ed.; Ottawa: Canadian Conference of Catholic Bishops, 1981).

30. Heggen, *Confession and the Service of Penance,* p. 105.

31. See Karl Rahner, "Bussandacht und Einzelbeichte" and "Busse und Beichte" in *Fragen der Kirche heute* (Adolph Exeler,

ed.; Würzburg: Echter Verlag, 1971), pp. 73–78, though the questions that follow go beyond Rahner's.

32. See, for example, Lentzen-Deis, *Busse als Bekenntnisvollzug*. The Congregation for Divine Worship has recommended this, particularly for those who have been away from the Church. See "Reflections on the *Rite of Christian Initiation of Adults*," Chapter 4 [*Documents on the Liturgy*, p. 763 (DOL 302, nos. 2496–2497)]. The November 30, 1972, draft of the RP suggested the possibility of liturgical celebrations extended throughout Lent. For other recent discussion, see Robert Blondell, "A Possible Solution," *Assembly* 10 (1983) 219–222; Joseph Slattery, "Restore the Ordo Paenitentium?—Some Historical Notes," *Living Light* 20 (1984) 248–253; and articles in *Hosanna* 1 (1982), No. 1. Frank C. Senn has proposed a similar discipline for use in Lutheran congregations; see his "Structures of Penance and the Ministry of Reconciliation," *Lutheran Quarterly* 25 (1973) 270–283.

33. Joseph Bernardin, "New Rite of Penance Suggested," *Origins* 13 (1983) 324–326. Though Cardinal Bernardin does not mention it, this fourth rite belongs in the Lent-Easter season.

34. For two articles offering context and method for dealing with such questions, see Edward K. Braxton, "The New Rite of Reconciliation in American Culture," and Peter E. Fink, "Investigating the Sacrament of Penance: An Experiment in Sacramental Theology," *Worship* 54 (1980) 206–220.

35. For a brief statement on lay ministries in penance, see my "Ministers of Sacramental Reconciliation," *Today's Parish* 8, No. 2 (February 1976), pp. 43–45.

36. See Walter Kasper, "Confession Outside the Confessional," *Concilium* 24 (1967) 31–42.

Bibliography

SOURCES

Acta Synodalia Sacrosancti Concilii Oecumenici Vaticani II. Rome: Typis Polyglottis Vaticanis, 1962– .

Archidiaconi Romani sermones tres de reconciliandis paenitenti- bus. Corpus Christianorum, Series Latina, v. 9. Turnhout and Paris: Brepols, 1957, pp. 355–363.

Bernhardi Cardinalis et Lateranensis Ecclesiae Prioris Ordo Of- ficiorum Ecclesiae Lateranensis. L. Fischer, ed. *Historische Forschungen und Quellen,* 2/3. Munich: 1916.

Codex Iuris Canonici. Auctoritate Ioannis Pauli II promulga- tus. Vatican City: Libreria Editrice Vaticana, 1983.

Il cosiddetto Pontificale di Poitiers. Aldo Martini, ed. Rome: Herder, 1979.

Cyprian. *Saint Cyprian, Letters (1–81). The Fathers of the Church,* v. 51. Washington, D.C.: Catholic University of America Press, 1964.

Denzinger, H. and A. Schönmetzer, eds. *Enchiridion Sym- bolorum, Definitionum et Declarationum.* 35th ed. Freiburg: Herder, 1967.

The Documents of Vatican II. Walter M. Abbott, ed. New York: Herder and Herder, 1966.

The Documents of Vatican II. Austin P. Flannery, ed. New York: Pillar Books, 1975.

Documents on the Liturgy, 1963–1979: Conciliar, Papal, and Curial Texts. Collegeville, Minn.: Liturgical Press, 1982.

Emendations in the Liturgical Books Following upon the New Code of Canon Law. Washington, D.C.: International Commission on English in the Liturgy, 1984.

Enchiridion Indulgentiarum: Normae et Concessiones. Rome: Typis Polyglottis Vaticanis, 1968.

The Epistles of St. Clement of Rome and St. Ignatius of Antioch. James A. Kleist, ed. *Ancient Christian Writers*, v. 1. New York: Newman Press, 1946.

Epistolae Romanorum Pontificum Genuinae. Andreas Thiel, ed. Brunsberg: Peter, 1868.

Hippolytus. "Apostolic Tradition." English text in Geoffrey J. Cuming, *Hippolytus: A Text for Students*. Bramcote: Grove Books, 1976.

The Irish Penitentials. Ludwig Bieler, ed. Dublin: Irish Institute for Advanced Studies, 1963.

John Paul II. *Reconciliatio et Paenitentia: On Reconciliation and Penance in the Mission of the Church Today*. Vatican City: Libreria Editrice Vaticana, 1984.

Liber Ordinum. M. Férotin, ed. Paris: Librairie de Firmin-Didot, 1904.

Liber Sacramentorum Romanae Aeclesiae Ordinis Anni Circuli. L. C. Mohlberg, ed. Rome: Herder, 1960.

Mansi, J. D., ed. *Sacrorum conciliorum nova et amplissima collectio*. 31 v. Florence: 1757–1798; Paris: 1901–1927.

Medieval Handbooks of Penance. J. T. McNeill and H. M. Gamer, eds. and trans. New York: Columbia University Press, 1938.

Migne, J.-P., ed. *Patrologiae cursus completus, Series Graeca*. 161 v. Paris: 1857–1866.

———. *Patrologiae cursus completus, Series Latina*. 221 v. Paris: 1844–1864.

North Italian Services of the Eleventh Century. C. Lambot, ed. London: Henry Bradshaw Society, 1931.

Les Ordines Romani du Haut Moyen Âge. Michel Andrieu, ed. 5 v. Louvain: Spicilegium Sacrum Lovaniense Administration, 1931–1961.

Ordo Paenitentiae. Rituale Romanum . . . Pauli VI. Editio typica. Rome: Typis Polyglottis Vaticanis, 1974.

Le Pontifical Romain au Moyen-Âge. Michel Andrieu, ed. *Studi e Testi,* 86–88, 99; 4 v. Vatican City: Biblioteca Apostolica Vaticana, 1938–1941.

Le Pontifical Romano-Germanique du Dixieme Siècle. Cyrille Vogel and Reinhard Elze, eds. *Studi e Testi,* 226–227; 2 v. Vatican City: Biblioteca Apostolica Vaticana, 1963.

Robert of Flamborough. *Liber Poenitentialis.* Francis Firth, ed. Toronto: Pontifical Institute of Medieval Studies, 1971.

Le sacramentaire gelasien d'Angoulême. Angoulême: Societé Historique et Archéologique, 1918.

Sacramentarium Veronense. L. C. Mohlberg, ed. *Rerum Ecclesiasticarum Documenta, Series Major, Fontes,* 1. Rome: Herder, 1956.

Sacrosanctum oecumenicum concilium vaticani II: Constitutiones, Decreta, Declarationes. Cura ac studio Secretariae Generalis Concilii Vaticani II. Rome: Typis Polyglottis Vaticanis, 1966.

The Sarum Missal. J. Wickham Legg, ed. Oxford: Clarendon Press, 1916.

Schmitz, H. J. *Die Bussbücher und die Bussdisciplin der Kirche.* Mainz: F. Kirchheim, 1883.

Les Statuta Ecclesiae Antiqua. Charles Munier, ed. Bibliotheque de l'Institut de Droit Canonique de l'Université de Strasbourg, 5; Paris: Presses Universitaires de France, 1960.

Tertullian. *Treatises on Penance.* William P. Le Saint, trans. *Ancient Christian Writers,* v. 28. New York: Newman Press, 1959.

Wasserschleben, F. W. H. *Die Bussordnungen der abendländischen Kirche.* Halle: Verlag Graeger, 1851; reprinted, Graz: Akademische Druck- u. Verlagsanstalt, 1958.

BOOKS

Anciaux, Paul. *The Sacrament of Penance.* New York: Sheed and Ward, 1962.

————. *La théologie de pénitence au XIIe siècle.* Louvain: Publications Universitaires de Louvain, 1948.

Arendt, Hans-Peter. *Busssakrament und Einzelbeichte: Die tridentinishchen Lehraussagen über das Sündenbekenntnis und ihre Verbindlichkeit für die Reform des Busssakramentes.* Freiburg: Herder, 1973.

Borobio, D. *La penitencia en la iglesia hispanica del siglo IV al VII.* Bilbao: 1978.

Braeckmans, Louis. *Confession et Communion au Moyen-Âge et au Concile de Trente.* Gembloux: Duculot, 1971.

Burghardt, Walter. *Towards Reconciliation.* Washington, D.C.: United States Catholic Conference, 1974.

Busse und Beichte. Ernst C. Suttner, ed. Drittes Regensburger Ökumenisches Symposium. Regensburg: Pustet, 1972.

La Celebrazione della penitenza cristiana. Atti della IX Settimana di Studio dell'Associazione Professori di Liturgia; Armeno (Novara), 25–29 agosto 1980. Turin: Marietti, 1981.

Commentary on The Rite of Penance. Study Text IV. Washington, D.C.: United States Catholic Conference, 1975.

Crichton, J. D. *The Ministry of Reconciliation.* London: Geoffrey Chapman, 1974.

Crotty, Robert and John Barry Ryan. *Commentaries on the Ritual Readings*. New York: Pueblo, 1982, pp. 77–151.

Dallen, James. "A Decade of Discussion on the Reform of Penance, 1963–1973: Theological Analysis and Critique." Unpublished S.T.D. dissertation. Catholic University of America, 1976.

Donnelly, Doris. *Putting Forgiveness into Practice*. Allen, Tex.: Argus Communications, 1982.

Falsini, Rinaldo. *I postcommuni del Sacramentario Leoniano*. Rome: 1964.

Forkman, Göran. *The Limits of the Religious Community: Expulsion from the Religious Community within the Qumran Sect, Rabbinic Judaism and Primitive Christianity*. Lund: Gleerups, 1972.

Frantzen, Allen J. *The Literature of Penance in Anglo-Saxon England*. New Brunswick, N.J.: Rutgers University Press, 1983.

Freburger, William. *Repent and Believe*. Notre Dame, Ind.: Ave Maria Press, 1972.

Funke, Felix. *Christliche Existenz zwischen Sünde und Rechtfertigung. Das Problem der Andachtsbeichte in der modernen Theologie*. Mainz: Grünewald, 1969.

Galtier, Paul. *De paenitentia: Tractatus dogmatico-historicus*. 9th edition. Rome: Pontifica Universitas Gregoriana, 1956.

General Absolution: Toward a Deeper Understanding. Chicago: Federation of Diocesan Liturgical Commissions, 1978.

Gula, Richard. *To Walk Together Again: The Sacrament of Reconciliation*. New York: Paulist Press, 1984.

Guzie, Tad and John McIlhon. *The Forgiveness of Sin*. Chicago: Thomas More Press, 1979.

Hebblethwaite, Margaret. *The Theology of Penance*. Butler, Wis.: Clergy Book Service, 1979.

Heggen, Franz. *Children and Confession*. London: Sheed and Ward, 1969.

———. *Confession and the Service of Penance*. Notre Dame, Ind.: University of Notre Dame Press, 1967.

Hellwig, Monika. *Sign of Reconciliation and Conversion*. Wilmington, Del.: Michael Glazier, 1982.

Journet, Charles. *Teologia delle indulgenze*. Rome: Ancora, 1966.

Jungmann, Josef. *Die lateinischen Bussriten in ihrer geschichtlichen Entwicklung*. Innsbruck: Rauch, 1932.

Kiely, B. *Psychology and Moral Theology*. Rome: Gregorian University Press, 1980.

Lea, Henry Charles. *A History of Auricular Confession and Indulgences in the Latin Church*. 2 v. Reprint, New York: Greenwood, 1968.

Lentzen-Deis, Wolfgang. *Busse als Bekenntnisvollzug. Versuch einer Erhellung der sakramentalen Bekehrung anhand der Bussliturgie des alten Pontificale Romanum*. Freiburg im Breisgau: Herder, 1968.

Lipinski, E. *La liturgie pénitentielle dans la Bible*. Paris: Éditions du Cerf, 1969.

Liturgie et Rémission des Péchés. Rome: Edizioni Liturgiche, 1975.

Lyonnet, Stanislaus and Léopold Sabourin. *Sin, Redemption and Sacrifice*. Rome: Pontifical Biblical Institute, 1970.

Meyer-Schene, Joseph. *Die häufige Beichte. Studie zur Literatur der letzten Jahrzehnte*. Vienna: Verlag der Herz-Jesu-Priester, 1968.

Murray, Sister Laurence. *Confession: Outmoded Sacrament? An Inquiry into Teenage Opinion*. London: Chapman, 1972.

The New Rite of Penance: Background Catechesis. Pevely, Missouri: Federation of Diocesan Liturgical Commissions, 1974.

Oakley, Thomas P. *English Penitential Discipline and Anglo-Saxon Law*. New York: Columbia University Press, 1923.

Orsy, Ladislas. *The Evolving Church and the Sacrament of Penance*. Denville, N.J.: Dimension Books, 1978.

Palmer, Paul F. *Sacraments and Forgiveness*. Westmınster, Maryland: Newman Press, 1959.

Pater, Giles. "Karl Rahner's Historico-Theological Studies on Penance: The Retrieval of Forgotten Truths." Unpublished Ph. D. dissertation. University of Notre Dame, 1977.

Penance and Reconciliation in the Mission of the Church. Washington, D.C.: National Conference of Catholic Bishops, 1984.

Penance Celebrations. The National Liturgical Office, ed. Ottawa: Canadian Conference of Catholic Bishops, 1981.

Poschmann, Bernhard. *Der Ablass im Licht der Bussgeschichte*. Bonn: Peter Hanstein Verlag, 1948.

———. *Paenitentia Secunda (Die abendländische Kirchenbusse im Ausgang des christlichen Altertums* and *Die abendländische Kirchenbusse im frühen Mittelalter)*. Bonn: Peter Hanstein Verlag, 1940.

———. *Penance and the Anointing of the Sick*. New York: Herder and Herder, 1964.

Prieur, Michael R. *The Sacrament of Reconciliation Today*. Bethlehem, Penn.: Catechetical Communications, 1973.

Rahner, Karl. *Allow Yourself to Be Forgiven: Penance Today*. Denville, N.J.: Dimension Books, 1978.

———. *Theological Investigations*, v. 15. New York: Crossroad, 1982.

The Renewal of the Sacrament of Penance. Committee Report; Catholic Theological Society of America, 1975.

The Rite of Penance: Commentaries. 3 v. Washington, D.C.: The Liturgical Conference, 1975–1978.

Schellens, Petrus J. *De satisfactione sacramentali, quatenus est problema pastorale.* Rome: Analecta Dehoniana, 1964.

Schlombs, Wilhelm. *Die Entwicklung des Beichtstuhls in der katholischen Kirche.* Düsseldorf: L. Schwann, 1965.

Schoonenberg, Piet. *Man and Sin: A Theological View.* Notre Dame, Ind.: University of Notre Dame Press, 1965.

Sottocornola, Franco. *A Look at the New Rite of Penance.* Washington, D.C.: United States Catholic Conference, 1975.

Swidler, Leonard. *Aufklärung Catholicism, 1780–1850: Liturgical and Other Reforms in the Catholic Aufklärung.* AAR Studies in Religion, 17. Missoula, Mont.: Scholars Press, 1978.

Teetaert, Amédée. *La Confession aux Laïques dans l'Église Latine.* Paris: Gabalda, 1926.

Tentler, Thomas N. *Sin and Confession on the Eve of the Reformation.* Princeton: Princeton University Press, 1977.

Thyen, H. *Studien zur Sündenvergebung im Neuen Testament und seinen alttestamentlichen und jüdischen Voraussetzungen.* Göttingen: Vandenhoeck und Ruprecht, 1970.

Uleyn, Arnold. *Is It I, Lord? Pastoral Psychology and the Recognition of Guilt.* New York: Holt, Rinehart and Winston, 1969.

Vogel, Cyrille. *La discipline pénitentielle en Gaule des origines à la fin du vii siècle.* Paris: Letouzey et Ané, 1952.

———. *Le Pécheur et la Pénitence au Moyen Âge.* Paris: Éditions du Cerf, 1969.

———. *Le pécheur et la pénitence dans l'église ancienne.* Paris: Editions du Cerf, 1966.

Vorgrimler, Herbert. *Busse und Krankensalbung*. Freiburg: Herder, 1978.

Watkins, Oscar D. *A History of Penance*. 2 volumes. New York: Longmans, Green, 1920; reprinted, 1960.

Xiberta, Bartholome F. *Clavis ecclesiae: De ordine absolutionis sacramentalis ad reconciliationem cum ecclesia*. Rome: Collegium Sancti Alberti, 1922.

ARTICLES AND ESSAYS

"A Request and a Reply." *Teaching All Nations* 4 (1967) 432–434.

Alszeghy, Zoltan. "La confessione dei peccati sacramentalmente perdonati." *Civiltà Cattolica* 130 (1979) III, 13–24.

Alszeghy, Zoltan and Mauricio Flick. "La dottrina tridentina sulla necessità della confessione." In *Magistero e Morale*. Bologna: Edizioni Dehoniana, 1970, pp. 103–192.

Amato, Angelo. "Il concilio di Trento e il nuovo 'ordo paenitentiae': Alcune considerazioni a proposito della legittimazione dogmatica dei nuovi riti di riconciliazione." *Ephemerides Liturgicae* 89 (1975) 282–293.

Anciaux, Paul. "Confession privée et célébration communautaire de la pénitence." *Collectanea Mechliniensia* 51 (1966) 606–617.

Aroustam, R. A. "Penitential Pilgrimages to Rome in the Early Middle Ages." *Archivum Historiae Pontificiae* 13 (1975) 65–83.

Babiak, Antonius. "Doctrina poenitentialis et administratio sacramenti poenitentiae tempore reformationis carolingiae." *Apolinaris* 30 (1957) 444–469, 31 (1958) 118–138.

Balen, T. J. van. "Das Sakrament der Beichte um die Wende des 13. Jahrhunderts." *Studia Moralia* 6 (1968) 295–350.

416

Beer, Peter J. "Trent's Temporal Punishment and Today's Renewal of Penance." *Theological Studies* 35 (1974) 467–481.

———. "What Price Indulgences? Trent and Today." *Theological Studies* 39 (1978) 526–535.

Bernardin, Joseph. "New Rite of Penance Suggested." *Origins* 13 (1983) 324–326.

Bernhard, Jean. "Excommunication et pénitence—sacrement aux deux premiers siècles de l'église. Contribution canonique." *Revue de Droit Canonique* 15 (1965) 265–281, 318–330; 16 (1966): 41–70.

Berrouard, Marie-François. "Pénitence de tous les jours selon saint Augustin." *Lumière et Vie* 13, No. 70 (November-December, 1964), pp. 51–74.

———. "La pénitence publique durant les six premiers siècles: Histoire et Sociologie." *Maison Dieu* 118 (1974) 92f.

Blondell, Robert. "A Possible Solution." *Assembly* 10 (1983) 218–221.

Borella, Pietro. "La Confessione al Mercoledi Santo." *Rivista Liturgica* 49 (1962) 244–250.

Braga, Carlo. "Il nuovo 'Ordo Paenitentiae.' " *Ephemerides Liturgicae* 89 (1975) 165–176.

Braxton, Edward K. "The New Rite of Reconciliation in American Culture." *Chicago Studies* 15 (1976) 185–198.

Brovelli, Franco. "Il nuovo 'Ordo Paenitentiae' alla luce della storia della liturgia." In *La Penitenza*. Quaderni di Rivista Liturgica, N.S. 3. Turin: Elle di Ci, 1976, pp. 136–166.

Browe, Peter. "Die Kinderbeichte im Mittelalter." *Theologie und Glaube* 25 (1933) 689–701.

———. "Die Kommunionvorbereitung im Mittelalter." *Zeitschrift für katholischen Theologie* 56 (1932) 375–415.

──────. "Die Pflichtbeichte im Mittelalter." *Zeitschrift für katholische Theologie* 57 (1933) 335–383.

Brulin, Monique. "Orientations pastorales de la pénitence dans divers pays." *La Maison Dieu* 117 (1974) 38–62.

Buckley, Francis J. "The Paschal Mystery and the Priest in the Sacrament of Penance." *Lumen Vitae* 31 (1976) 223–233.

──────. "Recent Developments in the Sacrament of Penance." *Communio* 1 (1974) 83–98.

Bussini, François. "L'intervention de l'assemblée des fidèles au moment de la réconciliation des pénitents d'après les trois 'postulationes' d'un archidiacre romain du Ve-VIe siècle." *Revue des Sciences Religieuses* 41 (1967) 29–38.

──────. "L'intervention de l'evêque dans la réconciliation des pénitents d'après les trois postulationes d'un archidiacre romain du Ve-VIe siècle." *Revue des Sciences Religieuses* 42 (1968) 326–338.

Champlin, Joseph M. "The Role and Qualities of a Good Confessor." *Homiletic and Pastoral Review* 75, No. 6 (March 1975), pp. 6–21.

Chapungco, A. "Teaching and Celebrating the Sacrament of Reconciliation in Seminaries." *Seminarium* 31 (1979) 706–720.

Chauvet, L.-M. "Pratiques pénitentielles et conceptions du péché." *Le Supplement* 120–121 (March 1977) 41–64.

Coless, Gabriel M. "The Sacrament of Penance: Creative Ferment." *Worship* 47 (1973) 463–472.

Connell, Francis J. "Common Confession Rite." *American Ecclesiastical Review* 156 (1967) 409–412.

──────. "Some Recent Statements on the Sacrament of Penance." *American Ecclesiastical Review* 155 (1966) 278–280.

Cooke, Bernard. "The Social Aspect of the Sacrament of Penance." *Proceedings of the Catholic Theological Society of America* 22 (1967) 173–183.

Cooper, Eugene J. "A Newer Look at the Theology of Sin." *Louvain Studies* 3 (1971) 259–307.

Coune, Michel and Robert Gantoy. "Une 'postulation dia-conale' pour la réconciliation des pénitents." *Paroisse et Liturgie* 49 (1967) 365–373.

Curran, Charles E. "The Sacrament of Penance Today." In *ibid., Contemporary Problems in Moral Theology*. Notre Dame, Ind.: Fides, 1970, pp. 1–96.

Dallen, James. "The Absence of a Ritual of Reconciliation in Celtic Penance." In *The Journey of Western Spirituality*. A. W. Sadler, ed. Chico, Cl.: Scholars Press, 1981, pp. 79–105.

———. "Church Authority and the Sacrament of Penance: The Synod of Bishops." *Worship* 58 (1984) 194–214.

———. "Eucharist and Penance," *Worship* 50 (1976) 324–328.

———. "The Imposition of Hands in Penance: A Study in Liturgical History." *Worship* 51 (1977) 224–247.

———. "Ministers of Sacramental Reconciliation," *Today's Parish* 8, No. 2 (February 1976), pp. 43–45.

———. "Penance and the Life Situation of the Penitent." In *The New Rite of Penance: Background Catechesis*. Pevely, MO: Federation of Dir esan Liturgical Commissions, 1975, pp. 23–33.

———. "Penitential Celebrations for Lent." *Renewal and Reconciliation*. Washington, D.C.: Archdiocese of Washington, 1975, pp. 39–60.

———. "Reconciliatio et Paenitentia: The Postsynodal Apostolic Exhortation." *Worship* 59 (1985) 98–116.

————. "Reflections on Penance." *Origins* 4 (1975) 525–528.

Dedek, John F. "The Theology of Devotional Confession." *Proceedings of the Catholic Theological Society of America* 22 (1967) 215–222.

De Molen, Richard L. "Childhood and the Sacraments in the Sixteenth Century." *Archiv für Reformationsgeschichte* 66 (1975) 49–71.

de Regis, P. "Confession and Spiritual Direction in the Oriental Church." In *The Sacrament of Penance*. Marie-Bruno Carra de Vaux Saint-Cyr., ed. Glen Rock, N.J.: Paulist Press, 1966, pp. 79–95.

Donovan, Kevin. "The History of Penance in the West." *Music and Liturgy* 1 (1974) 8–13.

————. "The New *Ordo Paenitentiae*." *Clergy Review* 59 (1974) 660–671.

————. "The New Penitential Rite." *The Way* 15 (1975) 295–302; 16 (1976): 57–65.

————. "Public Services of Penance." *Clery Review* 57 (1972) 827–843.

Dooley, Catherine. "Development of the Practice of Devotional Confession." *Questions Liturgiques* (1983) 89–117.

————. "From Penance to Confession: The Celtic Contribution." *Bijdragen* 43 (1982) 390–411.

Dörries, H. "The Place of Confession in Ancient Monasticism." *Studia Patristica* 5 (*Texte und Untersuchungen* 80) (1962) 284–308.

Douglas, James. "The Sacrament of Penance in Present-Day Orthodoxy." *Diakonia* 4 (1969) 211–226.

Duffy, Regis. "Concelebration of Penance and a Therapeutic Model." *Worship* 48 (1974) 258–269.

Duquoc, Christian. "Real Reconciliation and Sacramental Reconciliation." *Concilium* 61 (1971) 26–37.

Eppacher, Anton, "Die Generalabsolution. Ihre Geschichte (9–14. Jahrhundert) and die gegenwärtige Problematik im Zusammenhang mit den gemeinsamen Bussfeiern." *Zeitschrift für katholische Theologie* 90 (1968) 296–308, 385–421.

Fagerberg, H. and Hans Jorissen. "Penance and Confession." In *Confessing One Faith: A Joint Commentary on the Augsburg Confession by Lutheran and Catholic Theologians.* G. W. Forell and J. F. McCue, eds. Minneapolis: Augsburg, 1982, pp. 234–261.

Fink, Peter E. "Investigating the Sacrament of Penance: An Experiment in Sacramental Theology." *Worship* 54 (1980) 206–220.

Finnerty, D. Joseph. "What Does the New Ritual of Penance Expect of the Priest?" *Review for Religious* 35 (1976) 3–13.

Fourez, Gérard. "Towards a Truly Communal Christian Penance." *Lumen Vitae* 25 (1970) 657–664.

Funke, Felix. "Survey of Published Writings on Confession over the Past Ten Years." *Concilium* 61 (1971) 120–132.

Gallen, John. "General Sacramental Absolution: Pastoral Remarks on Pastoral Norms." *Theological Studies* 34 (1973) 114–121.

Galtier, Paul. "Pénitents et 'Converti': De la pénitence latine à la pénitence celtique," *Revue d'Histoire Ecclésiastique* 33 (1937) 5–26, 277–305.

———. "La réconciliation des pêcheurs dans la première épître a Timothée." *Recherches de Science Religieuse* 39 (1951) 317–322.

Gaupin, Linda. "More Frequent Communion, Less Frequent Confession." *Living Light* 20 (1984) 254–260.

Gerardi, P. "Eucarestia e penitenza, sacramenti di riconciliazione, nella dottrina del Concilio di Trento." *Rivista di
Teologia Morale* 5 (1973) 491–514.

Gogan, Brian. "Penance Rites of the West Syrian Liturgy:
Some Liturgical and Theological Implications." *Irish Theological Quarterly* 42 (1975) 182–196.

Gracia, Juan Antonio. "La eucaristia como purificacion y
perdon de los pecados en los textos liturgicos primitivos."
Phase 7 (1967) 65–77.

————. "Historia de la reforma del nuevo ritual." *Phase* 14
(1974) 11–22.

Greégoire, Paul. "The Use of Penance and the Sense of
Sin." *Doctrine and Life* 22 (1972) 32–34.

Gromer, Georg. "Zur Geschichte der Diakonenbeicht im
Mittelalter." In *Festgabe Alois Knöpfler*. Freiburg im Breisgau: 1917, pp. 159–176.

Gy, Pierre M. "Les bases de la pénitence moderne." *Maison Dieu* 117 (1974) 63–85.

————. "Le precepte de la confession annuelle et la necessité de la confession." *Revue des Sciences Philosophiques et
Théologiques* 63 (1979) 529–547.

Hancock, Robert and Robert Williams. "The Scholastic
Debate on the Essential Moment of Forgiveness." *Resonance* 1 (1965) 63–74.

Hardon, John A. "First Confession: An Historical and
Theological Analysis." *Église et Théologie* 3 (1972) 69–110.

Haughton, Rosemary. "Penance and Asceticism in the
Modern World." In *Sin and Repentance*. Denis F. O'Callaghan, ed. Staten Island: Alba House, 1967, pp. 73–92.

Havener, Ivan. "A Curse for Salvation—1 Corinthians
5:1–5." In *Sin, Salvation and the Spirit*. Daniel Durken, ed.
Collegeville, Minn. Liturgical Press, 1979, pp. 334–344.

Heggen, Franz. "The Service of Penance: A Description and Appreciation of Some Models." *Concilium* 61 (1971) 134–154.

Hennig, John. "Die kollektive Bussfeier im Lichte der jüdischen Tradition." *Heiliger Dienst* 4 (1970) 164–169.

Huftier, M. "Integrité de la confession ou démarche progressive vers la vie spirituelle." *L'Ami du Clerge* 76 (1966) 683–687.

Hughes, Kathleen. "Liturgical Reconciliation and Spiritual Growth." *Spirituality Today* 30 (1978) 211–224.

Hurley, Francis T. "Communal Absolution—Anatomy of a Decision." *America* 127 (1972) 203–206.

International Theological Commission. "Penance and Reconciliation." *Origins* 13 (1984) 513–524.

Jedin, Hubert. "La necessité de la confession privée selon le concile de Trente." *Maison Dieu* 104 (1970) 88–115.

Jimenez, Julio. "Reformas en el rito de la penitencia." *Teologia y Vida* 9 (1968) 135–146.

Jorissen, Hans. "Does the Teaching of the 'Confessio Augustana' about Repentance Stand in the Way of Its Recognition by the Catholic Church?" In *The Role of the Augsburg Confession: Catholic and Lutheran Views*. Joseph A. Burgess, ed. Philadelphia: Fortress, 1980, pp. 101–121.

Jounel, P. "La liturgie de réconciliation." *Maison Dieu* 117 (1974) 7–37.

Journet, Charles. "Théologie des indulgences." *Nova et Vetera* 4 (1966) 81–111.

Jungmann, Joseph A. "De actu poenitentiali infra missam inserto conspectus historicus." *Ephemerides Liturgicae* 80 (1966) 257–264.

―――. "Oratio super populum und altchristliche Büssersegnung." *Ephemerides Liturgicae* 52 (1938) 77–96.

————. "The Question of General Absolution." *Teaching All Nations* 4 (1967) 426–431.

Kasper, Walter. "Confession Outside the Confessional." *Concilium* 24 (1967) 31–42.

Kilmartin, Edward J. "Eucharist and Reconciliation" in "The Eucharist in Recent Literature." *Theological Studies* 32 (1971) 254–260.

Kirk, David. "Penance in the Eastern Churches." *Worship* 40 (1966) 148–155.

Laarhoven, J. van. "Een geschiedenis van de biechtvader." *Tijdschrift voor Theologie* 7 (1967) 375–422.

La Bonnardiere, A.-M. "Pénitence et réconciliation des pénitents d'après saint Augustin." *Revue des Études Augustiniennes* 13 (1967) 31–53, 249–283; 14 (1968) 181–204.

La Due, W. "The Age of Reason Re-Examined: The Sacraments of Marriage and Confession." *Living Light* 11 (1974) 564–571.

Larrabe, José Luis. "Renovacion posconciliar del sacramento de la penitencia." *Phase* 11 (1971) 459–478.

László, Stefan. "Sin in the Holy Church of God." In *Council Speeches of Vatican II*. Yves Congar et al., eds. New York: Sheed and Ward, 1964, pp. 29–31.

Leclercq, Jean. "Confession and Praise of God." *Worship* 42 (1968) 169–176.

————. "Confession et louange de Dieu chez sainte Bernard." *La Vie Spirituelle* 120 (1969) 588–605.

Lehmann, Karl. "General Absolution—Private Confession." *Communio* [International Catholic Review] 1 (1972) 319–322.

Ligier, Louis. "Dimension personelle et dimension communautaire de la pénitence en Orient." *Maison Dieu* 90 (1967) 155–188.

————. "Pénitence et eucharistie en Orient: Théologie sur une interférence de prières et de rites." *Orientalia Christiana Periodica* 29 (1963) 5–78.

————. "Le sacrement de pénitence selon la tradition orientale." *Nouvelle Revue Théologique* 89 (1967) 940–967.

Linley, Piers. "The Falling Number of Confessions—Development or Deviation?" *New Blackfriars* 51 (1970) 388–395, 433–442.

McAuliffe, Clarence. "Penance and Reconciliation with the Church." *Theological Studies* 26 (1965) 1–39.

McCarthy, "The Pastoral Practice of the Sacraments of Cleansing in the Legislation of the Visigothic Church." *Classical Folia* 24 (1970) 177–186.

McCue, James. "Penance as a Separate Sacramental Sign." *Concilium* 61 (1971) 55–64.

McGoldrick, Patrick. "Sin and the Holy Church." *Irish Theological Quarterly* 32 (1965) 3–27.

McNally, Robert E. "The Counter-Reformation's Views of Sin and Penance." *Thought* 52 (1977) 151–166.

McNeill, J. T. "Folk Paganism in the Penitentials." *Journal of Religion* 13 (1933) 450–466.

————. "Medicine for Sin as Prescribed in the Penitentials." *Church History* 1 (1932) 14–26.

McSorley, Harry. "Luther and Trent on the Faith Needed for the Sacrament of Penance." *Concilium* 61 (1971) 89–98.

McSweeney, J. "Reconciliation and Changing Attitudes to Sin." *The Furrow* 29 (1978) 636–640.

Marcen Tihista, J. A. "Liturgias penitenciales en el antiguo testamento." In *El sacramento de la penitencia.* Madrid: Consejo Superior de Investigaciones Cientificas, 1972, pp. 85–104.

Marrevee, William. "New Order of Penance: Is It Adequate?" *Église et Théologie* 7 (1976) 119–137.

Martinez Diez, Gonzalo. "Algunos aspectos de la penitencia en la iglesia visigodo-mozárabe," *Miscelanea Comillas* 49 (1968) 5–19

———. "Un tratado visigotico sobre la penitencia." *Hispania Sacra* 19 (1966) 89–98.

Merton, Thomas. "The Spiritual Father in the Desert Tradition." In Ibid., *Contemplation in a World of Action*. Garden City: Doubleday Image, 1973, pp. 282–305.

Meyer, Hans Bernhard. "Confession or Spiritual Direction?" In *Making Sense of Confession*. Otto Betz, ed. Chicago: Franciscan Herald Press, 1968, pp. 125–142.

———. "Zur Busspraxis nach dem Erscheinen des neuen Ordo Paenitentiae." *Liturgisches Jahrbuch* 26 (1976) 156–164.

Michaud-Quantin, Pierre. "Deux formulaires pour la confession du milieu du XIIIe siècle." *Recherches de Théologie Ancienne et Médiévale* 31 (1964) 43–62.

Miller, Charles E. "The Best of Three Rites." *Homiletic and Pastoral Review* 78, No. 3 (December 1977), pp. 55–58.

Murphy, Thomas J. "Sin and Reconciliation in a Time of Confusion." *Chicago Studies* 17 (1978) 371–383.

Murphy-O'Connor, Jerome. "Sin and Community in the New Testament." In *Sin and Repentance*. Denis O'Callaghan, ed. Staten Island, N.Y.: Alba House, 1967, pp. 18–50. Also in *The Mystery of Sin and Forgiveness*. Michael J. Taylor, ed. Staten Island, N.Y.: Alba House, 1971, pp. 55–89.

Nieuwenhuizen, M. van den. "De Eucharistie als Sakrament van de Vergeving." *Tijdschrift voor Theologie* 9 (1969) 178–195.

Nikolasch, Franz. "The Sacrament of Penance: Learning from the East." *Concilium* 61 (1971) 66–75.

Nocent, Adrien. "L'acte pénitentielle du nouvel 'Ordo Missae': Sacrement ou sacramental?" *Nouvelle Revue Théologique* 91 (1969) 956–976.

Nuttall, J.C. "The Spirit and Reconciliation." *Clergy Review* 68 (1983) 408–410.

Oakley, Thomas P. "Celtic Penance: Its Sources, Affiliations, and Influence." *Irish Ecclesiastical Record* 52 (1938) 147–164, 581–601.

———. "Cultural Affiliations of Early Ireland in the Penitentials." *Speculum* 8 (1933) 489–500.

O'Callaghan, Denis F. "The *Confiteor-Indulgentiam* and Forgiveness of Sin." *Irish Ecclesiastical Record* 160 (1966) 322–326.

Orsy, Ladislas M. "Communal Penance: Some Preliminary Questions on Sin and Sacrament." *Worship* 47 (1973) 338–345.

———. "General Absolution: New Law, Old Traditions, Some Questions." *Theological Studies* 45 (1984) 676–689.

O'Shea, Kevin F. "The Reality of Sin: A Theological and Pastoral Critique." *Theological Studies* 29 (1968) 241–259.

Payen, Jean Charles. "La pénitence dans le contexte culturel des XIIe et XIIIe siècles." *Revue des Sciences Philosophiques et Théologiques* 61 (1977) 399–428.

Peter, Carl J. "Dimensions of *Jus Divinum* in Roman Catholic Theology." *Theological Studies* 34 (1973) 227–250.

———. "Integral Confession and the Council of Trent." *Concilium* 61 (1971) 99–109.

———. "Integrity Today." *Communio* 1 (1974) 60–82.

———. "The New Norms for Communal Penance: Will They Help?" *Worship* 47 (1973) 2–10.

————. "Renewal of Penance and the Problem of God." *Theological Studies* 30 (1969) 489–497.

Piil, Mary Alice. "The Penitential Rite of the Mass." *Hosanna* 1 (1982), No. 1, pp. 28–31.

Pocknee, C. E. "Confirmation and the Reconciliation of Heretics and Apostates." *Church Quarterly Review* 166 (1965) 357–361.

Pompei, Alfonso. "Il movimento penitenziale nei secoli XII–XIII." *Collectanea Franciscana* 43 (1973) 9–40.

Power, David N. "Confession as Ongoing Conversion." *Heythrop Journal* 18 (1977) 180–190.

————. "The Sacramentalization of Penance." *Heythrop Journal* 18 (1977) 5–22.

Price, John E. and R. George Sarauskas, "Second Thoughts on the Rite of Reconciliation." *Chicago Studies* 18 (1979) 223–232.

Quinn, Edward. "Home Thoughts on Penance." *Month* 233, 2nd N.S. 5 (1972) 369–371.

Quinn, John J. "The Lord's Supper and Forgiveness of Sin," *Worship* 42 (1968) 281–291.

Rahner, Karl. "Bussandacht und Einzelbeichte. Anmerkungen zum Römischen Erlass über das Busssakrament." *Stimmen der Zeit* 190 (1972) 363–372.

————. "Busse und Beichte." In *Fragen der Kirche heute*. Adolph Exeler, ed. Würzburg: Echter Verlag, 1971, pp. 73–78.

————. "The Church of Sinners." In *Theological Investigations*, v. 6. Baltimore: Helicon, 1969, pp. 253–269.

————. "Forgotten Truths Concerning the Sacrament of Penance." In *Theological Investigations*, v. 2. Baltimore: Helicon, 1963, pp. 135–174.

————. "Justified and Sinner at the Same Time." In *Theological Investigations*, v. 6. Baltimore: Helicon, 1969, pp. 218–230.

————. "On the Official Teaching of the Church Today on the Subject of Indulgences." In *Theological Investigations*, v. 10. New York: Herder and Herder, 1973, pp. 166–198.

————. "Penance as an Additional Act of Reconciliation with the Church." In *Theological Investigations*, v. 10. New York: Herder and Herder, 1973, pp. 125–149.

————. "The Sinful Church in the Decrees of Vatican II." In *Theological Investigations*, v. 6. Baltimore: Helicon, 1969, pp. 270–294.

————. "Theology and the Church's Teaching Authority after the Council." *Theological Investigations* 9 (New York: Herder and Herder, 1972) 83–100.

Ramos-Regidor, José. " 'Reconciliation' in the Primitive Church and Its Lessons for Theology and Pastoral Practice Today." *Concilium* 61 (1971) 76–88.

Riga, Peter. "Penance in St. Leo the Great." *Église et Théologie* 5 (1974) 5–32.

————. "Penance in Saint Ambrose." *Église et Théologie* 4 (1973) 213–226.

————. "The Roman Liturgical Rite and Prayers of Reconciliation of the Fifth Century." *American Ecclesiastical Review* 167 (1973) 196–207.

Rigaux, Beda. " 'Lier et delier.' Les ministères de réconciliation dans l'église des temps apostoliques." *Maison Dieu* 117 (1974) 86–135.

Righetti, Mario. *Manuale di storia liturgica*. Milan: Editrice Ancora, 1950–1953; v. 4, pp. 170–322.

Rossi, L. "Quando la mancanza di confessori genera il caso di necessità." *Settimana del Clero*, July 30, 1972, p. 1.

Rouillard, Philippe. "L'enseignement du magistère sur le sacrement de la pénitence de 1964 à 1974." *Ephemerides Liturgicae* 89 (1975) 177–193.

———. "Indicazioni teologico-pastorali sul rito della penitenza negli interventi delle conferenze episcopali." In *La Celebrazione della penitenza cristiana*. Turin: Marietti, 1981, pp. 112–122.

Ruffini, Eliseo. "La prassi della 'confessione frequente di devozione.' Dalla teologia degli anni trenta all Novus Ordo Paenitentiae." *Scuola Cattolica* 104 (1976) 307–338.

Sabourin, Leopold. "La rémission des péchés: Écriture Sainte et pratique ecclésiale." *Science et Esprit* 32 (1980) 299–315. For an English summary, see "Forgiveness of Sin and Church Praxis." *Theology Digest* 29 (1981) 123–126.

Scanlan, Michael. "Penance as Prayer." In *The New Rite of Penance: Background Catechesis*. Pevely, Missouri. Federation of Diocesan Liturgical Commissions, 1974, pp. 36–39.

Schmitt, J. "Contribution à l'étude de la discipline pénitentielle dans l'Église primitive à la lumière des textes de Qumrân." In *Les Manuscripts de la Mer Morte*. Paris: Aubier, 1957, pp. 93–109.

Schrijnen, J. "Die Entwicklung der Bussdisziplin im Lichte der altchristlichen Kunst." In *Verspreide Opstellen*. Nijmegen: Dekker & Van de Vegt, 1939, pp. 277–294.

Senn, Frank C. "Structures of Penance and the Ministry of Reconciliation." *Lutheran Quarterly* 25 (1973) 270–283.

Sheets, John R. "Communal Penance and Private Confession: The New Directives." *Communio* 1 (1974) 99–102.

Slattery, Joseph. "Restore the Ordo Paenitentium?—Some Historical Notes." *Living Light* 20 (1984) 248–253.

Smiar, Nicholas P. "Notes on Byzantine Penance." *Resonance* 2 (1966) 97–105.

Sottocornola, Franco. "Les nouveaux rites de la pénitence. Commentaire." *Questions Liturgiques* 55 (1974) 89–136.

Stolzman, W. "Communion for Repenting Sinners?" *Clergy Review* 65 (1980) 322–327.

Studzinski, Raymond. "The Minister of Reconciliation: Some Historical Models." In *The Rite of Penance: Commentaries*, v. 3, *Background and Directions*. Nathan Mitchell, ed. Washington, D.C.: The Liturgical Conference, 1978, pp. 50–61.

Tanghe, D. A. "L'eucharistie pour la rémission des péchés." *Irenikon* 34 (1961) 165–181.

Tillard, J. M. R. "The Bread and Cup of Reconciliation." *Concilium* 61 (1971) 38–54.

———. "Pénitence et Eucharistie." *Maison Dieu* 90 (1967) 103–131.

van der Geest, C. "Die Generalabsolution in Papua-New Guinea." *Liturgisches Jahrbuch* 21 (1971) 174–176.

Vellian, Jacob. "The New Rite of Reconciliation: Understanding Its Newness from Eastern Tradition." *Ephemerides Liturgicae* 91 (1977) 377–381.

Vogel, Cyrille. "Composition légale et commutations dans le systèm de la pénitence tarifée." *Revue du Droit Canonique* 8 (1958) 289–318; 9 (1959) 1–39, 341–359.

———. "La discipline pénitentielle dans les inscriptions paléochrétiennes." *Rivista di Archeologia Cristiana* 42 (1966) 317–325.

———. "Une mutation cultuelle inexpliquée: Le passage de l'eucharistie communautaire a la messe privée." *Revue des Sciences Religieuses* 54 (1980) 230–250.

———. "La paenitentia in extremis chez saint Cesaire évêque d'Arles (503–542)." *Studia Patristica* 5 (1962) 416–423.

———. "Sin and Penance." In *Pastoral Treatment of Sin*. P. Delhaye et al., eds. New York: Desclée, 1968, pp. 260–282.

Vokes, F. E. "Penitential Discipline in Montanism." *Studia Patristica* 14 (1976) 62–76.

Vorgrimler, Herbert. "Mt. 16:18s et le sacrement de pénitence." In *L'homme devant Dieu. Melanges offert au Pere Henri de Lubac*. Paris: Aubier, 1963, pp. 51–61.

Wagnon, H. "Les 'Normae pastorales' pour l'administration de l'absolution sacramentelle générale." *Revue Théologique de Louvain* 4 (1973) 46–57.

Waterkeyn, Baudouin. "The Sacrament of Forgiveness Celebrated in Living Christian Communities." *Lumen Vitae* 37 (1982) 191–194.

Whitley, Cuthbert M. "Understanding and Attitudes: Some Suggestions for Appreciating Communal Penance." *Review for Religious* 30 (1971) 218–227.

OTHER LITERATURE CITED

Bouley, Allan. *From Freedom to Formula: The Evolution of the Eucharistic Prayer from Oral Improvisation to Written Texts*. Washington, D.C.: Catholic University of America Press, 1981.

Brown, Raymond. *The Community of the Beloved Disciple*. New York: Paulist Press, 1979.

———. *The Epistles of John*. Anchor Bible, 30. Garden City, N.Y.: Doubleday, 1982.

Coppens, Joseph. *L'imposition des mains*. Paris: Gabalda, 1925.

Delumeau, Jean. *Catholicism between Luther and Voltaire: A New View of the Counter-Reformation*. Philadelphia: Westminster, 1977.

Furberg, Ingemar. *Das Pater Noster in der Messe*. Lund: CWK Gleerups, 1968.

Greeley, Andrew M., William C. McCready, and Kathleen McCourt. *Catholic Schools in a Declining Church*. Kansas City: Sheed and Ward, 1976.

Greeley, Andrew M. and Peter H. Rossi. *The Education of American Catholics*. NORC Monographs in Social Research, No. 6. Chicago: Aldine, 1966.

Harnack, Adolph. *History of Dogma*. New York: Dover, 1961.

Leuchli, Samuel. *Power and Sexuality*. Philadelphia: Temple University Press, 1972.

Liturgical Music Today. Washington, D.C.: National Conference of Catholic Bishops, 1982.

The Lord's Prayer and Jewish Liturgy. Jakob J. Petuchowski and Michael Brocke, eds. New York: Seabury, 1978.

Manson, T. W. "The Lord's Prayer." *Bulletin of the John Rylands Library* 38 (1956) 99–113, 436–448

Mirgeler, Arthur. *Mutations of Western Christianity*. Notre Dame, Ind.: University of Notre Dame Press, 1964.

Morrisey, Francis G. "The Canonical Significance of Papal and Curial Pronouncements." Canon Law Society of America, n.d.

Music in Catholic Worship. Washington, D.C.: United States Catholic Conference, 1972.

Saliers, Don. "The Integrity of Sung Prayer." *Worship* 55 (1981): 290–303.

Talley, Thomas. "Liturgical Time in the Ancient Church: The State of Research." In *Liturgical Time*. Wiebe Vos and Geoffrey Wainwright, eds. Rotterdam: Liturgical Ecumenical Center Trust, 1982, pp. 35–51.

Index

Hippolytus, 30, 36, 42, 43, 50, 98
Holy Saturday, 346
Holy Thursday, 70, 72, 86ff., 120ff., 174, 346
Homosexuality, 354ff.
Hugh of St. Victor, 146

Ignatius Loyola, 160, 273
Ignatius of Antioch, 20ff.
Imposition of hands. See Laying on of hands.
Individualizing of sin and repentance, 73ff., 77, 108, 151ff., 157, 159ff., 178, 180ff., 262, 265, 271, 299, 359, 371
Indulgences, 53, 107, 125, 127, 140, 153, 156, 158, 168, 183, 216, 242, 284, 365. See also Martyr's letter.
Indulgentiarum doctrina, 216
Initiation, 24, 30ff., 36, 40, 47ff., 58, 61ff., 73, 85, 98, 100, 107, 257, 301, 319, 351ff., 390. See also Baptism.
Innocent I, Pope, 60, 64, 70, 84, 87
Integrity. See Confession, integral.
International Committee on English in the Liturgy, 221
International Theological Commission, 225, 264
Ireland, 101ff.
Irenaus of Lyons, 24, 28
Isidore of Seville, 81
Ius divinum, 170, 231, 282, 290, 378, 385

James, 16, 117
Jan Hus, 168
Jansenism, 2, 182ff., 187, 258, 270, 285
Jerome, 63, 70, 72
Jesus, 5ff., 8, 10, 159
John, 12ff.
John Chrysostom, 74, 104, 387
John Paul II, Pope, 199, 225ff., 238, 344, 355, 371, 376
John Wyclif, 168
Jonas of Orleans, 112
Judaism, 9ff., 17
Judgment, 8, 46, 52, 58ff., 142ff., 171, 178, 261ff., 281, 287, 307, 310, 329
Jurisdiction, 60, 125, 137, 153, 159, 164, 165, 268
Justin Martyr, 21, 85

442